C. P. CAVAFY

Collected Poems

ισ’ ἐντελῶς.   Καὶ τώρα πιὰ ζ
λη καθενὸς   καινούριου ἐραστ
η τὰ δικά του·   στὴν ἔνωσι μὲ
ιον ἐραστὴ   ζητεῖ νὰ πλανηθεῖ
αι ὁ ἴδιος νέος,   πὼς δίδεται

ασ’ ἐντελῶς,   σὰν νὰ μὴ ὑπῆρχ
θελε — εἶπ’ ἐκεῖνος —   ἤθελε
στιγματισμένη,   τὴν νοσηρὰ
στιγματισμένη,   τοῦ αἴσχους
αιρὸς ἀκόμη —   ὡς εἶπε — νὰ

ασ’ ἐντελῶς,   σὰν νὰ μὴ ὑπῆρχ
ν φαντασίαν,   ἀπὸ τὲς παραισ
λη ἄλλων νέων   τὰ χείλη του
νὰ αἰσθανθεῖ   ξανὰ τὸν ἔρωτό

C. P. CAVAFY

Collected Poems

TRANSLATED,
WITH INTRODUCTION AND COMMENTARY,
BY

DANIEL MENDELSOHN

ALFRED A. KNOPF
NEW YORK

—

2009

THIS IS A BORZOI BOOK
PUBLISHED BY ALFRED A. KNOPF

Introduction, notes and commentary, and translation
copyright © 2009 by Daniel Mendelsohn

Library of Congress Cataloging-in-Publication Data
Cavafy, Constantine, 1863–1933.
[Poems. English]
Collected poems / C.P. Cavafy ; translated, with inroduction and
commentary, by Daniel Mendelsohn.
p. cm.
"This is a Borzoi book."
ISBN 978-0-375-40096-4
1. Cavafy, Constantine, 1863–1933—Translations into English.
I. Mendelsohn, Daniel Adam, 1960–   II. Title.
PA5610.K2A2 2009
889'.132—dc22
2008034718

Manufactured in the United States of America
Published April 7, 2009
Second Printing, May 2009

CONTENTS

I

PUBLISHED POEMS

Poems 1905–1915

v

Poems 1916–1918

CONTENTS

Poems 1919–1933

CONTENTS

Poems Published 1897–1908

II

REPUDIATED POEMS
(1886–1898)

III

UNPUBLISHED POEMS
(1877?–1923)

CONTENTS

CONTENTS

Prose Poems

Poems Written in English

INTRODUCTION

The Poet–Historian

"Outside his poetry Cavafy does not exist." Today, seventy-five years after the death of "the Alexandrian" (as he is known in Greece), the judgment passed in 1946 by his fellow poet George Seferis—which must have seemed rather harsh at the time, when the Constantine Cavafy who had existed in flesh and blood was still a living memory for many people—seems only to gain in validity. That flesh-and-blood existence was, after all, fairly unremarkable: a middling job as a government bureaucrat, a modest, even parsimonious life, no great fame or recognition until relatively late in life (and even then, hardly great), a private life of homosexual encounters kept so discreet that even today its content, as much as there was content, remains largely unknown to us. All this—the ordinariness, the obscurity (whether intentional or not)—stands in such marked contrast to the poetry, with its haunted memories of passionate encounters in the present and its astoundingly rich imagination of the Greek past, from Homer to Byzantium, from the great capital of Alexandria to barely Hellenized provincial cities in the Punjab, that it is hard not to agree with Seferis that the "real" life of the poet was, in fact, completely interior; and that outside that imagination and those memories, there was little of lasting interest.

As the man and everyone who knew him have passed into history, the contrast between the life and the art has made it easy to think of Cavafy in the abstract, as an artist whose work exists untethered to a specific moment in time. This trend has been given impetus by the two elements of his poetry for which he is most famous: his startlingly contemporary subject (one of his subjects, at any rate), and his appealingly straightforward style. Certainly there have always been many readers who appreciate the so-called historical poems, set in marginal Mediterranean locales and long-dead eras and tart with *mondain* irony and a certain weary Stoicism. ("Ithaca gave you the beautiful journey; / without her you wouldn't have set upon the road. / But now she has nothing left to give you," he writes in what is perhaps his most famous evocation of ancient Greek culture, which tells us that the journey is always more important than the inevitably disappointing destination.) But it is probably fair to say that Cavafy's popular reputation currently rests almost entirely on the remarkably prescient way in which those other, "sensual" poems, as often as not set in the poet's present, treat the ever-fascinating and pertinent themes of erotic longing, fulfillment, and loss; the way, too, in which memory preserves what desire so often cannot sustain. That the desire and longing were for other men only makes him seem the more contemporary, the more at home in our own times.

As for the style, it is by now a commonplace that Cavafy's language, because it generally shuns conventional poetic devices—image, simile, metaphor, specialized diction—is tantamount to prose. One of the first to make this observation was Seferis himself, during the same 1946 lecture at Athens in which he passed judgment on Cavafy's life. "Cavafy stands at the boundary where poetry strips herself in order to become prose," he remarked, although not without admiration. "He is the most anti-poetic (or a-poetic) poet I know." Bare of its own nuances, that appraisal, along with others like it, has inevitably filtered into the popular consciousness and been widely accepted—not least, because the idea of a plainspoken, contemporary Cavafy, impatient with the frills and fripperies characteristic of his Belle Epoque youth, dovetails nicely with what so many see as his principal subject, one that seems to be wholly contemporary, too.

No one more than Cavafy, who studied history not only avidly but with a scholar's respect for detail and meticulous attention to nuance, would have recognized the dangers of abstracting people from their historical contexts; and nowhere is such abstraction more dangerous than in the case of Cavafy himself. To be sure, his work—the best of it, at any rate, which is as good as great poetry gets—is timeless in the way we like to think that great literature can be, alchemizing particulars of the poet's life, times, and obsessions into something relevant to a wide public over years and even centuries. But the tendency to see him as one of us, as someone of our own moment, speaking to us in a voice that is transparently, recognizably our own about things whose meaning is self-evident, threatens to take a crucial specificity away from him—one that, if we restore it to him, makes him seem only greater, more a poet of the future (as he once described himself). His style, to begin with, is far less prosaic, far richer and more musical, and indeed is rooted far more deeply in the nineteenth century—which, astoundingly it sometimes seems, he inhabited for more than half his life—than is generally credited. (Some readers will be surprised to learn that many of Cavafy's lyrics, until he was nearly forty, were cast as sonnets or other elaborate verse forms.) As for his subject, there is a crucial specificity there as well, one that tends to be neglected because it can strike readers as abstruse. Here I refer to those poems that are deliberately set in the obscurer margins, both geographical and temporal, of the Greek past: poems that, because they seem not to have much to do with our concerns today, are too often passed over in favor of the works with more obvious contemporary appeal.

The aim of the present translation and commentary is to restore the balance, to allow the reader to recapture some of that specificity of both content and, particularly, form. Any translation of a significant work of literature is, to some extent, as much a response to other translations of that work as to the work itself; the present volume is no exception. The most important and popular English translations of Cavafy in the twentieth century were those of John Mavrogordato (1951), Rae Dalven (1961), and Edmund Keeley and Philip Sherrard (1975); the latter in particular, with its briskly contemporary tone, its spare prosody, and its arresting use of Modern Greek spellings was instrumental in persuading a new and younger audience that Cavafy's "unmistakable tone of voice," as Auden memorably put it, was one worth listening to. And yet precisely because (as Auden went on to observe) that tone of voice seems always to "survive translation," I have focused my attention on other aspects of the poetry. In attempting to restore certain formal elements in particular, to convey the subtleties of language, diction, meter, and rhyme that enrich Cavafy's ostensibly prosaic poetry, this translation seeks to give to the interested reader today, as much as possible, a Cavafy who looks, feels, and sounds in English the way he looks, feels, and sounds in Greek. A Greek, to deal with first things first, that is not at all a straightforward and unadorned everyday language, but which, as

I explain below in greater detail, was a complex and subtle amalgam of contemporary and archaic forms, one that perfectly mirrored, and expressed, the blurring of the ancient and the modern that is the great hallmark of his subject matter. And a Greek, too, whose internal cadences and natural music the poet exploited thoroughly. There is no question that Cavafy in Greek is poetry, and beautiful poetry at that: deeply, hauntingly rhythmical, sensuously assonant when not actually rhyming. It seemed to me worthwhile to try to replicate these elements whenever it was possible to do so.

Cavafy's content also merits renewed attention—both the specific subjects of individual poems and also his larger artistic project, which in fact holds the historical and the erotic in a single embrace. For this reason I have provided extensive Notes in addition to a general Introduction. A necessary aspect of the project of presenting Cavafy anew to a public that enjoys poetry but is unlikely to be familiar with many of the eras and places where he likes to situate his poems (late Hellenistic Syria, say, or the fourteenth century in Byzantium; Seleucia, Cyrene, Tigranocerta) is to provide readers with the rich background necessary to decipher those works. Cavafy seems to have inhabited the remote past as fully as he inhabited the recent past, and so to appreciate his poems fully, with their nuances and, so often, their ironies—the latter in particular arising from the tension between what the characters in the poem knew while events were transpiring and what we know now, one or two millennia later—the reader also needs to be able to inhabit both of those pasts; to know what they knew then, and to know what we know now, too.

Readers will also find commentary on certain poems with subjects and settings that might not, at first, appear to require elucidation: poetic creation, erotic desire, the recent past. And yet however familiar or obvious to us the emotions that Cavafy describes may seem to be (the feeling of being "special"—of belonging to a rarefied elite—that comes with being a creative artist), or however self-evident or transparent the circumstances about which he writes, it is worth keeping in mind that the poet's presentation of such themes was often deeply marked by his reading in the poets and authors of his time—or unexpectedly indebted to his lifelong immersion in ancient history. Our understanding of an ostensibly simple short poem like "Song of Ionia," for instance—a poem that seems to revel straightforwardly in the fizzy possibility that even today the old gods still dart among the hills on the coast of Ionia—is deepened when we learn that it stemmed from the poet's poignant vision, while reading Gibbon's *Decline and Fall of the Roman Empire,* of the late Roman emperor Attalus (who was born in Ionia) "singing a touching song—some reminiscence of Ionia and of the days when the gods were not yet dead." By the same token, "But Wise Men Apprehend What Is Imminent," a poem about the special perception granted to certain gifted men, begins with an epigraph from an ancient biography of the first-century B.C. sage Apollonius of Tyana; but the reader who is given a note explaining who Apollonius was, without being made aware of the strong influence exerted by Baudelaire and the nineteenth-century French Parnassian school on the young Cavafy's thinking about poetry and "special" vision, is being deprived of a full appreciation of the poem.

That Apollonius poem, which comments implicitly on the role of the artist in the present even as it invokes a very ancient text, embodies a crucial aspect of the entire Cavafian oeuvre. Despite the persistent tendency to divide Cavafy's poems into two categories—scholarly poems set in the ancient world, and poems about sexual love set in a more or less recognizable present—there is an overarching and crucial coherence to the work as a whole, one we can grasp only when we unravel the meaning of the poet's famous description of himself as not "a poet only" but as a "poet-historian." To fail to appreciate his unique perspective, one that (as it were) allowed him to see history with a lover's eye, and desire with a historian's eye, is to be deprived of a chance to see the great and moving unity of the poet's lifelong project.

The Introduction that follows provides a brief survey of the life, in order to give readers a sense of who Cavafy was "outside his poetry"; then an extended critical appreciation of the work; and finally a discussion of certain technical issues—the handling of formal devices, the order in which the poems are here presented (always a thorny issue in the case of a poet who himself never published a complete collection of his poems), some smaller things. It is my hope that the essay will serve to do what an Introduction is supposed to do if we take seriously the etymology of the word, which is *to lead someone into something*—the something, in this case, being a destination every bit as worthwhile as the journey.

1

IN ONE SENSE, it was an unexceptional life—or, at least, no more exceptional or distinguished than the lives of certain other great poets, in whom the richness of the work stands in striking contrast to the relative uneventfulness of the life. (Emily Dickinson, say.) Constantine Petrou Cavafy—the Anglicized spelling of the Greek *Kavafis* was one that Cavafy and his family invariably used—was born in Alexandria in 1863, the youngest of seven surviving sons of parents whose families were not at all untypical of the far-flung Greek diaspora, with its hints of vanished empire. Their roots could be traced not only to the Phanar, the Greek community clustered around the Patriarchate in Constantinople, and to Nichori (Turkish Yeniköy) in the Upper Bosporus, but also to Caesarea, Antioch, and to Jassy, in present-day Moldavia. His father, Peter John Cavafy, was a partner in a flourishing family business devoted to corn and cotton export that eventually had offices in London and Liverpool as well as in several cities in Egypt; after moving from Constantinople to London, he finally settled in Alexandria, which was ruled at the time by the Muslim Khedive but had a large population of Europeans. There he would be considered one of the most important merchants in the mid-1850s—not coincidentally, a time when the Crimean War resulted in a steep rise in the price of grain. The poet's mother, Haricleia Photiades, the daughter of a diamond merchant from Constantinople, counted an archbishop of Caesarea and a Prince of Samos among her relations. At the height of their wealth and social success in Alexandrian society, the parents of the future poet had, in addition to their other servants, an Italian coachman and an Egyptian groom. Said Pasha, the Egyptian viceroy, paid attentions to Haricleia that were, if we are to judge from the photographs of her, purely a matter of politeness; Peter John received a decoration from the Khedive at the opening of the Suez Canal.

What effect the memory of such glory and prestige—carefully tended and endlessly polished by his mother long after she'd become a widow living in not very genteel poverty—might have had on her impressionable and imaginative youngest son, we can only guess at; but it is surely no accident that so much of Cavafy's poetry is torn between deep sentiment about the lost riches of the past and the intelligent child's rueful, sharp-eyed appreciation for the dangers of glib nostalgia. For his father's premature death, when Constantine was only seven, would bring hard times to Haricleia and her seven sons, from which the family fortunes would never really recover: Peter John had lived well but not wisely. For several years the widow Cavafy and her three younger sons ambled back and forth between Paris and London and Liverpool, relying on the generosity of her husband's brothers. They stayed in England for five years, where Cavafy acquired the slight British inflection that, we are told, accented his Greek. When it became clear that the surviving brothers had hopelessly bungled their own affairs, Haricleia returned to Alexandria in 1877, when Cavafy was fourteen. With the exception of a three-year sojourn in Constantinople, from 1882 to 1885, following the British bombardment of Alexandria (a response to Egyptian nationalist violence against some of the city's European inhabitants; the bombardment largely destroyed the family home), Cavafy would never live anywhere else again.

For some time, the life he lived there was, as he later described it to his friend Timos Malanos, a "double life." The poet had probably had his first homosexual affair around the age of twenty, with a cousin, during his family's stay in Constantinople; there is no question that he continued to act on the desires that were awakened at that time once he returned to Alexandria. By day, when he was in his middle and late twenties, he was his corpulent mother's dutiful son (he called her, in English, "the Fat One"), working gratis as a clerk at the Irrigation Office of the Ministry of Public Works in the hopes of obtaining a salaried position there. (This he eventually did, in 1892, remaining at the office with the famously Dantesque name—the "Third Circle of Irrigation"—until his retirement, thirty years later.) From seven–thirty to ten in the evening he was expected to dine with the exigent and neurotic Haricleia. Afterward, he would escape to the city's louche quarters. One friend recalled that he kept a room in a brothel on the Rue Mosquée

Attarine; another, that he would return from his exploits and write, in large letters on a piece of paper, "I swear I won't do it again." Like many bourgeois homosexual men of his era and culture (and indeed later ones) he seems to have enjoyed the favors, and company, of lower-class youths: another acquaintance would recall Cavafy telling him that he'd once worked briefly as a dishwasher in a restaurant in order to save the job of one such friend, who'd been taken ill. About the youths and men he slept with we know little. We do know, from an extraordinary series of secret notes that he kept about his habitual masturbation, that the amusing Alexandrian nickname for that activity—"39," because it was thought to be thirty-nine times more exhausting than any other sexual activity—was not entirely unjustified:

> And yet I see clearly the harm and confusion that my actions produce upon my organism. I must, inflexibly, impose a limit on myself till 1 April, otherwise I shan't be able to travel. I shall fall ill and how am I to cross the sea, and if I'm ill!, how am I to enjoy my journey? Last January I managed to control myself. My health got right at once, I had no more throbbing. 6 March 1897.

At about the same time he'd settled in his rather dreary job, he began to write and publish seriously. (He had been writing verse, in English and French as well as in Greek, since at least the age of fourteen; and the family's flight to Constantinople in 1882 inspired a journal that the nineteen-year-old Cavafy, already in love with literature, called *Constantinopoliad: An Epic,* which he soon abandoned.) Apart from that, the life he led, as he got older, wasn't noticeably different from that of many a midlevel provincial functionary. He enjoyed gambling, in moderation; he played the stock market, not without success. Apart from his constant and extensive reading of ancient and modern historians in a variety of languages, his tastes in literature were hardly remarkable. His library of about three hundred volumes contained a quantity of what his younger Alexandrian friend, the botanist J. A. Sareyannis, later recalled, with a palpable shudder, as "unmentionable novels by unknown and forgotten writers." An exception was Proust, the second volume of whose

Le Côté de Guermantes he borrowed from a friend not long after its publication. "The grandmother's death!" he exclaimed to Sareyannis. "What a masterpiece! Proust is a great writer! A very great writer!" (Interestingly, he was less enthusiastic about the opening of *Sodome et Gomorrhe,* which he dismissed as "pre-war.") He particularly enjoyed detective novels. Simenon was a favorite in his last years.

At the turn of the century, when he was in his early forties, he took a few trips to Athens, a city that was largely indifferent to him—as he, an Alexandrian, a devotee of the Hellenistic, the Late Antique peripheries, had always been indifferent to it, the great symbol of High Classicism. He likely fell in love there with a young littérateur called Alexander Mavroudis; but about this, like so much of his erotic life, we will never have more than the odd hint. A few years later—by now his mother had been dead for almost a decade—he came to live at the overstuffed apartment on Rue Lepsius (today the Cavafy Museum), where he would spend the rest of his life. For Sareyannis, who wrote a reminiscence of his friend for an Athens journal in 1944, it is only too clear that the poet's taste in decor was clearly no better than his taste in fiction:

> Cavafy's flat was on an upper floor of a rather lower-class, unkempt apartment house. Upon entering, one saw a wide hall laden with furniture. No walls were to be seen anywhere, as they were covered with paintings and, most of all, with shelves or Arabian *étagères* holding countless vases—small ones, large ones, even enormous ones. Various doors were strung along that hall; the last one opened onto the salon where the poet received his visitors. At one time I greatly admired that salon, but one morning in 1929, as I was passing by to pick up some collections of Cavafy's poetry to be delivered to friends of his in Paris, I waited alone there for quite a while and was able to study it detachedly. With surprise I realized for the first time that it was crowded with the most incongruous things: faded velvet armchairs, old Bokhara and Indian stuffs at the windows and on the sofa, a black desk with gilt ornament, folding chairs like those found in colonial bungalows, shelves on the walls and tables

with countless little columns and mother-of-pearl, a *koré* from Tanagra, tasteless turn-of-the-century vases, every kind of Oriental rug, Chinese vases, paintings, and so on and so on. I could single out nothing as exceptional and really beautiful; the way everything was amassed reminded me of a secondhand furniture store. Could that hodgepodge have been in the taste of the times? I had read similar descriptions of the homes of Anatole France and of Villiers de l'Isle Adam, who were also, both of them, lovers of beauty and gave careful attention to their writing. Whether Cavafy himself chose and collected those assorted objects or whether he inherited them, I do not know; what is certain is that Cavafy's hand, his design, could not be felt in any of that. I imagine that he just came slowly to love them, with time, as they were gradually covered with dust and memories, as they became no longer just objects, but ambiance. (tr. Diana Haas)

The cluttered, déclassé surroundings, the absence of aesthetic distinction, the startlingly conventional, to say nothing of middlebrow, taste: Cavafy's apartment, like his job, gave little outward sign of the presence of a great artistic mind—the place from which the poetry really came. The more you know about the life, the more Seferis's pronouncement that Cavafy existed only in his poetry seems just.

Most evenings, as he grew older, found him at home, either alone with a book or surrounded by a crowd of people that was, in every way, Alexandrian: a mixture of Greeks, Jews, Syrians, visiting Belgians; established writers such as the novelist and children's book author Penelope Delta, Nikos Kazantzakis, a critic or two, younger friends and aspiring writers. (Among the latter, eventually, was Alexander Sengopoulos, known as Aleko, who was very possibly the illegitimate son of one of Cavafy's brothers—acquaintances remarked on a striking family resemblance—and would eventually be his heir.) To these friends and admirers the poet liked to hold forth, in a voice of unusual charm and authority and in the mesmerizing if idiosyncratic manner memorably described by E. M. Forster, who met Cavafy during World War I, when Forster was working for the Red Cross in Alexandria. It was Forster who would do more than anyone to bring Cavafy to the attention of the English-speaking world, and it is to him that we owe the by-now canonical description of the poet as "a Greek gentleman in a straw hat, standing absolutely motionless at a slight angle to the universe." Cavafy, the novelist recalled,

> may be prevailed upon to begin a sentence—an immense complicated yet shapely sentence, full of parentheses that never get mixed and of reservations that really do reserve; a sentence that moves with logic to its foreseen end, yet to an end that is always more vivid and thrilling than one foresaw. . . . It deals with the tricky behaviour of the Emperor Alexius Comnenus in 1096, or with olives, their possibilities and price, or with the fortunes of friends, or George Eliot, or the dialects of the interior of Asia Minor. It is delivered with equal ease in Greek, English, or French. And despite its intellectual richness and human outlook, despite the matured charity of its judgments, one feels that it too stands at a slight angle to the universe: it is the sentence of a poet.

It was, in other words, a life that was a bit of a hybrid: the fervent, unseen artistic activity, the increasingly tame pleasures of a middling bourgeois existence, the tawdry *quartier,* the abstruse, rather baroque conversation. Not coincidentally, the latter pair of adjectives well describes a particular literary manner—characteristic of the Hellenistic authors who flocked to the era's cultural capital, and who were so beloved of Cavafy—known as "Alexandrian."

In 1932, Cavafy, a lifelong smoker, was diagnosed with cancer of the larynx. That summer he traveled to Athens for the tracheotomy that would deprive him forever of the famous voice; from that point on, he was forced to communicate in a distorted whisper and, later on, by means of penciled notes. He returned home in the autumn, after declining an invitation from his wealthy friend Antony Benakis, a collector and the brother of Penelope Delta, to stay with him in Athens. ("Mohammed Aly Square is my aunt. Rue Cherif Pasha is my first cousin, and the Rue de Ramleh my second. How can I leave them?")

After first refusing and then allowing himself to be visited by the Patriarch of the city, he died in the Greek Hospital in Alexandria on April 29, 1933, his seventieth birthday: an elegant concentricity, a perfect closure, that are nicely suggested by what is said to have been his last act. For we are told that on one of the pieces of paper that had become his sole mode of communication he drew a circle; and then placed a small dot in the middle of that circle. Whatever he may have meant by that glyph, certain people will recognize in it an apt symbol. It is the conventional notation, used by authors when correcting printer's proofs, for the insertion of a period, a full stop.

2

"In the poems of his youth and even certain poems of his middle age he quite often appears ordinary and lacking in any great distinction," Seferis remarked during his 1946 lecture—another rather severe judgment whose underlying shrewdness cannot be denied, when we go back to so many of the poems Cavafy wrote in his thirties and even early forties, with their obvious debts to other writers and thinkers, their evasions and obfuscations. And then, as Seferis went on to say, "something extraordinary happens." As will be evident by now, little about the external events of his life helps to account for that remarkable evolutionary leap; in this respect Cavafy resembles, more than a little, his near contemporary Proust, who similarly underwent a profound but invisible metamorphosis that, by his late forties, had transformed him from a dabbling littérateur into a major artist. Only by tracing the course of Cavafy's interior life, his intellectual development, from the 1890s to the 1910s is it possible to discern the path by which (to paraphrase that other great Greek poet again) Cavafy went from being a mediocre writer to a great one.

In the 1880s and 1890s, when he was in his twenties and thirties, Constantine Cavafy was a young man with modest literary ambitions, steadily writing quantities of verse as well as contributing articles, reviews, and essays, most in Greek but some in English (a language in which he was perfectly at home as the result of those adolescent years spent in England), on a number of idiosyncratic subjects, to Alexandrian and Athenian journals. ("Coral from a Mythological Viewpoint," "Give Back the Elgin Marbles," Keats's *Lamia*.) Such writings, as well as the historical poems that belong to this early period, already betray not only a deep familiarity with a broad range of modern historians, whom he read in Greek, English, and French, but also the meticulous attentiveness to primary sources in the original languages—the Classical and later Greek and Roman historians, the early Church Fathers, Byzantine chroniclers—that we tend to associate with scholars rather than poets.

The writings of those early years indicate that Cavafy was struggling to find an artistically satisfying way in which to unite the thematic strands that would come to characterize his work, of which the consuming interest in Hellenic history was merely one. (An interest, it is crucial to emphasize, that rather strikingly disdained the conventional view of what constituted "the glory that was Greece"—which is to say, the Archaic and Classical eras—in favor of the long post-Classical phase, from the Hellenistic monarchies through Late Antiquity to the fall of Byzantium.) There was, too, the poet's very strong identity as a product of the Greek diaspora, an Orthodox Christian and the scion of that once-distinguished Phanariote family who saw, in the thousand-year arc of Byzantine history, not a decadent fall from idealized Classical heights—the standard Western European attitude, crystallized by Gibbon—but a continuous and coherent thread of Greek identity that seamlessly bound the antique past to the present.

And, finally, there was homosexual sensuality. However tormented and secretive he may have been about his desire for other men, Cavafy came, after a certain point in his career, to write about that desire with an unapologetic directness so unsensational, so matter-of-fact, that we can forget that barely ten years had passed since Oscar Wilde's death when the first of these openly homoerotic poems was published. As the poet himself later acknowledged, he had to reach his late forties before he found a way to unify his passion for the past, his passion for "Hellenic" civilization, and his passion for other men in poems that met his rigorous standards for publication.

The earliest poems we have date to the poet's late teens, the period when he was sojourning with his mother's family in and around Constantinople. These include dutiful if unpersuasive exercises on Romantic themes (ecstatic encomia to the lovely eyes of fetching lasses; a Grecified adaptation of Lady Anne Barnard's ballad on love and loss in the Highlands) and, perhaps predictably, some flights of Turkish Orientalism, complete with smoldering beauties locked up in harems. As time passed, he was drawn more and more to recent and contemporary currents in Continental literature. The Parnassian movement of the 1860s and 1870s, in particular, with its eager response to Théophile Gautier's call for an "Art for Art's sake," its insistence on elevating polished form over earnest subjective, social, and political content, and particularly its invitation to a return to the milieus and models of the antique Mediterranean past, had special appeal. (That a number of Cavafy's poems from this period are sonnets is surely a testament to the influence of the Parnassians, who prized the form for its rigorous technical requirements.)

From the Parnasse it was but a short step to Baudelaire, a Greek translation of whose "Correspondences" constitutes part of one 1892 poem; and, ultimately, to Symbolism. It is not hard to see the allure that the French writer's elevation of the poet as a member of an elite—a gifted seer whose special perceptions were denied to the common mass—had for the young Cavafy, in whom a taste for the past, as well as a necessarily secret taste for specialized erotic pleasures, coexisted. Lines from the second half of "Correspondences According to Baudelaire" suggests how thoroughly the young Alexandrian had absorbed the lessons of the pioneering French modernist:

> Do not believe only what you see.
>
> The vision of poets is sharper still.
>
> To them, Nature is a familiar garden.
>
> In a shadowed paradise, those other
> people grope along the cruel road.

With Cavafy, the inevitably self-justifying preoccupation with the notion of a rarefied artistic elite ("Cavafy's attitude toward the poetic

vocation is an aristocratic one," wrote Auden, perhaps a trifle indul-
gently)—an attitude irresistible, as we might imagine, to a painfully
closeted gay man—was paralleled by a lifelong fascination with figures
gifted with second sight, extrasensory perception, and telepathic
knowledge. It found its ideal historical correlative in the first-century
A.D. magus and sage Apollonius of Tyana, about whom Cavafy pub-
lished three poems and, as the corpus of poems left unfinished at the
time of his death now makes clear, was working on the draft of another
toward the end of his life.

As with Baudelaire, the Parnassians, and the later Esoteric and Deca-
dent poets, the furious nineteenth-century obsession with progress,
fueled by the technological advances of the industrial age, found no
favor with the young Cavafy. His 1891 sonnet "Builders" not only makes
clear his allegiance to Baudelaire's worldview, but also sets the stage for
a poetic gaze that would, for so much of his life, be backward-glancing
in one way or another:

> . . . the good builders make haste
> all as one to shield their wasted labor.
> Wasted, because the life of each is passed
> embracing ills and sorrows for a future generation,
>
> that this generation might know an artless
> happiness, and length of days, and wealth, and wisdom
> without base sweat, or servile industry.
>
> But it will never live, this fabled generation;
> its very perfection will cast this labor down
> and once again their futile toil will begin.

The rejection of modern notions of progress, the inward- and back-
ward-looking gaze, inevitably led to a flirtation with Decadence and
Aestheticism as well. The same turbulently formative years of the 1890s
produced, for example, a coldly glittering poem, in quatrains, on
Salome, in which a young scholar, having playfully asked Salome for her
own head—and having been obeyed—"orders this bloodied thing to / be

taken from him, and continues / his reading of the dialogues of Plato";
one feels the spirit of Wilde hovering here. More important, the begin-
ning of that decade saw the composition of a cycle of eleven poems, all
but two of which we know by their titles alone, which were collected
under the heading "Byzantine Days"—Byzantium being a milieu much
beloved of the Decadents, who viewed it, of course, from the Western,
rather than Eastern, European point of view. Cavafy would come to
reject these poems as "unsuitable to his characters": only two survived
the later purge of his early work. It would be some time before he came
to appreciate fully just how well Byzantium would serve his artistic and
intellectual needs.

Indeed, by the end of the 1890s he was experiencing a profound
intellectual and artistic crisis that had been precipitated by his engage-
ment not with other poets, but with two historians. A series of reading
notes on Gibbon's *Decline and Fall of the Roman Empire,* made between
1893 (the year after he wrote the last of his "Byzantine Days" poems)
and 1899, indicates a serious ongoing engagement with the great
Enlightenment historian. The exasperated rejection of Gibbon's dis-
dainful view of Byzantium and Christianity that we find in those notes
betrays the strong influence exerted by the contemporary Greek histo-
rian Konstantinos Paparrigopoulos, whose *History of the Greek Nation*
expounded a Romantic-nationalist vision of a coherent Greek identity
continuing unbroken from ancient to Byzantine to modern times. It was
Cavafy's reading in these two historians that led him to reject his earlier,
rather facile use of history as merely the vehicle for bejeweled verses in
the Parnassian mode on "Ancient Days" (one of the thematic headings
into which he'd group his poems: others were "The Beginnings of
Christianity," "Passions," and "Prisons"), and inspired him to try to find a
way to integrate History and Poetry in a more intellectually and aes-
thetically serious way.

This intellectual crisis coincided with a devastating series of deaths
of friends and family members throughout the same decade (his two
closest friends, three of his six brothers, an uncle, his mother, and his
maternal grandfather would all die between 1886 and 1902) and with
what he obscurely referred to as a "crisis of lasciviousness," which may
or may not have had something to do with his intense attraction to

Alexander Mavroudis. Together, these cerebral, emotional, and erotic upheavals culminated in a dramatic reappraisal of his life's work thus far: the "Philosophical Scrutiny" of 1902–03, to which the poet, as he turned forty, ruthlessly subjected all of his poems written up to that point, both unpublished and published. (Hence the later appellation "Repudiated" for a group of poems that he'd already published by that time and subsequently disowned.) A contemporary note that he left reveals a writer at a moment that he recognizes as one of deep significance, even if he hasn't yet seen his way through to his ultimate destination:

> After the already settled Emendatory Work, a philosophical scrutiny of my poems should be made.
>
> Flagrant inconsistencies, illogical possibilities, ridiculous exaggeration should certainly be corrected in the poems, and where the corrections cannot be made the poems should be sacrificed, retaining only any verses of such sacrificed poems as might prove useful later on in the making of new work.
>
> Still the spirit in which the Scrutiny is to be conducted should not be too fanatical . . .
>
> Also care should be taken not to lose from sight that a state of feeling is true and false, possible and impossible at the same time, or rather by turns. And the poet—who even when he works most philosophically, remains an artist— gives one side, which does not mean that he denies the other, or even—though perhaps this is stretching the point—that he wishes to imply that the side he treats is the truest, or the one oftener true. He merely describes a possible and an occurring state of feeling—sometimes very transient, sometimes of some duration.
>
> Very often the poet's work has but a vague meaning: it is a suggestion: the thoughts are to be enlarged by future generations or his immediate readers: Plato said that poets utter great meanings without realizing them themselves . . .
>
> My method of procedure for this Philosophical Scrutiny

may be either by taking the poems one by one and settling them at once—following the lists and ticking each on the list as it is finished, or effacing it if vowed to destruction: or by considering them first attentively, reporting on them, making a batch of the reports, and afterwards working on them on the basis and in the sequence of the batch: that is the method of procedure of the Emendatory Work . . .

If a thought has really been true for a day, its becoming false the next day does not deprive it of its claim to verity. It may have been only a passing or a short-lived truth, but if intense and serious it is worthy to be received, both artistically and philosophically. (tr. Manuel Savidis)

This unsparing (if, typically, not unforgiving) self-examination was the portal to the poet's mature period, one in which the tripartite division that he had once used to categorize his work—into "philosophical" (by which he meant provocative of reflection), "historical," and "sensual" poems—began to disintegrate. The enriched and newly confident sense of himself as a Greek and as a man of letters that resulted from the intellectual crisis of the 1890s seems to have resulted in some kind of reconciliation with his homosexual nature, too. (The death of his mother might, in its own way, have been liberating in this respect.)

Indeed it is no accident that Cavafy himself dated this period to the year 1911—the year in which he published "Dangerous," the first of his poems that situated homoerotic content in an ancient setting. Nor is it a coincidence that the subject of this poem is a Syrian student living in Alexandria during the uneasy double reign of the sons of Constantine the Great, Constans and Constantius, in the fourth century A.D., at the very moment when the Roman Empire was segueing from paganism to Christianity. As if profiting from that uncertain moment, and reflecting it as well, the young man feels emboldened to give bold voice to illicit urges:

> Strengthened by contemplation and study,
> I will not fear my passions like a coward.
> My body I will give to pleasures,

to diversions that I've dreamed of,
to the most daring erotic desires,
to the lustful impulses of my blood, without
any fear at all.

Both the setting and the character are typical of what George Seferis described as the characteristic Cavafian milieu: "the margins of places, men, epochs . . . where there are many amalgams, fluctuations, transformations, transgressions." (The reader of his poems would, indeed, do well to observe how often, and how strikingly, we encounter the vocabulary of indirect placement—"nearby," "in front of," "by," "next to," "on the side"—in these poems. The titles alone of many betray this preoccupation with the edges of spaces: "In the Entrance of the Café," "The Mirror in the Entrance," "On the Outskirts of Antioch.") As he neared the age of fifty, Cavafy had at last found a way to write, without shame, about his desire—a way that suggestively conflated the various margins to which he had always been drawn: erotic, geographical, spatial, temporal.

The painfully achieved reconciliation of Gibbon's eighteenth-century, Enlightenment view of history and Paparrigopoulos's nineteenth-century, Romantic national feeling, coupled with a startlingly prescient twentieth-century willingness to write frankly about homosexual experience, made possible the "unique tone of voice," as the admiring Auden described it, that is the unmistakable and inimitable hallmark of Cavafy's work. Ironic yet never cruel, unsurprised by human frailty, including his own ("Cavafy appreciates cowardice also," Forster wrote, "and likes the little men who can't be consistent or maintain their ideals") yet infinitely forgiving of it, that tone takes its darker notes from the historian's shrewd appreciation for the ironies of human action (which inevitably result, as did the life-altering business misfortunes of his father and uncles, from imperfect knowledge, bad timing, missed opportunities, or simply bad luck); yet at the same time is richly colored by a profound sympathy for human striving in the face of impossible obstacles. (Which could be the armies of Octavian or taboos against forbidden desires.) And it is inflected, too, by the connoisseur's unsparing and unsentimental grasp of both the pleasures and the pain to which desire makes us vulnerable.

That appreciation, that sympathy, that understanding are, of course, made possible only by Time—the medium that makes History possible, too. As I have said, for many readers, even sophisticated ones, Cavafy is a poet who wrote essentially two kinds of poems: daringly exposed verses about desire, whose frank treatment of homoerotic themes put them decades ahead of their time—and make them gratifyingly accessible; and rather abstruse historical poems, filled with obscure references to little-known and confusingly homonymous Hellenistic or Byzantine monarchs, and set in epochs that one was never held responsible for learning and places that fringed the shadowier margins of the Mediterranean map. But to divide the poet's work in this way is to make a very serious mistake: Cavafy's one great subject, the element that unites virtually all of his work, is Time. His poetry returns obsessively to a question that is, essentially, a historian's question: how the passage of time affects our understanding of events—whether the time in question is the millennia that have elapsed since 31 B.C., when the Hellenophile Marc Antony's dreams of an Eastern Empire were pulverized by Rome (the subject of seven poems), or the mere years that, in the 1918 poem "Since Nine—," have passed since those long-ago nights that the narrator spent in bustling cafés and crowded city streets: a space of time that has since been filled with the deaths of loved ones whose value he only now appreciates, sitting alone in a room without bothering to light the lamp. What matters to Cavafy, and what so often gives his work both its profound sympathy and its rich irony, is the understanding, which as he knew so well comes too late to too many, that however fervently we may act in the dramas of our lives—emperors, lovers, magicians, scholars, pagans, Christians, catamites, stylites, artists, saints, poets—only time reveals whether the play is a tragedy or a comedy.

The references to long-vanished eras, places, and figures that we so often find in Cavafy's poetry, and which indeed are unfamiliar even to most scholars of Classical antiquity, are, for this reason, never to be mistaken for mere exercises in abstruse pedantry. Or, indeed, for abstruseness at all. A poem's casual allusion to, say, the autumnal thoughts of the Byzantine emperor Manuel Comnenus in the year 1180 functions quite differently from the way in which invocations of arcane material can function in (to take the well-known example of a contemporary) *The Waste Land* of T. S. Eliot—where the self-consciously rarefied quality of the numerous allusions is part of the texture of the poem, part of its Modernist project. Cavafy, by contrast, may be said simply to have inhabited his various pasts so fully that they are all equally present to him. Not for nothing are a striking number of his poems about nocturnal apparitions of those who have vanished into history. In "Caesarion," for instance, a poem written in 1914 and published in 1918—the intervening years, the years of the Great War, saw the publication of a number of poems on beautiful dead youths—the beautiful (as he imagines) teenage son of Caesar and Cleopatra materializes one night in the poet's apartment:

> Ah, there: you came with your indefinite
> charm . . .
>
> . . . .
> And I imagined you so fully
> that yesterday, late at night, when the lamp
> went out—I deliberately let it go out—
> I dared to think you came into my room,
> it seemed to me you stood before me.

Such apparitions do not always belong to the distant past. In "Since Nine—," published in 1918 and written the year before, an "apparition" of the poet's own "youthful body" suddenly materializes in front of him one evening as he sits alone in a darkened room; in an Unfinished Poem of the same period, first drafted in 1919, "It Must Have Been the Spirits," the poet's own soul, together with the image of a louche youth he'd encountered years ago in Marseille, takes form before his eyes, replacing a decor that is itself a suggestive mélange of past and present (a commonplace settee, a piece of Archaic Greek statuary). Although in the latter poem the narrator attributes his supernatural vision to the excess of wine he'd drunk the previous night—hence the title—such apparitions are, therefore, hardly anomalous in his creative life, and symbolize a crucial theme of the entire body of work: the presence of the past in our own present. To Cavafy, figures such as that of the dead princeling and the long-forgotten French boy all inhabit the same era—

the vastly arcing past that his own imagination inhabited so fully—and were therefore as alive and present to him as the whores who lived in the brothel below his apartment on the Rue Lepsius. ("Where could I better live?" he once remarked, in the worldly tone we recognize from his verse. "Under me is a house of ill repute, which caters to the needs of the flesh. Over there is the church, where sins are forgiven. And beyond is the hospital, where we die.") It is the responsibility of the reader to inhabit that past as fully as possible, too, if only during the brief space during which he or she explores these poems. Otherwise, the meaning of many of them will be obscure, if not opaque. And the reader who, put off by that opacity, seeks out the contemporary poems while skipping over the historical poems, is missing the point of Cavafy's work—is, like so many of his characters both real and imagined, mistaking the clouded part for the clear and illuminating whole.

The rich tension between furious human striving (political, intellectual, or erotic) in the present and the poignantly belated ability to assess the true significance of that striving indeed characterizes the most memorable of Cavafy's poems. It is there in "Nero's Deadline," in which the thirty-year-old emperor, freshly back in Rome from a trip to hedonistic Greece, never dreams that "beware the age of seventy-three," the Delphic oracle's stern warning to him, refers not to him but to his aged general, Galba, plotting revolt in Spain, who will replace him on the imperial throne. It is there, too, in the dazzled and uncomprehending gawking on the part of the citizens of Seleucia, in "One of Their Gods," who can't possibly know that the stupefyingly beautiful youth whom they see passing through the marketplace on the way to the red-light district is actually one of the Greek gods. Quite typically of the great mature poetry, the confusion of the hapless observers within the poem mirrors a purposeful and productive confusion, for the reader, as to what era we are in, and indeed what order of being—human? divine? real? mythological?—we are reading about:

> And as he disappeared beneath the arcades,
> among the shadows and the evening lights,
> making his way to the neighborhood that comes alive

> only at night—that life of revels and debauchery,
> of every known intoxication and lust—
> they'd wonder which of Them he really was
> and for which of his suspect diversions
> he'd come down to walk Seleucia's streets
> from his Venerable, Sacrosanct Abode.

Here we have another inscrutable apparition; and we have, too, the subtle, richly matured transformation of a theme from the early years: a message from the gods that only the elect can decipher.

The poet's predilection for the historian's perspective—his interest in the way in which the experiences of the present, always confusing as they occur, can only be properly understood in the future; which is to say, at the moment when the present has become the past—helps to explain why so many of the ostensibly erotic poems are, essentially, poems about the past, too. A significant number of poems about desire in the poet's own time (or his recent past) are, in fact, cast as *memories* of love, or of desire. More often than not, when this poet speaks longingly of "skin, as if of jasmine" or eyes that are a "deep blue, sapphirine," as he does in the 1914 lyric "Far Off," he does so not as most conventional love poets might extol the virtues of their beloveds, but in his own distinctive way—which is to say, he speaks of them as a memory so far off that we cannot be sure whether the details of skin and eyes that he recalls are quite accurate:

> I'd like to talk about that memory . . .
> But by now it's long died out . . . as if there's nothing left:
> because it lies far off, in the years of my first youth.
>
> Skin, as if it had been made of jasmine . . .
> That August—was it August?—evening . . .
> I can just recall the eyes: they were, I daresay, blue . . .
> Ah yes, blue: a deep blue, sapphirine.

Even in the most intensely erotic verses, poems in which the poet reveals that he knows "love's body . . . the lips, / sensuous and rose-colored, of drunkenness," as he does in the 1916 poem "One Night," the celebration of the physical turns out to be a memory:

> And there, in that common, vulgar bed
> I had the body of love, I had the lips,
> sensuous and rose-colored, of drunkenness—
> the rose of such a drunkenness, that even now
> as I write, after so many years have passed!,
> in my solitary house, I am drunk again.

This poet very seldom writes what we usually think of as love poetry; his verse, which if anything tends to be about desire, is also—if not primarily—about the way in which the passage of time makes possible the poetry about desire that we are reading.

That Cavafy saw not only desirable young men but desire itself through a historian's appraising eyes helps to account for a distinctive feature of his poetry. In sharp contrast to other Greek poets of his day, he notably shuns elaborate, exotic, or self-consciously "poetic" diction; his language, so famously plain, is striking above all for its lack of precision in descriptions of physical beauty—a choice of arresting significance in a poet greatly preoccupied with desire. More often than not he will resort to abstract adjectives—*oréos* and *émorfos,* "beautiful," *idanikós,* "ideal," *exaísia,* "exquisite," *idonikós,* "sensual," "voluptuous," *esthitikós,* "refined," "sensitive," "aesthetic"—where another poet might seek to evoke greater detail.

We very seldom know, in fact, just what the beautiful young men in so many of Cavafy's poems look like. In "One of Their Gods," the figure seen walking through the marketplace of a great city is simply "tall and perfectly beautiful"; in "Before Time Could Alter Them," the narrator's reverie about a long-ago affair whose premature end may have been a blessing (since it preserves the memory of the lovers' beauty "before Time could alter them"), the lover is described as a "beautiful boy," *oréo pedí.* And the climactic vision to which "Days of 1908" inexorably leads—a glimpse of a ravishing youth who is the subject of the narrator's fascinated gaze, after the boy has stripped for a seaside bathe—reveals only that he is

> flawlessly beautiful; a thing of wonder.
> His hair uncombed, rising from its peak;
> his limbs a little colored by the sun

What is of interest to Cavafy is not so much individual beauty, but the idea of beauty itself—what happens to it when it is filtered through the passage of many years. Significantly, one of the few poems to include some particulars of what a beautiful young man might actually look like is a poem about beauty in the abstract: the short lyric "I've Gazed So Much" (whose original title, it's worth noting, was "For Beauty"):

> At beauty I have gazed so much
> that my vision is filled with it.
> The body's lines. Red lips. Limbs made for pleasure.
> Hair as if it were taken from Greek statues:
> always lovely, even when it's uncombed,
> and falls, a bit, upon the gleaming brow.

The poet's descriptive vocabulary, then, while narrow, has the supreme advantage of imparting to his imaginations of the beautiful an abstract, philosophical dimension—and, perhaps more important, of forcing his reader to do what the historian must do, which is to apply his own imaginative powers to subjects of which, so often, few details are extant.

Indeed, if the desire that flares in so many of these poems has, more often than not, been extinguished, the compensation for all those vanished or disappointed or broken-off love affairs is an artistic one: for we are always reminded that the poem itself is the vehicle for the preservation of desire, and of beauty, that otherwise would have disappeared. This important theme has its roots in the young poet's debt to the Parnasse and to Baudelaire, with their elevation of the poet as a craftsman and seer whose gifts are denied to the common masses. A crucial aspect of this theme, developed as the poet evolved, was that the artistic creation ultimately has a life more substantial than the object that inspired it. Two decades after those early poems of the 1890s, with their heavy debt to those French poets, the theme recurs with greater subtlety, in suggestive ways. In the 1913 poem "In Stock," for instance, a jeweler—a stand-in for the poet, of course—fashions fabulous pieces that may mimic nature, but are symbols of the supremacy of his creative fantasy to any vulgar needs of the public:

> Roses from rubies, pearls into lilies,
> amethyst violets. Lovely the way that *he* sees,
>
> and judges, and wanted them; not in the way
> he saw them in nature, or studied them. He'll put them away
>
> in the safe: a sample of his daring, skillful work.
> Whenever a customer comes into the store,
>
> he takes other jewels out of the cases to sell—
> . . . .

And in another poem of virtually the same period, "Painted," written in 1914 and published in 1916, the theme of the superior powers of Art is again stressed. Here, however, it is not natural life but a beautiful boy who becomes the object of Art's transformative, and in this case healing, power:

> In this painting, now, I'm looking at
> a lovely boy who's lain down near a spring;
> it could be he's worn out from running.
> What a lovely boy; what a divine afternoon
> has caught him and put him to sleep.—
> Like this, for some time, I sit and look.
> And once again, *in* art, I recover from creating it.

Another twenty years later, the theme of the artist's observing gaze and creative powers as the indispensable vehicles for both an emotionally charged reverie and a creative commemoration has its most sublime expression in the magnificent late poem "Days of 1908," published the year before the poet's death. Here, the beautiful but down-at-the-heels young Alexandrian, full of his schemes to make, win, or borrow money (a character we have met before, to be sure), never dreams, as he strips for his seaside swim, that the beauty by which he may well end up making his living will be immortalized in unimagined ways by the poem's anonymous speaker. Or, rather, by Time itself, since the "you" to whom this speaker addresses himself is, in fact, the days of the long-past summer of 1908:

> Your vision preserved him
> as he was when he undressed, when he flung off
> the unworthy clothes, and the mended underwear.
> And he'd be left completely nude; flawlessly beautiful;
>   a thing of wonder.
> His hair uncombed, springing back;
> his limbs a little colored by the sun
> from his nakedness in the morning at the baths,
>   and at the seashore.

The hotly yearning heart, with its ambitions, its strivings; the coolly assessing mind, to which those yearnings can appear so puny, even absurd, when measured against the epic forces of history and time and chance. Beauty, yes—the red lips, the jasmine skin, the sapphire eyes: but we can only know that beauty, know about the red and jasmine and sapphire, because of the assessing, measured gaze of the observing artist who beheld and touched and looked; and remembered. The rich, perfervid, sensuous present of most lives is lost forever to recollection: only the living memory of that past, memory that is itself alchemized into something permanent, and permanently beautiful, by poetry, "preserves" them forever. The past and the present; the past *in* the present. Small wonder that Cavafy, toward the end of his life, insisted that "plenty of poets are poets only, but I am a historical poet." Those last two words are one way of rendering what he said in Greek, which was *piitís istorikós;* but the adjective *istorikós* can also be a substantive, "historian." There is no way to prove it, but I suspect that what he meant was precisely what his work makes clear: that he was a "poet-historian."

3

THE READER WHO takes the time to immerse himself in Cavafy's rich and idiosyncratic poetic world should be aware of certain technical features, not least because they raise questions about the aims and strategies of any given translation.

One of the techniques of which Cavafy made use to convey the suggestive interplay of past and present so important to his work is one that poses particularly thorny difficulties for the English translator. As a Greek author writing at the turn of the last century, Cavafy had available to him two quite different registers of the language: demotic Greek, the vernacular spoken by the people, and the far more formal *Katharevousa,* or "pure" Greek, the high language of literature, intellectual life, and officialdom. (The accent falls on the third syllable.) This artificial form of the language, invented at the turn of the nineteenth century by an eminent literary and political figure who had studied Classics, grafted much of the vocabulary and many of the more complicated grammatical forms of Classical Greek onto the everyday language as a means of "purifying" it of non-Greek elements that had accreted during centuries of foreign influence and occupation; its adoption was, therefore, a political gesture as much as anything else. Katharevousa became the official language of the state, and was used in newspapers, official publications, and government edicts. It was, moreover, de rigueur in institutions of higher learning.

Katharevousa savored, then, of official culture, the classical past, and high art. (To Forster, it "has tried to revive the classical tradition, and only succeeds in being dull.") Just as Cavafy began writing, however, katharevousa—after having achieved preeminence over the years as the primary vehicle for literary expression, one increasingly characterized by an elaborate diction and style—was being rejected by the so-called Generation of 1880, a literary movement led by the prolific poet, dramatist, and critic Kostas Palamas, who advocated the use of demotic in literature. Cavafy's earliest works were written in katharevousa, but in the early 1890s he had begun using demotic; the unpublished poem

"Good and Bad Weather" (1893) was the first poem written entirely in demotic.

And yet he often chose not to write entirely in demotic. A distinctive feature of Cavafy's style—perhaps *the* distinctive feature—is that he continued to mingle katharevousa diction and grammar (as well as pure Classical Greek words from time to time, to say nothing of citations from ancient texts) with demotic. The result is a poetry that has a unique and inimitable texture, very often plain and admirably direct but starched, too, with a loftier, more archaic and ceremonious language— like the talk of a fluent and charming raconteur (like Cavafy himself) that is sprinkled with locutions from the King James Bible. For this reason, it is a mistake to overemphasize, as many critics and admirers (and translators) have done, the laconic plainness of Cavafy's diction; such an emphasis fails to convey the frequent strangeness of the diction, the "unique and cunning alloy," as the great English travel writer and Hellenophile Patrick Leigh Fermor so marvelously put it in his essay "Landmarks in Decline,"

> in which the fragments of legal diction and ancient Greek and inscriptions on tombs and old chronicles—one can almost hear the parchment creak and the flutter of papyrus— are closely haunted by the *Anthology* and the Septuagint; it is contained in a medium demotic perversely stiffened with mandarin and beaten at last into an instrument of expression which is austere and frugal in the extreme.

Those strange irruptions of mandarin stiffness deserve to be heard. When, in "Philhellene," Cavafy ends a monologue by a vulgar eastern potentate—eager to indulge in superficial shows of Hellenic style despite that fact (which his monologue inadvertently betrays) that he is crassly disdainful of its substance—with an awkward shift into Classical Greek (on the word "unhellenized," no less), he tells us more about the speaker's pretensions than a laborious exposition could.

The deployment of this hybrid language—a verbal expression, you could say, of that larger and abiding fascination with margins, amalgams, cultural "alloys"—is, indeed, crucial for the interpretation of many poems. Two examples, one from a poem that treats a contemporary erotic theme, the other from a poem with an ancient setting, will help illuminate Cavafy's subtle technique, while showing my own strategies for rendering them in English.

The 1928 poem "Days of 1909, '10, and '11" treats a favorite theme: the squalid life of an impoverished young man whose spectacular beauty stands in stark contrast to his humble circumstances—and, in this case, to his convenient morals. (We're told that the lovely blacksmith's assistant is willing to sell his favors, if necessary, in order to buy a coveted tie or expensive shirt.) In the poem's final stanza, the narrator wonders whether even ancient Alexandria, famed for its louche and comely youths, could claim a young man as lovely as this down-at-the-heels boy. Here, the contrast between the allure of the youths in the glittering ancient city and that of a common blacksmith's boy is suggestively conveyed by the shift in tone between the adjective used of the former, *perikallis,* and the noun used of the latter, *agori:* for the former is a rather high-flown katharevousa word taken directly from the Ancient Greek (which I translate by means of the rather archaic "beauteous") while the latter is a quite ordinary noun: "kid."

Even more strikingly, in "The Seleucid's Displeasure," first written in 1910 and published in 1916, a large part of the meaning of the entire poem rests on the difference between a katharevousa and a demotic word, both of which mean the same thing. Set in the second century B.C., as the Hellenistic monarchies founded after the death of Alexander were crumbling before an emergent Rome, the poem treats the painful disappointment felt by one Greek monarch, Demetrius I Soter of the Seleucid house in Asia, on hearing that his Egyptian counterpart, Ptolemy VI, had cast aside his royal dignity and traveled to Rome as a supplicant in order to appeal for help in a dynastic struggle against his brother. The first two stanzas evoke Demetrius's grandiose regard for the dignity "befitting . . . an Alexandrian Greek monarch": to the impoverished Ptolemy he offers lavish clothing, jewels, and a retinue for his presentation to the Senate.

The Seleucid monarch's attitude is pointedly contrasted with Ptolemy's canny appreciation for political realities; he knows that he's likelier to obtain Roman aid if he appears humble when he makes his

appeal. His abject willingness to come down off his royal pedestal is bril-
liantly evoked in the Greek. In the first line of the stanza he is described
as having come for the purposes of *epaiteia,* a noun with roots in Classical
and Byzantine Greek that means everything from "a request" to "beg-
ging"; but in the last line, the verb used for the reason for his visit is the
demotic *zondanevo,* "to beg." Hence the shift from the high to the demotic
forms, both words meaning the same thing, itself beautifully reflects the
demotion in his status from an ostensibly independent ruler to a suppli-
cant reliant on the power of others. In my rendering of these lines, I have
attempted to suggest this tonal shift by using an abstruse term in the first
instance, and a familiar, monosyllabic word in the second:

> But the Lagid, who had come a mendicant,
> knew his business and refused it all:
> He didn't need these luxuries at all.
> Dressed in worn old clothes, he humbly entered Rome,
> and found lodgings with a minor craftsman.
> And then he presented himself to the Senate
> as an ill-fortuned and impoverished man,
> that with greater success he might beg.

As these two examples indicate, I have tried to convey distinctions
between katharevousa and demotic, when possible, by using high Lati-
nate forms in the case of the former, and ordinary, plain Anglo-Saxon
derivations in the case of the latter—an imperfect, but I hope sugges-
tive, means of conveying this vital aspect of Cavafy's technique. In
certain cases, moreover ("Philhellene," for one), I have used British
spellings when rendering katharevousa, since these—as indeed with the
archaic spellings of certain words that Cavafy often favored—instantly
and quite effectively (to the American eye) signal a different, often elite
cultural milieu, which is part of katharevousa's flavor.

There are other stylistic matters, resulting in other choices I have made,
with which the reader should be acquainted. However much Cavafy's
language may eschew the devices—metaphor, simile, figurative and
"lyrical" language—that we normally associate with poetry, his verse, in

Greek, is unmistakably musical. This music results principally from two stylistic features, which I have taken pains, whenever possible, to reproduce.

The first is meter. Very often Cavafy's lines have a strong iambic rhythm; very often, too, he favors a five-beat line that English speakers are familiar with—as Cavafy himself was, from his deep reading of British poets. (There is, indeed, a distinctly English cast to many of his poems, as commentators have observed.) Although he will often preserve a strict iambic pentameter, he just as often loosens the line when it suits his purposes. In "Nero's Deadline," for instance, we first learn about the Delphic oracle's warning (that the emperor should "beware the age of seventy-three"), as the direct object of the verb "heard," in a line with a strictly iambic beat with precisely ten syllables (I have marked the stresses with acute accents):

> *tou Dhélfikoú mantíou tón khrismó*
> the prophecy of the Delphic Oracle

Here, the preciseness of the meter vividly suggests the ineluctable character of the oracle itself. By contrast, the first line of the second stanza, in which the poet describes how Nero returns to Rome from a pleasure trip to Athens exhausted by his sensual indulgences, Cavafy maintains a five-beat line while padding it with five extra syllables:

> *Tóra stin Rhómi tha epitrépsei kourasménos lígo*
> Now to Rome he'll be returning a little bit wearied

The subtle loosening of the line nicely conveys the relaxation of the self-involved Nero, who is blithely unaware that his days of aesthetic and erotic pleasure are numbered.

These strong and suggestive rhythms structure much of the verse, from the early sonnets of the 1890s to the poems of his last decade; without them, the poetry, already devoid of the usual devices, might well seem flat-footed in a way that indeed reminds us that both the Ancient and the Modern Greek word for prose, *pezos,* literally means "pedestrian"—that is, language that lumbers along arhythmically rather than dancing. Fortunately for the English translator, English itself falls quite naturally into the rhythms that Cavafy favored.

Cavafy is, indeed, endlessly inventive with his meters. In certain early lyrics, for example "La Jeunesse Blanche" (1895) and "Chaldean Image" (1896), the very elaborate metrical schemes betray the young poet's infatuation with the Continental poetry of the day; while in others, like the Repudiated Poem "A Love" (1896), we hear the thrumming fifteen-syllable beat characteristic of the Greek popular songs so beloved of this poet. (In a famous 1904 poem, "Waiting for the Barbarians," Cavafy rather suggestively casts the anxious questions of the speakers in this "Greek" rhythm, while the answers that come back are in "English" iambics.) One particularly noteworthy metrical innovation can be observed in a number of lyrics composed in what George Seferis, in commenting on these poems, referred to as a "tango" rhythm. Each line of these poems is composed of two half lines of three beats each; the lines are separated by white space. Hence, for instance, the opening of "In Despair" looks like this:

Ton ékhas' éndhelós.   *Ke tóra piá zití*
sta khília káthenós   *kenoúriou erastí*
ta khília tá diká tou . . .

He's lost him utterly.   And from now on he seeks
in the lips of every new   lover that he takes
the lips of that one: *his.*

These tango poems, in striking contrast to their jaunty meter (which is striking in itself), are more often than not about devastating disappoint-ment or frustrated desire: for instance, "In the Taverns," in which a rejected lover consoles himself by "wallowing" in the demimonde of Beirut; "Temethus, an Antiochene: 400 A.D.," in which the verses of a poet "suffering in love" are "heated" because the historical figure he writes about is merely a stand-in for his lover; or "On the Italian Seashore," a historical poem in which an Italian youth of Greek descent stands "pensive and dejected" as he watches Roman troops unload the booty from their conquest of Greece in 146 B.C. Because this rhythm has such great technical and thematic significance, it seemed to me worthwhile to attempt to reproduce it, where possible.

The second crucial aspect of Cavafy's prosody is rhyme. The well-intentioned Forster couldn't have been more wrong when, in introducing the Alexandrian's poems to his British audience, he claimed that "they are all short poems, and unrhymed." The great majority of Cavafy's youthful output of the late 1880s and throughout the 1890s was strictly rhymed; many of those poems, as I have mentioned, are cast as sonnets (most as Italian sonnets), and adhere closely to all of the conventions of that form. Although it is true that as Cavafy matured his verse became freer, he continued to employ rhyme to potent effect for the rest of his career. Examples from three poems—one from the 1890s, another from the early 1910s (which is to say, after the Philosophical Scrutiny, the moment when the poet stood on the threshold of his mature work) as well as a very late one—show how important this device remained for him from the beginning to the end of his career.

"Walls," a crucial early poem written in 1896 and published the following year, combines, with a marvelous complexity and subtlety, two crucial aspects of Cavafy's technique: his early penchant for strict rhyme, and his pointed manipulation of tensions between katharevousa and demotic. It consists of eight lines, rhymed *a-b-a-b-c-d-c-d*:

> Without pity, without shame, without consideration
> they've built around me enormous, towering walls.
>
> And I sit here now in growing desperation.
> This fate consumes my mind, I think of nothing else:
>
> because I had so many things to do out there.
> O while they built the walls, why didn't I look out?
>
> But no noise, no sound from the builders did I hear.
> Imperceptibly they've shut me from the world without.

The rhymes (which in Greek are strictly homophonous) effectively convey the prisonlike feeling of being locked in; and indeed the poet listed this poem under the thematic heading "Prisons." But there is far more going on here. For in the case of each set of rhymes but one, the first rhymed word is katharevousa, while the second is demotic, or is at least neutral: hence for example line 1 (literally, "without consideration, without pity, without shame") ends with the katharevousa word αἰδώ, "shame," which is pronounced *ehdhó,* while line 3 (literally, "And I sit and lose all hope now here") ends with the demotic word ἐδώ, "here," which has the identical pronunciation. In the first two couplets, moreover, the katharevousa usages are associated with the oppressive "them" (*without shame, walls*), while the demotic usages are associated with the imprisoned "I" (*here, this fate*). The only pairing in which the rhymed words are both in the demotic is that of lines 6 and 8. The former (literally, "O while they built the walls, how could I not pay attention?") ends with the verb *proséxo,* "pay attention"—but to the Greek ear, the word is indistinguishable from the prepositional phrase *pros éxo,* "towards the outside": which is to say, the very direction in which the speaker failed to look. (To the Greek ear, it sounds as if the line is going to be something like, "O while they built the walls, why didn't I look towards the outside?") In my translation I have tried to convey this provocative confusion by translating the first word by means of the casual English expression "look out," which has the further advantage of enabling the loaded repetition, which we find in the Greek, of the word "out."

Similarly, the two eight-line stanzas that make up "The City," which Cavafy published in 1910 after fifteen years of constant revision of an earlier version, and which he selected as the opening poem for his 1905–15 collection (and which is, therefore, the first of his poems that his readers encounter), follow a strict rhyme scheme, in this case a-b-b-c-c-d-d-a. Here, as before, he employs a strict homophonous end-rhyme to hammer home a crucial point. The first stanza provides a useful example:

> You said: "I'll go to some other land, I'll go to some other sea.
> There's bound to be another city that's better by far.
> My every effort has been ill-fated from the start;
> my heart—like something dead—lies buried away;
> How long will my mind endure this slow decay?
> Wherever I look, wherever I cast my eyes,

> I see all round me the black rubble of my life
> where I've spent so many ruined and wasted years."

In line 4 a desperately frustrated youth describes his heart as something that, like a corpse, lies "buried" (*thaméni,* the last word in the line in the original), and in the following line he asks, with great anguish, how long his mind will remain in a state of stagnation; the sound of the last words of this line in the Greek, *tha méni,* "will remain," are indistinguishable from those of *thaméni,* inextricably linking the boy's abject feeling of being buried alive to a predicament that is indeed desperate. For as we learn, he will in fact remain in Alexandria for the rest of his life, imprisoned by a hopeless, soul-destroying drudgery. The return in each stanza's final line to the rhyme with which the stanza begins (*khalassa,* "wasted"/*thalassa,* "sea") is, moreover, itself indicative of the way in which the boy is trapped, doomed always to return to "the same place." There is no forward motion in the rhymes, as there is no forward motion in his life.

In the late poem "Days of 1908," to recur to a by-now-familiar example of so many of Cavafy's most characteristic themes and techniques, rhyme is similarly used to great effect. The first three lines, for instance, quickly sketch a portrait of the dire economic position of the beautiful young man whom the narrator will later see naked on the beach:

> *Ton khróno ekeínon vréthike khorís dhouliá*
> That year he found himself without a job;

> *ke sinepós zoúsen ap' ta khartiá*
> and so he made a living from cards,

> *apó to távli, ké ta daneiká.*
> from backgammon, and what he borrowed.

The triple repetition of accented final syllables ending in a short *a,* which I have attempted to mimic here, conveys the dreary monotony of the boy's endless quest for money. The conclusion of the poem shows a similar interest in exploiting the potential of rhyme. The two penultimate stanzas are composed of three lines each, the sequence of end-rhymes in the first repeated by that in the second:

> His clothes were in a dreadful state.
> There was one suit that he would always wear,
> a suit of a very faded cinnamon hue.
>
> Oh days of the summer of nineteen hundred eight,
> your vision, quite exquisitely, was spared
> that very faded cinnamon-colored suit.

But here, the similarity in sound is pointedly belied by a crucial difference in sense. The first of these two stanzas describes the shabby state of the boy's clothes, as observed by the poet, while the second declares that Time itself (the apostrophized "days of 1908") has been spared the sight of that ugliness—and will, as we learn in the final stanza, already quoted above, redeem the boy's tawdry circumstances by preserving forever the vision of his beauty once it has been stripped of the dreadful clothes.

As these few examples will indicate, a primary concern of the present translation is to try—as much as possible, and without contorting the English—to convey this vital element of Cavafian prosody. As these examples also show, I have made use of off-rhymes, assonance, consonance, and slant-rhymes when strict rhymes were difficult to achieve in English, in the belief that readers should be able to feel the formal elements of Cavafy's verse whenever possible.

A short word on Cavafy's striking use of enjambment—the way he allows a sentence or thought to continue past a line break—is in order, because this device, too, puts interesting demands on the translator.

Cavafy's use of this device is the more noteworthy because he is quite happy to eschew it altogether, as he does, for instance, in the poems "Whenever They Are Aroused" and "In the Church." In the latter (which I quote below in its entirety), published probably in 1912, the lack of any spillover from line to line gives the poem just the right incantatory, ecclesiastical feel:

I love the church—its labara,
the silver of its vessels, its candelabra,
the lights, its icons, its lectern.

When I enter there, inside of a Greek Church:
with the aromas of its incenses,
the liturgical chanting and harmonies,
the magnificent appearance of the priests,
and the rhythm of their every movement—
resplendent in their ornate vestments—
my thoughts turn to the great glories of our race,
to our illustrious Byzantinism.

With this we might compare another, historical poem of 1912, "Alexandrian Kings." Here Cavafy describes the magnificent ceremony, staged in Alexandria by Antony and Cleopatra in 34 B.C., at which the power-hungry royal couple publicly proclaimed Cleopatra's still-small sons (aged thirteen, six, and two) the rulers of a number of foreign possessions stretching far into Asia—an event that demonstrated the couple's international aspirations, even as the ironic contrast between the magnificence of the honorifics and the tender age of their recipients, made much of in this poem, highlights the ruthless ambition of the royal parents.

Cavafy's characteristic interest in the ironies of this occasion is evident precisely in his use of enjambment. Take, for instance, the first few lines of the poem:

The Alexandrians came out in droves
to have a look at Cleopatra's children:
Caesarion, and also his little brothers,
Alexander and Ptolemy, who for the first
time were being taken to the Gymnasium.

The first instance of enjambment—"came out in droves / to have a look"—underscores the ardent curiosity of the local populace, and hence emphasizes the dazzling nature of the occasion (while hinting at

the locals' cynicism about political displays, which is, in fact, empha-
sized later on in the poem). The second instance—"who for the first /
time were being taken"—places extraordinary emphasis on the noun
time by separating it from its adjective, *first,* which is also thereby
emphasized: an emphasis that reminds us of the youth and inexperience
of the children who are being so cynically exploited by their parents.

To turn to a work from the poet's latest phase, the final stanza of the
great 1930 poem "The Mirror in the Entrance" suggests how Cavafy
continued to hone his handling of this technique. The poem describes
an occasion on which a beautiful youth employed by a tailor makes a
delivery to a wealthy home; while he waits for a receipt, alone in the
vestibule, he approaches an old mirror and fixes his tie, unaware that the
mirror itself—here a double for the poet—is, as it were, "watching" him.
The poem ends with a description of the mirror's feelings:

> But the ancient mirror, which had seen and seen again,
> throughout its lifetime of so many years,
> thousands of objects and faces—
> but the ancient mirror now became elated,
> inflated with pride, because it had received upon itself
> perfect beauty, for a few minutes.

Except for the final two lines, each line is a grammatically independent
unit ending with some kind of punctuation—a comma or a dash. Com-
ing at the end of this series of discrete phrases, the penultimate line,
which can only be logically and grammatically completed by the line
that follows, takes on a tremendous drama and excitement: by with-
holding the object of the verb "received" until the next line, the poet
gives the all-important word "beauty" an enormous climactic force.

Given the importance of this technique in Cavafy's prosody, the
meticulous care with which he constructed each line, I've tried to struc-
ture the English of these translations so that it achieves the same effect.

One final note, concerning a choice on my part that might strike some
readers as controversial. In rendering Greek names from the Classical,
Hellenistic, Late Antique, and Byzantine past, I have consistently chosen

to eschew a phonetic rendering of the way those names sound in Greek, opting instead to adopt the traditional, Latinate forms—which is to say, the forms that will be familiar to English speakers. To my mind, mimicking the contemporary Greek pronunciation of the names of the historical or pseudohistorical characters is, at best, inappropriate and indeed unhelpful in an English translation. When the Greek eye sees the name Ἰουστινιανός, the person brought to mind is the person brought to mind when the eye of an English-speaking person comes across the name "Justinian"; transliterating it as "Ioustinianos" is to obscure, rather than translate, Cavafy's text.

Worse, a misguided allegiance to the sound of Modern Greek can lead to a serious misrepresentation of a poem's deeper meanings. To take "The Seleucid's Displeasure" once more: certain translators have chosen to render the title of this poem as "The Displeasure of Selefkidis"—that last word being an accurate phonetic reproduction of what the Greek word Σελευκίδης, which indeed appears in the poem's title, sounds like. But this choice conveys the entirely false impression that "Selefkidis" is someone's name, whereas, as we know, the word refers here to a member of the Seleucid *dynasty*—someone whose name was, in fact, Demetrius. The word "Seleucid" in this poem is therefore a crucial part of its meaning, one that rests on our ability to grasp the great, if rather pathetic, pride that Demetrius took in the fact that he was a Hellenistic monarch—a *Seleucid*. A fluent speaker and tireless reader of English, Cavafy himself was familiar with the Latinate forms of these names from his extensive reading in English works of history and philology—Gibbon, J. B. Bury, many others—and used these forms himself when writing in English. Not least for that reason, I have done the same.

4

THE PRESENT VOLUME collects all of the known poetic work of Cavafy (with the exception of five translations that he made as a young man from various languages into Greek, which it seemed pointless to retranslate). A second, companion volume offers the first English translations, with full commentary, of the thirty nearly complete drafts that the poet left among his papers at his death, a body of work now known as the Unfinished Poems (to which I occasionally refer in the Notes to this volume).

The manner in which Cavafy's poetry is presented in the following pages merits brief comment. Although he published a small number of verses, most of them when he was young, in literary journals and annu-als, Cavafy had for most of his career a highly idiosyncratic method of presenting his poems, and never published a definitive collection of them in book form. He preferred, instead, to have poems printed at his own expense as broadsheets or in pamphlets, which he would distribute to a select group of friends and admirers. Among other things, this method allowed the poet to treat every poem as a work in progress; friends recalled that he often went on emending poems after they had been printed. In an essay called *Independence,* the poet articulated what was clearly a kind of anxiety about the finality associated with publication:

> When the writer knows pretty well that only very few vol-umes of his edition will be bought . . . he obtains a great freedom in his creative work. The writer who has in view the certainty, or at least the probability of selling all his edition, and perhaps subsequent editions, is sometimes influenced by their future sale . . . almost without meaning to, almost without realizing—there will be moments when, knowing how the public thinks and what it likes and what it will buy, he will make some little sacrifices—he will phrase this bit differently, and leave out that. And there is nothing more destructive for Art (I tremble at the mere thought of it) than that this bit should be differently phrased or that bit omitted.

Still, after a time he would periodically order modest printings of book-lets that contained small selections of the poems, arranged thematically. The first of these, *Poems 1904,* contained just fourteen poems; a second, *Poems 1910,* added seven more, and a later manuscript of that booklet (known, because the poet copied it out by hand as a gift to his friend and heir, as the "Sengopoulos Notebook") added one more early poem— "Walls"—which had been written in 1897 and much anthologized, bringing the total to twenty-two. These and subsequent booklets (and sometimes the poems in them) were constantly being revised, added to, and subtracted from: hence *Poems 1910* became *Poems (1909–1911)*, and then *Poems (1908–1914)*, and so on, according to which works the poet had decided to add or remove.

By the time Cavafy died, there were three such collections in circulation. Two were bound, and arranged thematically: *Poems 1905–1915*, containing forty poems (the dates refer to the year of first publication) and *Poems 1916–1918*, containing twenty-eight poems. The third, *Poems 1919–1932*, a collection of sixty-nine poems arranged chronologically by date of first publication, was merely a pinned-together sheaf of individual sheets. These 137 poems, together with one poem that Cavafy had corrected for the printer in the weeks before his death, "On the Outskirts of Antioch," and sixteen early poems from the Sengopoulos Notebook that had not already been collected in *Poems 1905–1915*, are the 154 poems that appeared in the first commercial collection of his work, lavishly published (in a chic Art Deco style) in Alexandria two years after Cavafy's death, edited by Rika Sengopoulou, the first wife of his heir.

Although this group of poems is now often referred to as "the Canon"—a word, one suspects, that would have caused Cavafy to raise an eyebrow, given his sardonic appreciation for the difference between the judgments we pass and those that history passes—I refer to them here as the Published Poems, since these are the works that this most fastidious of poets published, or approved for publication, during his own lifetime, precisely as he wanted them to be read. They appear here in the following order: (1) *Poems 1905–1915;* (2) *Poems 1916–1918;* (3) *Poems 1919–1933* (including "On the Outskirts of Antioch"); a fourth section, which I have entitled "Poems Published 1897–1904," offers the contents of the Sengopoulos Notebook, minus of course the six poems that already appear in *Poems 1905–1915*. (It is worth remembering that Cavafy was eager to take *Poems 1910,* the basis for the Sengopoulos Notebook, out of circulation in the years after its publication.) It is true that this presentation of the latter group wrests them from the poet's careful thematic arrangement, in which each poem is meant to comment on and, as it were, converse with its neighbor; but it would be awkward, to say nothing of pedantic, to repeat six poems in two successive sections. For the sake of readers who want to experience the Sengopoulos Notebook as Cavafy arranged it, I have included, before this final section of the Published Poems, a list of the poems giving the order in which they appeared in the Notebook.

Because they were works about which the poet had mixed feelings, I have decided to place the remaining poems, some of which are very early, after those that the poet approved for publication, in roughly chronological order—which is to say, first the twenty-seven Repudiated Poems, originally published between 1886 and 1898, and subsequently renounced by the poet; and then the Unpublished Poems. The latter is a group of seventy-seven texts (including three written in English) that Cavafy completed but never approved for publication, and which he kept among his papers, many of them bearing the notation "Not for publication, but may remain here." The first of these was written when the poet was around fourteen; the last was written in 1923, when he was sixty. Thirteen found their way into print after World War II, and a complete scholarly edition of the entire group, edited by George Savidis, was published in Athens, in 1968. A subsequent edition, published by Mr. Savidis in 1993, gives to them a new name, "Hidden Poems," but I have retained the old designation, "Unpublished," both in my text and in my notes, since I believe that "unpublished" adequately suggests the poet's attitude toward those works without introducing speculative psychological overtones. In the present volume I have included translations of all seventy-four of the Unpublished Poems that were written in Greek, as well as the texts of the three poems Cavafy wrote in English, since they are original works; I have omitted from the present translation the poet's five translations into Greek of works in other languages, of which three are from English. Readers will also find translations of the three remarkable Prose Poems.

A final word, about the presentation of the poems. As we know, the dates of composition and subsequent publication of Cavafy's poems is often suggestive: it surely meant something that he spent fifteen years returning to and polishing "The City" before he chose to publish it. According to Sarayannis,

Cavafy himself told me that he never managed to write a poem from beginning to end. He worked on them all for years, or often let them lie for whole years and later took them up again. His dates therefore only represent the year when he judged that one of his poems more or less satisfied him.

Given the importance of those dates, I have chosen to note them at the bottom of the page(s) on which the poems appear in the main portion of this text, rather than cluttering the notes at the back with one-line items ("Written in 1917, published in 1918"). To do so, I have adopted the following system of notation. When known, the year of original composition (and of subsequent rewriting, if there was one and if we know when it occurred) appears in *italics;* the year (or years) of publication appear in roman type. Hence, for example, in the case of the Published Poem "Song of Ionia," of which an early version was written at some point before 1891 and then published in 1896, only to be subsequently revised in 1905 and published in its final form in 1911, the notation reads as follows: [*<1891;* 1896; *1905;* 1911].

In the case of the Unpublished Poems—the date of whose first publication, long after the poet's death, does not, by contrast, shed any light on his feelings or intentions—I have merely added the date of composition, in parentheses, after the title of each poem: a choice that, I think, has the virtue of marking those poems visually as different from those that Cavafy himself chose to publish—however he may have subsequently felt about them. Readers today are, indeed, likely to find more to admire, or at the very least to learn from, in the Repudiated and Unpublished Poems than Cavafy himself would have suspected.

But then, as he himself knew so well, Time is the final arbiter—of literary reputations, as well as other things. In the second of the essays he wrote about Cavafy, in the hopes of alerting English speakers to a poet "whose attitude to the past did not commend him to some of his contemporaries," E. M. Forster, writing in 1951, recalled a conversation he had with the poet in 1918:

Half humorously, half seriously, he once compared the Greeks and the English. The two peoples are almost exactly alike, he argued; quick-witted, resourceful, adventurous. "But there is one unfortunate difference between us, one little difference. We Greeks have lost our capital—and the results are what you see. Pray, my dear Forster, oh pray, that you never lose your capital."

"His words made one think," Forster went on, after ruefully observing that, while British insolvency had seemed impossible in 1918, the passage of three decades and a world war had made "all things possible." Now, when nearly twice as many decades have passed since Forster wrote those words, there is once more occasion to "think" about the themes—the unexpected faltering of overconfident empires; the uneasy margins where West and East meet, sometimes productively but often not; how easy it is, for polities as well as for people, to "lose one's capital"—which once again turn out to be not "historical" but, if anything, very contemporary indeed; themes that the "very wise, very civilized man" kept returning to, knowing full well, as historians do, that the backward glance can, in the end, be a glimpse into the future.

PRONUNCIATION OF
PROPER NAMES

The rhythm and assonance of Cavafy's poetry depends in many cases on the correct pronunciation of proper names; fortunately, a more or less standard pronunciation of Greek and Byzantine names as traditionally spelled in English, which I have chosen to follow, often allows for scansion and sound patterns not dramatically different from the ones produced by the Modern Greek pronunciation of those names.

- The consonant combination *ch,* representing the Greek letter χ, is generally pronounced as a hard *c* or *k* whether at the beginning of a word or in the middle; hence the name *Charmides* is *KAHR-mih-deez,* not *Tchar-mih-deez.*

- An initial *i* is consonantal, pronounced as a *y:* hence the name *Iases* is pronounced *Yah-SEEZ.* Otherwise, the vowel *i* is pronounced *ee,* and never rhymes with the word *eye.*

- The final *-es* in masculine nouns and names is invariably voiced, and pronounced *eez,* like the *-es* at the end of the name *Socrates.* Hence the name *Mebes* is pronounced *Meebeez,* never *Meebs.*

- In the case of Classical Greek names, the final *e* in feminine nouns and names is always sounded as *ay:* hence the name *Stratonice* is *Strah-toe-NEE-kay.* In the case of Byzantine names, the final *e* is pronounced as *ee:* hence the second part of the empress Anna Dalassene's name is *Dah-lah-see-NEE,* never *Dah-lah-SEEN.*

I

PUBLISHED POEMS

Poems 1905–1915

The City

You said: "I'll go to some other land, I'll go to some other sea.
There's bound to be another city that's better by far.
My every effort has been ill-fated from the start;
my heart—like something dead—lies buried away;
How long will my mind endure this slow decay?
Wherever I look, wherever I cast my eyes,
I see all round me the black rubble of my life
where I've spent so many ruined and wasted years."

You'll find no new places, you won't find other shores.
The city will follow you. The streets in which you pace
will be the same, you'll haunt the same familiar places,
and inside those same houses you'll grow old.
You'll always end up in this city. Don't bother to hope
for a ship, a route, to take you somewhere else; they don't exist.
Just as you've destroyed your life, here in this
small corner, so you've wasted it through all the world.

[*1894*; 1910]

5

The Satrapy

What a pity, given that you're made
for deeds that are glorious and great,
that this unjust fate of yours always
leads you on, and denies you your success;
that base habits get in your way,
and pettinesses, and indifference.
How terrible, too, the day when you give in
(the day when you let yourself go and give in),
and leave to undertake the trip to Susa,
and go to the monarch Artaxerxes,
who graciously establishes you at court,
and offers you satrapies, and the like.
And you, you accept them in despair,
these things that you don't want.
But your soul seeks, weeps for other things:
the praise of the People and the Sophists,
the hard-won, priceless "Bravos";
the Agora, the Theatre, and the victors' Crowns.
How will Artaxerxes give you *them,*
how will you find *them* in the satrapy;
and what kind of life, without them, will you live.

[*1905;* 1910]

But Wise Men Apprehend What Is Imminent

The gods perceive what lies in the future, and mortals, what occurs in the present, but wise men apprehend what is imminent.

—PHILOSTRATUS, *Life of Apollonius of Tyana*, VIII, 7

Mortal men perceive things as they happen.
What lies in the future the gods perceive,
full and sole possessors of all enlightenment.
Of all the future holds, wise men apprehend
what is imminent. Their hearing,

sometimes, in moments of complete
absorption in their studies, is disturbed. The secret call
of events that are about to happen reaches them.
And they listen to it reverently. While in the street
outside, the people hear nothing at all.

[*1896*; 1899; <1915]

7

Ides of March

Of glory be you fearful, O my Soul.
And if you are unable to defeat
your ambitions, then hesitantly, guardedly
pursue them. And the further you proceed,
the more searching, the more attentive must you be.

And when at last you reach your apogee—a Caesar;
and cut the figure of one who's much renowned,
then take heed more than ever as you go out on the street,
a man of power, conspicuous with your retinue,
when someone approaches you out of the crowd,
a certain Artemidorus, bringing a letter,
and hurriedly says "Read this right away,
it's something important that concerns you,"
don't fail to stop; don't fail to put off
all talk and business; don't fail to
brush off all and sundry who salute and fawn
(you can see them later); let even
the Senate wait, and find out at once
the weighty contents of Artemidorus's letter.

[*1906*; 1910]

Finished

Deep in fear and in suspicion,
with flustered minds and terrified eyes,
we wear ourselves out figuring how
we might avoid the certain
danger that threatens us so terribly.
And yet we're mistaken, that's not it ahead:
the news was wrong
(or we didn't hear it; or didn't get it right).
But a disaster that we never imagined
suddenly, shatteringly breaks upon us,
and unprepared—no time left now—we are swept away.

[*1910*; 1911]

The God Abandons Antony

When suddenly, at midnight, there comes the sound
of an invisible procession passing by
with exquisite music playing, with voices raised—
your good fortune, which now gives way; all your efforts'
ill-starred outcome; the plans you made for life,
which turned out wrong: don't mourn them uselessly.
Like one who's long prepared, like someone brave,
bid farewell to her, to Alexandria, who is leaving.
Above all do not fool yourself, don't say
that it was a dream, that your ears deceived you;
don't stoop to futile hopes like these.
Like one who's long prepared, like someone brave,
as befits a man who's been blessed with a city like this,
go without faltering toward the window
and listen with deep emotion, but not
with the entreaties and the whining of a coward,
to the sounds—a final entertainment—
to the exquisite instruments of that initiate crew,
and bid farewell to her, to Alexandria, whom you are losing.

[*1910*; 1911]

Theodotus

If you are among the truly elect,
watch how you achieve your predominance.
However much you're glorified, however much
your accomplishments in Italy and Thessaly
are blazoned far and wide by governments,
however many honorary decrees
are bestowed on you in Rome by your admirers,
neither your elation nor your triumph will endure,
nor will you feel superior—superior how?—
when, in Alexandria, Theodotus brings you,
upon a charger that's been stained with blood,
poor wretched Pompey's head.

And do not take it for granted that in your life,
restricted, regimented, and mundane,
such spectacular and terrifying things don't exist.
Maybe at this very moment, into some neighbor's
nicely tidied house there comes—
invisible, immaterial—Theodotus,
bringing one such terrifying head.

[<*1911*; 1915]

Monotony

On one monotone day one more
monotone, indistinct day follows. The same
things will happen, then again recur—
identical moments find us, then go their way.

One month passes bringing one month more.
What comes next is easy enough to know:
the boredom from the day before.
And tomorrow's got to where it seems like no tomorrow.

[*1898*; 1908]

Ithaca

As you set out on the way to Ithaca
hope that the road is a long one,
filled with adventures, filled with discoveries.
The Laestrygonians and the Cyclopes,
Poseidon in his anger: do not fear them,
you won't find such things on your way
so long as your thoughts remain lofty, and a choice
emotion touches your spirit and your body.
The Laestrygonians and the Cyclopes,
savage Poseidon; you won't encounter them
unless you stow them away inside your soul,
unless your soul sets them up before you.

Hope that the road is a long one.
Many may the summer mornings be
when—with what pleasure, with what joy—
you first put in to harbors new to your eyes;
may you stop at Phoenician trading posts
and there acquire the finest wares:
mother-of-pearl and coral, amber and ebony,
and heady perfumes of every kind:
as many heady perfumes as you can.
Many Egyptian cities may you visit
that you may learn, and go on learning, from their sages.

Always in your mind keep Ithaca.
To arrive there is your destiny.
But do not hurry your trip in any way.
Better that it last for many years;
that you drop anchor at the island an old man,
rich with all you've gotten on the way,
not expecting Ithaca to make you rich.

Ithaca gave you the beautiful journey;
without her you wouldn't have set upon the road.
But now she has nothing left to give you.

And if you find her poor, Ithaca didn't deceive you.
As wise as you will have become, with so much experience,
you will understand, by then, these Ithacas; what they mean.

[*1910*; 1911]

As Much As You Can

And even if you cannot make your life the way you want it,
this much, at least, try to do
as much as you can: don't cheapen it
with too much intercourse with society,
with too much movement and conversation.

Don't cheapen it by taking it about,
making the rounds with it, exposing it
to the everyday inanity
of relations and connections,
so it becomes like a stranger, burdensome.

[*1905;* 1913]

Trojans

Our efforts, those of the ill-fortuned;
our efforts are the efforts of the Trojans.
We will make a bit of progress; we will start
to pick ourselves up a bit; and we'll begin
to be intrepid, and to have some hope.

But something always comes up, and stops us cold.
In the trench in front of us Achilles
emerges, and affrights us with his shouting.—

Our efforts are the efforts of the Trojans.
We imagine that with resolve and daring
we will reverse the animosity of fortune,
and so we take our stand outside, to fight.

But whenever the crucial moment comes,
our boldness and our daring disappear;
our spirit is shattered, comes unstrung;
and we scramble all around the walls
seeking in our flight to save ourselves.

And yet our fall is certain. Up above,
on the walls, already the lament has begun.
They mourn the memory, the sensibility, of our days.
Bitterly Priam and Hecuba mourn for us.

[1900; 1905]

King Demetrius

Not like a king, but like an actor, he exchanged his showy robe of state for a dark cloak, and in secret stole away.

—PLUTARCH, *Life of Demetrius*

When the Macedonians deserted him,
and made it clear that it was Pyrrhus they preferred
King Demetrius (who had a noble
soul) did not—so they said—
behave at all like a king. He went
and cast off his golden clothes,
and flung off his shoes
of richest purple. In simple clothes
he dressed himself quickly and left:
doing just as an actor does
who, when the performance is over,
changes his attire and departs.

[*1900*; 1906]

17

The Glory of the Ptolemies

I'm the Lagid, a king. The possessor absolute
(with my power and my riches) of pleasure.
There's no Macedonian, no Eastern foreigner
who's my equal, who even comes close. What
a joke, that Seleucid with his vulgar luxe.
But if there's something more you seek, then simply look:
the City is our teacher, the acme of what is Greek,
of every discipline, of every art the peak.

[*1896; 1911; 1911*]

The Retinue of Dionysus

Damon the artisan (none as fine
as he in the Peloponnese) is
fashioning the Retinue of Dionysus
in Parian marble. The god in his divine
glory leads, with vigor in his stride.
Intemperance behind. Beside
Intemperance, Intoxication pours the Satyrs wine
from an amphora that they've garlanded with vines.
Near them delicate Sweetwine, his eyes
half-closed, mesmerizes.
And further down there come the singers,
Song and Melody, and Festival
who never allows the hallowed processional
torch that he holds to go out. Then, most modest, Ritual.—
That's what Damon is making. Along with all
of that, from time to time he gets to pondering
the fee he'll be receiving from the king
of Syracuse, three talents, quite a lot.
When that's added to the money that he's got,
he'll be well-to-do, will lead a life of leisure,
can get involved in politics—what pleasure!—
he too in the Council, he too in the Agora.

[*1903*; 1907]

19

The Battle of Magnesia

He's lost his former dash, his pluck.
His wearied body, very nearly sick,

will henceforth be his chief concern. The days
that he has left, he'll spend without a care. Or so says

Philip, at least. Tonight he'll play at dice.
He has an urge to enjoy himself. Do place

lots of roses on the table. And what if
Antiochus at Magnesia came to grief?

They say his glorious army lies mostly ruined.
Perhaps they've overstated: it can't all be true.

Let's hope not. For though they were the enemy, they were kin to us.
Still, one "let's hope not" is enough. Perhaps too much.

Philip, of course, won't postpone the celebration.
However much his life has become one great exhaustion

a boon remains: he hasn't lost a single memory.
He remembers how they mourned in Syria, the agony

they felt, when Macedonia their motherland was smashed to bits.—
Let the feast begin. Slaves: the music, the lights!

[*1913*; 1916]

20

The Seleucid's Displeasure

The Seleucid Demetrius was displeased
to learn that a Ptolemy had arrived
in Italy in such a sorry state.
With only three or four slaves;
dressed like a pauper, and on foot. This is why
their name would soon be bandied as a joke,
an object of fun in Rome. That they have, at bottom,
become the servants of the Romans, in a way,
the Seleucid knows; and that those people give
and take away their thrones
arbitrarily, however they like, he knows.
But nonetheless at least in their appearance
they should maintain a certain magnificence;
shouldn't forget that they are still kings,
that they are still (alas!) called kings.

This is why Demetrius the Seleucid was annoyed,
and straightaway he offered Ptolemy
robes all of purple, a gleaming diadem,
exceedingly costly jewels, and numerous
servants and a retinue, his most expensive mounts,
that he should appear in Rome as was befitting,
like an Alexandrian Greek monarch.

But the Lagid, who had come a mendicant,
knew his business and refused it all;
he didn't need these luxuries at all.

Dressed in worn old clothes, he humbly entered Rome,
and found lodgings with a minor craftsman.
And then he presented himself to the Senate
as an ill-fortuned and impoverished man,
that with greater success he might beg.

[*1910*; 1916]

Orophernes

He, who on the four-drachma piece
seems to have a smile on his face,
on his beautiful, refined face,
he is Orophernes, son of Ariarathes.

A child, they chased him out of Cappadocia,
from the great ancestral palace,
and sent him away to grow up
in Ionia, to be forgotten among foreigners.

Ah, the exquisite nights of Ionia
when fearlessly, and completely as a Greek,
he came to know pleasure utterly.
In his heart, an Asiatic still:
but in his manners and in his speech a Greek,
bedecked with turquoise, yet Greek-attired,
his body scented with perfume of jasmine;
and of Ionia's beautiful young men
the most beautiful was he, the most ideal.

Later on, when the Syrians came
to Cappadocia, and had made him king,
he threw himself completely into his reign,
that he might enjoy some novel pleasure each new day,

that he might horde the gold and silver, avaricious,
that over all of this he might exult, and gloat
to see the heaped-up riches glittering.
As for cares of state, administration—
he didn't know what was going on around him.

The Cappadocians quickly threw him out.
And so to Syria he fled, to the palace of
Demetrius, to entertain himself and loll about.

Still, one day some unaccustomed thoughts
broke in on his total idleness:
he remembered that through his mother, Antiochis,
and through that ancient lady, Stratonice,
he too descended from the Syrian crown,
he too was very nearly a Seleucid.
For a while he emerged from his lechery and drink,
and ineptly, in a kind of daze,
cast around for something he might plot,
something he might do, something to plan,
and failed miserably and came to nothing.

His death must have been recorded somewhere and then lost.
Or maybe history passed it by,
and very rightly didn't deign
to notice such a trivial thing.

He, who on the four-drachma piece
left the charm of his lovely youth,
a glimmer of his poetic beauty,
a sensitive memento of an Ionian boy,
he is Orophernes, son of Ariarathes.

[*1904*; 1916]

Alexandrian Kings

The Alexandrians came out in droves
to have a look at Cleopatra's children:
Caesarion, and also his little brothers,
Alexander and Ptolemy, who for the first
time were being taken to the Gymnasium,
that they might proclaim them kings
before the brilliant ranks of soldiers.

Alexander: they declared him king
of Armenia, of Media, of the Parthians.
Ptolemy: they declared him king
of Cilicia, of Syria, of Phoenicia.
Caesarion was standing well in front,
attired in rose-colored silk,
on his chest a garland of hyacinths,
his belt a double row of sapphires and amethysts,
his shoes laced up with white
ribbons embroidered with pink-skinned pearls.
Him they declared greater than the boys:
him they declared King of Kings.

The Alexandrians were certainly aware
that these were merely words, a bit of theatre.

But the day was warm and poetic, the sky pale blue,
the Alexandrian Gymnasium

a triumphant artistic achievement,
the courtiers' elegance exceptional,
Caesarion all grace and beauty
(Cleopatra's son, of Lagid blood):
and the Alexandrians rushed to the festival,
filled with excitement, and shouted acclaim
in Greek, and in Egyptian, and some in Hebrew,
enchanted by the lovely spectacle—
though of course they knew what they were worth,
what empty words these kingdoms were.

[*1912*; 1912]

Philhellene

Take care the engraving's artistically done.
Expression grave and majestic.
The diadem better rather narrow;
I don't care for those wide ones, the Parthian kind.
The inscription, as usual, in Greek:
nothing excessive, nothing grandiose—
the proconsul mustn't get the wrong idea,
he sniffs out everything and reports it back to Rome—
but of course it should still do me credit.
Something really choice on the other side:
some lovely discus-thrower lad.
Above all, I urge you, see to it
(Sithaspes, by the god, don't let them forget)
that after the "King" and the "Savior"
the engraving should read, in elegant letters, "Philhellene."
Now don't start in on me with your quips,
your "Where are the Greeks?" and "What's Greek
here, behind the Zágros, beyond Phráata?"
Many, many others, more oriental than ourselves,
write it, and so we'll write it too.
And after all, don't forget that now and then
sophists come to us from Syria,
and versifiers, and other devotees of puffery.
Hence unhellenised we are not, I rather think.

[*1906; 1912*]

28

The Steps

On an ebony bed that is adorned
with eagles made of coral, Nero sleeps
deeply—heedless, calm, and happy;
flush in the prime of the flesh,
and in the beautiful vigor of youth.

But in the alabaster hall that holds
the ancient shrine of the Ahenobarbi
how uneasy are his Lares!
The little household gods are trembling,
trying to hide their slight bodies.
For they've heard a ghastly sound,
a fatal sound mounting the stairs,
footsteps of iron that rattle the steps.
And, faint with fear now, the pathetic Lares,
wriggle their way to the back of the shrine;
each jostles the other and stumbles
each little god falls over the other
because they've understood what kind of sound it is,
have come to know by now the Erinyes' footsteps.

[*1893*; 1897; *1903*; 1909]

Herodes Atticus

Ah, Herodes Atticus, what glory is his!

Alexander of Seleucia, one of our better sophists,
on arriving in Athens to lecture,
finds the city deserted, since Herodes was
away in the country. And all of the young people
followed him out there to hear him.
So Alexander the sophist
writes Herodes a letter
requesting that he send back the Greeks.
And smooth Herodes swiftly responds,
"I too am coming, along with the Greeks."

How many lads in Alexandria now,
in Antioch, or in Beirut
(tomorrow's orators, trained by Greek culture)
when they gather at choice dinner parties
where sometimes the talk is of fine intellectual points,
and sometimes about their exquisite amours,
suddenly, abstracted, fall silent.
They leave their glasses untouched at their sides,
and they ponder the luck of Herodes—
what other sophist was honored like this?—
whatever he wants and whatever he does

the Greeks (the Greeks!) follow him,
neither to criticize nor to debate,
nor even to choose any more; just to follow.

[*1900; 1911;* 1912]

Sculptor from Tyana

As you will have heard, I'm no beginner.
Lots of stone has passed between my hands.
And in Tyana, my native land,
they know me well. And here the senators
commission many statues.

                    Let me show
a few to you right now. Notice this Rhea;
august, all fortitude, quite archaic.
Notice the Pompey. The Marius,
the Aemilius Paullus, and the African Scipio.
The likenesses, as much as I was able, are true.
The Patroclus (I'll touch him up soon).
Near those pieces of yellowish
marble there, that's Caesarion.

And for some time now I've been involved
in making a Poseidon. Most of all
I'm studying his horses: how to mold them.
They must be rendered so delicately that
it will be clear from their bodies, their feet,
that they aren't treading earth, but racing on water.

But this work here is my favorite of all,
which I made with the greatest care and deep feeling:
him, one warm day in summer
when my thoughts were ascending to ideal things,
him I stood dreaming here, the young Hermes.

[*1893; 1903;* 1911]

The Tomb of Lysias the Grammarian

Just there, on the right as you go in,
in the Beirut library we buried him:
the scholar Lysias, a grammarian.
The location suits him beautifully.
We put him near the things that he
remembers maybe even there—glosses, texts,
apparatuses, variants, the multivolume works
of scholarship on Greek idiom. Also, like this,
his tomb will be seen and honored by us
as we pass by on our way to the books.

[*1911*; 1914]

Tomb of Eurion

Inside of this elaborate memorial,
made entirely of syenite stone,
which so many violets, so many lilies adorn,
Eurion lies buried, so beautiful.
A boy of twenty-five, an Alexandrian.
Through the father's kin, old Macedonian;
a line of alabarchs on his mother's side.
With Aristoclitus he took his philosophical instruction;
rhetoric with Parus. A student in Thebes, he read
the sacred writings. He wrote a history
of the Arsinoïte district. This at least will endure.
Nevertheless we've lost what was most dear: his beauty,
which was like an Apollonian vision.

[*1912*; 1914]

That Is He

Unknown, the Edessene—a stranger here in Antioch—
writes a lot. And there, at last, the final canto has
appeared. Altogether that makes eighty-three

poems in all. But the poet is worn out
from so much writing, so much versifying,
the terrific strain of so much Greek phrasing,
and every little thing now weighs him down.

A sudden thought, however, pulls him out
of his dejection—the exquisite "That is he"
which Lucian once heard in a dream.

[*1898*; 1909]

Dangerous

Said Myrtias (a Syrian student
in Alexandria; during the reign
of the *augustus* Constans and the *augustus* Constantius;
partly pagan, and partly Christianized):
"Strengthened by contemplation and study,
I will not fear my passions like a coward.
My body I will give to pleasures,
to diversions that I've dreamed of,
to the most daring erotic desires,
to the lustful impulses of my blood, without
any fear at all, for whenever I will—
and I will have the will, strengthened
as I'll be with contemplation and study—
at the crucial moments I'll recover
my spirit as it was before: ascetic."

[?; 1911]

37

Manuel Comnenus

The emperor Lord Manuel Comnenus
one melancholy morning in September
sensed that death was near. The court astrologers
(those who were paid) were nattering on
that he had many years left yet to live.
But while they went on talking, the king
recalls neglected habits of piety,
and from the monastery cells he orders
ecclesiastical vestments to be brought,
and he puts them on, and is delighted
to present the decorous mien of a priest or friar.

Happy are all who believe,
and who, like the emperor Lord Manuel, expire
outfitted most decorously in their faith.

[*1905*; 1916]

In the Church

I love the church—its labara,
the silver of its vessels, its candelabra,
the lights, its icons, its lectern.

When I enter there, inside of a Greek Church:
with the aromas of its incenses,
the liturgical chanting and harmonies,
the magnificent appearance of the priests,
and the rhythm of their every movement—
resplendent in their ornate vestments—
my thoughts turn to the great glories of our race,
to our illustrious Byzantinism.

[*1892; 1901; 1906; 1912?*]

Very Rarely

He's an old man. Worn out and stooped,
crippled by years, and by excess,
stepping slowly, he moves along the alleyway.
But when he goes inside his house to hide
his pitiful state, and his old age, he considers
the share that he—*he*—still has in youth.

Youths recite his verses now.
His visions pass before their animated eyes.
Their healthy, sensuous minds,
their well-limned, solid flesh,
stir to his own expression of the beautiful.

[*1911*; 1913]

In Stock

He wrapped them up carefully, neatly
in green silken cloth, very costly.

Roses from rubies, pearls into lilies,
amethyst violets. Lovely the way that *he* sees,

and judges, and wanted them; not in the way
he saw them in nature, or studied them. He'll put them away,

in the safe: a sample of his daring, skillful work.
Whenever a customer comes into the store,

he takes other jewels from the cases to sell—fabulous things—
bracelets, chains, necklaces, rings.

[*1912*; 1913]

Painted

To my craft I am attentive, and I love it.
But today I'm discouraged by the slow pace of the work.
My mood depends upon the day. It looks
increasingly dark. Constantly windy and raining.
What I long for is to see, and not to speak.
In this painting, now, I'm gazing at
a lovely boy who's lain down near a spring;
it could be that he's worn himself out from running.
What a lovely boy; what a divine afternoon
has caught him and put him to sleep.—
Like this, for some time, I sit and gaze.
And once again, *in* art, I recover from creating it.

[*1914*; 1916]

Morning Sea

Here let me stop. Let me too look at Nature for a while.
The morning sea and cloudless sky
a brilliant blue, the yellow shore; all
beautiful and grand in the light.

Here let me stop. Let me fool myself: that these are what I see
(I really saw them for a moment when I first stopped)
instead of seeing, even here, my fantasies,
my recollections, the ikons of pleasure.

[?; 1916]

Song of Ionia

Because we smashed their statues all to pieces,
because we chased them from their temples—
this hardly means the gods have died.
O land of Ionia, they love you still,
it's you whom their souls remember still.
And as an August morning's light breaks over you
your atmosphere grows vivid with their living.
And occasionally an ethereal ephebe's form,
indeterminate, stepping swiftly,
makes its way along your crested hills.

[*1886*; 1896; *1905*; 1911]

In the Entrance of the Café

Something they were saying close to me
drew my attention to the entrance of the café.
And I saw the lovely body that looked as if
Eros had made it using all his vast experience:
crafting with pleasure his shapely limbs;
making tall the sculpted build;
crafting the face with emotion
and leaving behind, with the touch of his hands,
a feeling in the brow, the eyes, and the lips.

[*1904?; >1915*]

One Night

The room was threadbare and tawdry,
hidden above that suspect restaurant.
From the window you could see the alley,
which was filthy and narrow. From below
came the voices of some laborers
who were playing cards and having a carouse.

And there, in that common, vulgar bed
I had the body of love, I had the lips,
sensuous and rose-colored, of drunkenness—
the rose of such a drunkenness, that even now
as I write, after so many years have passed!,
in my solitary house, I am drunk again.

[*1907*; 1916]

Come Back

Come back often and take hold of me,
beloved feeling come back and take hold of me,
when the memory of the body reawakens,
and old longing once more passes through the blood;
when the lips and skin remember,
and the hands feel like they're touching once again.

Come back often and take hold of me at night,
when the lips and skin remember . . .

[*1904; 1909; 1912*]

Far Off

I'd like to talk about that memory . . .
But by now it's long died out . . . as if there's nothing left:
because it lies far off, in the years of my first youth.

Skin, as if it had been made of jasmine . . .
That August—was it August?—evening . . .
I can just recall the eyes: they were, I daresay, blue . . .
Ah yes, blue: a deep blue, sapphirine.

[*1914*; 1914]

He Swears

Now and then he swears   to begin a better life.
But when the night comes on   with its own counsels,
its own compromises,   and with its promises:
but when the night comes on   with a power of its own,
of a body that desires and demands, he returns,
lost, once more to the same fateful pleasure.

[*1905*; >1915]

I Went

No restraint. I surrendered completely and I went.
To gratifications that were partly real,
partly careening within my mind—
I went in the illuminated night.
And I drank powerful wines, just as
the champions of pleasure drink.

[*1905*; 1913]

Chandelier

In a small and empty room, four lone walls,
covered in a cloth of solid green,
a beautiful chandelier burns and glows
and in each and every flame there blazes
a wanton fever, a wanton need.

In the small room, which has been set
aglow by the chandelier's powerful flames,
the light that appears is no ordinary light.
The pleasure of this heat has not been fashioned
for bodies that too easily take fright.

[*1895*; 1914]

Poems 1916–1918

Since Nine—

Half past twelve. The time has quickly passed
since nine o'clock when I first turned up the lamp
and sat down here. I've been sitting without reading,
without speaking. With whom should I speak,
so utterly alone within this house?

The apparition of my youthful body,
since nine o'clock when I first turned up the lamp,
has come and found me and reminded me
of shuttered perfumed rooms
and of pleasure spent—what wanton pleasure!
And it also brought before my eyes
streets made unrecognizable by time,
bustling city centres that are no more
and theatres and cafés that existed long ago.

The apparition of my youthful body
came and also brought me cause for pain:
deaths in the family; separations;
the feelings of my loved ones, the feelings of
those long dead which I so little valued.

Half past twelve. How the time has passed.
Half past twelve. How the years have passed.

[*1917*; 1918]

Comprehension

The years of my youth, my pleasure-bent existence—
how plainly do I see their meaning now.

What useless, foolish regrets . . .

But I didn't see their meaning then.

In the dissolute life I led in my youth
my poetry's designs took shape;
the boundaries of my art were drawn.

That is why the regrets were never firm.
And my resolutions—to master myself, to change—
would keep up for two weeks at the most.

[*1895*; 1917/1918]

In the Presence of the Statue of Endymion

On a chariot of white, drawn by four
snow-white mules caparisoned in silver,
I have arrived at Latmus from Miletus. I sailed over
from Alexandria in a purple trireme to perform
holy rites for Endymion, sacrifices and libations.
Behold the statue. With rapture I now look upon
the fabled beauty of Endymion. My slaves
empty panniers of jessamine; and well-omened acclamations
have awakened the pleasure of ancient days.

[*1895*; 1916]

Envoys from Alexandria

They hadn't seen, in Delphi, such beautiful gifts in centuries
as those that were sent by the two, the Ptolemies,
the rival brother kings. Ever since the priests accepted them,
though, they've been worried about the oracle. To frame it
with finesse they'll need all of their expertise:
which of the two, two such as these, must be displeased.
And they convene at night, secretly,
to confer about the Lagid family.

But look, the envoys have come back. They take their leave.
Returning to Alexandria, they say. They no longer have
need of oracles. The priests are overjoyed to hear this
(it's understood they'll keep the fabulous gifts)
but they're also bewildered in the extreme,
clueless as to what this sudden lack of interest means.
For yesterday the envoys had grim news of which priests are unaware:
At Rome the oracle was handed down; destinies were meted there.

[1915; 1918]

Aristobulus

The palace is in tears, the king's in tears,
King Herod inconsolably laments,
the entire country is in tears for Aristobulus
who so needlessly, accidentally drowned
playing in the water with his friends.

And also when they hear the news elsewhere,
when it gets as far as Syria,
even many of the Greeks will be distressed:
the poets and the sculptors all will mourn,
for the renown of Aristobulus had reached them,
and any vision of theirs of what a youth could be
never matched the beauty of this boy.
What statue of a god could Antioch boast
that was the like of this boy of Israel?

The Throne Princess laments and weeps:
his mother, the greatest of the Jewesses.
Alexandra laments and weeps over the calamity.—
But when she finds herself alone her anguish alters.
She groans; she seethes; she swears; she calls down curses.
How they made a fool of her! How they gulled her!
How, in the end, they had got their way!
They've laid the house of the Hasmoneans in ruins.

How did he manage it, that criminal of a king;
that charlatan, that miscreant, that scoundrel?
How did he manage it? What a diabolical plan,
for Mariamne not to have noticed a thing.
Had Mariamne noticed, or suspected,
she'd have found a way to save her little brother;
she's queen after all, she could have managed something.
How they'll gloat now, how they'll exult in secret,
those spiteful women, Cypros and Salome;
those vile trollops, Cypros and Salome.—
And to be powerless, to be compelled
to pretend as though she believed their lies;
to be unable to go to the people,
to go outside and cry out to the Jews,
to tell, to tell how the murder had been done.

[*1916*; 1918]

Caesarion

In part to ascertain a certain date
and in part to while away the time,
last night I took down a collection
of Ptolemaic inscriptions to read.
The unstinting laudations and flatteries
are the same for all. All of them are brilliant,
glorious, mighty, beneficent;
every undertaking utterly wise.
As for the women of the line, they too,
all the Berenices and the Cleopatras, are wonderful too.

When I successfully ascertained the date
I'd have finished with the book, if a tiny,
insignificant reference to King Caesarion
hadn't attracted my attention suddenly. . . . . . .

Ah, there: you came with your indefinite
charm. In history there are only a few
lines that can be found concerning you;
and so I could fashion you more freely in my mind.
I fashioned you this way: beautiful and feeling.
My artistry gives to your face
a beauty that has a dreamy winsomeness.
And so fully did I imagine you

that yesterday, late at night, when the lamp
went out—I deliberately let it go out—
I dared to think you came into my room,
it seemed to me you stood before me: as you must have been
in Alexandria after it had been conquered,
pale and wearied, perfect in your sorrow,
still hoping they'd have mercy on you,
those vile men—who whispered "Surfeit of Caesars."

[*1914*; 1918]

Nero's Deadline

Nero wasn't worried when he heard
the prophecy of the Delphic Oracle.
"Let him beware the age of seventy-three."
He still had time to enjoy himself.
He is thirty years old. It's quite sufficient,
this deadline that the god is giving him,
for him to think about dangers yet to come.

Now to Rome he'll be returning a little wearied,
but exquisitely wearied by this trip
which had been endless days of diversion—
in the theatres, in the gardens, the gymnasia. . . .
Evenings of the cities of Achaea . . .
Ah, the pleasure of naked bodies above all . . .

So Nero. And in Spain, Galba
was secretly assembling his army and preparing it:
the old man, seventy-three years old.

[*1915*; 1918]

Safe Haven

Emes, a young man of twenty-eight, came by a Tenian
ship (meaning to learn the incense trade) to this Syrian
haven. But during the voyage he took sick,
and just after he had disembarked,
he died. His burial, the very cheapest kind,
took place there. A few hours before he died,
he whispered something about "home" and "elderly parents."
But no one knew who they might have been;
nor what his native land might be, in all the wide Greek world.
Better this way. For this way, while
he lies dead in this safe haven,
his parents will keep hoping he's still alive.

[*1917*; 1918]

One of Their Gods

Whenever one of Them would cross Seleucia's
marketplace, around the time that evening falls—
like some tall and flawlessly beautiful boy,
with the joy of incorruptibility in his eye,
with that dark and fragrant hair of his—
the passersby would stare at him
and one would ask another if he knew him,
and if he were a Syrian Greek, or foreign. But some,
who'd paid him more attention as they watched,
understood, and would make way.
And as he disappeared beneath the arcades,
among the shadows and the evening lights,
making his way to the neighborhood that comes alive
only at night—that life of revels and debauchery,
of every known intoxication and lust—
they'd wonder which of Them he really was
and for which of his suspect diversions
he'd come down to walk Seleucia's streets
from his Venerable, Sacrosanct Abode.

[*1899*; 1918]

Tomb of Lanes

The Lanes whom you loved is not here, Marcus,
in the tomb where you come to cry, and stay for hours and hours.
The Lanes whom you loved you have much closer to you,
at home, when you shut yourself in and look at his picture:
it preserves some part of what was precious in him,
it preserves some part of what you'd loved.

Remember, Marcus, how you brought the famed
Cyrenian painter back from the proconsul's palace,
and with what artful cunning he attempted
to persuade you both, no sooner had he seen your friend,
that he simply *had* to do him as Hyacinth
(which would make his portrait so much better known).

But your Lanes didn't loan out his beauty like that;
and objecting firmly he told him to represent
neither Hyacinth nor anyone else,
but Lanes, son of Rhametichos, an Alexandrian.

[*1916*; 1918]

Tomb of Iases

Here I lie: Iases. Throughout this great city I was renowned
for being the most beautiful boy.
Admired by men of deep learning—and also by the less profound,
the common folk. Both gave equal joy

to me. But they took me so often for a Narcissus or a Hermes
that excess wore me out, and killed me. Passerby,
if you're an Alexandrian you won't judge me. You know the yearnings
of our life; what heat they hold; what pleasures most high.

[*1917*; 1917]

In a City of Osrhoene

From the tavern brawl they brought him back to us, wounded—
our friend Rhemon, around midnight yesterday.
Through the windows we'd left open all the way
the moon illumined his beautiful body on the bed.
We're a hodgepodge here: Syrians, Greeks, Armenians, Medes.
Rhemon too is such a one. But yesterday, as the moon
shone its light upon his sensuous face
we were put in mind of Plato's Charmides.

[*1916*; 1917]

Tomb of Ignatius

Here I'm not the Cleon who's renowned
in Alexandria (where they aren't easily impressed)
for my fabulous houses, for my gardens,
for my horses and for my chariots,
for the diamonds and the silks I wore.
Far from it: here I'm not that Cleon.
May those twenty-eight years be erased.
I am Ignatius, a Lector, who very late
came to my senses. But still I lived ten blessed months
in the serenity and security of Christ.

[*1916*; 1917]

In the Month of Hathor

With difficulty I read   upon this ancient stone
"O Lo[r]d Jesus Christ."   I can just discern a "So[u]l."
"In the mon[th] of Hathor"   "Leuciu[s] went to his re[s]t."
Where they record his age   "The span of years he li[ve]d"
the Kappa Zeta is proof   that he went to his rest a youth.

Amidst the erosion I see   "Hi[m] . . . Alexandrian."
Then there are three lines   radically cut short;
but some words I can make out—   like "our t[e]ars," "the pain,"
"tears" again further down,   and "grief for [u]s, his [f]riends."
In love, it seems to me,   Leucius was greatly blessed.
In the month of Hathor   Leucius went to his rest.

[*1917*; 1917]

70

For Ammon, Who Died at 29 Years of Age, in 610

Raphael, they want you to compose
some verses as an epitaph for the poet Ammon.
Something very artistic and polished. You'll be able,
you're the perfect choice, to write what's suitable
for the poet Ammon, one of our own.

Certainly you'll talk about his poetry—
but do say something, too, about his beauty,
about the delicate beauty that we loved.

Your Greek is always beautiful and musical.
But now we want all of your craftsmanship.
Into a foreign tongue our pain and love are passing.
Pour your Egyptian feeling into a foreign tongue.

Raphael, you verses should be written
so that they have, you know, something of our lives within them,
so that the rhythm and every phrasing makes it clear
that an Alexandrian is writing of an Alexandrian.

[*1915*; 1917]

71

Aemilian Son of Monaës, an Alexandrian, 628–655 A.D.

From my speech, and looks, and from my mien
I shall make an excellent panoply;
and so I'll stand before those wicked men
without fear, without debility.

They will want to harm me. But none of those
who come close to me will ever see
where my vulnerable places are, my wounds,
beneath the falsehoods that will cover me.—

Boastful words of Aemilian son of Monaës.
I wonder if he ever made that suit of armor?
In any event, he didn't wear it much:
At twenty-seven, in Sicily, he died.

[*1898?*; 1918]

Whenever They Are Aroused

Try to keep watch over them, poet,
for all that few of them can be restrained:
Your eroticism's visions.
Place them, partly hidden, in your phrases.
Try to keep hold of them, poet,
whenever they're aroused within your mind,
at night or in the brightness of midday.

[*1913*; 1916]

To Pleasure

Joy and balm of my life the memory of the hours
when I found and held on to pleasure as I wanted it.
Joy and balm of my life—for me, who had no use
for any routine enjoyment of desire.

[*1913*; 1917]

I've Gazed So Much—

At beauty I've gazed so much
that my vision is filled with it.

The body's lines. Red lips. Limbs made for pleasure.
Hair as if it were taken from Greek statues:
always lovely, even when it's uncombed,
and falls, a bit, upon the gleaming brow.
Faces of love, exactly as
my poetry wanted it . . . in the nights of my youth,
secretly encountered in my nights. . . .

[*1911*; 1917]

In the Street

His appealing face, somewhat pallid;
his chestnut eyes, looking tired;
twenty-five years old, but looks more like twenty;
with something artistic about his clothes
—something in the color of the tie, the collar's shape—
aimlessly he ambles down the street,
as if still hypnotized by the illicit pleasure,
by the very illicit pleasure he has had.

[*1913*; 1916]

The Window of the Tobacco Shop

Nearby the illuminated window
of a tobacco shop they stood, in the midst of many others.
Quite by chance their glances happened to meet,
and timorously, hesitantly expressed
the illicit longing of their flesh.
Later, on the pavement, a few nervous steps—
until they smiled, and nodded very faintly.

And afterward the closed carriage. . . .
the sensitive nearing of their bodies;
the hands as one, the lips as one.

[*1907;* 1917]

Passage

What he timidly imagined in his school days, is opened up,
revealed to him. And he makes the rounds, stays out all night,
gets swept up in things. And as is (for our art) only right,
pleasure rejoices in his fresh, hot blood,
an outlaw sensual abandon overcomes
his body; and his youthful limbs
give in to it.
            And so a simple boy
becomes, for us, worth looking at, and passes through the High
World of Poetry, for a moment—yes, even he;
this aesthete of a boy, with his blood so fresh and hot.

[*1914*; 1917]

In Evening

At any rate it wouldn't have lasted long. Years
of experience make that clear to me. But still, Fate
came and ended things in too much of a hurry.
The life of loveliness was brief.
But how powerful our perfumed unctions were,
how exquisite the bed in which we lay,
to what pleasure we gave our bodies away.

A reverberation of the days of pleasure,
a reverberation of those days drew near me,
something we two had in youth, the fire;
once more I took a letter in my hands,
and read it over and over, till the light had failed.

And I went out onto the balcony, melancholy—
went out so I might clear my head by seeing at least
a little of this town I love so well,
some little movement in the street, and in the shops.

[*1916*; 1917]

Gray

Looking at an opal of medium gray,
I remembered two beautiful gray eyes
that I saw; it must be twenty years ago. . . .

. . . .

For one month we were in love.
Then the departure, for Smyrna I daresay,
to get work there, and we never saw each other again.

Those gray eyes—if they're alive—will have lost their beauty;
the beautiful face will have fallen into ruins.

O my memory, keep them as they were.
And, memory, whatever you can bring back from that love of mine,
whatever you can, bring back to me tonight.

[*1917*; 1917]

Below the House

Yesterday while strolling through a neighborhood
on the edge of town, I passed below the house
I used to go in when I was very young.
There Eros had taken possession of my body
with his exquisite force.

And yesterday
as I passed along that ancient street,
suddenly everything was made beautiful by desire's spell:
the shops, the pavements, the stones,
and walls, and balconies, and windows;
there was nothing ugly that remained there.

And while I was standing, gazing at the door,
and standing, tarrying by the house,
the foundation of all my being yielded up
the sensual emotion that was stored inside.

[*1917*; 1919]

The Next Table

Can't be more than twenty-two years old.
And yet I'm sure that, just about the same
number of years ago, I enjoyed that very body.

It's not at all a flaring of desire.
And I only came to the casino a little while ago;
I haven't even had time to drink a lot.
This very body: I enjoyed it.

And if I don't remember where—one slip doesn't signify.

Ah there, sitting at the next table now:
I recognize each movement—and beneath the clothes
I see once more the naked limbs I loved.

[*1918*; 1919?]

Remember, Body

Body, remember not just how much you were loved,
not just the beds where you have lain,
but also those longings that so openly
glistened for you in eyes,
and trembled in voices—and some
chance obstacle arose and thwarted them.
Now that it's all finally in the past
it almost seems as if you gave yourself to
those longings, too—remember how
they glistened, in eyes that looked at you;
how they trembled in voices, for you; remember, body.

[*1916*; 1917/1918]

Days of 1903

I never found them, ever again—all so quickly lost . . .
the poetic eyes, the pallid
face. . . . in the gloaming of the street. . . .

I've not found them since—things I came to have completely by chance,
things that I let go so easily;
and afterwards, in anguish, wanted back.
The poetic eyes, the pale face,
those lips, I haven't found them since.

[*1909*; 1917]

Poems 1919–1933

The Afternoon Sun

This room, how well I know it.
Now it's being rented out, with the one next door,
for commercial offices. The entire house has now become
offices for middlemen, and businessmen, and Companies.

Ah, this room, how familiar it is.

Near the door, here, was the sofa,
and in front of it a Turkish rug;
Close by, the shelf with two yellow vases.
On the right—no, opposite, a dresser with a mirror.
In the middle, the table where he'd write;
and the three big wicker chairs.
Near the window was the bed
where we made love so many times.

They must be somewhere still, poor things.

Near the window was the bed:
the afternoon sun came halfway up.

. . . At four o'clock in the afternoon, we'd parted
for one week only . . . Alas,
that week became an eternity.

[*1918*; 1919]

To Stay

One in the morning it must have been,
or half past one.
                    In a corner of that dive;
in back of the wooden partition.
Apart from the two of us, the place completely empty.
A kerosene lamp barely shed some light.
The vigilant servant was sleeping by the door.

No one would have seen us. But
we were so on fire for each other
that caution was beyond us anyway.

Our clothes were half undone—we weren't wearing much,
since it was blazing hot, a heavenly July.

Delight in flesh amidst
clothes half undone:
quick baring of flesh—the image of it
has crossed twenty-six years; and now has come
to stay here in this poetry.

[*1918*; 1919]

Of the Jews (50 A.D.)

Painter and poet, runner and thrower,
Endymion's beauty: Ianthes, son of Antonius.
From a family close to the Synagogue.

"The days that I most value are the ones
when I abandon the aesthetic quest,
when I forsake the beauty and rigor of the Hellenic,
with its overriding preoccupation
with perfectly formed and perishable white limbs.
And I become what I would like
always to remain: of the Jews, of the holy Jews, the son."

A bit too heated, this declaration of his. "Always
remain of the Jews, of the holy Jews—"

But he didn't remain one at all.
the Hedonism and Art of Alexandria
made the boy into their devotee.

[*1912*; <1919?]

Imenus

". . . it should be loved all the more,
the pleasure that's attained unwholesomely and in corruption;
only rarely finding the body that feels things as *it* wants to—
the pleasure that, unwholesomely and in corruption, produces
a sensual intensity, which good health does not know . . ."

A fragment of a missive
from the youth Imenus (of patrician stock), infamous
in Syracuse for dissipation,
in the dissipated times of Michael the Third.

[*1915; 1919;* 1919]

Aboard the Ship

It certainly resembles him, this small
pencil likeness of him.

Quickly done, on the deck of the ship:
an enchanting afternoon.
The Ionian Sea all around us.

It resembles him. Still, I remember him as handsomer.
To the point of illness: that's how sensitive he was,
and it illumined his expression.
Handsomer, he seems to me,
now that my soul recalls him, out of Time.

Out of Time. All these things, they're very old—
the sketch, and the ship, and the afternoon.

[*1919*; 1919]

Of Demetrius Soter (162–150 B.C.)

His every expectation turned out wrong!

He used to imagine that he'd do celebrated deeds,
would end the shame that since the time of the Battle
of Magnesia had ground his homeland down.
That Syria again would be a mighty power,
with her armies, with her fleets,
with her great encampments, with her wealth.

He endured it, grew embittered in Rome
when he sensed, in the conversation of his friends,
the scions of the great houses,
in the midst of all the delicacy and *politesse*
that they showed toward him, toward the son
of King Seleucus Philopator—
when he sensed that nonetheless there was always a hidden
disdain for the dynasties of the Greek East:
which were in decline, not up to serious affairs,
quite unfit for the leadership of peoples.
He'd withdraw, alone, and grow indignant, and swear
that it wouldn't be the way they thought, at all.
Look, *he* has the will:
would struggle, would do it, would rise up.

If only he could find a way to reach the East,
manage to get away from Italy—

and all of this power that he has
in his soul, all this vehemence,
he'd spread it to the people.

Ah, if only he could be in Syria!
He was so little when he left his homeland
that he only dimly remembers what it looks like.
But in his thoughts he's always studied it
like something sacred you approach on bended knee,
like an apparition of a beautiful place, like a vision
of cities and of harbors that are Greek.—

And now?
              Now, hopelessness and dejection.
They were right, those lads in Rome.
It's not possible for them to survive, the dynasties
that the Macedonian Conquest had produced.

No matter: he himself had spared no effort;
as much as he was able, he'd struggled on.
Even in his black discouragement,
there's one thing that still he contemplates
with lofty pride: that even in defeat
he shows the same indomitable valor to the world.

The rest—was dreams and vain futility.
This Syria—it barely even resembles his homeland;
it is the land of Heracleides and of Balas.

[*1915*; 1919]

93

If Indeed He Died

"Where has he gone off to, where did the Sage disappear?
Following his many miracles,
and the great renown of his instruction
which was diffused among so many peoples,
he suddenly went missing and no one has learned
with any certainty what has happened
(nor has anyone ever seen his tomb).
Some have put it about that he died in Ephesus.
But Damis didn't write that. Damis never
wrote about the death of Apollonius.
Others said that he went missing on Lindos.
Or perhaps that other story is
true, that his assumption took place on Crete,
in the ancient shrine of Dictynna.—
But nonetheless we have the miraculous,
the supernatural apparition of him
to a young student in Tyana.—
Perhaps the time hasn't come for him to return,
for him to appear before the world again;
or metamorphosed, perhaps, he goes among us
unrecognized.— But he'll appear again
as he was, teaching the Right Way. And surely then
he'll reinstate the worship of our gods,
and our exquisite Hellenic ceremonies."

So he daydreamed in his threadbare lodging—
after a reading of Philostratus's
"Life of Apollonius of Tyana"—
one of the few pagans, the very few
who had stayed. Otherwise—an insignificant
and timid man—he, too, outwardly
played the Christian and would go to church.
It was the period during which there reigned,
with the greatest piety, the old man Justin,
and Alexandria, a god-fearing city,
showed its abhorrence of those poor idolators.

[*1897; 1910; 1920; 1920*]

Young Men of Sidon (400 A.D.)

The actor whom they'd brought to entertain them
declaimed, as well, a few choice epigrams.

The salon opened onto the garden;
and had a delicate fragrance of blooms
that was mingled together with the perfumes
of the five sweetly scented Sidonian youths.

Meleager, and Crinagoras, and Rhianus were read.
But when the actor had declaimed
"Here lies Euphorion's son, Aeschylus, an Athenian—"
(stressing, perhaps, more than was necessary
the "valour far-renowned," the "Marathonian lea"),
at once a spirited boy sprang up,
mad for literature, and cried out:

"Oh, I don't like that quatrain, not at all.
Expressions like that somehow seem like cowardice.
Give—so I proclaim—all your strength to your work,
all your care, and remember your work once more
in times of trial, or when your hour finally comes.
That's what I expect from you, and what I demand.
And don't dismiss completely from your mind
the brilliant Discourse of Tragedy—

96

that Agamemnon, that marvelous Prometheus,
those representations of Orestes and Cassandra,
that *Seven Against Thebes*—and leave, as your memorial,
only that you, among the ranks of soldiers, the masses—
that you too battled Datis and Artaphernes."

[*1920*; 1920]

That They Come—

One candle is enough.   Its faint light
is more fitting,   will be more winsome
when come Love's—   when its Shadows come.

One candle is enough.   Tonight the room
can't have too much light.   In reverie complete,
and in suggestion's power,   and with that little light—
in that reverie: thus   will I dream a vision
that there come Love's—   that its Shadows come.

[?; 1920]

Darius

The poet Phernazes is working on
the crucial portion of his epic poem:
the part about how the kingdom of the Persians
was seized by Darius, son of Hystaspes. (Our
glorious king is descended from him:
Mithridates, Dionysus and Eupator.) But here
one needs philosophy; one must explicate
the feelings that Darius must have had:
arrogance and intoxication, perhaps; but no—more
like an awareness of the vanity of grandeur.
Profoundly, the poet ponders the matter.

But he's interrupted by his servant, who comes
running and delivers the momentous intelligence:
The war with the Romans has begun.
Most of our army has crossed the border.

The poet stays, dumbfounded. What a disaster!
How, now, can our glorious king,
Mithradates, Dionysus and Eupator,
be bothered to pay attention to Greek poems?
In the middle of a war—imagine, Greek poems.

Phernazes frets. What bad luck is his!
Just when he was sure, with his "Darius,"
to make his name, and to reduce his critics,
those envious men, to silence at long last.
What a setback, what a setback for his plans!

And if it had only been a setback: fine.
But let's see if we are really all that safe
in Amisus. It's not a spectacularly well-fortified land.
The Romans are most fearsome enemies.
Is there any way we can get the best of them,
we Cappadocians? Could it ever happen?
Can we measure up to the legions now?
Great gods, protectors of Asia, help us.—

And yet in the midst of all his upset, and the disaster,
a poetic notion stubbornly comes and goes—
far more convincing, surely, are arrogance and intoxication;
arrogance and intoxication are what Darius would have felt.

[<*1897?*; *1917*; *1920*]

Anna Comnena

She laments in the prologue to her *Alexiad,*
Anna Comnena laments her widowhood.

Her soul is in muzzy whirl. "And with
freshets of tears," she tells us, "I deluge
mine eyes. . . . Alack the breakers" of her life,
"alack for the upheavals." Anguish burns her
"unto the very bones and marrow and rending of my soul."

Nonetheless the truth seems to be that she knew one
mortal grief alone, that power-loving woman:
that she had only one profound regret
(even if she won't acknowledge it), that supercilious Greekling:
for all of her dexterity she didn't manage
to secure the Throne; instead he took it
practically right out of her hands, that upstart John.

[*1917*; 1920]

Byzantine Noble, in Exile, Versifying

Let the dilettantes call me dilettante.
In serious matters I have always been
most diligent. And on this I will insist:
that no one has a better knowledge of
Church Fathers or Scripture, or the Synodical Canons.
On every question that he had, Botaniates—
every difficult ecclesiastical matter—
would take counsel with me, me first of all.
But since I've been exiled here (curse that spiteful
Irene Ducas) and am frightfully bored,
it's not at all unseemly if I divert myself
by crafting verses of six or seven lines—
divert myself with mythological tales
of Hermes, and Apollo, and Dionysus,
or the heroes of Thessaly and the Peloponnese;
or with composing strict iambic lines
such as—if I do say so—the litterateurs
of Constantinople don't know how to write.
That strictness, most likely, is the reason for their censure.

[*1921*; 1920]

Their Beginning

The fulfillment of their illicit pleasure
is accomplished. They've risen from the bed,
and dress themselves quickly without speaking.
They emerge separately, covertly, from the house. And while
they walk rather uneasily in the street, it seems
as if they suspect that something about them betrays
what kind of bed they'd fallen into just before.

Nonetheless, how the artist's life has gained.
Tomorrow, the day after, or through the years he'll write
powerful lines, that here was their beginning.

[*1915*; 1921]

Favour of Alexander Balas

Oh I'm not put out because my chariot's
wheel was smashed, and I'm down one silly win.
I shall pass the night among fine wines
and lovely roses. All Antioch is mine.
I am the most exalted of young men.
I'm Balas's weakness, the one he worships.
Tomorrow, you'll see, they'll say the race wasn't proper.
(But if I were vulgar, and had secretly given the order—
they'd even have placed my crippled chariot first, the flatterers.)

[*1916?*; 1921]

Melancholy of Jason, Son of Cleander: Poet in Commagene: 595 A.D.

The aging of my body and my looks
is a wound from a terrible knife.
I have no means whatsoever to endure it.
Unto you I turn, Art of Poetry,
you who know something of drugs;
of attempts to numb pain, in Imagination and Word.

It's a wound from a terrible knife.—
Bring on your drugs, Art of Poetry,
which make it impossible—for a while—to feel the wound.

[*1918?*; 1921]

Demaratus

The theme, "The Character of Demaratus,"
which Porphyry has suggested to him in conversation,
the young scholar outlined as follows
(intending, afterwards, to flesh it out rhetorically).

"At first the courtier of King Darius, and then
a courtier of King Xerxes;
and now accompanying Xerxes and his army,
to vindicate himself at last: Demaratus.

"A great injustice had been done to him.
He *was* the son of Ariston. Shamelessly
his enemies had bribed the oracle.
Nor did they fail to deprive him of his throne;
but when at last he yielded, and decided
to resign himself to living as a private person
they had to go and insult him before the people,
they had to go and humiliate him, in public, at the festival.

"And so it is that he serves Xerxes with such great zeal.
Accompanying the enormous Persian army
he too will make his return to Sparta;
and, a king once more, how swiftly
he will drive him out, will degrade
that conniving Leotychides.

"And so his days pass by, full of concerns:
giving the Persians counsel, explaining to them
what they need to do to conquer Greece.

"Many worries, much reflection, which is why
the days of Demaratus are so dreary.
Many worries, much reflection, which is why
Demaratus doesn't have a moment's pleasure;
since pleasure isn't what he's feeling
(it's not; he won't acknowledge it;
how can he call it pleasure? it's the acme of his misfortune)
when everything reveals to him quite clearly
that the Greeks will emerge victorious."

[*1904; 1911; 1921*]

I Brought to Art

I'm sitting and musing.   I brought to Art
longings and feelings—   some half-glimpsed
faces or lines;   some uncertain mem'ries
of unfulfilled loves.   Let me submit to it.
It knows how to shape   the Form of Beauty;
almost imperceptibly   filling out life,
piecing together impressions,   piecing together the days.

[*1921*; 1921]

From the School of the Renowned Philosopher

He remained Ammonius Saccas's student for two years;
but of philosophy and of Saccas he grew bored.

Afterward he went into politics.
But he gave it up. The Prefect was a fool;
and those around him solemn, pompous stiffs;
their Greek horribly uncouth, the wretches.

His curiosity was aroused,
a bit, by the Church: to be baptized,
to pass as a Christian. But he quickly
changed his mind. He'd surely get in a row
with his parents, so ostentatiously pagan:
and they'd immediately put an end—an awful thought—
to his extremely generous allowance.

Still, he had to do something. He became an habitué
of the depraved houses of Alexandria,
of every secret den of debauchery.

In this, fortune had been kind to him:
had given him a form of highest comeliness.
And he delighted in that heavenly gift.

For at least another ten years yet
his beauty would endure. After that—
perhaps to Saccas he would go once more.
And if in the meantime the old man had died,
he'd go to some other philosopher or sophist;
someone suitable can always be found.

Or in the end, it was possible he'd even return
to politics—admirably mindful
of his family traditions,
duty to one's country, and other pomposities of that sort.

[*1921*; 1921]

Maker of Wine Bowls

On this mixing-bowl   of the purest silver—
which was made for the   home of Heracleides,
where great elegance   always is the rule—
note the stylish blooms,   and the brooks, the thyme;
and in the middle I put   a beautiful young man,
naked, sensuous;   he still keeps one leg,
just one, in the water.—   O Memory, I have begged
to find in you the best   of guides, that I might make
the face of the youth I loved   as it really was.
This has proved to be   very difficult since
some fifteen years have passed   since the day on which
he fell, a soldier, in   the defeat at Magnesia.

[*1903; 1912;* 1921]

Those Who Fought on Behalf of the Achaean League

You brave, who fought and fell in glory:
who had no fear of those who'd conquered everywhere.
You blameless, even if Diaeus and Critolaus blundered.
Whensoever the Greeks should want to boast,
"Such are the men our race produces," is what they'll say
about you. That's how marvelous the praise for you will be.—

Written in Alexandria by an Achaean:
in the seventh year of Ptolemy, the "Chickpea."

[*1922*; 1922]

For Antiochus Epiphanes

The young Antiochene   said to the king,
"In my heart there beats   a single precious hope:
the Macedonians again,   Antiochus Epiphanes,
the Macedonians are back   in the great fight again.
If only they would win—   I'll give to anyone who wants them
the horses and the lion,   the Pan made out of coral,
and the elegant mansion,   and the gardens in Tyre,
and everything else you've given me,   Antiochus Epiphanes."

Maybe he was moved   a little bit, the king.
But he recalled at once   his father and his brother,
and so made no response.   Some eavesdropper might
go and repeat something.—   Anyway, as expected,
at Pydna there swiftly came   the horrible conclusion.

[*1911?; 1922;* 1922]

113

In an Old Book

In an old book—about a hundred years old—
I found, neglected among the leaves,
a watercolour with no signature.
It must have been the work of a very powerful artist.
It bore the title "Representation of Love."

But "—of the love of extreme sensualists" would have been more fitting.

For it was clear as you looked at this work
(the artist's idea was easily grasped)
that the youth in this portrait wasn't meant
for those who love in a somewhat wholesome way,
within the limits of what is strictly permitted—
with his chestnut-brown, intensely colored eyes;
with the superior beauty of his face,
the beauty of unusual allures;
with those flawless lips of his that bring
pleasure to the body that it cherishes;
with those flawless limbs of his, made for beds
called shameless by the commonplace morality.

[*1892?*; 1922]

In Despair

He's lost him utterly.   And from now on he seeks
in the lips of every new   lover that he takes
the lips of that one: his.   Coupling with every new
lover that he takes   he longs to be mistaken:
that it's the same young man,   that he's giving himself to *him*.

He's lost him utterly,   as if he'd never been.
The other wished—he said—   he wished to save himself
from that stigmatized   pleasure, so unwholesome;
from that stigmatized   pleasure, in its shame.
There was still time, he said—   time to save himself.

He's lost him utterly,   as if he'd never been.
In his imagination,   in his hallucinations
in the lips of other youths   he seeks the lips of that one;
He wishes that he might   feel his love again.

[*1923*; 1923]

Julian, Seeing Indifference

"Seeing, then, that there is great indifference
among us toward the gods"—he says with that solemn affect.
Indifference. But what then did he expect?
Let him organize religion as much as he pleased,
let him write the high priest of Galatia as much as he pleased,
or to others like him, exhorting, giving directions.
His friends weren't Christians: that much is certain.
But even so they weren't able to
play the way that he did (brought up as a Christian)
with the system of a new religion,
ridiculous in theory and in practice.
In the end they were Greeks. *Nothing in excess,* Augustus.

[*1923?*; 1923]

Epitaph of Antiochus, King of Commagene

After she returned from his funeral, greatly bereaved,
the sister of him who had temperately and sweetly lived—
the exceedingly scholarly Antiochus, king
of Commagene—she wanted an epitaph for him.
And the Ephesian sophist Callistratus—who sojourned
often in the principality of Commagene,
and who in the royal household had been
so pleasantly and frequently received—
wrote it, at the suggestion of Syrian courtiers,
and sent it to her aged ladyship.

"May the renown of Antiochus the benevolent king
be meetly extolled, O Commagenians.
He was the provident captain of the land.
The life he lived was just, and wise, and gallant.
The life he lived, still more, was that finest thing: Hellenic—
mankind holds no quality more precious:
among the gods alone does anything surpass it."

[*1923?*; 1923]

Theater of Sidon (400 A.D.)

A respectable citizen's son—   above all else, a beauteous
youth who belongs to the theatre,   agreeable in so many ways:
I now and then compose,   in the language of the Greeks,
exceedingly daring verses,   which I circulate
very secretly, of course—   gods! they mustn't be seen
by those who prate about morals,   those who wear gray clothes—
verses about a pleasure   that is select, that moves
toward a barren love   of which the world disapproves.

[*1923?*; 1923]

Julian in Nicomedia

Foolhardy doings, full of risks.
The encomia for the ideals of the Greeks.

The white magic and the visits to the pagans'
temples. The raptures over the ancient gods.

The frequent conversations with Chrysanthius.
The theories of the (quite clever) philosopher Maximus.

And look at the result. It's obvious that Gallus
is very anxious. Constantius is suspicious.

Ah, his advisors weren't wary in the least.
This story's gone too far, Mardonius says,

and it's got to stop at once, all this furore.—
Julian is going back, a Lector once more,

to the church at Nicomedia,
where, loudly and with considerable

piety, he reads the holy Scriptures,
and at his Christian reverence the people wonder.

[*1892?*; *1924?*; 1924]

Before Time Could Alter Them

They were very pained   when they parted company.
They themselves didn't want it;   it was just the way things were.
The need to make a living   was forcing one of them
to go far away—   New York or Canada.
Certainly their love   wasn't the same as before;
the attraction had been   gradually diminished,
its attraction had been   very much diminished.
But still, that they should part—   that they didn't want.
It was just the way things were.—   Or perhaps it was that Fate
was something of an artist,   separating them now
before their feeling died away,   before Time could alter them:
Each one, for the other,   will be as if he'd stayed
twenty-four years old,   the exquisite lad.

[*1924?*; 1924]

He Came to Read—

He came so he could read. Lying open
are two or three books: historians and poets.
But he'd barely read for ten minutes,
when he put them aside. On the sofa
he's half asleep. He's completely devoted to books—
but he's twenty-three years old, and very handsome;
and this afternoon desire has come
to his flawless flesh, and to his lips.
To his flesh, which is beauty entire,
the fever of desire has come;
without foolish shame about the form of its enjoyment. . . .

[*1924?*; 1924]

The Year 31 B.C. in Alexandria

From his little village near the city's outskirts,
still dusted with his journey's dirt,

the peddler arrives. He hawks his wares—
"Incense!" "Gum!" "The finest oil!" "Scent for your hair!"—

through the streets. But the tremendous stir,
and the music, and parades, won't let him be heard.

The mob shoves him, drags him, knocks him down.
And at the height of his confusion, when he asks "What on earth is
      going on?"

someone tosses him the palace's gargantuan lie:
that victory in Greece belongs to Antony.

[*1917; 1924; 1924*]

122

John Cantacuzenus Triumphs

He sees the fields of which he's still the master,
with their corn, their livestock, with their fruitful
trees. And further off the house of his forefathers,
filled with clothes and costly furnishings, and silver.

They'll take it all—Christ Jesus!—now they'll take it all.

He wonders whether Cantacuzenus will have pity
if he goes and falls at his feet. They say he's lenient,
extremely lenient. But those around him? The army?—
or should he prostrate himself and plead with Lady Irene?

Dullard! To have gotten tangled up with Anna's faction—
curse the day that Lord Andronicus ever
married her. Have we seen any success
come from her conduct, any humankindness?
Even the Westerners no longer value her:
Her plans are ridiculous, her strategy absurd.
While from the City they were threatening the world,
Cantacuzenus laid them low, Lord John laid them low.

And to think he'd planned to go over to Lord John's
side! And he'd have done it, too. And he'd be happy now,
still a great noble, solidly established,

if the bishop hadn't persuaded him at the last minute,
with his hieratic pushiness,
with his faulty information from start to finish,
and with his promises, and his foolishness.

[1924]

Temethus, an Antiochene: 400 A.D.

Verses by young Temethus,   suffering in love.
Entitled "Emonides"—   Antiochus Epiphanes'
dearly loved companion;   a surpassingly comely
youth of Samosata.   But if the verses were
heated, deeply moving   it's because Emonides
(who belongs to that   ancient period:
year one-thirty-seven   of the Greeks' dominion!—
perhaps a little earlier)   was added to the poem
simply as a name;   quite fitting, all the same.
A love of Temethus   is what the poem expresses,
fine and worthy of him.   We who are initiates,
his most intimate friends;   we who are initiates
we know who it is   for whom the lines were written.
The clueless Antiochenes   read only "Emonides."

[1925]

125

Of Colored Glass

One detail in particular greatly moves me
about the crowning, in Blachernae, of John Cantacuzenus
and Irene, Andronicus Asen's daughter.
As they had very little in the way of precious stones
(our wretched dominion's poverty was great)
they wore artificial ones. A heap of bits of glass,
scarlet, green, or blue. There was nothing
that was abject or unsuitable
in my eyes about those little pieces
of colored glass. On the contrary, they look
like a piteous protestation against
the unjust misfortune of those who were being crowned.
They are the symbols of what was fitting for them to have,
of what above all it was right for them to have
at their crowning: for a Lord John Cantacuzenus,
for a Lady Irene, Andronicus Asen's daughter.

[1925]

The 25th Year of His Life

He frequently goes into the tavern
where they'd met each other the month before.
He enquired; but there was nothing they could tell him.
From their words, he understood he'd met
a character who was totally unknown;
one of the many unknown and suspect
youthful figures who would pass through there.
He nonetheless goes to the tavern frequently, at night,
and sits and looks toward the entrance;
he grows weary looking toward the entrance.
Perhaps he'll come in. Tonight, perhaps he'll come.

For close to three weeks this is what he does.
His mind has grown sick with wantonness.
On his mouth the kisses have remained.
All his flesh is suffering from the ceaseless yearning.
The feel of the other's body is upon him.
He wants to be as one with it again.

Not to betray himself: this is what he strives for, of course.
But sometimes he's almost indifferent.—
Besides, he knows what he's exposing himself to,
he's made up his mind. It's not unlikely that the life he's living
will lead him to some devastating scandal.

[*1918?*; 1925]

On the Italian Seashore

Cemus, son of Menedorus,   a young Italiote,
passes through his life   immersed in his amusements:
this is what they're used to,   the youths of Greater Greece,
who have been brought up   with enormous wealth.

But today he is extremely   (contrary to his nature)
broody and dejected.   Close to the seashore,
in deepest melancholy,   he sees that they're unloading
the vessels with the plunder   from the Peloponnese.

Spoils of the Greeks: the pillage from Corinth.

O surely it is not   permissible today,
it isn't possible   for the young Italiote
to have any desire   at all for his amusements.

[1925]

In the Boring Village

In the boring village where he works—
an employee in a general
store; extremely young—and where he's waiting
for another two or three months to pass,
for another two or three months till business tapers off,
so he can make for the city and throw himself
straight into its bustle and amusements:
in the boring village where he's waiting—
he fell into his bed this evening sick with desire,
all his youth inflamed with carnal yearning,
with beautiful intensity, all his beautiful youth.
And pleasure came into his sleep; within
his sleep he sees and possesses the shape, the flesh he wanted. . . .

[*1925*; 1925]

Apollonius of Tyana in Rhodes

On the subject of proper education and instruction
Apollonius was conversing with a
young man who was building a luxurious
residence in Rhodes. "For my part, when I enter"
the Tyanean said in closing, "a temple, however small,
I should very much prefer to see inside
a statue made of ivory and of gold
than, in a big one, something made of clay, something common."—

That "clay" and that "common"; so revolting:
humbug that has already deceived
some (who lack sufficient training). That clay and that common.

[*1925*; 1925]

Cleitus's Illness

Cleitus, an extremely amiable
boy of twenty-three or thereabouts—
with the best of educations, with a rare Greek culture—
is gravely ill. The fever has got him,
the one that's swept through Alexandria this year.

The fever also found him morally wracked,
anguished because his friend, a certain young actor,
has ceased loving him and wanting him.

He's gravely ill, and his parents are terrified.

And a certain old housemaid who raised him
is also full of fear for Cleitus's life.
In her terrible anxiety
she is put in mind of an idol
she once worshipped as a girl, before she came here as a maid
to the home of eminent Christians, and herself became a Christian.
She secretly takes some cakes, and wine, and honey.
She brings them before the idol. She chants as many
litanies as she recalls: the bits from either end, the middles. The foolish
        woman
doesn't realize that it matters little to the black demon
whether a Christian is or isn't cured.

[1926]

131

In a Municipality of Asia Minor

The tidings of the outcome of the naval battle, at Actium,
were rather unexpected, to be sure.
But there's no need to draft a new inscription.
The name alone need change. Instead of (there,
in the final lines) "Having saved the Romans
from that calamitous Octavian,
a man who's like a parody of Caesar,"
now we'll put "Having saved the Romans
from that calamitous Marc Antony."
The entire text fits beautifully.

"To the conqueror, the most glorious,
unsurpassed in every martial action,
astounding for his political achievements,
on behalf of whom the people fervently prayed
for the triumph of Marc Antony"
here, as we said, the switch: "of Caesar,
considering him the finest gift of Zeus—
to the powerful protector of the Greeks,
who benevolently reverences all Greek customs,
is beloved in every region that is Greek,
so richly worthy of encomia,
and of the narration of his deeds at length
in the Greek tongue, both in verse and prose:
in the Greek tongue, which is the bearer of renown,"
etcetera, etcetera. It all fits brilliantly.

[1926]

Priest of the Serapeum

The good old man my father
the one who always loved me just the same,
the good old man my father I now mourn,
who died two days ago, a bit before the break of day.

O Jesus Christ, that I might observe
the commandments of your most holy church
in every deed of mine, in every word,
in every thought, is my endeavor
every day. And from those who deny you
I turn my face.— But now I mourn:
I lament, O Christ, for my father
for all that he was—dreadful to utter it—
a priest at the accursed Serapeum.

[1926]

In the Taverns

In the public houses   and in the lowest dives
of Beirut I wallow.   I didn't want to stay
in Alexandria: not I.   Tamides has left me;
he went off with the Eparch's   son so he could get
a villa on the Nile,   a palace in the city.
It wouldn't do for me   to stay in Alexandria.—
In the public houses   and the lowest dives
of Beirut I wallow.   In low debauchery
I spend my sordid hours.   The only thing that saves me,
like a lasting beauty,   like a perfume that
has stayed on my flesh,   is that, for two years,
Tamides was all mine,   the most exquisite youth,
all mine—not for a house,   nor a villa on the Nile.

[1926]

A Great Procession of Priests and Laymen

A procession of priests and laymen,
representing every walk of life,
moves through the streets, the squares, and gates
of the illustrious city of Antioch.
At the head of the grand, imposing procession
a beautiful youth clad all in white holds the Cross,
his hands raised high: our power and our hope, the Holy Cross.
The pagans, who were so arrogant before,
now diffident and timid, hastily
shrink back from the great procession.
Far from us, far from us may they stay
(as long as they continue to deny their error). The Holy Cross
moves ahead. In all the neighborhoods
where Christian people live in piety
it is the bearer of consolation and joy:
they emerge, the pious folk, at the doorways of their houses
and full of jubilation reverence it—
the power, the salvation of the universe, the Cross.—

This is an annual Christian holiday.
But today, behold, it ends more gloriously.
The empire has been saved at last.
The most accursed, most execrable
Julian is king no more.

For the most pious Jovian let us pray.

[*1892?*; *1917?*; *1926*]

135

Sophist Departing from Syria

Learned sophist, you   who are quitting Syria
and have in mind to write   about Antioch,
it's fitting that you mention   Mebes in your work.
Mebes the renowned,   who's undeniably
the most beauteous youth,   the one who's most beloved,
in all of Antioch.   No one of the other
youths who lead that life—   none of them is paid
as highly as he is.   In order to have Mebes
for only two or three days,   they very often give him
up to a hundred staters.—   I said, In Antioch:
but also in Alexandria,   but also even in Rome,
you cannot find a youth   as desirable as Mebes.

[1926]

Julian and the Antiochenes

The Chi, so they say, in no wise harmed the city, nor did the Kappa . . .
Finding ourselves interpreters . . . we learned that letters were the initials
of names, and that the former meant Christ, and the latter, Constantius.

—Julian, *Misopogon*

Was it ever possible for them to give up
their beautiful way of life; the rich array
of their daily entertainments; their glorious
theater where was born a union of Art
and the erotic predilections of the flesh!

Immoral to a point—quite likely to a great extent—
that they were. But they had the satisfaction that their way of life
was the *much discussed* life of Antioch,
pleasure-bent, absolutely elegant.

To give up all of that, and turn to *what,* precisely?

His airy prattle concerning the false gods,
his wearisome braggadocio;
his childish fear of the theatre;
his graceless prudishness; his ridiculous beard.

O certainly they preferred the Chi,
O certainly they preferred the Kappa; a hundred times more.

[1926]

Anna Dalassene

In the chrysobull that Alexius Comnenus issued
to honor his mother in a most distinguished way,
the Lady Anna Dalassene, so very wise—
remarkable for her deeds, her mores—
there can be found a miscellany of praise:
among which, let us here relate
one beautiful, noble phrase,
"No one ever uttered 'mine' or 'thine,' those chilly words."

[1927]

Days of 1896

He debased himself completely.   An erotic inclination,
very much forbidden   and held in great contempt
(innate, all the same)   was the reason why:
the society he lived in   was extremely priggish.
He had gradually lost   what little money he had;
afterwards his position,   then his reputation.
He was nearing thirty   and had never held
a job for even a year,   at least that anyone knew of.
Sometimes he would meet   his expenses by
playing go-between   in deals considered shameful.
He ended up the sort   who, if you were seen with him
often, you'd likely be   extremely compromised.

But that's not all of it;   that wouldn't be fair.
The memory of his beauty   deserves a great deal more.
There's another way of looking   and, if seen that way,
he strikes you as attractive;   strikes you as the simple, true
child of desire   who, above his honor
and his reputation,   placed, without a thought,
the unsullied pleasure   of his unsullied body.

Above his reputation?   But society, which was
so extremely priggish   had such foolish values.

[1925; 1927]

Two Young Men, 23 to 24 Years Old

Since half past ten he'd waited at the café,
expecting him to appear before too long.
Midnight came and went—and still he waited.
Half past one had come and gone: the café
had emptied out entirely, almost.
He grew bored of reading the newspapers
mechanically. Of his three poor shillings
only one was left: during his long wait
he'd squandered all the rest on coffee and cognac.
He smoked all the cigarettes he had.
All the waiting was exhausting him. Because,
alone as he had been for many hours, he
began to be possessed by irksome thoughts
about the wayward life that he was living.

But when he saw his friend come in—all at once
the weariness, the boredom, the thoughts all fled.

His friend brought some unexpected news:
In the card game he'd won sixty pounds.

Their handsome faces, their exquisite youth,
the sensitive love that they shared between them,
was refreshed, revived, invigorated by
the sixty pounds from the game of cards.

All joy and potency, feeling and beauty,
they went—not to the houses of their upstanding families
(where, at any rate, they were no longer wanted):
to a certain one they knew, and rather special,
to a house of vice they went, and asked for
a bedroom, and expensive drinks, and they drank again.

And when the expensive drinks had all been drained,
and when it was close to four o'clock in the morning,
happy, they gave themselves to love.

[1927]

Greek Since Ancient Times

Antioch goes boasting   about her splendid buildings,
and her lovely streets;   about the marvelous
countryside around her,   and the great number of
those who dwell inside her.   She boasts that she's the seat
of illustrious kings;   and about the artists
and scholars that she has,   as well as hugely rich
and very canny merchants.   But most incomparable
of all, Antioch   boasts that she's a city
that's been Greek since ancient times;   a relative of Argos:
through Ionê, a city   founded by the Argive
colonists in honor   of the daughter of Inachus.

[1927]

Days of 1901

This was the thing about him that stood out:
that even with all of his loose living,
and such a vast experience of the sensual;
for all that it was usually the case
that his attitude was so well-fitted to his age,
there would be moments—to be sure,
extremely rare—when the impression that
he gave was one of flesh almost untouched.

The beauty of his nine-and-twenty years,
which had been assayed so much by pleasure,
reminded one at moments, strangely enough,
of a lad who—somewhat awkwardly—for
the first time gives his pure body up to love.

[<*Oct. 1927*; 1927]

You Didn't Understand

On the subject of our religious beliefs—
the fatuous Julian said, "I read it up, I understood it,
I looked down on it." As if he'd wiped us out
with that "looked down" of his, ridiculous man.

But quips like that don't hold much weight with us
Christians. "You read it up, but didn't understand; had you understood,
you'd not have looked down on it" we straightaway replied.

[1928]

A Young Man, Skilled in the Art of the Word— in His 24th Year

Keep working however you can, brain.—
A one-sided passion is wasting him away.
He is in a maddening situation.
He kisses the beloved face each day,
his hands upon those most exquisite limbs.
Never before has he loved with such great
passion. But what's missing is the beautiful fulfillment
of love; what's missing is the fulfillment
which both of them must long for with the same intensity.

(They're not equally devoted to abnormal pleasure; not both of them.
He alone is utterly possessed by it.)

And he wastes away, his nerves completely shot.
Besides, he's out of work; that makes things worse.
With a bit of trouble he borrows some
small sums of money (which he practically
has to beg for, sometimes) and barely gets by.
He kisses the lips he worships: he takes his pleasure
upon the exquisite body—which, however,
he now feels is merely acquiescing.
And then he drinks and smokes; he drinks and smokes;
and drags himself around the cafés all day long,
wearily drags the wasting of his beauty.—
Keep working however you can, brain.

[1928]

145

In Sparta

King Cleomenes didn't know, he didn't dare—
he didn't how to say such a thing
to his mother: that Ptolemy was demanding,
as a guarantee for their agreement, that she too be sent
to Egypt to be held there as a hostage;
a very humiliating, unseemly affair.
He was always on the verge of speaking; and would always hesitate.
He was always about to tell; and would always stop.

But the extraordinary woman understood him
(she'd already heard some rumors about it anyway),
and encouraged him to tell her everything.
And she laughed; and said of course she'd go.
And indeed rejoiced that she could,
in her old age, be of use to Sparta still.

As for humiliation—but she was totally indifferent.
Of course a Lagid arriviste like that
was incapable of comprehending the Spartan spirit;
and so his arrogant demand could not,
in fact, humiliate an Eminent
Lady such as she: mother to a Spartan king.

[1928]

146

Portrait of a Young Man of Twenty-Three Done by His Friend of the Same Age, an Amateur

He finished up the portrait   yesterday at noon. Now
he studies it in detail.   He did him in a gray
jacket, all unbuttoned,   a deep gray. Without
any vest or tie.   In a shirt of rose;
so a little of   the beauty of the chest,
the beauty of the throat,   might show through a bit.

The right side of his brow   is almost totally
covered by his hair,   by his beautiful hair
(which is combed the way   he fancies it this year).
The note is utterly   the voluptuous one
that he wanted to strike   when he did the eyes,
when he did the lips . . .   That mouth of his, the lips
made for the fulfillment   of a choice eroticism.

[1928]

147

In a Large Greek Colony, 200 B.C.

That things in the Colony aren't going as one might wish
not the slightest doubt at all remains,
and though, despite it all, we're getting ahead,
perhaps the time has come, as more than a few have said,
for us to bring in a Political Reformer.

Still, the obstacle, the quandary,
is that they always make a palaver
out of everything, these Reformers.
(It would be a blessing if no one ever
had need of them.) They investigate
everything, look into every corner,
and immediately dream up radical reforms,
and demand that they be enacted straightaway.

They also have a penchant for sacrifices.
You must give up that property of yours;
for you to own it is a risky business:
it's precisely properties like this that ruin Colonies.
You must give up that source of revenue
and also this one, which is connected with it,
and this third one, too: a natural consequence.
They are substantial, but what is to be done?
the liability they create is harmful to you.

And as they proceed with their investigation,
they keep finding waste, and call for its elimination;
things, however, that are hard to do without.

And when, all being well, they complete their mission,
every detail squared away and whittled down,
and they leave, taking appropriate compensation,
let's see if anything's left, after
such a great display of surgical skill.—

Perhaps the time hasn't yet arrived.
Let's not force it: haste is dangerous.
Premature measures often bring remorse.
Certainly, regrettably, the Colony has its share of foolishness.
But what human affair is without its flaws?
And when all is said and done, we're getting ahead.

[1928]

149

Potentate from Western Libya

Overall he was well liked in Alexandria,
during the ten days that he sojourned there,
Aristomenes, the son of Menelaus,
the potentate from Western Libya.
Like his name, his attire, too, quite suitably, was Greek.
He gratefully received his honors, although
he didn't court them; he was unpretentious.
He'd spend his time shopping for Greek books,
history and philosophy especially.
Above all, however: a person of few words.
He must have been a deep thinker, it was widely said,
and for such men it's only natural not to talk too much.

No deep thinker was he; no anything.
A commonplace, laughable sort of person.
He took a Greek name, dressed like the Greeks,
learned, more or less, to behave like the Greeks;
and in his heart he dreaded that by some chance
he'd lose the goodish impression that he'd made
by speaking a terribly barbaric Greek
and that the Alexandrians would poke fun at him,
as is their wont, horrid people.

For this reason he confined himself to a few words,
frightfully attentive to his declensions and his accent;
and grew bored to death, with all those
conversations piled up inside him.

[1928]

Cimon Son of Learchus, 22 Years Old, Teacher of Greek Letters (in Cyrene)

"My end came for me   when I was content.
Hermoteles had me   for his inseparable friend.
In my final days,   for all that he pretended
that he wasn't worried,   I could often sense that
his eyes were wet with tears.   When he thought that I
had dozed off for a while,   he fell, like one distraught,
at the side of my bed.   But we two were young men
both of the same age,   twenty-three years old.
Fate is a betrayer.   Perhaps some other passion
might have taken Hermoteles   quite away from me.
I ended my days well: in undivided love."

This epitaph for Marylus   son of Aristodemus,
who died a month ago   in Alexandria:
I received it as I mourned him,   I, his cousin Cimon.
The writer sent it to me,   a certain poet I know.
He sent it to me since   he knew I was a relation
of Marylus: he knew   nothing else at all.
My soul is full of pain   pain for Marylus.
We two had grown up   together, like two brothers.
I'm deep in melancholy.   His untimely death
has completely snuffed   every bit of rancor
that I bore Marylus;   every bit of rancor
even though he stole   Hermoteles' love;
even though, if Hermoteles   wanted me back again,
it would hardly be the same.   I know my own character,

how sensitive it is.   The image of Marylus
will always come between us,   and I'll imagine that
he's saying to me, Look here,   now you're satisfied.
Look, you've got him back,   just as you'd longed for, Cimon.
Look, you no longer have   a reason to malign me.

[*1913?*; 1928]

On the March to Sinope

As Mithridates, glorious and powerful,
the lord of great cities,
master of mighty armies and fleets,
made his way to Sinope, he passed along a road
deep in the countryside, quite out of the way,
where a soothsayer had his dwelling-place.

Mithridates sent an officer of his
to inquire of the seer how much more wealth he would acquire
in the future, how many other forces.

He sent an officer of his, and afterwards
proceeded on the march to Sinope.

The soothsayer withdrew into a secret room.
After about a half an hour he came out
very much concerned, and told the officer:
"An adequate discernment I could not make.
Today is not a day that's suitable.
I saw some shadowy things. I didn't understand them well.—
But the king should rest content, in my opinion, with all he has.
Any more than that will bring him danger.
Remember, officer, to tell him this:
with all that he has, by god, let him rest content!
Fate keeps unexpected changes in store.

Go tell this to King Mithridates:
all too seldom one finds the noble friend
of his forebear, someone who just in time writes with his spear
upon the dust the words that saved him *Flee, Mithridates.*"

[1928]

Days of 1909, '10, and '11

He was the son of a much put-upon, impoverished
sailor (from an island in the Aegean Sea).
He worked at a blacksmith's. He wore threadbare clothes;
his workshoes split apart, the wretched things.
His hands were completely grimed with rust and oil.

Evenings, when he was closing up the shop,
if there was anything he was really longing for,
some tie that cost a little bit of money,
some tie that was just right for a Sunday,
or if in a shop window he'd seen and yearned for
some beautiful shirt in mauve:
one or two shillings is what he'd sell his body for.

I ask myself whether in antique times
glorious Alexandria possessed a youth more beauteous,
a kid more perfect than he—for all that he was lost:
for of course there never was a statue or portrait of him;
thrown into a blacksmith's poor old shop,
he was quickly spoiled by the arduous work,
the common debauchery, so ruinous.

[1928]

Myres: Alexandria in 340 A.D.

When I learned the dreadful news, that Myres was dead,
I went to his house, for all that I am loath
to go inside the homes of Christians,
above all those in mourning, or on feast-days.

I stood there in a corridor. I didn't want
to go in any further, since I perceived
that the kinsmen of the dead man were looking at me
with evident dismay, and with displeasure.

They had him in a large room
a part of which I saw from where I stood
off to the side: all expensive carpets,
and services of silver and of gold.

I stood crying on one side of the corridor.
And I was thinking that our gatherings and outings
wouldn't be worth much, without Myres, from now on;
and was thinking that I'd no longer see him
at our splendid and outrageous all-night revels,
enjoying himself, and laughing, and declaiming lines
with that perfect feel he had for Greek rhythm;
and was thinking that I'd lost forever more
his beauty, that I'd lost forever more
the youth whom I once worshipped to distraction.

Some old women, near me, were speaking softly
about the last day that he was alive—
the name of Christ always on his lips,
a cross that he was holding in his hands.—
Later on there came into the room
four Christian priests, and they fervently
recited prayers and orisons to Jesus,
or to Mary (I don't know their religion very well).

We knew, of course, that Myres was a Christian.
From the very first we knew it, when
two years ago he joined our little band.
But he lived his life completely as we did.
Of all of us, the most devoted to his pleasures;
squandering lavish sums on his amusements.
Blithely untroubled by what people thought,
he threw himself eagerly into street brawls late at night,
whenever our gang chanced upon a rival gang.
Never once did he speak about his religion.
In fact, there was one time when we told him
that we were taking him with us to the Serapeum.
But he seemed to be unhappy with
this little joke of ours: I remember now.
Ah, and two other times now come to mind.
When we were making libations to Poseidon,
he pulled out of our circle, and turned his gaze elsewhere.
When one of us, in his enthusiasm,
said, May our company ever be under
the favor and protection of the great,
the all-beautiful Apollo—Myres murmured
(the others didn't hear) "except for me."

Their voices raised, the Christian priests
were praying for the soul of the young man.—
I stood observing with how much diligence,
and with what intense attention
to the protocols of their religion, they were preparing
everything for the Christian funeral rite.
And all of a sudden I was seized by a queer
impression. Vaguely, I had the feeling that
Myres was going far away from me;
had a feeling that he, a Christian, was being united
with his own, and that I was becoming
a stranger to him, very much a stranger; I sensed besides
a certain doubt coming over me: perhaps I had been fooled
by my passion, had always been a stranger to him.—
I flew out of their horrible house,
and quickly left before their Christianity
could get hold of, could alter, the memory of Myres.

[1929]

Alexander Jannaeus, and Alexandra

Successful and completely satisfied,
King Alexander Jannaeus
and his wife, Queen Alexandra,
parade—with musicians in the lead,
and all manner of magnificence and luxe—
parade through the streets of Jerusalem.
They have brought to a brilliant conclusion the work
that the great Judah Maccabee had started,
along with his four illustrious brothers;
and which had continued resolutely in the midst
of many dangers and of many hardships.
By now, nothing unseemly remained.
Gone was any trace of subservience
to the arrogant rulers of Antioch. See how
King Alexander Jannaeus,   .
and his wife Queen Alexandra,
are the equals of the Seleucids in every respect.
Good Jews, pure Jews, pious Jews: this above all.
But, inasmuch as circumstances require,
conversant, too, in the Greek tongue;
and acquainted, too, with both Greek and Hellenizing
rulers—but as equals, let there be no mistake.
Truly, they have brought to a brilliant conclusion,
have brought to a spectacular conclusion
the work that the great Judah Maccabee had started
along with his four illustrious brothers.

[1929]

Beautiful, White Flowers As They Went So Well

He went into the café   where they used to go together.
Here his friend had said   just three months ago:
"We haven't got a cent.   We two are so poor
that we've come to this—   the cheapest spots in town.
I'll put it to you straight: I can't keep going out
with you. Someone else—   *listen*—wants me now."
That someone else had promised   him two suits and some
silken handkerchiefs.—   To get him back again
his friend made quite a fuss,   and came up with twenty pounds.
He came back to him   for the twenty pounds.
But not just only that: for their old affection,
and for their old love,   and for their old feelings.
That "someone" was a liar,   a real low character.
He'd had only one   suit made for him and
that, begrudgingly: he had to plead a thousand times.

But he no longer wants   any suits at all
nor indeed wants any   silken handkerchiefs,
neither twenty pounds,   not even twenty pence.

They buried him on Sunday,   at ten o'clock in the morning.
They buried him on Sunday: scarcely a week ago.

On his shabby coffin   he laid some flowers,
beautiful, white flowers   as they went so well
with his beauty and   his two-and-twenty years.

When at night he went—   he happened to have some business,
something absolutely vital—   into the café where
they used to go together: a dagger in his heart,
that dismal black café,   where they used to go together.

[1929]

Come Now, King of the Lacedaemonians

Cratesicleia did not condescend to let
the people see her crying and lamenting;
magnificent she went about, and silent.
Never did her imperturbable mien reveal
her dejection or her torment.
But even so, for a moment she could not hold back:
and before she went aboard the ship to go to Alexandria,
she took her son to the temple of Poseidon,
and when they found themselves alone she clasped him to her bosom
and kept kissing her son, who was "tormented," says
Plutarch, "and in a state of very great distress."
Still, her strong character prevailed:
pulling herself together, the remarkable woman
said to Cleomenes "Come now, O king
of the Lacedaemonians, and when we go forth
from here, let no one see us weeping
nor doing anything that is unworthy of
Sparta. This alone is ours to do;
our fortunes go howsoever the god provides."

And onto the ship she went, making her way to that "provides."

[1929]

In the Same Space

House, coffeehouses, neighborhood: setting
that I see and where I walk; year after year.

I crafted you amid joy and amid sorrows:
out of so much that happened, out of so many things.

And you've been wholly *remade into feeling;* for me.

[1929]

The Mirror in the Entrance

In the entrance hallway of that sumptuous home
there was an enormous mirror, very old;
acquired at least eighty years ago.

A strikingly beautiful boy, a tailor's assistant,
(on Sunday afternoons, an amateur athlete),
was standing with a package. He handed it
to one of the household, who then went back inside
to fetch a receipt. The tailor's assistant
remained alone, and waited.
He drew near the mirror, and stood gazing at himself,
and straightening his tie. Five minutes later
they brought him the receipt. He took it and left.

But the ancient mirror, which had seen and seen again,
throughout its lifetime of so many years,
thousands of objects and faces—
but the ancient mirror now became elated,
inflated with pride, because it had received upon itself
perfect beauty, for a few minutes.

[1930]

165

He Asked About the Quality—

From within the office where he'd been taken on
to fill an insignificant, ill-paid position
(eight pounds a month at best: bonuses included)
he emerged, when he'd finished the solitary task
at which he'd been stooped the entire afternoon.
He left at seven, and then strolled slowly along,
and dawdled in the street.— Handsome;
interesting, too: in a way that showed he'd realized
a maximal yield from his senses.
He'd just turned twenty-nine, the month before.

He dawdled in the street, and in the shabby
alleyways that led to where he lived.

As he passed before a little store
where the goods that were for sale were
shoddy, low-priced things for laborers,
he saw a face within, he saw a shape;
they urged him on and he went in, as if keen
on seeing colored handkerchiefs.

He asked about the quality of the handkerchiefs,
and what they cost; in a voice that was choked,
almost stifled by his yearning.

So, too, the answers that came back:
distracted, in a voice kept very low,
secretly concealing consent.

Now and then they'd talk about the merchandise—but
their sole aim: for their hands to touch
atop the handkerchiefs; for their faces to
draw near, and their lips, as if by chance.
Some momentary contact of their limbs.

Quickly and secretly, so the proprietor
wouldn't notice, sitting there in back.

[1930]

Should Have Taken the Trouble

It's gotten so I'm practically homeless and broke.
This deadly city, Antioch,
has devoured all my money:
deadly, with its ruinous way of life.

But I'm young and in the best of health.
With an astounding mastery of Greek
(I know—by heart—Aristotle, Plato:
any orator, any poet, anyone you say.)
I know a thing or two about the army,
and have connections among the mercenary leaders.
I'm on pretty good terms with the High Command as well.
I stayed six months in Alexandria, last year;
am fairly well acquainted (and this is useful) with what goes on there:
the "Malefactor"'s schemes, the dirty deals, and so forth.

Which is why I think I'm totally
qualified to be of service to this country,
my beloved homeland, Syria.

In whatever job they give me I'll try hard
to be useful to this country. That's my plan.
And if they trip me up again with their machinations—
we know who our fine friends are; enough said for now;
if they trip me up, am I to blame?

I'll solicit Zabinas first off,
and if that fool doesn't appreciate me
I'll go to his archrival, Grypus.
And if that idiot doesn't take me either,
off I go at once to Hyrcanus.

One of the three, in any case, is bound to want me.

And my conscience isn't troubled by the fact
that I'm so completely indifferent to my choice.
All three of them harm Syria just the same.

But, given what I've come to, am I to blame?
I'm just a wretch who's trying to get by.
The almighty gods should have taken the trouble
to create a fourth man, who was good.
With pleasure I'd have gone along with him.

[1930]

According to the Formulas of Ancient Greco-Syrian Magicians

"What distillation is there to be found, from magic
herbs," an aesthete said,
"what distillation, made according to the formulas
of ancient Greco-Syrian magicians,
that could, for one day (if its power can't
last more than that), or just a little while,
bring me back the age of twenty-three
again; bring my friend at twenty-two years old
back to me again—his beauty, and his love.

"What distillation is there to be found, made according to the formulas
of ancient Greco-Syrian magicians
that, in keeping with this movement back in time,
might even bring us back our little room once more."

[1931]

In 200 B.C.

"Alexander son of Philip and the Greeks except the
       Lacedaemonians"—

We can very easily imagine
how utterly indifferent they were in Sparta
to that inscription. "Except the Lacedaemonians,"
but of course. Spartans weren't for
being led around and ordered about
like prized retainers. Anyway
a panhellenic expedition without
a king of Sparta taking the command
wouldn't have seemed of much account to them.
Oh most certainly "except the Lacedaemonians."

That's one point of view. Without a doubt.

So: except the Lacedaemonians at Granicus;
and at Issus afterwards; and in the final
battle, where they swept away the fearsome army
which the Persians had assembled at Arbela:
which had set out from Arbela for victory, and was swept away.

And from that amazing panhellenic expedition,
crowned with victory, everywhere acclaimed,
famed throughout the world, illustrious
as no other has been illustrious,

without any rival: we emerged,
a new world that was Greek, and great.

We: the Alexandrians, the Antiochenes,
the Selucians, and the numerous
other Greeks of Egypt and of Syria,
and in Media, and in Persia, and all the others.
With their far–flung realms,
with the nuanced policy of judicious integration.
And the Common Greek Language
which we've taken as far as Bactria, as far as the Indians.

Let's talk about Lacedaemonians now!

[*1916?*; 1931]

Days of 1908

That year he found himself without a job;
and so he made a living from cards,
from backgammon, and what he borrowed.

A job, at three pounds a month, at a little stationer's,
had been offered to him.
But he turned it down without the slightest hesitation.
It wouldn't do. It wasn't a wage
for him, a young man with some education, twenty-five years of age.

Two or three shillings a day was what he'd get, sometimes not.
What could the boy possibly earn from cards and backgammon
in the coffeehouses of his class, the common ones,
however cleverly he played, however stupid the partners he chose?
And loans—then there were those loans.
It was rare that he'd manage a crown, more often it was half;
sometimes he'd settle for shillings.

Sometimes for a week, occasionally more,
when he was spared the horror of staying up till dawn,
he'd cool off at the baths, with a swim at morning.

His clothes were in a dreadful state.
There was one suit that he would always wear,
a suit of a very faded cinnamon hue.

Oh days of the summer of nineteen-hundred eight,
your vision, quite exquisitely, was spared
that very faded cinnamon-colored suit.

Your vision preserved him
as he was when he undressed, when he flung off
the unworthy clothes, and the mended underwear.
And he'd be left completely nude; flawlessly beautiful; a thing of
        wonder.
His hair uncombed, springing back;
his limbs a little colored by the sun
from his nakedness in the morning at the baths, and at the seashore.

[1921?; 1931]

On the Outskirts of Antioch

We were mystified in Antioch when we learned
of the latest antics Julian had got up to.

Apollo had laid it all out for him, at Daphne!
He didn't want to give an oracle (we couldn't care less!),
he had no intention of speaking prophetically, unless they first
purified his sanctuary in Daphne.
They irritate him, he explained—the dead, his neighbors.

In Daphne there are many burials.—
One among those who'd been entombed there
was the miraculous—the glory of our church—
the sainted, the all-triumphant martyr Babylas.

He's the one the false god hinted at, the one he fears.
As long as he senses him nearby, he dares not
issue any oracles: not a word.
(They tremble before our martyrs, those false gods do.)

The impious Julian girded himself for action:
he lost his temper and kept shouting: "Dig him up, move him,
take him away, this Babylas, at once.
You there, do you hear? Apollo's irritated.
Dig him up, take hold of him at once.

Exhume him, put him wherever you like.
Take him out, get him out of here. You think I'm joking?
Apollo said his sanctuary must be purified."

We took it out, we took the holy relic somewhere else.
We took it out, we took it in love and in honor.

And since then, the sanctuary has done so *very* well.
Without the slightest delay, an enormous fire
broke out: a terrifying fire:
and the sanctuary and Apollo both burned up.

The idol is ash: something to sweep up with the trash.

Julian exploded and he put it about—
what else could he do?—that the fire was set
by the Christians, by us. Let him talk.
It hasn't been proved. Let him go and talk.
The essential thing is that he exploded.

[*1932–1933; 1935*]

Poems Published 1897–1908

CONTENTS OF
THE SENGOPOULOS NOTEBOOK

(Poems already published in Poems 1905–1915 *are italicized.)*

Voices

Imagined voices, and beloved, too,
of those who died, or of those who are
lost unto us like the dead.

Sometimes in our dreams they speak to us;
sometimes in its thought the mind will hear them.

And with their sound for a moment there return
sounds from the first poetry of our life—
like music, in the night, far off, that fades away.

[*1894; 1894; 1903; 1904*]

Longings

Like the beautiful bodies of the dead who never aged,
shut away inside a splendid tomb by tearful mourners
with roses at their head and jasmine at their feet—
that's what longings look like when they've passed away
without being fulfilled, before they could be made complete
by just one of pleasure's nights, or one of its shimmering mornings.

[*1904*; 1904/5]

Candles

The days of the future stand before us
like a row of little lighted candles—
golden, warm, and vibrant little candles.

The days that have gone by remain behind us,
a melancholy line of candles now snuffed out;
the closest still give off their smoke,
cold candles, melted down, bent out of shape.

I don't want to see them; their appearance saddens me,
and I'm saddened, too, to recall their former light.
I look in front of me, at my lighted candles.

I don't want to turn around lest I see and tremble at
how quickly the darkened line is growing longer,
how quickly the snuffed-out candles multiply.

[*1893*; *1899*]

An Old Man

In the noisy café, right in the middle,
an old man sits bent over the table;
his newspaper in front of him, with no one for company.

And in his contempt for his wretched old age,
he thinks how very little he enjoyed
the years when he had strength, and wit, and beauty.

He knows he's aged a lot: he feels it, sees it.
And even so, the moment when he was young seems
like yesterday. How brief a span, how brief a span.

And he brooded on the way that Prudence had duped him:
and how he'd always trusted—so stupidly!—
the lie she told: "Tomorrow. You have lots of time."

He remembers the impulses he bridled; and how
much joy he sacrificed. His foolish caution, now,
is mocked by each lost opportunity.

. . . But all this thinking, all this remembering
makes the old man dizzy. And leaning
on the table in the café, he falls asleep.

[*1894*; 1897]

183

Prayer

The sea took into her depths a sailor's life.—
Unaware, his mother goes and lights

a taper before the image of Our Lady
that the weather might be fair, and his return speedy—

while at the wind she always strains her ears.
But as she prays the ikon hears,

solemn and full of mourning,
knowing that the son she awaits won't be returning.

[*1896; 1898*]

Old Men's Souls

Inside their old bodies, so wasted away,
the souls of old men sit around.
How woebegone the poor things are, and
how bored by the wretched life they live.
How afraid they are of losing it and how they love it,
these bewildered and contradictory
souls, which sit around—tragicomic—
inside their old hides, so worn away.

[*1898*; 1901]

The First Step

To Theocritus one day the young
poet Eumenes was complaining:
"By now two years have passed since I've been writing
and I've only done a single idyll so far.
It's the only work that I've completed.
O woe is me, I see how high it is,
Poetry's stairway; very high indeed.
And from where I stand, on this first step,
I shall never ascend. Unhappy me!"
Theocritus replied: "The words you speak
are unbecoming; they are blasphemies.
Even if you are on the first step, you ought
to be dignified and happy.
To have got this far is no small thing;
what you have done is a glorious honor.
Even that first step, even the first,
is very far removed from the common lot.
In order for you to proceed upon this stair
you must claim your right to be
a citizen of the city of ideas.
It is difficult, and rare as well,
to be entered into that city's rolls.
In its agora you'll find Legislators
whom no mere adventurer can fool.
To have got this far is no small thing;
what you have done is a glorious honor."

[*1895*; *1899*]

Interruption

It's we who interrupt the work of the immortals,
we hasty, inexperienced creatures of a moment.
In the palaces of Eleusis and of Phthia
Demeter and Thetis initiate good works
amidst high flames and dense smoke.
But Metaneira always comes rushing in from the
royal halls, her hair disheveled, terrified,
and Peleus always takes fright, and interferes.

[*1900*; 1901]

Thermopylae

Honor to all of those who in their lives
have settled on, and guard, a Thermopylae.
Never stirring from their obligations;
just and equitable in all of their affairs,
but full of pity, nonetheless, and of compassion;
generous whenever they're rich, and again
when they're poor, generous in small things,
and helping out, again, as much as they are able;
always speaking nothing but the truth,
yet without any hatred for those who lie.

And more honor still is due to them
when they foresee (and many do foresee)
that Ephialtes will make his appearance in the end,
and that the Medes will eventually break through.

[*1901*; 1903]

Che Fece . . . Il Gran Rifiuto

For certain people there comes a day
when they are called upon to say the great Yes
or the great No. It's clear at once who has
the Yes within him at the ready, which he will say

as he advances in honor, in greater self-belief.
He who refuses has no second thoughts. Asked
again, he would repeat the No. And nonetheless
that No—so right—defeats him all his life.

[*1899*; 1901]

The Windows

In these shadowed rooms, in which I pass
gloomy days, up and down I pace
that I might find the windows.—For a window
to be open would be a consolation.—
But there are no windows, or I can't
find them. And perhaps it's best I don't.
Perhaps the light will be a new oppression.
Who knows what new things it will show.

[*1897*; 1903]

Walls

Without pity, without shame, without consideration
they've built around me enormous, towering walls.

And I sit here now in growing desperation.
This fate consumes my mind, I think of nothing else:

because I had so many things to do out there.
O while they built the walls, why did I not look out?

But no noise, no sound from the builders did I hear.
Imperceptibly they shut me off from the world without.

[*1896*; 1897]

191

Waiting for the Barbarians

—What is it that we are waiting for, gathered in the square?

    The barbarians are supposed to arrive today.

—Why is there such great idleness inside the Senate house?
    Why are the Senators sitting there, without passing any laws?

    Because the barbarians will arrive today.
    Why should the Senators still be making laws?
    The barbarians, when they come, will legislate.

—Why is it that our Emperor awoke so early today,
    and has taken his position at the greatest of the city's gates
    seated on his throne, in solemn state, wearing the crown?

    Because the barbarians will arrive today.
    And the emperor is waiting to receive
    their leader. Indeed he is prepared
    to present him with a parchment scroll. In it
    he's conferred on him many titles and honorifics.

—Why have our consuls and our praetors come outside today
    wearing their scarlet togas with their rich embroidery,
    why have they donned their armlets with all their amethysts,

and rings with their magnificent, glistening emeralds;
why should they be carrying such precious staves today,
maces chased exquisitely with silver and with gold?

> Because the barbarians will arrive today;
> and things like that bedazzle the barbarians.

—Why do our worthy orators not come today as usual
  to deliver their addresses, each to say his piece?

> Because the barbarians will arrive today;
> and they're bored by eloquence and public speaking.

—Why has this uneasiness arisen all at once,
  and this confusion? (How serious the faces have become.)
  Why is it that the streets and squares are emptying so quickly,
  and everyone's returning home in such deep contemplation?

> Because night has fallen and the barbarians haven't come.
> And some people have arrived from the borderlands,
> and said there are no barbarians anymore.

And now what's to become of us without barbarians.
Those people were a solution of a sort.

[1898; 1904]

Betrayal

We laud many things in Homer, but this we cannot commend. . . . nor Aeschylus when his Thetis says that Apollo, singing at her wedding,

> spoke at length of her great offspring,
> untouched by illness and of very long life.
> And then he said my life was blessed by the gods
> and sang a paean, wishing me all joy.
> And I had hoped that Phoebus's divine mouth
> would be truthful, since it brims with prophetic art:
> But although he sang these things himself, . . .
> . . . . it was he who killed
> my child.

—PLATO, *Republic* 2

When Thetis and Peleus were being wed,
Apollo rose at the fabulous bridal
banquet, and he blessed the newlyweds
in the offspring that would issue from their union.
He said: Never shall an illness touch him
and he will have long life.— And as he said it,
Thetis greatly rejoiced, because the words
of Apollo, who knew so much of prophecies,
seemed to her a surety for her child.
And as Achilles was growing up, and his
beauty was the glory of Thessaly,
Thetis would remember what the god had said.
But then one day there came old men with tidings,
and told her of the killing of Achilles in Troy.
And Thetis rent asunder her purple clothes
and she cast off the bracelets and the rings

from her body and dashed them to the ground.
And in her grief she remembered ancient things:
and asked them what the wise Apollo was doing,
where he'd wandered off to, the poet who at feasts
spoke so superbly, where he'd wandered off to, the prophet,
while they were slaying her son in his first youth.
And the old men replied to her that Apollo,
he himself, had descended into Troy,
and with the Trojans he had killed Achilles.

[*1903*; 1904]

The Funeral of Sarpedon

Zeus is deep in mourning. Sarpedon
was slain by Patroclus. And now they're rushing in,
Menoeteus's son along with the Achaeans,
to seize the body and defile it.

By no means will Zeus consent to this.
His beloved son—whom he allowed
to perish; such was the Law—
will receive his honors at least in death.
And lo, he sends Phoebus down to the plain,
with instructions on how the body should be seen to.

With reverence and with sorrow, Phoebus lifts
the hero's body and takes it to the river.
Of all the dust and gore he washes it clean;
closes up the wound, so that he leaves
no traces visible; he pours perfumes
ambrosial upon him; and in splendid
garments, Olympian, he clothes him.
He whitens the skin; with a mother-of-pearl
comb he combs the hair of deepest black.
The beautiful limbs he arranges, and lays them out.

Now he resembles a young king, a charioteer,
in his twenty-fifth year, or his twenty-sixth,
who is resting now, since he has won,

with a chariot all of gold and the swiftest steeds,
the trophy in a contest of wide renown.

After Phoebus had fulfilled his mission
in this way, he called for the two brothers
Sleep and Death, and he commanded them
to take the body to the rich land of Lycia.

And toward the rich land there, toward Lycia
they made their way on foot, the two brothers
Sleep and Death, and when at last they reached
the portal of the royal house
they handed over the body, now made glorious,
and returned then to their other cares and tasks.

And when they received it there, in the house, there began—
with processions, and honors, and laments,
and with unstinting libations from sacred vessels,
with everything as it is meet—the mournful burial;
and afterward the city's expert artisans,
and the craftsmen famed for the work they did in stone
came and made the tomb and the grave-stele.

[*1892?*; 1898; *1908*; 1908]

197

The Horses of Achilles

When they saw Patroclus had been killed,
 he who'd been so brave, and strong, and young,
 the horses of Achilles began to weep:
 their immortal nature was indignant
 at this work of death, which it now beheld.
They'd shake their heads and toss their flowing manes,
  and with their feet they'd stamp the ground and grieve
 for Patroclus who they knew was lifeless—undone—
shabby flesh by now—his spirit vanished—
 left without defenses—without breath—
returned from life unto the great Nothing.

  Zeus beheld the tears of the immortal
 horses and grieved. "At Peleus's marriage,"
 he said, "I should never have committed such great folly.
 Better never to have given you away, my
 unhappy horses! What business have you down here
with wretched humanity, the plaything of fate.
  You, for whom neither death nor old age lie in wait,
 are oppressed by passing misfortunes. Men have snared you
 in their afflictions."—And yet their tears,
  for the everlasting calamity
 of death, the noble creatures kept on shedding.

[*1896*; 1897]

198

II

REPUDIATED POEMS

(1886–1898)

Brindisi

Exhausted by the world's seductive instability,
inside this cup of mine I've found tranquility;
Life and hope within it I enclose, and longings:
      give ye me to drink.

Here, distant from the woes of life, and from its storms,
I'm like a sailor who's been rescued from the whelm,
and finds himself aboard a ship that's safe in harbor:
      give you me to drink.

O! heat of wine salubrious, you send away
every icy influence: nor envy's chill, nor hate's,
nor shame's, nor calumny's comes near to me:
      give ye me to drink.

No longer do I look upon the graceless truth stripped nude.
I enjoyed another life, I have a world that's new;
and now I find myself upon the spreading field of dreams—
      give, give me to drink!

And if it's poison, and I find the bitterness
of death within it, I have yet found happiness,
delight, and joy, and exaltation in the poison:
      give ye me to drink!

[1886]

The Poet and the Muse

THE POET

To what good, to what avail did fate desire
that I be made a poet, though I be weak?
Vain are my words; the sounds of my lyre
are not true, even those most sweet.

If I wish to hymn a noble sentiment,
glory and virtue are, I sense, but dreams.
Wherever I gaze, I find discouragement,
and everywhere my foot is tripped in thorns.

The earth's a shadowed sphere: cold, devious.
The world's inveigling image are my lays.
Love do I hymn, and joy; wretched burlesque,
wretched lyre, of every cozenage the prey!

THE MUSE

You are no liar, poet. The world you see
is the true one. Only your lyre's chords
recognize what's true; and only they
toward that life will be your trusty guides.

You serve the god. To you he gave the part
of beauty and of spring. Mellifluous
song flows from your lips, of incenses you are
the treasure-house, the voice on high, the golden promise.

If the earth is hid in shadow, do not fear.
Do not think the gloom a constant one.
Friend, to pleasures, blossoms, valleys are you near:
have courage, and step forth. Behold the dawn!

'Tis but a delicate mist affrights your vision.
Kind nature prepares for you beneath her gown
a wreath of roses, violets, noble narcissus,
aromatic recompense for your song.

[1886]

Builders

Progress is a giant edifice—each hefts
his stone: one words, counsels, another
deeds—and every day it lifts its head
higher. Should some tempest, some sudden

storm approach, the good builders make haste
all as one to shield their wasted labor.
Wasted, because the life of each is passed
embracing ills and sorrows for a future generation,

that this generation might know an artless
happiness, and length of days, and wealth, and wisdom
without base sweat, or servile industry.

But it will never live, this fabled generation;
its very perfection will cast this labor down
and once again their futile toil will begin.

[1891]

Word and Silence

idhâ kân al-kalâm min fiḍḍa, al-sukût min dhahab

—ARAB PROVERB

"Silence is golden and the word is silver."

What impious man pronounced such blasphemy?
What blind, mute Asiatic, to blind, mute destiny
sluggishly resigned? Who is the wretched fool who,
a stranger to humanity, outraging virtue,
said the soul's a chimera, the word is silver?
The only godlike gift we have, encompassing
everything—rapture, sorrow, joy, and love:
in all our bestial nature, the only human thing!
        You, the one who calls it silver, you put no trust
in the future which dissolves the silence, mystic utterance.
You do not bask in wisdom, progress charms you not;
with ignorance—golden silence—you are content.
You are ill. Insensate silence is a grievous illness,
while the warm, the sympathetic Word is health.
Silence is shadow and night; the Word is day.
Word is truth, life, immortality.
        Let's speak, let's speak—silence suits us not
since we were fashioned in the image of the Word.
Let's speak, let's speak—because there speaks in us
thought divine, unsubstanced discourse of the soul.

[1892]

Sham-el-Nessim

Our pale Misiri
the sun, with arrows full
of bitterness and spite, burns up and flays,
and wears her out with thirst and with affliction.
Our sweet Misiri,
in gladsome festival,
is drunk, forgets, bedecks herself, is gay,
and heaps her scorn upon the tyrant sun.

Glad Sham-el-Nessim, a blameless country fête,
announces the spring.
Alexandria and her milling streets are emptied.
The good Egyptian wants to celebrate
glad Sham-el-Nessim, and becomes a nomad.
From everywhere the thronged

formations of the revelers pour out. Khabari
is full, and dreamy, azure Mahmoudiya.
The Mex and Muharram Bey are full, and Ramleh.
The country boroughs vie to host the carts
in which the crowds of happy people come
in sober, calm good cheer.

Because the Egyptian, even in his fêtes,
keeps hold of his sobriety.

He decks his fez with flowers; but his face
is immobile. He hums a droning ditty,
mirthful. In his thought there's gaiety,
          very little in his movements.

Our Misiri possesses no rich verdure,
          nor pleasant streams nor founts,
it has no lofty peaks with spreading shade.
But it does have magic blossoms which fall burning
from Ptah's flambeaux; and myrrhs that emanate
          obscure aromas, among which nature faints.

Encircled by admirers the sweet *moganni*
          of widest fame is warmly lauded.
In his trembling voice love's agonies
sigh; his bitter ballad inveighs against
the flighty Fatma or the harsh Eminah,
          or Zeinab, who is so very wicked.

The tents, all shady, and the cold sorbets
          put the swelter and the dust to flight.
The hours flee like minutes, like racing steeds
upon a level plain; their brilliant manes,
gaily spreading out over the fête,
          gild Sham-el-Nessim, the glad.

          Our pale Misiri
          the sun, with arrows full
of bitterness and spite, burns up and flays,

and wears her out with thirst and with affliction.
        Our sweet Misiri,
        in a gladsome festival,
gets drunk, forgets, bedecks herself, is gay,
and heaps her scorn upon the tyrant sun.

[1892]

Bard

Far from the world, poetic magic makes him drunk;
        all the world, for him, is lovely verse.
For her bard, Imagination built a house: strong,
        incorporeal, which fortune will not jar.

You will say: "A cold and futile life. Foolishness
        to think that life's the pleasurable sounds
of a flute and nothing else" or "Hard-heartedness
        afflicts the man who's never been worn down

by the pain of life's travail." And yet your judgment
        is error and injustice. His nature is god-sent.
Judge not in your reasoned, blind affliction.

The walls of his house are magic emerald—
        and in them voices whisper: "Friend, be tranquil:
reflect and sing. Take heart, mystic apostle!"

[1892]

Vulnerant Omnes, Ultima Necat

The metropolis of Bruges, which of old a powerful
Flemish duke had built and lavishly endowed,
a clock-tower has, with portals all of silver,
which has told the time for many centuries.

Said the clock-tower: "My life is cold
       and hard and gray.
Every day on earth's the same to me.
Friday and Saturday, Sunday, Monday
are indistinct. I live—but do not hope.
The sole diversion, the sole variety
in my fateful, harsh monotony,
       is the world's decay.
While I dully turn my hands, as in a stupor,
to me the fraud of every earthly thing's revealed.
Ending, downfall everywhere. The din of tireless battle,
moanings roar all round me—and I conclude that
All my hours wound; the last one kills."

The Archbishop heard this brazen speech
and said: "Clock-tower, your talk's off-key,
unsuited to your ecclesiastic, elevated rank.
How is it that this wicked way of thinking

entered your mind? O heretic idea, absurd!
       An age-old boredom
must have cast a fog around your spirit.
       From the Lord
the chorus of the hours received another mission.
Each one rekindles; the final one gives birth."

[1893]

Good and Bad Weather

It irks me not if winter
spreads fog, and cloudiness, and cold outside.
Within me it is springtime, true delight.
Laughter is a wholly golden ray of sun,
there is no garden that compares to love,
all snows are melted by the warmth of song.

What use is it if springtime
sprouts flowers and sows verdant lawns outside!
I've winter in me when my heart feels woe.
The brightest sun is darkened by lamenting,
when you're in grief, May is like December,
tears are colder than the coldest snow.

[1893]

Timolaus the Syracusan

Timolaus is the premier musician
of the premier city in all of Sicily.
Throughout this Western Greece of ours the Greeks
from Neapolis, and from Massalia,
from Tarentum, from Panormus, and Akragas,
and from any other cities of Hesperia
whose shores are crowned with Hellenism,
converge en masse in Syracuse
to attend the concerts of the famed musician.
Preëminent in the lyre and the kithara,
he is skilled as well upon the piffero,
the tenderest of tender flutes. He draws
from the douçaine a plangent melody.
And when he takes the psalterium in his hands
its chords bring forth the poetry
of sultry Asia—an initiation
into voluptuous and dulcet reverie,
fragrance of Ecbatana and Ninus.

. . . .

. . . .

But amidst the many accolades,
amid the gifts of many talents' worth,
the goodly Timolaus is utterly wretched.
Ruddy Samian does not hearten him,
and by his silence he insults the symposium.
An indefinable grief takes hold of him,

grief for his great insufficiency.
He senses that his instruments are empty,
even as his soul is filled with music.
Painfully, persistently he struggles
to find an outlet for the mystic sounds.
His most perfect harmonies remain
silent and concealed inside of him.
The crowd in its enthusiasm marvels at
the very things he censures and contemns.
The clamorous sound of accolades disturbs him,
and amid the gifts of many talents' worth
distractedly he stands there, the musician.

[1894]

Athena's Vote

When justice is devoid of a solution,
when men's judgment finds no way, and needs
a higher succour and enlightenment,
the judges, feeble, small, fall silent,
and the compassion of the Gods decides.

To the citizens of Athens thus spoke Pallas:
"Your law-court I did found. Neither Hellas
nor another state will e'er attain
another that is worthier. Jurymen,
show yourselves worthy of it. Spurn
unseemly passions. Let mercy
walk with justice. And if your
judgment is severe, let it be pure
as well—chaste, like flawless diamond.
Let your work be a guide to what is good
and noble; and let it manage
prudently. Never foolish vengeance."

Deep in feeling, the citizens replied:
"O Ladyship, our mind cannot find
sufficient tribute of our thankfulness
for your splendid benefaction."

The goddess,
gray of eye, responded: "Mortal men,

the Divinity seeks of you no recompense.
Virtuous be ye, and take ye no one's side:
this suffices me. Jurymen, I have, besides,
guarded as my right a single vote."

Said the jurymen: "Seeing you inhabit
the starry firmament, Goddess, how is it
that you will vote among us here?"

                              "Be not
vexed by this confusion. In my voting
I am temperate. But should there come a moment
when you are sundered into factions two,
some for, others against, then you,
without my leaving the halls of heaven,
will make use of my vote. O citizens,
my desire is that clemency be shown
always to the one who is accused. Within
the heart of your Athena dwells forgiveness:
great, hereditary, limitless,
an instinct from Metis, the coronet
of the highest wisdom in the firmament."

[1894]

The Inkwell

The poet's sacred, honorable inkwell,
　　　you, from whom a world entire comes forth,
every time a form passes close by you
　　　it comes back with some charm that is new.
Your ink—where did it find those mythic
treasures! Every drop, as it trickles on the page,
　　　sets yet another diamond for us
　　　among the jewels of the imagination.

Those words, who taught you them, which you send forth
　　　all throughout the world, and which thrill us;
our children's children too will read them still
　　　with the same emotion, the same fervor.

Those words, where did you find them, which to our ears
　　　while sounding as if heard for the first time,
do not yet seem to be completely strange—
　　　our hearts must have known them in another life.

The pen you moisten seems to be a hand
　　　that goes around the clock of the soul.
It reckons and fixes the moments of feeling,
　　　it reckons and alters the hours of the soul.

The poet's sacred, honorable inkwell,
　　　you, from whose ink a world entire comes forth,

I'm put in mind, now, of how many people will
         stay lost within you, when the deep
slumber comes one night to take the poet.
The words will always be there; but what strange hand
   will have the power to find and bring them to us!
   You, faithful to the poet, will refuse it.

[1894]

Sweet Voices

Those voices are the sweeter which have fallen
        forever silent, mournfully
resounding only in the heart that sorrows.

In dreams the melancholic voices come,
        timorous and humble,
and bring before our feeble memory

the precious dead, whom the cold cold earth
        conceals; for whom the mirthful
daybreak never shines, nor springtimes blossom.

Melodious voices sigh; and in the soul
        our life's first poetry
sounds—like music, in the night, that's far away.

[1894]

Elegy of the Flowers

The flowers that are loveliest, blossom in summer.
And of all the flowers in the field it seems
the most beautiful is youth. And yet it wilts
quickly, and once it goes is not reborn;
the lilacs sprinkle it with tears of dew.

The flowers that are loveliest, blossom in summer.
But the eyes that look at them are not the same.
And other hands, on other bosoms, place them.
The same months come, except they seem like strangers.
The faces have changed, and do not recognize them.

The flowers that are loveliest, blossom in summer.
But they do not always tarry with our joy.
Some gladden us, others make us bitter.
They sprout upon the tombs whereon we weep,
even as they tint our gladsome fields.

Summer has come back, and all the fields are blooming.
But from the window it is hard to reach.
And the pane grows ever smaller, disappears.
The exhausted eye grows clouded, then it shuts.
Our weary legs are heavy, do not support us.

Not all the fields will bloom for us this year.
The lilies of forgotten August crown us,
nimbly the bygone years return,
beloved shadows beckon to us sweetly
and send our beggar heart sweetly to sleep.

[1895]

Hours of Melancholy

The happy sully Nature.
The earth's a realm of grief.
The dawn weeps tears of unknown woe.
The orphaned evenings, pallid, grieve.
And the soul that is elect sings mournfully.

In breezes I hear sighing.
In violets I see blame.
I feel the rose's painful life;
the meadows filled with cryptic woe.
And in the woodland thick a sobbing sounds.

Mankind lauds the happy.
And poets false extol them.
But Nature's gates are closed to those
who, heartless and indifferent, laugh,
laugh: strangers in a miserable land.

[1895]

Oedipus

The Sphinx has fallen on him
with teeth and claws unsheathed
and with all her nature's savagery.
At her first onslaught Oedipus fell down,
terrified, at first, by her appearance—
until now he'd never have imagined
a countenance like this, such speech as this.
But though the monster ramps with both her feet
upon the breast of Oedipus,
he recovered swiftly—nor does he in the least
fear her now, since he has
the answer ready and will vanquish her.
And yet he takes no pleasure in this victory.
His eye, with melancholy filled,
does not behold the Sphinx, but sees beyond
the narrow road that goes to Thebes
and will come to its conclusion at Colonus.
And in his soul there is a clear foreboding
that there the Sphinx will speak to him again
with much more difficult and with far greater
riddles for which there isn't any answer.

[1896]

Ode and Elegy of the Streets

The footfalls of the first passerby;
the first peddler's lively shouting;
the first windows opening,
the first door—these are the song
of the streets in the morning.

The steps of the last passerby;
the last of the peddlers shouting;
the doors and windows shutting—
are the elegiac sound
of the streets in the evening.

[1896]

Near an Open Window

In the stillness of an autumn night,
I sit near an open window,
for entire hours, in a perfect,
voluptuous tranquility.
The gentle rainfall of the leaves descends.

The keening of the perishable world
resounds within my perishable nature,
but is a dulcet keening, rising like a prayer.
My window opens up an unknown
world. A fount of fragrant memories,
unutterable, appears before me.
Against my window wings
are beating—chill autumnal exhalations
approach me and encircle me
and in their holy tongue they speak to me.

I feel vague and wide-embracing
hopes; and in the hallowed silence
of creation, my ears hear melodies,
hear the crystalline, the mystic
music of the chorus of the stars.

[1896]

A Love

However much you speak of it, misfortune does not fade away.
But there are woes that will not rest at peace within the heart.
To emerge, and by their plaint to spend themselves, they yearn.

Antony was in love with me, and I in love with him.
And he gave his word to me that he'd not take another!
And yet he was so very poor, and he had a lofty pride.
So it was he up and went off in an ill-starred ship
in the hope of finding work, of acquiring a trade.
He wanted to become a sailor, and one day a captain,
and thereafter to be married with his heart at peace.

Ah, not a single year was spared, before my father fell
and broke his leg, and his right arm.
My mamma then fell sick. Whatever we still had,
a little bit of ancient copper, a little bit of silver,
some small bits of jewelry that my mother had been saving
were sold off for a pittance.
                              Our misfortune soon became
the talk of the entire village. In all of the great houses
they spread the news about, and from his mansion Stavros
would often come, both as a friend and as protector
into our home . . . and looked at me, and love was in his eyes.

My father was not working; mamma did not embroider.
I was working night and day and pouring out my eyesight
and still did not succeed in eking out their daily bread.
Stavros was a wealthy man and had a generous heart.
Simply—without swaggering, without giving himself airs—
and secretly, he gave to them that they might have to eat.
And my soul rejoiced for my poor parents—and wept for my poor self.
It did not tarry very long, the hapless day on which
he stood nearby me in the field, and took my hand
and stood there looking at me . . . I was trembling like a leaf
because I knew well what he wanted, and I loved him not . . .
The words were hesitating on my lips—until he said:
"Phroso, do you not—for their sake—condescend to have me?"

No, my heart intoned to me, still seeking Antony.
But a North Wind, tempestuous, had risen heavily
and they were saying that his boat was lost on unknown seas.
Ah, how was it that the harsh, empoisoned lie crept out! . . .
Ah, wretched me, how shall I live then, weeping night and day! . . .

My father had much talk with me, in order to persuade me.
But my good mother never said a single word to me,
but merely looked into my eyes, and grief and poverty
poured down from her. I lost whatever strength I had.
I could not bear it. I gave my hand to him. My heart
had been buried deep within the sea.

All the village maidens envied me my fortune
in marrying a wealthy man, a great aristocrat—
I, who was country maid, I who was so poor.

Never had the village seen a wedding that was grander
than ours was. Young and old alike gathered together
to clap their eyes upon the lucky bride of the great lord.
They strewed the road with lilacs and with roses.
Dancing and music were everywhere, and songs and groaning boards.
For me it was night. All were wearing black.

Four months only had passed since I had married him,
and one evening, when I was standing by the door
of my house, I saw in front me the shade of Antony.
To me it seemed he was a dream, I trusted not my eyes,
until he said to me "My love, why are you sorrowing?
Our troubles now are ended, I have come to marry you."

Bitterly, bitterly I welcomed him, and told him everything.
And I clasped his hands, as once before, in mine,
and kissed him as I had before, and wept upon his neck.
I told him that I loved no other man but him . . .
I told him they'd deceived me, that I believed
that in the tempest he had drowned . . . That only for the sake
of my mother, of my father had I wed . . . That with him
I would have gladly chosen troubles, poverty, and scorn
over all the wealth there is on earth, that another brought . . .
I told him that I loved him now as I first did, but now
my love's an unquenched fire that burns me,
now I know that he will never, never, never
be mine, nor I be his . . . and I told him that,
if anything remained of our old love,
he must swear that he would never see me more while I yet lived . . .

And I said other things, said other things. Things I do not recall.
My head was burning up. My wits had fled from me.

Now everything is ended forevermore. My life's gone black.
This world will have no joy for me, ever again.
Would that death would take me! . . . And yet how could I die—
I have a wound within my heart, but I am ever young.

[1896]

Remembrance

The gods die not. What dies is the belief
      of the thankless mortal mob.
The gods are deathless. Silver clouds conceal
      them from our vision.
O sacred Thessaly, they love You still,
      their souls recall You still.
In the gods, as in us, memories bloom,
      their first love's pulse.
When amorous daybreak kisses Thessaly,
      vividness of lives divine
passes through her atmosphere; and an airy shape
      sometimes darts across her hills.

[1896]

The Death of the Emperor Tacitus

Tacitus the emperor is ailing.
In his deep old age he was unable
to resist the ravages of war.
In his sickbed at the hateful camp
at miserable Tyana—so remote!—

he remembers his Campania, his beloved,
the garden, and the villa, and the morning
promenades—his life six months ago—
And calls down curses in his agony
on the Senate, on the spiteful Senate.

[1897]

The Eumenides' Footfalls

Nero is asleep inside his palace
calm, unconscious, and content—
blooming with the heartiness of flesh
and the lovely vigor of his youth.

But his Lares are uneasy.
The little hearth-gods are atremble,
and seek to hide their trifling bodies,
to diminish them, to make them disappear.
Because they heard a ghastly crash—
a Hellish crash, a fatal crash—
coming from the stairway, and straight off
the fearful Lares, their frail divinity
all fainted dead away,
divined, perceived, recognized
the dreadful footfalls of the Eumenides.

[1897]

The Tears of Phaëthon's Sisters

Like light in matter, like a diaphanous
gold is amber, which mankind holds so precious.—
When a ghastly power, furious,
envious of Phaëthon, from the crest

of the heavens cast him down headlong,
his sisters came, decked out in their weeds,
to Eridanus, to his watery tomb,
and day and night they mourned in misery.

And with them too all mortal men lamented
the vanity of reveries too proud.
O heartless fate, O hateful destiny,
Phaëthon has fallen from the clouds!

Let us live among our lowly hearths,
humble men, and be content with little;
let us cast out yearnings from our hearts,
let every motion heavenward desist.

They wept him ever, miserable maids,
Phaëthon's sisters ever wept for him,
and in every one of Eridanus's bends
their images, so pallid, were reflected.

With profound emotion the earth did take
the sacred teardrops of the seven maidens
and hoarded them. When the seventh day
came round, and when the eighth dawn glistened,

their many, many weepings were transformed
into an everlasting scintillation
and metamorphosed into gleaming amber.
O choicest stone! o goodly lamentation!

Noble lament, enviable lament,
filled with love and filled with luster,—
estimable sisters, who with tears of light
mourned the youth who on earth was loveliest.

[1897]

Ancient Tragedy

Ancient tragedy, ancient tragedy
is as holy and vast as the heart of the universe.
One people gave it birth, one Greek city,
but it took wing straightaway, and set its stage
      in heaven.

In the theatre of Olympus, in its worthy dust,
Hippolytus, Ajax, Alcestis, Clytemnestra
tell the story of our terrible, cruel life
and upon the ruinous earth there falls a drop
      of divine pity.

The Athenian people saw and marveled at
tragedy in its earliest incarnation.
Tragedy grew up beneath the sapphirine
theatre of the sky. There it had an audience
of immortals. And the gods, upon great thrones
of purest adamant, would listen in ineffable
pleasure to the beautiful lines of Sophocles,
the rhythms of Euripides, the grandeur of Aeschylus,
the Attic phantasies of graceful Agathon.
The actors in these lofty plays, equally worthy,
were the Muses, Hermes, and the skilled Apollo,
beloved Dionysus, Athena and Hebe.
And the vaults of heaven were filled with poetry.

The monologues resounded, eloquent and mournful;
the choruses too, untiring founts of harmony;
and the clever dialogue with its pithy phrases.
Piously, all nature kept its silence, lest the clamor
of the storm disturb the godlike pageant.
Unmoving and pious, air, and earth, and ocean
kept watch over the quiet of the great gods.
And now and then an echo from above would come to them,
an incorporeal garland of some lines,
with the gods' "Bravo, bravo" mingled with the trimeters.
And air to earth, and aged Lady Earth to the sea would say:
"Silence, silence; let us listen. In the heavenly
theatre they're concluding the performance of Antigone."

Ancient tragedy, ancient tragedy
is as holy and vast as the heart of the universe.
One people gave it birth, one Greek city,
but it took wing straightaway, and set its stage
          in heaven.

In the theatre of Olympus, in its worthy dust,
Hippolytus, Ajax, Alcestis, Clytemnestra
tell the story of our terrible, cruel life
and upon the ruinous earth there falls a drop
          of divine pity.

[1897]

236

Horace in Athens

In the bedchamber of the hetaera Leah,
where all is style and wealth, a downy bed,
a youth, with jasmine upon his hands, is speaking.
His fingers are adorned with many gems,

and he wears a snow-white silk himation
picked out in scarlet, in the eastern fashion.
His speech is Attic of the purest strain
but a gentle stress in his pronunciation

betrays a trace of Tiber and of Latium.
The young man is avowing his adoration,
and silently she listens, the Athenian,

to her lover Horace, so mellifluent;
and stupefied, she sees new worlds of Beauty
within the passion of the great Italian.

[1897]

Voice from the Sea

The sea exhales a hidden voice—
    a voice that enters
into our heart and moves it,
    and gladdens it.

The sea intones a tender song for us,
a song that is composed by three great poets,
    the sun, the air and sky.
She sings it with that godlike voice of hers,
when the summer weather spreads upon her shoulders
    the calm, as if a veil.

Her melody bears messages endewed
to souls. She brings to mind lost youth,
    without bitterness or grief.
Of loves that passed she speaks quietly,
forgotten feelings once more come alive
    within the waves' respiring so sweet.

The sea intones a tender song to us,
a song composed by three great poets,
    the sun, the air and sky.
And when you look upon its wetted plain,
when you see her sward which never ends,
    the field that is both near and very far,

full of yellow flowers that the light sows
as if it were a gardener, joy seizes you,
       intoxicates you, and exalts your heart.
And if you are young, the yearning for the sea
will course within your veins; the wave will say
a word of its love to you, and it will dip
       your love in mysterious perfume.

The sea exhales a hidden voice—
       a voice that enters
into our heart and moves it,
       and gladdens it.

A song is it, or the plaint of those who drowned?—
the tragic plaint of those who died,
       who have for shrouds the chilly foam,
and lament for their wives, and for their children,
for their parents and their empty nests,
       while the bitter ocean thrashes them,

dashes them on rocks and jagged stones,
in seaweed wraps them, drags them, hurls them out,
       and they, as if still living, hasten
with their eyes wide open, terrified,
and their hands outstretched and wild
       in their final agony.

A song is it, or the plaint of those who drowned?—
the tragic plaint of those who died
       and are yearning for a grave with Christian rites.

A tomb, where relatives will sprinkle tears,
and with flowers will adorn the hands so dear,
        and where the sun casts warm, compassionate light.

A tomb, over which th' Immaculate Cross stands guard,
where every now and then some priest will go
        to burn some incense and to say a prayer.
The widow brings him, remembering her husband,
or a son, or sometimes, too, a mourning friend.
They commemorate the dead; and the pardoned
        soul more peacefully now slumbers.

[1898]

The Tarentines Have Their Fun

Theatres filled, music everywhere;
here debauch and lechery, and there
contests for the athletes and philosophers.
Dionysus's statue is embellished with a crown
unwithering. No corner of the land remains unstrewn
with offerings. The people of Tarentum have their fun.

But the Senators withdraw from all of these
and glowering say many angry things.
And each barbarian toga as it leaves
seems to be a storm-cloud, threatening.

[1898]

The Funeral of Sarpedon

Zeus's heart is full of agony.
Patroclus has laid Sarpedon low.

The God has reverenced the will of Destiny.
But the father grieves for his misfortune.

The invincible son of Menoeteus,
and the Achaeans, bellowing like lions,
are trying to seize the corpse, and toss it
to the crows and dogs to dine upon.

But Zeus will not condone this degradation.
He will not let them insult the body of
his well-beloved and highly-honored son.

Behold, Phoebus descends from his chariot
to the earth, by command divine.
His hands sublime make safe the corpse
of Sarpedon, and to the river
carry it and lave it piously.
The dust and blood, congealed, are washed away
and the features of the just and courageous hero are revealed.
Upon the carcase Phoebus lavishly
pours the perfumes of ambrosia
and covers it up with Olympian,

immortal garments. He closes up
the gaping wound in his chest. He sets
the limbs in a peaceful and winsome array.
His skin glistens. A gleaming comb
combs his locks, abundant locks
and black, which not a single white
hair has sullied yet.

He looks like a young athlete
in repose—like a young lover
dreaming of pleasure and of cupids
with azure wings and celestial
bows—like a young and blessed bridegroom,
fortunate among all his agemates,
who, without groom-gifts, has won a lovely bride.

Having brought his mission to an end the God
calls Sleep and Death, the brothers, and commands them
to bear Sarpedon back to wide-spreading Lycia.

So in their fatherly and tender arms
they took him, Sleep and Death,
with sorrow and love and with care
lest the grave tranquility of the corpse's face
be disturbed, lest the splendor of
the manly body suffer any harm.

The Lycians profoundly reverenced
the Gods in their dreadful indifference,
and they collected their goodly lord,

dead in spirit, but radiant in form,
vigorous, and fragrant, and at peace.

They reared for him a monument of marble,
and upon its base in an inscription
skilled sculptors told the story of the victories
of the hero, and of his many campaigns.

[1898]

III

UNPUBLISHED POEMS
(1877?–1923)

The Beyzade to His Lady-Love (1884)

I love you. . . . but if you are a humble fisher's lass,
are your eyes bright, for that, a whit the less,
is your hand not whiter still than milk is white,
is your body with amorous graces not replete?
Lineage, name, I utterly forget them all,
a slave before you I, the prince's son, do fall!

I love you. . . . and when I see you on the bloomy lea
dancing with the village lads vivaciously
I envy them, and o'er my harsh fate keen,
that I your slave forever cannot be.
Betwixt us fate has placed a bar abhorred:
relentless generations of dragomans and lords!

Dünya Güzeli *(1884)*

This vision is true, the mirror does not lie:
there is no other on earth as fair as I.
My eyes possess the brilliancy of gems,
close to coral's hue my lips do come,
with double rows of pearls my mouth is graced.
My body has great charm, my foot they praise,
and snowy hands and throat, my silken hair. . . .
       but what does it avail?

Since in this hateful harem I am immured
who can see my beauty, in all the world?
The jealous foe who casts her poisoned look
at me, or vile eunuchs; and the blood
freezes in my veins when my contemned
husband draws near. Prophet, Master mine,
forgive my heart that cries aloud in pain,
      If only I were Christian!

Had I been born a Christian I should be free
to show myself to all, both night and day;
the men in wonder, women jealously
would behold my beauty and agree,—
Nature won't again produce my like.
When I set out in my calèche to ride
the crowds would fill up Stamboul's streets
      that each might look on me.

When, My Friends, I Was in Love . . . *(1885)*

When, my friends, I was in love—
'twas many years ago—
I dwelt not in the world that other
mortal men called home.

Poetic was the fantasy
I had; if it deceived,
it yet wrought a felicity
ardent and alive.

Whatsoe'er my eye would see
offered a rich sight;
my lover's nest appeared to be
a palace in my eyes.

She'd wear a dress of calico,
oh it was very cheap;
to me, at first, I swear to you,
of silk it seemed to be.

On her hands two bracelets poor
served for ornament;
to me they seemed a grand parure
of lordly provenance.

About her head she wore a mass
of blossoms from the hills;
what garland ever was there that,
for me, adorned as well?

The walks where we together went
always gentle were:
they either had no brambles then,
or they were hid by earth.

Today the genius moves me not
of orators and sages
as much as just a single nod
of hers in bygone days.

When, my friends, I was in love—
'twas many years ago—
I dwelt not in the world that other
mortal men called home.

Nichori *(1885)*

Stranger, when you see a town where nature smiles
and where a girl as lovely as a rose is hidden near
every plane tree—you must stop there. Stranger,
        you have reached Nichori.

And if, when evening comes, you go outside to stroll
and find before you walnut trees—do not proceed
any further on your way. Where else could you seek
        a place more lovely than Nichori?

Nowhere else on earth are springs as fresh as these,
mountains elsewhere do not have our hills' nobility,
and you will be inebriated by earth's perfume alone
        if you stay a while in Nichori.

Do not hope to find, elsewhere, the greenery
that you will see there. From the hilltop look and see
the plains below and say you could not love
        this, our little Nichori.

Do not think, O Stranger, that I love hyperbole.
There are many places that have rich and fruitful fields.
But there is something special, as you'll certainly agree,
        about the fruit and flowers of Nichori.

If you should wish to go with me inside the church
of the Virgin of Coumariés, forgive my zealotry
when I am there. Prayers, I daresay, win a different
grace in pious Nichori.

If you cannot stay, O Stranger, then before you leave,
you must go, one Sunday, to the Quay of Gregory;
peace, and youth, and joy you'll see, and you will know
what it is, our Nichori.

Song of the Heart *(1886)*

With you, I think, all that is pleasant smiles on me,
in the mirror of your eyes there is reflected joy.
Stay, my light, and still I have not told you even half
of all that presses down upon my heart so amorous,
that rushes to my lips with just a single look from you.
If you wish it, do not speak to me, or say enchanting
words of love and adoration. 'Tis enough that you're nearby,
that I tell you that I want you, that I'm near you, that the morning
dew that you breathe in, I breathe in, too; and if you find
that these too are excessive, 'tis enough I merely see you!

To Stephanos Skilitsis (1886)

If souls, as they tell us, are immortal,
perhaps your spirit wanders near us, Stephanos,
and feels contentment when you hear your name
upon our lips, and when our faithful thoughts
are stirred by your beloved memory.

Stephanos, you've not been parted from us by the grave:
from us, with whom you nearly shared your life.
As children we would play together; our childish woes
and our joys we'd feel together; and then, young men,
we discovered life's first pleasures all as one—
till two days ago, Stephanos, two days ago, and now
we have borne you, cold, to your last abode.

But no. You're with us. The stone upon your grave
will be, for us, a delicate veil, diaphanous.
And though you're lost to your friends' eyes, their souls,
and memories, and hearts, will always see you
and keep you, Stephanos, their inseparable friend.

Correspondences According to Baudelaire (1891)

Aromas inspire me as music does,
as rhythm does, as do beautiful words,
and I delight when, in harmonious
verses, Baudelaire expresses
what the amazed spirit, even dimly,
feels amidst its sterile stirrings.

"A temple is what Nature is, where living
pillars every now and then pronounce
muddled words. Man goes through the center
of the crowded groves of symbols, which
observe him with familiar gazes.

"As drawn-out echoes, which from far away
commingle in a gloomy unity,
so, in a unity boundless as the dark
and as the light, there correspond
colors, noises, and aromas.

"There are fragrances as dewy as
the skin of children; as sweet as oboes;
grassy as meadows.
                    "Others are
rich, corrupt, triumphant:
they sing of the transports of the mind

and of the senses; they contain the outpouring
of infinite things—like ambergris,
and musk, gum benjamin, and frankincense."

Do not believe only what you see.

The vision of poets is sharper still.

To them, Nature is a familiar garden.

In a shadowed paradise, those other
people grope along the cruel road.
The sole illumination, which like a fleeting
spark will sometimes light their way
at night, is a short-lived feeling of
a chance and irresistible approach—
brief nostalgia, momentary shiver,
dream of the sunrise hour, a joy
that has no cause, suddenly flowing
into the heart and just as suddenly fleeing.

[Fragment of an untitled poem] (1892)

. . . .

one day of the dead girl, the phantom of a day.
Who he was, this inhuman man, history does not say.
Who Rhamanakti's killer was, I do not know.

A sullen Persian governor insulting a people enslaved
as retaliation and as vengeance for the way
he is himself insulted by those who are in power;
or a supercilious Greek who sees in all the world
nothing but his Greece, and for a poor barbarian girl's
tender feelings has no thought, nor for her innocent life's
final yearning, so innocent.

. . . .

"Nous N'osons Plus Chanter les Roses" *(1892)*

Fearing what is commonplace,
I stifle many of my words.
In my heart are written many
poems; and I love the lays
that are there interred.

O first, pure, only liberty
of youth, penchant for pleasure!
O sweet drunkenness of senses!
I fear lest base banality
your forms divine dishonour.

Indian Image *(1892)*

Our universe has four great gates,
     which four angels keep.
One is North; across is South;
     the others West and East.

The gate of the East is radiant nacre;
     in front, an angel bright
wears a diamond crown and belt
     and stands upon pure agate.

South's gate is purple amethyst.
     Its guardian angel holds
a magic staff of dark sapphire,
     and his feet are hid
by a turquoise cloud.

     Upon a shore
     with fine red seashells spread
the Western angel stands and guards
     the gate of coral rare.
With hand-made roses is he wreathed,
     each rose of ruby pure.

The Northern gate is built of gold,
     its throne the entrance fronts

. . . .

Pelasgian Image (1892)

An ancient Giant in earth's innards dwells.
      Thirty are his hands
and his feet are thirty. His enormous neck
      thirty heads upholds
and each has twenty of the sharpest eyes
      for which the deepest gloom
of deepest earth is as the lighted day.
      He is idle, is indifferent.
He has unnumbered treasures; and great mines
      of silver, diamonds, gold.
His rare riches, his extraordinary riches
      he coolly watches with
his six hundred eyes, but sometimes, to enliven
      a century or so, he counts it.
And it comes to bore him, and two years yawn wide,
      and tired, he falls asleep.
His sleep continues for entire centuries;
      every dream a generation.
But of a sudden, with a start he wakes. Ephialtes—
      offspring of raw matter—
has disturbed his sleep, reflecting in the blurry
      mirror of his cold
callous thoughts unknown and dreadful phantoms.
      Then he unfolds
his monstrous limbs and with his sixty hands and feet
      strikes, kicks, the vault. And earth

is shaken from its groundwork; cities fall down,
        and all the rivers flood,
and fires flow like breakers down from the mountains.
        The earth opens and closes
and people tumble down and are entombed within.
        But now the giant stirs
awake, and as he rubs his monstrous orbs he sees
        that so much tumult
and so much confusion were absurd, all for
        a cheap shadow of a dream.
At his cowardice he laughs, at his great terror,
        and peaceful goes to bed
again, and with his thirty mouths he smiles.

The Hereafter (1892)

I believe in the Hereafter. Material appetites
or love for the real don't beguile me. It's not habit
but instinct. The heavenly word will be added

to life's imperfect sentence, otherwise inane.
Respite and reward will follow upon action.
When sight is closed forever more to Creation,

the eye will be opened in the presence of the Creator.
An immortal wave of life will flow from each and every
Gospel of Christ—wave of life uninterrupted.

The Mimiambs of Herodas *(1892)*

Waiting, hidden for thousands of years
within the gloom of Egypt's earth
beneath a silence so desperate
those charming mimiambs were bored to tears;

But now those times have passed away,
from the North have come savants;
the iambs' tomb, their oblivion
are at an end. Their accents gay

return us to the jollity
of Greek streets and agoras;
and with them we enter the vigorous
life of a curious society.—

A bawd most wicked straightaway
meets us; she would lead astray
a faithful wife! But Metriche
knows how to keep her honor safe.

Then we spy another churl
who runs a certain establishment
and furiously charges a Phrygian
with corrupting his—School for Girls.

Two chatterers, elegant ladies,
visit the shrine of Asclepius;
the tastiest of their tête-à-têtes
enliven the temple enormously.

Into the leatherer's shop we go—
lovely things heaped up in piles,
here you'll find the latest styles—
accompanied by our fair Metrô.

Yet how much of these scrolls has been effaced;
how often a tart and graceful verse
has become the meal of vile worms.
Unhappy Herodas, who was made
for gaiety and for repartée—
has come to us so badly hurt!

Azure Eyes (1892)

Not for contempt were these luminaries bright
      born, lovely Circassian lass.
Not of anger, but of joy and love the lights,
        generous givers of delight,
         of pleasure the sweet promise.

Had they been made to spite an errant heart,
      and for destruction;
had they been earthward sent by an angry god;
      they would have some

other shape, and the heavens' gentle firmament
      would not have lent its tender color,
the beneficent sun would never have consented
        to grant them the flame so radiant
        from its body of love and of fire.

The Four Walls of My Room (1893)

. . . .

I know that they are all impoverished,
that these friends of mine should have
other ornaments, more distinguished
and more numerous, more grand.

But what do these words mean?
My walls have finer manners;
not for any gifts do they love me.
They are not like men.

Besides, they know they'll hold
my possessions for but a moment,
and me as well. My joys and woes
and whatever I have here below

will pass quickly. To gifts like these
the sturdy walls are indifferent.
They are long-lived and of my brief
life they ask for nothing.

Alexandrian Merchant *(1893)*

I sold the rancid barley very dear.
This Rome is the kingdom of sheer
profit. And in April I arrived:
I've lost no time. In April I shall leave.

To me the sea seems rather tiresome;
enormous clouds are covering the sun.
So what? For me each rock is but a shell,
every ocean like a level field.

I have no fear of winds aslant the air.
At hurricanes I scoff, and laugh at wrecks.
Broad-boulevarded Alexandria

will greet me safe. . . . Mates, look out there!
Off the jug! Treating himself—the cheek!
After the voyage the soul thirsts for Samian.

The Lagid's Hospitality *(1893)*

King Ptolemy Philopator royally
plays host to Medon the sophist—
the king takes great pride in his guest,
researcher of the powers of the soul.

At another time, the sophist, very poor
in noxious Rome, offered a great
potentate his work. The latter said: "Take
this *mna* and go. It's drivel and I'm bored."

"O insolence, insolence! Studying the infinite,
I inscribed each searing sentiment,
all of my heart, into that

papyrus. . . ." But in his scorn for the dictator
he kept his wingèd utterances short.—
Do honor to Ptolemy Philopator.

In the Cemetery *(1893)*

When to the cemetery memory
directs your steps,
worship the sacred mystery
of our darkling future, devoutly.
Lift up your mind to the Lord.
Before you
the most narrow bed of slumbers infinite
lies beneath the pity of Jesus.

Our beloved religion hallows our memorials,
hallows our death.
For the pagans' gifts and ceremonials
and sacrifices she has no love.
Without any foolish offerings
of gold,
the most narrow bed of slumbers infinite
lies beneath the pity of Jesus.

Priam's March by Night *(1893)*

Sorrow in Ilium, and lament.
                The land
of Troy in bitter hopelessness and fear
for great Hector, Priam's son, sheds tears.

The lamentation loudly, heavily resounds.
                       Not a soul
remains in Troy who is not yet in grief,
who has no care for Hector's memory.

But so much lamentation is utterly useless,
                       foolish
in a city so ill-fortuned;
fate implacable is deaf as stone.

Priam, despising helplessness,
              from his
treasury removes the gold; he adds
cauldrons, carpets, mantles; and

cloaks and tripods, a gleaming pile
                of veils
and whatever else appears appropriate,
and heaps them up inside his chariot.

He wants, with this ransom, to regain
                              his son's
body from his terrifying enemy,
and honor it with venerable obsequy.

In the taciturn night he leaves.
                    He says
little. Now his only thought is this:
that his chariot be swift, swift.

The road before him stretches gloomily.
                              Pitiably
the wind laments and groans.
Far off croaks an ill-omened crow.

Here, the bark of a dog is heard;
                         a hare
passes over there, swift as a whisper.
The king his horses spurs, spurs.

The shadows on the battlefield are astir,
                                   sinister,
and have no idea why, in such a rush,
Dardanides is heading for the ships

of Argive murderers, and Achaeans
                         malign.
But the king pays no attention to this;
'tis enough that his chariot be swift, swift.

Epitaph *(1893)*

Stranger, by the Ganges here I lie, a man
who lived a life of lamentation, toil, and pain;
a Samian, I ended in this thrice-barbaric land.
This grave close by the riverside contains

many woes. Undiluted lust for gold
drove me into this accursed trade.
I was shipwrecked on the Indian coast and sold
as a slave. Well into old age

I wore myself out, worked until I breathed no more—
deprived of Greek voices, and far from the shore
of Samos. What I suffer now is not, therefore,

fearful; and I voyage down to Hades without grief.
There among compatriots I shall be.
And forever after I shall speak in Greek.

Displeased Theatregoer *(1893)*

"I am leaving, leaving. Do not hold me back.
I'm a martyr to ennui and to revulsion."
"But stay a while for Menander's sake.
What a pity if you miss it." "You insult me.

"Menander's are they, then, these weak *données,*
these unpolished verses, this childish speech?
Let me leave this theatre straightaway
so I can go home—with no little relief.

"The Roman air has ruined you utterly
Instead of condemning, you timidly
acclaim, applaud this uncouth—what's his name?

Gabrence, Terence?—one whose only talent
is for composing those Latin Atellans;
yet nonetheless he hungers for Menander's fame."

Before Jerusalem *(1893)*

Now they've come before Jerusalem.
Passions, avarice, and ambition,
as well as their chivalrous pride
have swiftly slipped from their souls.

Now they've come before Jerusalem.
In their ecstasy and their devoutness
they've forgotten their quarrels with the Greeks;
they've forgotten their hatred of the Turks.

Now they've come before Jerusalem.
And the Crusaders, so daring and invincible,
so vehement in their every march and onslaught,
are fearful and nervous and are unable
to go further; they tremble like small children,
and like small children weep, all weep,
as they behold the walls of Jerusalem.

Second Odyssey *(1894)*

DANTE, *Inferno,* Canto XXVI
TENNYSON, "Ulysses"

A second Odyssey and a great one, too,
greater than the first perhaps. But alas,
without a Homer, without hexameters.

Small was his ancestral house,
small was his ancestral town,
and all his Ithaca was small.

Telemachus's affection, the faithfulness
of Penelope, the years of his father's old age,
his old companions, the people's unswerving love,
the blessed repose of the house
entered like rays of joy
into the heart of the seafarer.
And like rays they sank.
                              Inside of him
there awakened the thirst for the sea.
He hated the air of dry land.
Phantasms of the West
disturbed his sleep at night.
Nostalgia took hold of him:
for voyages, and early-morning
arrivals in harbors which,
with what joy, you enter for the first time.

Telemachus's affection, the faithfulness
of Penelope, the years of his father's old age,
his old companions, the people's unswerving love,
and the peace and repose
of the house—they all bored him.

                              And he left.

When Ithaca's headlands
slipped away bit by bit before him
and he voyaged westward at full sail,
towards Iberia, towards the Heraclean pillars,—
far from every Achaean sea,—
he felt that he lived once again, that
he'd slipped the burdensome bonds
of things that were known and familiar.
And his heart, adventuress,
exulted coldly, empty of love.

He Who Fails *(1894)*

He who fails, he who falls down low:
how difficult for him to learn poverty's
new language and new manners.

Poor unfamiliar houses, how will he enter them!—
with what a heart will he go along the street
and when he finds himself before his door where will he find
the strength to touch the bell.
For the lowly need for bread
and for shelter, how will he say his thank-you's!
How will he greet the chilly eyes
that reveal that he's a burden!
His haughty lips, how will they now
begin to speak so humbly;
and his lofty head, how will he bend it!
How will he hear the talk that mangles
his ears with every word—and even then
you must make out as if you do not sense them
as if you are simple and do not understand.

The Pawn *(1894)*

Often, when I see them playing chess,
my eye will follow a Pawn
as bit by bit he finds a path
and finally reaches the last row.
He goes to the end with such eagerness
you'd venture to say that surely here
his pleasures and rewards will begin.
He encounters many hardships on the way.
Foot soldiers hurl their lances aslant;
the castles hit him with their flat
lines; inside of their two squares
swift knights wheel round
craftily trying to snare him;
and here and there, a threat at an angle:
across his path there comes a pawn
dispatched from the enemy's camp.

But he wriggles out of all these dangers
and at last attains the final row.

How triumphantly he reaches it,
this terrifying row, the very last;
how eagerly he has come close to death!

For here the Pawn will die,
for this alone he has struggled.
On behalf of the queen, who will save us:
to resurrect her from her tomb
he fell into the underworld of chess.

Dread *(1894)*

At night, O Christ my Lord,
protect for me my soul and my mind
when about me there begin to roam
Beings and Things that have no name
and they run with fleshless feet around my room
and make a circle round my bed that they might see me—
and gaze upon me as though they know me
cackling voicelessly because they've frightened me.

I know it, yes, they lie in wait for me
as though they were mulling over the foul times
when perhaps I crept along with them—in the murk,
entangled with those beings and with those things.
And they're frenzied to think those times will come again.
But they won't come again; for I am saved,
in Christ's name I have been baptized.

I tremble when at night I sense,
when I feel that there in the dense
gloom their eyes are staring down at me. . . .
Hide me from their sight, my Lord.
And when they speak or croak, do not allow
any of their blasphemies to reach my ears,
lest it happen that they bring to my soul
some dreadful reminder of the hidden things they know.

In the House of the Soul *(1894)*

Deeper, at the deepest part in the House of the Soul,
Where they come and go and sit around a fire,
The Passions with their women's faces.

—RODENBACH

In the House of the Soul the Passions wander—
    beautiful women gowned
in silks, and sapphires crown their heads.
From the door of the house to its innermost depths they command
all of the chambers. Within the grandest—
    on nights when their blood is inflamed—
they dance and they drink with their hair unbound.

Outside the chambers, pale and poorly dressed
    in a bygone era's garments,
  the Virtues wander and in bitterness listen
to the merrymaking of their drunken companions.
To the glass of the windows they press their faces
    and, contemplative, they watch in silence
the lights, the jewels, and the blossoms of the dance.

Rain *(1894)*

. . . .

two slender trees
a little garden has;
and there the water makes
a parody of the land—
going into shoots
which have no mystery;
watering the roots
which have a sickly juice;
running into foliage
that, tied up with thread,
glum and melancholy
hang upon the windows;
and wanly washing off
the plants that in their pots
a careful housewife has
ordered row by row.

Rain, which little children
gaily look upon
inside a toasty room,
and as the water swells
and falls more heavily,
they clap their hands and jump.
Rain, which old men hear
with forbearance glum,

with boredom and ennui;
since instinctively
they have no love at all
for rain-drenched earth and shadows.

Rain, rain—ever more
violently comes the rain.
But I can no longer see.
Because of all that wet
the windowpane fogged up.
Upon its surface the
scattered drops of rain
run, and slip, stretch out
go up and then go down
and one of them will splotch
and one of them's a blur.
And the street by now is hardly
visible in the mist;
so too, in a watery rime,
the houses and the carriages.

La Jeunesse Blanche *(1895)*

Most beloved, white our youth,
   ah our white, our snowy youth,
  which is boundless, and is very brief,
   opening above us like an angel's wings!. . . .
     It is all worn out, loves everything;
and melts away and swoons upon the white horizons.
Ah it goes there and is lost upon the white horizons,
       goes forever.

Forever, no. It will return,
   will come round again, return.
  With its limbs so white, its white allure,
  our youth so white will come to take us.
    It will hold us in its hands of white,
and in a fragile winding-shroud, of whiteness formed,
in a snowy winding-shroud of whiteness formed,
       will cover us.

Distinguishing Marks *(1895)*

For different lands are rich in different crops and cattle; the horse distin-
guishes the Thessalian . . . but the product of this city is reason, and man.

—HIMERIUS

Every land has its distinguishing mark.
Particular to Thessaly are horsemanship and horses;
      what marks a Spartan
      is war's season; Media has

      its tables with their dishes;
hair marks the Celts, the Assyrians have beards.
      But the marks that distinguish
      Athens are Mankind and the Word.

Eternity *(1895)*

The Indian Arjuna, a goodly and mild king,
hated slaughter. He never went to war.
But the dreadful god of war was greatly vexed—
(diminished was his glory, his temples emptied)—
and went in great anger to the palace of Arjuna.
The king took fright and said: "Great god,
forgive me if I cannot take a human life."
In contempt the god replied: "You think yourself
more just than I? By words be not deceived.
No life is ever taken. Know you then that no one
is ever born, that no one ever dies."

Confusion *(1896)*

My soul, in the middle of the night,
is confused and paralyzed. Outside:
       its life comes into being outside itself.

And it awaits the improbable dawn.
And I await, am worn down, and am bored,
       even I, who am in it or with it.

Salome *(1896)*

Upon a golden charger Salome bears
   the head of John the Baptist
     to the young Greek sophist
who recoils from her love, indifferent.

The young man quips, "Salome, your own
   head is what I wanted them to bring me."
     This is what he says, jokingly.
And her slave came running on the morrow

holding aloft the head of the Beloved,
   its tresses blond, upon a golden plate.
     But all his eagerness of yesterday
the sophist had forgotten as he studied.

He sees the dripping blood and is disgusted.
   He orders this bloodied thing to
     be taken from him, and he continues
his reading of the dialogues of Plato.

Chaldean Image *(1896)*

Before the god Ea created mankind, the earth was full of
      the abominable races
of Apsu—who for bodies had abysses infinite—
      and Mummu Tiamat's wet chaos.
In those days there were Warriors with the bodies of birds;
      Folk with human bodies
and the heads of crows; and Breeds of great, enormous bulls
      with the heads of men;
and dogs that bayed all night and all the livelong day who had
      four bodies and the tails
of fish.—The good Ea and all our other gods wiped out
      those creatures
before they set mankind inside of Paradise (from which
      alas!, how pitiably they fell).

Julian at the Mysteries *(1896)*

But when he found himself amid the darkness,
amid the terrifying depths of the earth,
in the company of godless Greeks,
and saw the disembodied forms emerge before him
with apparitions, and with brilliant lights,
for a moment he was afraid, this youth,
and an instinct from his pious years
returned, and he made the sign of the cross.
Immediately the Forms disappeared.
The visions were gone—the lights went out.
The Greeks sneaked glances at each other.
And the young man said: "Did you see that marvel?
My dear companions, I am afraid.
I am afraid, my friends, I want to go.
Did not you see the spirits straightaway
vanish at the moment when I made
the blessed shape of the cross?"
There was much guffawing from the Greeks.
"For shame, for shame that you should speak such words
to us, who are philosophers and sophists.
If you like, go tell such things to the man
of Nicomedia, and tell them to his priests.
Before you there appeared the greatest gods
of our illustrious Greece.
And if they left, do not think for a minute
that they were frightened by a gesture.

It's merely that when they saw you make
that extremely base and boorish shape
their noble nature was repelled,
and they left and held you in contempt."
This is what they said, and from his fear,
which was holy and blessed,
the foolish man recovered, and was persuaded
by the godless words of the Greeks.

The Cat *(1897)*

The cat is distasteful to ordinary people.
Magnetic and mysterious, it wearies their
   frivolous minds; nor do they place any
     value on its charming manners. [   ]
  [   ]
  [   ]

But the soul of a cat is its lordly pride.
Liberty, its blood and its nerves.
   Its gaze is never cast down.
     In the constant concealment of its passions,
   in the clarity, the serenity
   and beauty of its stances, the discipline

of its movements, how delicate a purity of feeling
may be found. When cats day dream or slumber
   a spectral chill surrounds them.
     Then, perhaps, the ghosts of olden times

roam around them. Perhaps this vision
leads them to Bubastis; where their holy places
   flourished once, and Ramessid ritual crowned them,
     and their every movement was an augury for the priests.

The Bank of the Future *(1897)*

In order to make my difficult life more secure
I shall be issuing very few drafts
on the Bank of the Future.

I doubt that it possesses very great assets.
And I've begun to fear that in the first crisis
it will suddenly stop making payments.

Impossible Things *(1897)*

There is one joy alone, but one that's blessed,
one consolation only in this pain.
How many thronging vulgar days were missed
because of this ending; how much ennui.

A poet has said: "The loveliest
music is the one that cannot be played."
And I, I daresay that by far the best
life is the one that cannot be lived.

Addition *(1897)*

Whether I am happy or unhappy, I don't calculate.
But one thing always I joyfully keep in sight—
that in the great addition (the addition of those I hate)
that comprises such great numbers, I don't count
as one of the many units there. I wasn't numbered in the great
addition. And for me that delight is sufficient.

Garlands *(1897)*

Absinthe, datura, and hypoceme,
aconite, hellebore, and hemlock—
all of the bitter and poisonous—
give up their leaves and their terrible flowers
that they might become the great garlands
that are placed on the radiant altar—
ah, the shining altar of Malachite stone—
of the Passion both dreadful and sublime.

Lohengrin *(1898)*

The goodly king feels pity for Elsa
and to the Herald he turns.

The Herald calls out, and the trumpets sound.

Ah king, I bid thee once again,
let the Herald call out one more time.

The Herald sounds the summons one more time.

                                        I beg you,
I fall at your feet. Have mercy on me, mercy.
He is far away, very far, and does not hear.
Now, this one last time, let the Herald
sounds the summons. Perhaps he will appear.

                              The Herald
sounds the summons once again.

                        And see,
something white shone out on the horizon.
It has appeared, appeared—it is the swan.

Oh our misfortune, Oh misfortune, when
the king feels pity and turns mechanically

to his Herald, without very much hope.
And the Herald cries out, and the trumpets sound.

    And again he cries out and the trumpets sound;
    and again he cries out and the trumpets sound;
    but Lohengrin never comes.

And nonetheless faith would have kept the watch, inviolate.

Suspicion *(1898)*

And who shall say the worst.
(Better for it never to be uttered.)
Who will come to tell us (Let's not listen to him.
Let's not listen to him. They'll have tricked him)
the unjust accusation; and then
the challenge, another challenge from the Herald,
the glorious arrival of Lohengrin—
swan, and magic sword, and holy Grail—
and in the end the single combat,
in which he was defeated by Telramund.

Death of a General (1899)

Death stretches out his hand
and touches a glorious general's brow.
That evening a paper reveals the news.
A great crowd fills the sick man's house.

His pain has paralyzed his limbs
and his tongue. He turns his gaze
and stares a long while at familiar things.
Serene, he recalls the heroes of olden days.

On the outside—he is covered by silence and stillness.
Inside—he's devoured by envy for life, by cowardice,
leprous pleasure, foolish spite, fury, malice.

He groans deeply.—He's expired.—The voice of every
citizen laments. "His death has ruined our city!
Virtue has died with him, O woe is me!"

The Intervention of the Gods (1899)

Heartily know / . . . / The gods arrive.

—EMERSON

RÉMONIN.—He'll disappear at the crucial time; the gods will intervene.

Mme DE RUMIÈRES.—As in ancient tragedies? (Act II, sc. i)

Mme DE RUMIÈRES.—What is the matter?

RÉMONIN.—The Gods have arrived. (Act V, sc. x)

—ALEXANDRE DUMAS, FILS, *L'Etrangère*

This will happen now, and later that;
and later still, in a year or two (as I reckon it),
affairs will be such, and manners such.
We won't fret about the distant future.
What we'll attempt is something better.
And we'll ruin whatever we attempt;
we'll so entangle our affairs that we'll end up
in deep confusion. And then we'll stop.
That will be the hour for the gods to work.
They always come, the gods. They will descend
from their machines, and some they'll save,
others they will violently, suddenly raise
by the middle; and when they've brought some order
they will withdraw.—And then this man will do this,
and that man that; and in time the others
will do as they see fit. And so we will start over.

King Claudius *(1899)*

To far-off parts my mind now makes its way.
I walk around the streets of Elsinore,
I wander in the squares, and I remember
her most mournful history, that luckless king,
whom his nephew slew because of some imagined suspicions.

In all the houses of the poor they secretly
(because they were in fear of Fortinbras)
wept for him. A lover of quiet, and mild
was he; and he loved peace (the land had suffered much
from the battles of his predecessor).
He behaved with courtesy to all,
to great and small. High-handedness
he reviled, and he always sought
counsel about the kingdom's affairs
from people who were sober and experienced.

Why his nephew killed him
they never said with any certainty.
He suspected him of a murder.
The basis of his suspicion was this:
that when, one night when he was walking on
one of the ancient battlements,
he reckoned that he saw a ghost
and with the ghost he had a conversation.

And from the ghost, presumably, he learned
of certain accusations against the king.

It must have been excitement of the imagination,
to be sure, some trick played on his eyes.
(The prince was nervous to extremes.
When he was studying in Wittenberg his fellow
students took him for a lunatic.)

A few days afterwards he went to see
his mother, so that they could have a talk
about some family matters. And suddenly
just as he was talking he became excited
and began to shout, and to cry aloud
that the ghost had appeared in front of him.
But his mother didn't see a thing.

And on that very day he killed
an aged nobleman without any cause.
Since anyway the prince was due to leave
for England in a day or two,
the king hastened his departure
hurry-scurry, so that he might save him.
But everyone was so indignant
about the horrifying murder that rebels rose up
and tried to storm the palace gates
together with the son of the murdered man
the nobleman Laertes (a young man
who was brave, and was ambitious, too:

some of his friends cried out "Long live
King Laertes!" in the confusion).

When later the place had quieted down
and the king had been laid out in his grave,
murdered by his nephew (the prince didn't go to England;
during the journey he escaped from the ship),
a certain Horatio come forward
and tried, by means of detailed explanations,
to vindicate the prince. He said the trip to England
had been a secret plot, and that an order
had been given to kill him there.
(This, however, was never clearly proved.)
He talked, moreover, of wine that had been poisoned,
wine that had been poisoned by the king.
This, it is true, Laertes also said.
But couldn't he have been lying? couldn't he be deceived?
And when did he say it? When he had been wounded,
and was dying and his mind was wandering
and it seemed that he was raving.
As for the poisoned weapons,
later it appeared that the king
hadn't poisoned them at all,
Laertes alone had poisoned them.
But Horatio, whenever it seemed necessary,
would even produce the ghost as a witness.
The ghost said this, said that!
The ghost did this and that!

Even as they heard him saying these things,
most of them, in their consciences,

felt sorry for their goodly king
whom they had slain with phantoms and fairy tales,
so unjustly, and who now was gone.

But Fortinbras, who had profited
and had so easily acquired the throne,
gave great weight and serious attention
to everything that Horatio said.

The Naval Battle (1899)

We were annihilated there at Salamis.
Let us say oá, oá, oá, oá, oá, oá.
Ecbatana and Susa belong to us,
and Persepolis—the loveliest of places.
What were we doing there at Salamis
hauling our fleets and doing battle at sea?
Now we shall return to our Ecbatana
to our Persepolis, and to Susa.
We shall go, but shan't enjoy them as once we did.
Otototoi, otototoi: this battle at sea,
why must it be, why must it be sought out?
Otototoi, otototoi: why must
we pick ourselves up, abandon everything,
and go there to do battle so wretchedly at sea.
Why is it thus: as soon as someone owns
illustrious Ecbatana, and Susa,
and Persepolis, he straightaway assembles a fleet
and goes forth to battle the Greeks at sea.
Ah yes, of course: let's not say another word:
otototoi, otototoi, otototoi.
Ah yes, indeed: what's left for us to say:
oá, oá, oá, oá, oá, oá.

When the Watchman Saw the Light *(1900)*

Winters, summers the Watchman sat upon the roof
of the Atreids and watched. Now he's got good news
to tell. Far away he saw the fires kindle.
And he is glad; besides, his labor's ended.
Arduous it is, both day and night,
in heat and cold, to have to look for lights
beyond Arachnaeum. Now the longed-for sign
has appeared. When happiness arrives
it gives a lesser joy than anyone
expects. But clearly there is one
thing we gained: we've rid ourselves of hopes
and expectations. Many things will happen
to the Atreids. One need not be wise,
since the Watchman saw the light, to surmise
that much. So let's not overdo it.
The light is good; good are those en route;
and all they say and do is also good.
So let us pray things turn out well. And yet
Argos is capable of making do without
Atreids. Royal houses aren't everlasting.
People, certainly, will be saying all sorts of things.
As for us, let's listen. But we won't be taken in
by "the Indispensable," by "the One and Only," by "the Great."
They always find another straightaway
who's indispensable, the one and only, and great.

The Enemies *(1900)*

To the Consul came three sophists who wished to bring him
    greetings.
The Consul placed them close to him and told them to be
    seated.
He spoke to them politely. And then to them, in jest,
he said they should be worried. "What makes men envious
is Fame. One's rivals are writers, too. You have enemies."
Of the three men one replied in words most serious.

"Those who are our enemies today will never harm us.
Our enemies will come afterwards, those who are the new sophists.
When we, by then so very old, shall pitiably be laid
to rest and some of us will be in Hades. Our present-day
words and works will seem quite strange (and even comical
perhaps) because our enemies will change what is "sophistic,"
and style, and trends. Precisely as I myself once did,
and they as well; all of us who so transformed the past.
All of what we represented as beautiful and sound
the enemies will reveal as being ludicrous and groundless
repeating the same things differently (without any great bother).
Just as we ourselves once said the old words in another manner."

Artificial Flowers (1903)

I do not want narcissuses that are real—nor do lilies
    please me, nor do roses that are real.
The gardens they adorn are trite and common. To me
    their flesh gives bitterness, weariness, and grief—
      Their perishable beauties tire me.

Give me artificial blooms—the glories of porcelain and metal—
which shrivel not and do not rot, with forms that do not age.
    Blooms of the exquisite gardens of another place,
    where Theories and Rhythms dwell, and Knowledges.

The blooms I love are fashioned of glass or gold:
    of a faithful Art, the faithful gifts;
dyed in colors more lovely than the natural,
    worked with nacre and with enamel,
      with idealized leaves and shoots.

They take their grace from Taste, most wise and pure;
in the earth they did not sprout, nor filthily in slime.
    If they have no aroma, perfumes shall we pour,
    and burn the incenses of sentiment before them.

Strengthening *(1903)*

Whoever longs to make his spirit stronger
should leave behind respect and obedience.
Some of the laws are ones that he will keep,
but for the most part he will contravene
both laws and ethics, and he will leave behind
the norms that are received, inadequate.
Many things will he be taught by pleasures.
He will never fear the destructive act;
half the house must be demolished.
Thus will he grow virtuously into knowledge.

September of 1903 *(1904)*

At least let me be deceived by delusions, now,
so that I might not feel my empty life.

And I was so close so many times.
And how I froze, and how I was afraid;
why should I remain with lips shut tight;
while within me weeps my empty life,
and my longings wear their mourning black.

To be, so many times, so close
to the eyes, and to the sensual lips,
to the dreamed of, the beloved body.
To be, so many times, so close.

December 1903 *(1904)*

Even though I may not speak about my love—
I may not talk about your hair, or your lips, or your eyes;
still, your face, which I keep inside my soul;
the sound of your voice, which I keep inside my mind;
the September days that dawn within my dreams:
my words and phrases take their shape and color from these,
whatever subject I may touch upon, whatever idea I may be speaking of.

January of 1904 (1904)

Ah this January, this January's nights,
when I sit and refashion in my thoughts
those moments and I come upon you,
and I hear our final words, and hear the first.

This January's despairing nights,
when the vision goes and leaves me all alone.
How swiftly it departs and melts away—
the trees go, the streets go, the houses go, the lights go:
it fades and disappears, your erotic shape.

On the Stairs *(1904)*

As I was going down the shameful stair,
you came in the door, and for a moment
I saw your unfamiliar face and you saw me.
Then I hid so you wouldn't see me again, and you
passed by quickly as you hid your face,
and stole inside the shameful house
where you likely found no pleasure, just as I found none.

And yet the love you wanted, I had to give you;
the love I wanted—your eyes told me so,
tired and suspicious—you had it to give me.
Our bodies sensed and sought each other out;
our blood and skin understood.

But we hid from each other, we two, terrified.

In the Theatre *(1904)*

I grew bored with looking at the stage,
and raised my eyes to the loge.
And there inside a box I saw you
with your queer beauty, and your spoilt youth.
And straightaway there came back to my mind
all they'd told me about you, that afternoon,
and my thoughts and my body were stirred.
And whilst I gazed enchanted
at your weary beauty, at your weary youth,
at your discriminating attire,
I imagined you and I depicted you,
in just the way they'd talked about you, that afternoon.

Poseidonians *(1906)*

. . . like the Poseidonians in the Tyrrhenian Gulf whom it befell that, although of Greek origin, they became utterly barbarized, becoming Tyrrhenians or Romans, and changing their language along with many of their customs. Yet to this day they observe a certain Greek holiday, during which they gather together and recall the ancient names and customs; after which, lamenting loudly to each other and weeping, they depart.

—ATHENAEUS

The Greek language the Poseidonians
had forgotten after centuries of intermingling
with Tyrrhenians and Latins, and other foreigners.
The one ancestral feature they retained
was a Greek festival, with elaborate rites,
with lyres and oboes, with contests and garlands.
It was their custom, at the festival's conclusion,
to tell each other of their ancient practices
and to pronounce Greek words again,
which but a few of them any longer understood.
And their holiday would always end in melancholy.
For they'd remember then that they too were Greeks—
they too Italiotes, once upon a time.
And now how far they'd fallen, what had they become
that they should live and speak like barbarians,
removed—disastrous fate!—from the culture of the Greeks.

The End of Antony (1907)

But when he heard that the womenfolk were weeping
and were keening for his pitiable state—
madame with her Oriental flailings,
and the slave-girls with their barbarous Greek—
the lofty pride within his soul
awoke, his Italian blood was sickened,
and it all seemed strange to him, indifferent,
everything he'd blindly worshipped until then—
all his frenetic Alexandrian life—
and he said "They ought not weep for him. It is not fitting.
But to glorify him, rather, it behooves them,
he who had turned out to be great lord,
and had amassed so many goods, so many riches.
And now if he has fallen, he falls not humbly,
but as a Roman by a Roman was he vanquished."

27 June 1906, 2 P.M. *(1908)*

When the Christians brought him to be hanged,
the innocent boy of seventeen,
his mother, who there beside the scaffold
had dragged herself and lay beaten on the ground
beneath the midday sun, the savage sun,
now would moan, and howl like a wolf, a beast,
and then the martyr, overcome, would keen
"Seventeen years only you lived with me, my child."
And when they took him up the scaffold's steps
and passed the rope around him and strangled him,
the innocent boy, seventeen years old,
and piteously it hung inside the void,
with the spasms of black agony—
the youthful body, beautifully wrought—
his mother, martyr, wallowed on the ground
and now she keened no more about his years:
"Seventeen days only," she keened,
"seventeen days only I had joy of you, my child."

Hidden *(1908)*

From all I did and from all I said
they shouldn't try to find out who I was.
An obstacle was there and it distorted
my actions and the way I lived my life.
An obstacle was there and it stopped me
on many occasions when I was going to speak.
The most unnoticed of my actions
and the most covert of all my writings:
from these alone will they come to know me.
But perhaps it's not worth squandering
so much care and trouble on puzzling me out.
Afterwards—in some more perfect society—
someone else who's fashioned like me
will surely appear and be free to do as he pleases.

Hearing of Love (1911)

On hearing of a powerful love tremble and be moved
like an aesthete. But then, contented,
remember how many your imagination fashioned for you: those
first: and then the others—lesser—that in your life you've
experienced and enjoyed, those more real, and tangible.—
You were not deprived of loves like these.

"The Rest Shall I Tell in Hades
to Those Below" (1913)

"Indeed," said the proconsul, as he closed the book,
"this line is very lovely, and quite right;
Sophocles wrote it in a deeply philosophical light.
How much we'll have to say there, how much we'll say there,
and how vastly different we'll appear.
All that here we hold in, like wakeful guards,
the wounds and secrets that we shut inside,
with weighty anguish each and every day,
freely, there, and clearly we shall say."

"Add to that," the sophist said, half-smiling,
"if they talk like that down there, whether they still care."

That's How *(1913)*

In this obscene photograph, which is secretly
sold in the street (so the police won't see),
in this smutty photograph
how could there be a face like this,
of dreams; how could you be here.

Who knows what debased, sordid life you must lead;
how horrid the surroundings must have been
when you posed so they could photograph you;
what a tawdry soul yours must be.
But given all of this, and more, to me you remain
the face that comes in dreams, a figure
fashioned for and dedicated to Greek pleasure—
that's how you are for me still and how my poetry speaks of you.

Homecoming from Greece (1914)

So we're getting closer to arriving, Hermippus.
The day after tomorrow, I daresay; so said the captain.
At least we're sailing on our seas:
waters of Cyprus, of Syria, and of Egypt,
waters of our beloved fatherlands.
Why so silent? Ask your heart:
as we drew ever farther from Greece,
weren't you happier, too? Why fool ourselves?—
surely that wouldn't be fitting for a Greek.

Let's admit the truth from here on in:
we too are Greek—what else could we be?—
but with loves and with emotions that are Asia's,
but with loves and with emotions
that now and then are alien to Greek culture.

It's not becoming to us, Hermippus, to us philosophers
to resemble certain of our lesser kings
(remember how we'd laugh at them
when they'd come to have a look at our Schools)
beneath whose exteriors, so ostentatiously
Hellenized and (dare I say!) Macedonian,
some Arabia peeps out every now and then,
some Media that cannot be reined in;
with what comical contrivances the poor things
labor so that nobody will notice.

Ah no, such things don't become us.
For Greeks like us such pettiness won't do.
Of the blood of Syria and of Egypt
that flows in our veins, let's not be ashamed;
let us revere it, and let us boast of it.

Fugitives *(1914)*

Always Alexandria remains herself. Walk a little down
the straight road that comes to an end at the Hippodrome,
you'll see palaces and monuments that will astound you.
For all the harm it's suffered in its wars,
for all that it's diminished, still a marvelous place.
And then, with the excursions, and the books,
and with the various studies, the time does pass.
In the evening we gather at the shore,
the five of us (all with our fictitious
names, of course) and some other Greeks
of those few who have remained in the city.
Now and then we'll talk about church matters (they seem
rather Latin here), now and then about literary matters.
Two days ago we were reading Nonnus's lines.
What images, what rhythm, what language, what harmony.
In our eagerness, we marveled at the Panopolite.
So the days pass, and our sojourn
is not unpleasant, since, naturally,
it isn't something that's going to last forever.
We've had good reports, and whether something
is going on in Smyrna now, or in April
our allies will set forth from Epirus, our plans
are working, and we'll easily throw out Basil.
And it will be our turn from there on in.

Theophilus Palaeologus *(1914)*

The final year is this one. The final Greek
emperor is this one. And alas
what dismal things they're saying all around him.
In his desperation, in his pain
the Lord Theophilus Palaeologus
says "I'd rather die than live."

Ah, Lord Theophilus Palaeologus,
how much of the yearning of our race, how much of its exhaustion
(how much weariness from injustice and persecution)
those five tragic words of yours contained.

And I Got Down and I Lay There in Their Beds *(1915)*

When I went inside the house of pleasure
I didn't linger in the parlor where they celebrate
conventional desires, with some decorum.

The rooms I went to were the secret ones
and I got down and I lay there in their beds.

The rooms I went to were the secret ones,
the ones they think it shameful even to name.
But for me there was no shame—for if there were
what kind of poet, what kind of craftsman would I be?
Better to abstain completely. That would be more in keeping,
much more in keeping with my poetry
than going to the common parlor for my pleasure.

Half an Hour *(1917)*

I never had you, nor will I have you
ever, I daresay. A couple of words, a closeness
as in the bar two days ago, and nothing else.
It is, I don't deny, a pity. But we who belong to Art
sometimes—with intensity of mind, and of course only
for a little while—create a pleasure
that gives the impression of being almost real.
So it was in the bar two days ago—with a good deal of help,
besides, from some merciful alcohol—
I had half an hour that was utterly erotic.
And it seems to me you understood,
and you stayed somewhat longer purposely.
It was rather necessary, that. Because
for all the imagination, for all that liquor's a magician,
I needed to see your lips as well,
needed to have your body close to me.

House with Garden *(1917)*

I wanted to have a house in the country
with a very large garden—not so much
for the flowers, the trees, and the greenery
(certainly there will be that, too; it's so lovely)
but for me to have animals. Ah to have animals!
Seven cats at least—two completely black,
and, for contrast, two as white as snow.
A parrot, quite substantial, so I can listen to him
saying things with emphasis and conviction.
As for dogs, I do believe that three will be enough.
I should like two horses, too (ponies are nice).
And absolutely three or four of those remarkable,
those genial animals, donkeys,
to sit around lazily, to rejoice in their well-being.

A Great Feast at the House of Sosibius *(1917)*

Lovely was my afternoon, extremely
lovely. The oar grazes, very lightly,

the Alexandrian sea, sweetly calm; caresses it.
We need a respite like this: our toils oppress us.

Let's look at things innocently, serenely, every now and then.
But evening's fallen, regrettably. Look, I drank up all the wine,

not a single drop remains inside my flask.
It's time we returned to other things, alas!

A celebrated house (the famed Sosibius and his nice
spouse; let's put it that way) invites us to a feast.

We must go back again to all our dirty tricks—
and once more enter the dreary fray of politics.

Simeon *(1917)*

I know them, yes, those new poems of his.
All Beirut is passionate about them.
I'll take a careful look at them another day.
Today I cannot, since I'm rather upset.

Certainly he's better versed in Greek than Libanius.
But even better than Meleager? I don't believe so.

Ah, Mebes, so what of Libanius! and so what of books!
and all such trivialities! . . . . . Mebes, yesterday I was—
quite by chance it happened—at the foot of Simeon's pillar.

I slipped in among the Christians
who were praying silently and worshipping,
and kneeling down; but since I'm not a Christian
I didn't have their serenity of mind—
and I was trembling all over, and suffering;
and I was horrified, upset, deeply distressed.

Ah, don't smile; thirty-five years, just think—
winter, summer, night and day, thirty-five
years he's been living atop a pillar, martyring himself.
Before we were born—I'm twenty-nine years old,
and you, I daresay, are younger than I—
before we were born, imagine it,

Simeon went up onto the pillar
and ever since he's stayed there before his God.

Today I have no head for work.—
Except for this, Mebes: better if you say
that, whatever the other sophists say,
I myself acknowledge Lamo
as first among the poets of Syria.

The Bandaged Shoulder *(1919)*

He said that he'd hit a wall, or that he'd fallen.
But probably there was another reason
for the wounded, bandaged shoulder.

With a rather forceful motion,
so he could take down from a shelf some
photographs that he wanted to see close up,
the bandage came undone and a little blood flowed.

I bound the shoulder up again, and over the binding
I lingered somewhat; for he wasn't in pain,
and I liked looking at the blood. Matter
of my love, is what that blood was.

When he left I found, in front of the chair,
a bloodied scrap of cloth, part of the bandage,
a scrap that looked like it should go straight into the trash;
and which I took upon my lips,
and which I kept for a long while—
the blood of love upon my lips.

Coins *(1920)*

Coins with Indian inscriptions.
Those of the most powerful monarchs,
of Evoukratindaza, of Strataga,
of Menandraza, of Heramaïaza.
That's how the scholarly book conveys to us
the Indian writing on one side of the coins.
But the book shows us the other side as well,
that is, moreover, the right side,
with the figure of the king. And how quickly he stops there,
how a Hellene is moved as he reads the Greek,
Hermaeus, Eucratides, Strato, Menander.

It Was Taken *(1921)*

These days I've been reading popular songs,
about the struggles of the klephts and about their wars,
congenial matters: all our own, and Greek.

I've also been reading the laments over the fall of the City
"They took the City, took her; took Salonica."
And the Voice, while the two of them were chanting,
"On the left the king, on the right the patriarch,"
was heard and said that they must henceforth cease,
"Cease ye priests with your books and close the gospels"
they took the City, took her; took Salonica.

But the song that touched me far more than the others
was the one of Trebizond, with its unusual language
and the suffering of those Greeks so far away
who maybe always believed that we'd still be saved.

But woe, the fateful bird "from t' City is y-commen"
with "a paper all a-writ upon its wing
nor did it settle in the vineyard nor in the little garden
but went and settled on the cypress's root."
The prelates were unable (or unwilling) to read it;
"See, Johnny, O, the widow's son" takes the paper himself,
and he reads it and laments.
"Now he reads now weeps now beats upon his breast.
Alack for us, O woe for us, Romany is taken."

From the Drawer (1923)

I had in mind to place it on a wall of my room.

But the dampness of the drawer damaged it.

I won't put this photograph in a frame.

I ought to have looked after it more carefully.

Those lips, that face—
ah if only for a day, only for an
hour their past would return.

I won't put this photograph in a frame.

I'll endure looking at it, damaged as it is.

Besides, even if it weren't damaged,
it would be annoying to be on guard lest some
word, some tone of voice betrayed—
if they ever questioned me about it.

Prose Poems

The Regiment of Pleasure *(1894–1897?)*

Do not speak of guilt, do not speak of responsibility. When the Regiment of Pleasure passes by, with music and flags; when the senses quiver and tremble, whoever stands apart is foolish and impertinent: whoever does not rush to join the good crusade, to the conquest of pleasures and of passions.

All the laws of morals—as ill-considered as they are ill-constructed—are naught and cannot stand fast even for a moment, when the Regiment of Pleasure passes by accompanied by music and by flags.

Do not let a single shadowy virtue stop you. Do not believe that a single commitment binds you. Your duty is to give in, give in always to your longings, which are the most perfect creations of perfect gods. Your duty is to fall in, a faithful soldier, with simplicity of heart, when the Regiment of Pleasure passes by accompanied by music and by flags.

Do not shut yourself inside your house and deceive yourself with theories of justice, with the superstitions about reward held by ill-made societies. Do not say, My toil is worth so much, and so much I'm due to enjoy. Since life is an inheritance and you had nothing to do to earn it, so an inheritance, too, must Pleasure necessarily be. Do not shut yourself inside your house; but keep the window open, completely open, so that you might hear the first sounds of the passing of the soldiers, when there arrives the Regiment of Pleasure accompanied by music and by flags.

Do not be deceived by the blasphemers who tell you that

this service is risky and toilsome. Service to Pleasure is a constant joy. It exhausts you, but it exhausts you with heavenly intoxications. And when at last you fall down in the street, even then your fate is to be envied. When your funeral procession passes by, the Shapes that your longings fashioned will cast tulips and white roses on your coffin, and onto their shoulders the youthful Gods of Olympus will lift you, and they will entomb you in the Cemetery of the Ideal where the mausoleums of poetry gleam white.

Ships *(1895–1896?)*

From Imagination onto Paper. Difficult the passage, risky the sea. The distance seems short at first sight, and yet even so how great a journey it is, and how harmful sometimes to the ships that undertake it.

The first sort of damage stems from the exceedingly fragile nature of the merchandise that the ships transport. In the marketplaces of the Imagination, the greatest number and the most beautiful of the objects are created of delicate glasses and porcelains translucent, and even with all the care in the world many shatter on the journey, and many shatter when they are unloaded ashore. All of the damage of this sort is irreparable, since it is out of the question for the ship to turn back and take aboard objects of comparable quality. It is impossible to find the same shop that sold them. The marketplaces of the Imagination have shops that are grand and opulent, but not of any great duration. Their transactions are brief, they dispose of their merchandise swiftly, and they are immediately liquidated. It is very rare for a ship to return and find the same exporters of the same goods.

Another sort of damage stems from the capacities of the ships themselves. They set out from the harbors of the prosperous mainlands heavy with cargo, and then when they find themselves upon the open sea they are forced to toss away a part of the cargo in order to save the whole. Hence virtually no ship manages to deliver intact precisely as many treasures as it had taken aboard. Those that were tossed away are, to be sure, the goods of lesser value, but sometimes it happens that sailors, in their great haste, make a mistake and toss into the sea some articles of great value.

Upon their arrival at the white harbor of paper, new sacrifices are required once again. The customs officials come and examine one item and ponder whether they should send the cargo back; they deny permission for another item to be unloaded; and of certain objects only a small quantity is admitted. The country has its laws. Not all goods have free entry and smuggling is strictly forbidden. The importation of wine is prohibited, since the lands from which the ships come make wines and spirits from grapes that grow and mature in more generous climates. The customs officials have no desire at all for these beverages. They are extremely intoxicating. They are not suitable for all heads. Besides there is an association in this country that has the monopoly on wines. It manufactures liquids having the color of wine and the taste of water, and you can drink them all day long without getting giddy in the slightest. It is an old association. It enjoys an excellent reputation, and its shares are always overvalued.

But we should be happy that the ships put into harbor, should be so even with all of those sacrifices. For when all is said and done, thanks to great vigilance and great care, the number of objects shattered or cast overboard during the duration of the voyage is limited. Also, while the laws of the country and the customs regulations are oppressive in many respects, they are not completely restrictive, and a great part of the cargo is, in fact, unloaded. And the customs officials are not infallible, and various of the prohibited articles get through, inside deceptive containers which have been labeled one way on the outside but contain something else within, and several fine wines are imported for select drinking parties.

There is something else that is more distressing still; more distressing still. Sometimes certain enormous ships pass by, with décors of coral and with ebony masts, with tremendous white and scarlet banners flying, filled with treasure, and do not even approach the harbor either because all of the goods that they carry are forbidden or because the harbor does not have sufficient depth to receive them. And so they continue along on their course. A following wind breathes upon their silken sails, the sun glazes the brilliance of their golden prows, and they move away tranquilly and magnificently, move away forever from us and from our narrow harbor.

Fortunately they are very rare, those ships. Barely two or three do we see in all our lives. And we forget them quickly. As radiant as the sight of them is, so swift is the forgetting of them. And when a few years have passed, if some day—while we sit inertly looking at the light or listening to the silence—there should by chance return to our mind's ear some rousing stanzas, we do not recognize them at first and we torment our memory in order to recall where we heard them before. After a great deal of effort the ancient recollection wakens and we recall that those stanzas are from the hymn that the sailors were chanting, beautiful as the heroes of the *Iliad,* when the grand, the heavenly ships passed by and proceeded on their way going—who knows where.

Clothes *(1894–1897?)*

Inside a chest or inside a wardrobe of precious ebony I shall arrange and keep the clothing of my life.

The garments of azure. And then the scarlet, those most beautiful of all. And afterwards the yellow. And finally the azure once again, but far more faded, these latter, than the first.

I shall watch over them with devotion and great regret.

When I come to wear black garments, and dwell inside a black house, inside a dark room, every now and then I will open the chest with joy, with yearning, and with despair.

I will see the garments and will remember the great celebration which will, by then, be completely finished.

Completely finished. The furniture in disarray strewn throughout the great halls. Plates and glasses shattered on the ground. All of the candles burned down to the ends. All of the wine drunk up. All of the guests gone away. A few who are tired will sit all alone, like me, inside houses that are dark—others, more tired still, will have gone to sleep.

Poems Written in English

[More Happy Thou, Performing Member]

(1887?—1882?)

More happy thou, performing Member,
Who hast not need of wit's keen temper;
Thou standst on every side possessed
Of what Parnassus boasts as best.
On thy right sits, chief in wisdom's college,
Profound experience crowned with knowledge.
And further on, historic lore,
With erudition's ample store.
Third on thy right, imagination
Holds by no means a humble station.
But in thy front a dazzling light
Obscures your wavering mortal sight.
How shall I praise this man so blessed
Above the poor lot of the rest?
Diplomacy, Religion, Art,
Of Letters also every part,
Find in his penetrating eye,
Judgment which no man dares belie.
No one stands with him on a par,
Except of wits the transcendent star,
To whose seat, on thy left hand side,
My duteous homage I shall guide.

The tide of wit for ever flows
From his high throne. Now bellicose,
Fiery; now laughing and jocose.

And as men always persecute
True worth when joined to mind acute,
Against him anger is directed
When aught of wrong has been detected;
And all inspired by exasperation
Shout for a speedy situation.
Then, sole amid the increasing noise,
His wit to fruitful ends employs—
Silences every accusing voice
By proofs that none denies.—

      Be happy, Foreman, with thy station
Which offers wit and information
For every question and occasion.
Have always thy untiring sight
On thy left and on thy right;
Study each conduct and be taught
From every word and every thought.
What to believe & what to say—
When to say "yes" & when to say "nay,"
What to eat and what to drink,
What on everything to think,
How to dress and how to talk,
How to sleep and how to walk
For every human thing is brought
To perfection, and is taught
In this Pancosmium of Thought.—

Leaving Therápia (1882)

Good-bye to Therápia & joys of the hotel—
Good dinners that make you exultingly swell,
Good beds that refresh you from the toil of the day
Fine sights near which you'd wish ever to stay—
To all these good things the time is well nigh
      I must bid a Good-Bye!

However Catíkioy's opposite shore
I must hail tho' by far more simple & poor:
But they say what is simple is good at the heart
And where goodness is we may well spare art:
So at humble Catíkioy let us not rail
      But bid it All Hail!

Darkness and Shadows (1882?)

A transcription from the French of C. F. C.

Through smiling meadows ripening into gold,
And flowers engendered in new life and beauty
I wandered lithlessly. On every side
The hand beneficient of labour ruled;
And everywhere the people well content
With Nature's gifts prolific, nothing more
Desired, nor tempted Sorrow with the search
For things unprofitable, vain, obscure.

  In harmony and the celestial peace of love
They lived: and thriving reaped the fruits of toil.
They knew not envy, hatred nor despair;
Nor chained their minds to the dull misery
Of discontent, distrust and little faith.
Mercy and virtue, strength and hope were theirs;
Their minds in splendour shone alike the Sun.

  Behold however darkness seized the earth.
Darkness interminable, awful night,
And opaque shadows veiled the light of day.
Deep night like that which lay upon the seas
In the beginning of the World and Time;
Deep night that tamed the wild beasts of the field
Dismally wailing in the covert woods;
Deep night confounding into one all hues;

Deep night and endless, driving men to madness,
Making them blind and sorrowful to death.

And thereupon the multitudes began
In lamentations to reproach the Lord
With his injustice, speaking in this wise:
"Almighty, thou art good and merciful;
Almighty, we have seen and known thy love;
Almighty, we do know thee to be just.
Shew us, Father, wherein lies our sin
That we may chastise our iniquities!
An evil hour hath meted out to us
The direst of calamities: our babes
Are borne into the world in darkness, blind.
Thou hast deprived us of the fairest gift
In thy Creation. With the breath of life
Thy love awarded us the light of day;
But life in darkness is akin to death:
And death we pray Thee grant us if the light
Hath faded from the world for evermore!"—

It came to pass that God attended them,
And thus to the celestial Chorus spake:
"Of what doth man complain? And whence these tears?
He hath found favour in mine eyes. Behold
I have awarded him the joys of Heaven,
And cleansed his soul of its impurities.
The shadows that erewhile his mind obscured
Have I expelled and driven otherwhere."

But Michael mindful of man's happiness
Spake answering: "Thy mercy's great, O Lord;
The shadows that erewhile man's mind obscured
Hast Thou expelled and driven otherwhere.
But lo! So numerous were these, that now
They veil the Sun, and their obscurity
Hath wrapt the world in deep and endless night."

The Father of all Goodness, at these words,
Smiled, and his Spirit bade upon the earth
Descend. Forthwith a voice like thunder spake:

"Your vices and your sins were numberless,
Your hearts were hardened in iniquity,
Your minds darkened.—These evils were ye spared;
For I have chased the shadows, cleansed your souls.
But lo! So numerous were they, that now
They veil the Sun & their obscurity
Hath wrapt the world in deep and endless night."—

Together cried the multitudes, one voice:
"Almighty, thou art good and merciful.
Restore our minds to darkness, but vouchsafe
The essence of our life, the light of day!"—

And the Spirit answered: "Be it as ye will.
Behold, no longer is the Sun obscured."—

Once more the stars shone in the firmament,
The earth and deep lay bathed in luminence,
The mind of man in night's obscurity!—

NOTES

IMPORTANT CAVAFIAN CHARACTERS

A small number of historical figures and families recur so frequently in Cavafy's poetic landscape that readers would do well to get to know them before undertaking a reading of the poems—or, indeed, of these Notes. Accordingly, I have provided general introductions to this crucial handful of "Cavafian Characters" immediately below, before the Notes themselves. This is partly to give the reader a generous sense of who these people and dynasties are before he or she reads, in greater detail, about the specific incidents described in the poems and explained in the Notes; also, having an easily consulted concise biography of these characters will spare the reader having to scramble within the Notes to find the necessary information whenever one of these important and oft-encountered characters appears.

Otherwise, the Notes are straightforward. As the information about publication dates appears in the text of the poems itself, I have omitted discussion of the dates of composition and publication unless the details bear importantly on our understanding of the poem. The specific words or phrases from the text of a poem that seem to require explanation in the Notes— names of people or places, dates, etc.—appear in small capital letters.

All translations are mine unless otherwise indicated; translations of Cavafy's "Notes on Poetics and Ethics" quoted in the Introduction and the Notes are by Manuel Savidis.

Mark Antony, Triumvir and Ruler of the Roman East

MARCUS ANTONIUS (MARC ANTONY), soldier, statesman, co-ruler of Rome during the turbulent times when the Republic was crumbling, friend of Julius Caesar and lover and then husband of Cleopatra of Egypt, and above all a Roman who was besotted with all things Greek— not least, the greatest metropolis of the Greek-speaking East, Alexandria—is the subject of seven of Cavafy's poems. It is not difficult to see why he exerted such a fascination on the poet. This remarkable figure, in whose biography a considerable personal brilliance contrasted with an ultimate failure in a way that particularly appealed to Cavafy (as witness his poems about the Byzantine emperor John Cantacuzenus, below), embodied the tensions between Greek and Roman culture, between the rising Europe of the West and the more sophisticated, often decadent and multicultural East, to which the poet would return so often, in so many ways. Cavafy's special interest in what it meant to be Greek over the centuries was also excited by this complicated figure, a Roman who was irresistibly drawn to, and eventually absorbed by, Hellenistic culture.

Marc Antony was born in 83 B.C., as dramatic political and social upheavals in the Roman Republic were setting the stage for violent civil war that would result in the creation of the Empire—events in which Antony himself was to play a decisive role. After an apparently turbulent youth, he served in Palestine and Egypt in his mid-twenties, and soon after became attached to the staff of Julius Caesar, whose interests at home and abroad Antony vigorously supported. After the assassination of Caesar in 44 B.C., Antony shared supreme power at Rome with Caesar's adopted son, Octavian (later the emperor Augustus), and Marcus Lepidus as one of the *triumviri,* the three supreme leaders of the state; as part of his duties, he oversaw the reorganization of the eastern portion of Rome's empire.

It was during this phase of his career that Antony met Cleopatra, in the year 41 B.C., when she was twenty-eight and he forty-two. This remarkable, shrewd, ambitious, and brilliant queen had already been the lover of Julius Caesar, to whom she had borne a son, Caesarion (the subject of Cavafy's "Caesarion"); with her Antony began a relationship soon after their meeting, and she bore him twins, Alexander Helios and Cleopatra Selene, the year after they met. By 37 B.C., the alliance between Antony and Cleopatra had become political as well as personal: as Antony, supreme Roman leader in the East and increasingly enamored of Greek and Eastern ways, restored to Egypt certain portions of its former empire—even portions that belonged, properly speaking, to Rome—Cleopatra put Egypt's resources at Antony's disposal. In 34 B.C. the couple celebrated an elaborately symbolic ceremony known as the

"Donations," during which Cleopatra and her children were recognized as the rulers of an empire comprising all the lands that had been conquered by Alexander the Great three centuries before. The ceremony (to which Cavafy returns in his poem "Alexandrian Kings") was filled with religious and cultural symbolism, and suggested a revival of the Alexandrian vision of Greek empire in the East.

Following the Donations, relations between Antony and his fellow *triumvir* Octavian worsened dramatically, and the next year there was a bitter exchange of accusations between the two powerful men. Among other things, Octavian in Rome published the (alleged) contents of Antony's will, in which the Roman soldier asked to be buried in his beloved Alexandria; this was taken, as Octavian knew it would be, as a gross insult to Roman sensibilities. Finally, in 32 B.C., Octavian declared war on Cleopatra—and, therefore, on Antony. After their defeat by Octavian and his fleet at the Battle of Actium in 31 B.C., Antony and Cleopatra both committed suicide (in August of the following year). Ironically, Antony and Octavian would remain intertwined through their descendants: through his two daughters, both called Antonia, Marc Antony was an ancestor of the emperors Gaius ("Caligula"), Claudius, and Nero, and of Messalina, the adulterous wife of Claudius who was eventually executed for her sexual excesses.

Apollonius of Tyana, Sage and Magician

The first-century A.D. sage and miracle worker APOLLONIUS OF TYANA (a town in the Roman province of Cappadocia, in central Asia Minor) was a figure of lasting fascination for Cavafy, who during his lifetime published three works about the remarkable Apollonius—"But Wise Men Apprehend What Is Imminent" (*1896*; *1899*; *1915*), "If Indeed He Died" (*1897*; *1910*; *1920*), "Apollonius of Tyana in Rhodes" (*?*; *1925*)—and left the draft of another, "Among the Groves of the Promenades," now published as one of the Unfinished Poems. This cycle of poems makes clear the poet's great intimacy with our primary source for the life of Apollonius, which itself is one of the most remarkable works of Greek literature under the Roman Empire: the sprawling, rather baroque *Life of Apollonius of Tyana* by the third-century littérateur Flavius

Philostratus, episodes from which provide the inspiration for all of Cavafy's Apollonius poems.

An itinerant Neopythagorean philosopher who lived through much of the first century A.D., Apollonius is reported to have traveled widely, as far as Ethiopia and India; these travels inevitably give Philostratus's *Life* much of its vivid, *Odyssey*-like color. After his death, Apollonius became renowned both for his defiance of Roman despots—the climax of the first half of the *Life* is a confrontation with Nero; the climax of the second half, a confrontation with Domitian—and for his magical powers, which were said to have included the ability not only to heal the sick and raise the dead, but to see into the near future. (Philostratus's *Life,* composed as Christianity was rising to its ultimate power in Roman society, much later became a useful text for those seeking to present the philosophical and miracle-working Oriental Greek as a pagan rival to Christ.) For instance, the sage of Tyana is said not only to have had a telepathic vision of the assassination of Domitian (the subject of "Among the Groves of the Promenades"), but also to have predicted a plague that struck the city of Ephesus in Asia Minor. It was, in fact, this prediction that was later held against him when he was accused by an Egyptian enemy of various crimes and impieties, among them sorcery. Apollonius was subsequently tried before the notoriously cruel emperor Domitian (Titus Flavius Domitianus, 51–96 A.D.). In the *Life,* whose relationship to the historical truth is, to be sure, often casual, the trial scene—a grand occasion for displays of rhetorical pyrotechnics—takes up nearly all of the final book.

Already in an 1892 essay on Keats's *Lamia* (a poem that takes its *donnée* from Philostratus's tale of a lady vampire), Cavafy refers to the *Life of Apollonius* as a "storehouse of poetic material," and indeed two of the four Apollonius poems can be confidently dated to the mid- to late 1890s, just a few years later. This was the decade in which, as the scholar Diana Haas has shown in great detail in her important study of the religious issues in Cavafy's early work (*Le problème religieux dans l'oeuvre de Cavafy: Les années de formation [1882–1905],* Sorbonne, 1996), the poet was struggling to find a way to write meaningfully about religious belief, and the work of this period indeed betrays an interest in the supernatural, the uncanny, and telepathic knowledge that was to last his entire life. (They are also phenomena that recur in the fin-de-siècle Continental poetry—Symbolist, Esoteric, Decadent—that influenced him so strongly in those years.) That interest is evident not only in the many poems treating those themes (and hardly only in connection with Apollonius: see, for example, "Theodotus," "Since Nine—," "Caesarion," and the Unfinished Poems "Athanasius" and "From the Unpublished History") but also in his taste for tales of the fantastic (cf. his own ghost story, "In Broad Daylight") and in his belief, greatly influenced by the Parnassians and articulated with particular emphasis in a number of the early poems, that the poet was a kind of seer gifted with second sight. (See, for instance, the Unpublished Poem "Correspondences According to Baudelaire.")

Cavafy's religious crisis of the 1890s suggests a further explanation for the origins of his interest in Apollonius during those years. This was when he was trying to arrive at a unified vision of Hellenic identity from the Hellenistic monarchies through the fall of Constantinople to his own day—a vision, ultimately, that would allow him to synthesize Greek history, the Orthodox faith (from the early Christian era to his own time), and also a pagan homoeroticism. It is in this context that we do well to recall the Italian historian Arnoldo Momigliano's observation that the supernaturally gifted pagan hero of the *Life of Apollonius of Tyana* was, in fact, a figure whose literary influence can be felt in St. Athanasius's *Life of Saint Anthony,* the prototype for the Christian hagiography. Apart from his considerable inherent interest, then, Apollonius is a crucial figure because, as Cavafy surely understood, he is yet another link in a chain that binds the pagan and Christian Greek worlds.

It should be said, too, with respect to the *Life of Apollonius of Tyana,* that the biographer was of as great an interest to Cavafy as the subject was. Flavius Philostratus (ca. 170–240 A.D.) was a distinguished man of letters, of Greek origin, and a favorite of Julia Domna, wife of the emperor Septimius Severus; it was at her request that the *Life* was written. Cavafy's championing of Philostratus may therefore be seen as deeply connected to his sense of himself as a "Hellenistic" figure—an inhabitant of Greater Greece, a passionate heir to Greek culture living far from mainland Greece itself. An almost prickly impatience with the cultural snobberies of the European intellectual establishment (with its almost exclusive focus on "high" Classicism and Athens) is, indeed, evident in the *Lamia* article:

> Foreign scholars generally speak condescendingly about Philostratus and his works, just as they speak condescendingly about many writers of the decadent phase, as they are accustomed to call it, of Greek literature.

Julian the Apostate

The Roman emperor JULIAN (331?–363 A.D.), called "THE APOSTATE" because of his efforts to restore the newly Christianized Roman Empire to pagan worship, is the figure who more than any other preoccupied Cavafy's creative mind throughout his career. In the work he prepared for publication, there are six Julian poems: "Julian, Seeing Indifference," "Julian in Nicomedia," "A Great Procession of Priests and Laymen," "Julian and the Antiochenes," "You Didn't Understand," and "On the Outskirts of Antioch"; the Unpublished Poems give us "Julian at the Mysteries"; and the publication, in 1994, of the texts of the poet's Unfinished Poems adds to this already substantial cycle an extraordinary trove of four more works, which can be confidently dated to between 1920 and 1926: "Athanasius," "The Bishop Pegasius," "The Rescue of Julian," and "Hunc Deorum Templis"; there are also fragments of an untitled poem beginning "Fifteen years had passed . . . ," which also has Julian as its theme. Twelve poems in all, then, devoted to one complex and enigmatic figure who evoked in Cavafy an unflagging if negative fascination. Given Cavafy's supreme preoccupation with the character of Greek identity as transmitted from the pagan ancient world through Byzantine Christianity to the present day, his preoccupation with the apostate emperor, struggling to reimpose pagan worship, is not difficult to understand.

Born probably in 331 A.D., Flavius Claudius Julianus was the son of Constantine the Great's half brother, Julius Constantius; as befitted a member of the newly Christian Imperial Family, the young Julian was raised as a Christian, and even ordained a Lector in the church (the office held by the title character in "Tomb of Ignatius"). His childhood was marred by a trauma that had a great effect on his emerging character, which, for all of the young man's intellectual precociousness (and, later, his undeniable military ability and administrative canniness), was secretive, distrustful, high-handed, and often contemptuous of opposition and criticism. In 337, on the death of his half uncle Constantine the Great, many members of Julian's immediate family were executed, most likely on order of the new emperor, Constantine's son Constantius II, who undoubtedly saw in the profusion of half uncles and half cousins a source of future rivalries. The six-year-old Julian and his twelve-year-old half brother, Gallus, were spared apparently only because of their extreme youth. (For their rescue by Christian priests, an act about which the adult Julian showed an appalling lack of gratitude, see the Unfinished Poem "The Rescue of Julian.")

Julian's childhood and adolescence were solitary: from the ages of eleven to seventeen he lived in exile on the royal estate of Macellum in Cappadocia, carefully watched over by Constantius's agents. But an early exposure to the pagan classics by a beloved teacher provided the impetus for what would become a lifelong obsession with the pre-Christian Greek culture that he later sought to champion. The combination of the psychologically traumatizing loss of virtually his entire family, his precarious political position vis-à-vis his cousin, the Christian emperor, and the solace that the solitary, bookish youth clearly found in the Greek classics all help to explain Julian's susceptibility, later in adolescence, to the less rational, more mystical branches of Neoplatonic teachings, with their emphasis on portents, signs, and divine magic or theurgy. By the time he was twenty, in 351, he seems to have been fully converted to paganism, although he successfully concealed his religious inclinations until his accession to the throne ten years later. This patient and calculating duplicity held particular fascination for Cavafy (as witness, for instance, "Julian in Nicomedia" and the Unfinished Poem "The Bishop Pegasius")—not least, it seems safe to assume, because it resonated with the rather different but equally necessary caution and self-concealment with which Cavafy, as a homosexual, was painfully familiar, as many of his earlier poems witness.

This two-facedness served Julian well for the rest of his life. As a result of the intervention of Constantius's wife, the empress Eusebia, who seems to have had a soft spot for the young prince, Julian was recalled from exile, and late in 355, at the age of twenty-four, he was granted the title of Caesar by his cousin the emperor and given a military command in Gaul, where rebellious tribes had been a thorn in Constantius's side for some time. Over the next several years he proved himself an able commander and resoundingly defeated the Germanic tribes of the Alammani and the Franks, restoring the Roman frontier on the Rhine. Made uneasy, no doubt, by his young cousin's military successes and popularity with his legions—but also sorely pressed in his own military adventures against the Persians—Constantius early in 360 sent an emissary to Julian demanding that he send between one-third and one-half of his army to serve under Constantius in the East. This was the pretext for the open break with his cousin that Julian had been waiting for: in Paris, instigated very likely by Julian and his few intimates, the troops acclaimed him Augustus, but open civil war was avoided when Constantius II died in 361, as Julian was marching to meet him.

Julian's reign was a short one: he was killed in battle in the spring of 363 as he was retreating from a major campaign against the Persians. But his rule nonetheless betrayed the single-minded ruthlessness and subtle duplicity that had characterized his youth and young manhood. Vigorous fiscal and bureaucratic reforms, while in many ways salubrious, were also cunningly contrived to deprive Christian prelates of property and power while reviving a model of civic administration based on that of the Classical Greek city-states; similarly, although his restoration of status and real power to pagan cults was balanced by an ostensible refusal to persecute Christians, his occasional solicitousness toward certain Christian clerics usually had purely political motivations; Christian professors were, moreover, forbidden to teach the classics, and certain Christian clerics were in fact persecuted.

Indeed, despite a nostalgic yearning for the culture of the great Classical past that would have seemed, at first glance, to make Julian a sympathetic figure in the eyes of Cavafy, the Apostate is a figure for whom the poet has no little disdain—even contempt. For Julian's paganism was characterized by an asceticism and puritanical outlook that one might rather have expected from the early church fathers, and that was distinctly at odds with Cavafy's own hard-won and humane celebration of sensuality. For Cavafy, it was the pleasure-loving and indulgent Christians of the fourth century A.D., with their taste for luxury and leisure, for horse racing and the theater, who were the truer heirs to the pagan culture of the Greek east. The strange and sharp ironies of Cavafy's use of this figure are well summed up in the evaluation of the scholar G. W. Bowersock in his biography of Julian:

> There was nothing romantic or colourful about the paganism which Julian proposed to establish in the place of the religion of Constantine. Its austerity and the fanatical zeal of its advocate portended the end of the way of life which had not only replaced the old paganism but actually absorbed its *joie de vivre*. The deadly earnestness of Julian was manifest and unwelcome.

John VI Cantacuzenus, Emperor of Byzantium

The fourteenth-century Byzantine emperor JOHN VI CANTACUZENUS (ca. 1295–June 15, 1383; reigned 1347–1354), the brilliant, talented, and ultimately failed "reluctant emperor," has been much admired by historians since his own time, from his contemporary, the verbose but not unintelligent chronicler Nicephorus Gregoras ("he would have been one of the greatest of Byzantine emperors") to Gibbon, who greatly respected his adherence to principle despite the enormous temptations of ambition, to John Julius Norwich, who in his 1995 study *Byzantium: The Decline and Fall* refers to Cantacuzenus as "a man of integrity, courage, high intelligence and a rare degree of political vision." In Cavafy's work he emerges as a representative of the kind of person for whom this poet consistently expresses admiration no matter what period he may have belonged to: someone who upholds the standards and values of his culture even as that civilization crumbles around him. He is the subject of four significant poems, two Published and two Unfinished, which together constitute an important cycle within the poet's oeuvre: "John Cantacuzenus Triumphs" (1924), "Of Colored Glass" (1925), "The Patriarch" (February 1925), and "On Epiphany" (December 1925).

Cantacuzenus, the scion of a wealthy and powerful family who rose to the supreme political position of Great Domestic, was the loyal friend, closest adviser, and general of Emperor Andronicus III Palaeologus. When Andronicus died in 1341, he left a son (later John V), aged nine; his will directed that Cantacuzenus be regent for the minor sovereign. However, his regency was almost immediately challenged by a powerful faction at court led by the tremendously ambitious Admiral Apocaucus ("bold and subtle, rapacious and profuse," says Gibbon) and the scheming Patriarch of the church, John XIV Calecas. (Cantacuzenus, ironically, had been responsible for the elevation of both men; in a letter cited by Nicephorus Gregoras in his chronicle, a source Cavafy was well familiar with, Cantacuzenus bitterly reminded Calecas that he had helped him secure the patriarchate in 1334.) These men together persuaded the widowed empress, Anna of Savoy, that her dead husband's friend was planning to usurp the throne (something he could easily have done on Andronicus's death, had he wished); after Anna claimed control of the boy herself, the three began a campaign of vicious harassment against Cantacuzenus and his party that ultimately resulted in the civil war of 1341–1347.

The interlude proved to be one of the most disastrous and demoralizing in the history of the empire: during the six years before Cantacuzenus returned in triumph and took the throne for himself, Anna and her party, who had no experience of governance and few ideas about how to rule the empire they had appropriated, laid waste the empire's treasuries and seriously damaged the economy, made alliances with Genoa and Venice that would prove to weaken Byzantium considerably, and went as far as to pawn the crown jewels to the Venetians, for 30,000 ducats. (As a result of the latter outrage, Cantacuzenus and his queen were forced to wear regalia made of paste during their coronation, an episode that furnishes the material for "Of Colored Glass.") Among the many grotesqueries to which the coalition of the weak empress and her power-hungry advisers descended was a desperate promise to the pope by the Italian-born Anna that she and they would embrace the Roman faith in return for his support—although this promise was made in letters that may well have been forged in Anna's name by the impressively unscrupulous Apocaucus, with an eye to eventually discrediting her and seizing the throne for himself.

Although Cavafy, as we know from his reading notes to Gibbon, was often impatient with the latter's disdainful view of Byzantium, the two men are united in their admiration for Cantacuzenus, who even as he was forced into open rebellion by the outrages committed against himself, his friends, and his family by Anna and her party, clung to the forms of law, insisting, when he was declared emperor in October 1341, that no crowning take place, and that he was merely protecting the rights of the young John. ("But even in this act of revolt, he was still studious of loyalty; and the titles of John Palaeologus and Anne of Savoy were proclaimed before his own name and that of his wife Irene.")

In time, Cantacuzenus prevailed. He possessed enormous wealth of his own—sufficient, Gibbon reports, to equip a fleet of seventy ships out of his own funds—and was supported by powerful allies in central and northern Greece; eventually, he also had Serbian and Turkish troops at his disposal. In Constantinople, meanwhile, Anna was in trouble. In 1345 Apocaucus was murdered by some opponents whom he had had imprisoned; later, after discovering to her great rage that Calecas had been trying secretly to conclude a peace agreement with Cantacuzenus, Anna had the Patriarch deposed on trumped-up theological charges. She had at last achieved sole rule, but her triumph was short-lived: in February 1347, immediately after the deposition of Calecas, John Cantacuzenus stormed his way into the city and, with remarkable but characteristic evenhandedness, forced the empress to accept quite reasonable terms, which stipulated that he be crowned emperor, with her son, the fifteen-year-old John Palaeologus, as co-emperor. ("John Cantacuzenus Triumphs" takes the form of a monologue by a disappointed supporter of Anna and the Patriarch; to such former enemies Cantacuzenus showed admirable generosity.) His wife, the great noblewoman Irene Asenina—daughter of a powerful aristocrat, Andronicus Asen, granddaughter of the Bulgarian tsar John III, and great-granddaughter of Michael VIII, emperor and founder of the Paleologue dynasty—was crowned with him, and their daughter Helena was simultaneously married to the teenage John V. And so, as Gibbon dryly puts it, "Two emperors and three empresses were seated on the Byzantine throne."

However, by 1352 relations between the two co-emperors had deteriorated (not least, Gibbon tells us, because "Constantinople was still

attached to the blood of her ancient princes; and this last injury acceler-
ated the restoration of the rightful heir"), and another civil war broke
out. This time, Cantacuzenus was defeated by John V, and in 1354 he was
forced to abdicate. He thereafter became a monk, calling himself Joa-
saph, and during his monastic retirement devoted himself to matters
theological ("he sharpened a controversial pen against the Jews and
Mahometans," Gibbon reports) and to writing his admirably meticulous
and reflective (although inevitably self-justifying) memoirs in four
books, the *Historiai,* or "Histories." These were modeled, in part,
on Thucydides' work; the Unfinished Poem "On Epiphany" rather
poignantly refers to them. The quality of having persisted in his political
life with no little dignity against tremendous odds, and of then having
retreated from the world stage with an equal decorum, clearly capti-
vated Cavafy's imagination. We might compare the poet's apparent
approval for the quiet abdication of Demetrius Poliorcetes in "King
Demetrius," and, by contrast, his disdain for the self-serving quality of
the histories written by the scheming Anna Comnena in her forced
retirement, in "Anna Comnena."

The fact that all of the Cantacuzenus poems date to the mid-1920s sug-
gests, to my mind, a final and particularly bitter layer of irony, one of
which Cavafy, like any student of late Byzantine history, would have
been well aware: for this date suggests that at some level, the Can-
tacuzenus cycle was, at least in part, inspired by the disastrous conclu-
sion of the Greco-Turkish War of 1919–1922. This war arose out of the
irredentist concept of the *Megali Idea,* or "Great Idea," the longstanding
nationalist Greek dream (and a cornerstone of foreign policy almost
since the establishment of the independent Greek state in the 1820s) of
a "Greater Greece" encompassing large Greek Christian communities,
such as that in Izmir (Smyrna), living under Turkish domination in Asia
Minor. The war began with a massive Greek landing at Smyrna, and at
first went well for the Greeks; but as Turkish resistance stiffened, the
tide began to turn. The years 1921 and 1922 saw reverses for the
Greeks, starting in the interior and moving toward the coast, a trajec-
tory that culminated in the Turks' recapture of Smyrna and their atro-
cious massacre of the Christian population of that city in September

1922. A month later an armistice was concluded, and the following year saw the harrowing exchange of populations between the two implacably hostile states. Cavafy's friend Polis Modinos recalled how, a few days after the Smyrna disaster, he found the poet alone at home, sitting grief-stricken in his usual chair. Presently Cavafy exclaimed, "Smyrna is lost! Ionia is lost! The Gods are lost! . . ." Unable to go on, he simply wept in silence.

The bitter relations between Greeks and Turks in the 1920s, the failed fantasy of a pure Greek territorial dominion over Greeks, the specter of Ottoman control over European Christians: Cavafy the historian in the twentieth century would have acutely understood the ironic significance that John Cantacuzenus's story, in the fourteenth century, had for these themes. For in order to gain the upper hand against Apocaucus's forces, Cantacuzenus had successfully concluded an alliance with the Ottoman emir Orhan (cemented by a controversial marriage between his daughter, Theodora Cantacuzene, and the Muslim leader); but the use of many thousands of Turkish troops, who successfully fought for John in his war against Anna and Apocaucus in the early 1340s and then again, a decade later, helped John in his campaign in the Balkans, was the step that led to the establishment of a permanent Turkish presence in the European continent, and eventually resulted in the Ottoman conquest of the Balkans. Hence John, whom Cavafy warmly describes in one of the poems in this cycle as "the glory of our [Byzantine] race," may be seen as being ultimately responsible for the defeat of that race—a conclusion to which Gibbon had also bitterly come:

> To acquire the friendship of their emirs, the two factions vied with each other in baseness and profusion: the dexterity of Cantacuzene obtained the preference: but the succor and victory were dearly purchased by the marriage of his daughter with an infidel, the captivity of many thousand Christians, and the passage of the Ottomans into Europe, the last and fatal stroke in the fall of the Roman empire.

That fall was the cultural, ideological, and historical disaster which the "Megali Idea" was meant, in some large sense, to correct: a great idea which, as we know—and as Cavafy knew, when he was working on these poems—ended in the dreadful disaster that "lost Ionia."

The Hellenistic Dynasties

A significant number of Cavafy's poems treat, in some detail, monarchs belonging to the various royal houses of the Hellenistic era (conventionally dated from the death of Alexander the Great, in 323 B.C., after which those monarchies were established, to the death of Cleopatra, in 30 B.C., at which point the last of the independent dynasties, that of Egypt, was absorbed into Rome). Detailed comment about individual characters can be found in the Notes to the poems themselves, but any reader who wishes to read the poet's work with comprehension should have at least a general grasp of this complex and convoluted era. For Cavafy, the Hellenistic world, in which local cultures across the breadth of Asia had been hybridized with Greek influences, and which eventually would come into conflict with the emerging power of Rome to the west (which would ultimately defeat and absorb those cultures), was a rich matrix of material that allowed him to explore, first, the meaning of Hellenic identity, and also to reflect on the nature of power, the vagaries of fate, and the ironies of history.

When Alexander died in Babylon at the age of thirty-three, he had neither left a son nor indicated clearly who among his loyal generals his successor was to be. (In response to the inevitable question of succession, he is said on his deathbed to have uttered the words *tôi kratistôi,* "to the strongest"; it being highly improbable that he wanted to incite the rivalries that would, indeed, later tear his empire apart, it seems far likelier that what he actually said was *tôi Kraterôi,* "to Craterus," his loyal general.) Within a year, the first of three Wars of Succession that would radically change the political map of the world over the next two decades had begun. When the last of those struggles was over, three new realms had been carved out of the carcass of Alexander's world empire, ruled by three dynasties: the Antigonids, who first controlled the eastern portions of Asia Minor and part of Syria, and eventually became the ruling house of Macedon itself, Alexander's homeland; the Seleucids, who ended up controlling most of Alexander's Asian conquests, from Anatolia in the west to India in the east; and the Lagids, the dynastic name of the Ptolemaic kings of Egypt (because its founder's father had been called Lagus: the ending -*id* in Greek means "son of" or, more broadly, "descendant of").

The ANTIGONIDS were so-called because they were descended from Alexander's general Antigonus the One-Eyed (382–301 B.C.). Antigonus had been made governor of much of Asia Minor during Alexander's lifetime; after the latter's death, he received even more of that vast territory. During the next decade, Antigonus made several spectacular bids to take control of even more of the former empire, from Egypt to central Asia; he was killed, at the age of eighty-one, in one of the many battles he waged to this end. Eventually, however, his descendants did become the rulers of Macedon. Among them were Demetrius Poliorcetes ("the Besieger"), the subject of the poem "King Demetrius"; Philip V, who would support the Romans against the Seleucid emperor Antiochus III, the subject of "The Battle of Magnesia"; and Perseus, whose defeat by the Romans in 168 B.C. brought an end to the Antigonid house and to Macedonian independence, and who is referred to in a number of poems, including "For Antiochus Epiphanes."

The SELEUCIDS were descended from Seleucus (ca. 358–281 B.C.), an officer in Alexander's army who had become the commander in chief of the army of Alexander's general Perdiccas. The ruthlessly ambitious Seleucus later helped to assassinate Perdiccas in a bid for power for himself; under a treaty concluded with the other Successors in 320, he received the territory of Babylon but, as a result of both military aggression (including a defeat of Antigonus the One-Eyed) and canny diplomacy, he eventually expanded his empire to include a vast stretch of territory from Asia Minor and Syria (including the territory that would later become Judea) in the west, to India in the east—the largest by far of the successor states. The descendants of Seleucus (later given the epithet *Nicator,* "Conqueror") include a number of monarchs named Seleucus, Antiochus, and Demetrius, several of whom are the subjects of Cavafy's poems: see, for instance, "The Seleucid's Displeasure," "Of Demetrius Soter," "For Antiochus Epiphanes," and the Unfinished Poem "Antiochus Cyzicenus."

The LAGIDS were the ruling dynasty of Egypt from 305 B.C., when the house was founded by Alexander's general (and, according to some, half brother) Ptolemy I (367–283 B.C.), until the suicide of his distant descendant Cleopatra VII. All of the pharaohs of the house bore the name Ptolemy; their queens, who in the Egyptian tradition were often also their sisters, most often were named Cleopatra and Berenice. Ptolemy I had been named ruler of Egypt immediately following Alexander's death; alone among the Successors, his ambitions never got the best of him, and during the Wars of Succession he showed himself content to secure his power base in Egypt and the surrounding areas. In 305 B.C. he declared himself pharaoh; but his bid for supreme power had begun two decades earlier, when he hijacked the funeral cortege that was meant to take Alexander's body back to Macedon. Ptolemy eventually placed the meticulously embalmed body in a magnificent mausoleum in Alexandria, the great Hellenic city that Alexander had founded and which would become a second Athens, the leading city of the Hellenistic world. The dynasty founded by this shrewd old man would become distinguished for the spectacular corruption and ruthlessness showed by its incestuous members. Many of Cavafy's poems are devoted to the Lagids, particularly those who figured in the complex power plays between Rome and the Successor states: for example, "Envoys from Alexandria," "The Seleucid's Displeasure," and "Caesarion."

PUBLISHED POEMS

Poems 1905–1915

The City *pg. 5*

Cavafy wrote an early version of this poem (entitled "In the Same City") in 1894 and worked on it for the next fifteen years; it was finally published in the magazine *Nea Zoe* in April 1910.

It is easy to see why the poet, in arranging his first printed collection, chose this poem and the one that follows, "The Satrapy," as the portals through which readers must pass in order to encounter his work: between them, they embrace his important themes, which would be developed, teased out, varied, and elaborated in the poems that follow. "The Satrapy," like so many historical poems, contemplates the meaning of success and failure in life through the (often ironic) perspective of historical hindsight. In "The City," the problem of the unfulfilled or failed life also emerges as a central preoccupation, but one perceived through the lens not of time but of place: here, the individual is seen within the frame of the metropolis and its overpowering aura. A comment by the poet concerning this important poem has been preserved:

> The man who has ruined his life will try in vain to live it again better, more ethically . . . The city, an imaginary city, will prevent and follow him and wait for him with the same streets and the same quarters.

A note from April 1907 makes it clear that the importance of the city in question lay in the dense network of emotional associations that it conjures in the poet's mind—something that could be as true of a marginal city such as Alexandria in the early twentieth century (however frustrating its provincialism could be) as it was of the great contemporary metropolises:

> I have grown accustomed to Alexandria, and it is quite prob-able that even if I were rich I would stay here. But, despite this, how it constricts me. What an impediment, what a bur-den a small town is—what an absence of freedom.
>
> I would stay here (then again I am not completely sure if I would remain) because it is like a homeland, because it is associated with the memories of my life.
>
> Yet, how necessary for a man like me—so particular—is a big city.

If anything, the circumscribed life of a provincial city had its artistic advantages. Another crucial and related theme in "The City" is what Cavafy, in a letter to his friend Pericles Anastassiades that accompanied an autographed copy of the poem, referred to as "ennui":

> There is a class of poems whose role is "suggestif." My poem comes under that head. To a sympathetic reader—sympa-thetic by culture—who will think over the poem for a minute or two, my lines, I am convinced, will suggest an image of the deep, the endless "desésperance" [desperation] which they contain "yet cannot all reveal."

George Seferis, in his journals (whose title in Greek, *Meres,* "Days," self-consciously echoes the title of many of Cavafy's poems), recalls a con-versation that took place in April 1939, when he and Constantine Dimaras, later the century's great scholar of Modern Greek literature, were attempting to characterize Cavafy's poetry to André Gide, who was unfamiliar with it. Dimaras said it was "lyric"; Seferis claimed it was "didactic." Dimaras then read "The City" aloud to Gide, who turned to Seferis and said, "Now I understand what you meant by the word 'didactic.' "

The Satrapy

SATRAPY was the technical term given to the large administrative districts, comprising whole provinces, into which the Persian Empire was divided; in the time of Darius the Great, who reigned in the fifth century B.C. and was the Persian ruler who invaded Greece in 490 B.C. (as described in Herodotus's *Persian Wars*), the empire was divided into twenty satrapies.

SUSA was the capital of Persia under the Achaemenid dynasty, to which Darius belonged; the dynasty ruled Persia from the mid-sixth century B.C. until the death of Darius III in 330 B.C., following his defeat in battle by Alexander the Great.

ARTAXERXES was the name given to several important Persian monarchs, beginning with Artaxerxes I (reigned 464–424 B.C.), who was the grandson of Darius the Great: his father, Xerxes, Darius's son, led the second major invasion of Greece, also described by Herodotus.

Cavafy himself, in one of his "Self-Commentaries," asserted that the addressee of this poem is meant to be an artist or even a scientist, and not a public figure:

> The poet is not necessarily thinking of Themistocles or Demaratos or any other political character . . . the person intended is entirely symbolic, and we must rather take him to be an artist or man of learning who after failures and disappointments abandons his art and goes to Susa and Artaxerxes, that is changes his life and in another way of life finds luxury (which is a sort of happiness) but it cannot satisfy him. The line in parenthesis is important: *the day when you let yourself go, and you give in,* for it is the base of the whole poem because of the hint that the hero too easily lost heart, that he exaggerated the events, and was in too much of a hurry to take the road to Susa.

Still, the context of the poem and its reference to Artaxerxes strongly suggests that the poet had at least, at some point, been inspired by the later history of the fifth-century B.C. Athenian politician Themistocles (ca. 528–462 B.C.). As commander of the allied fleet during the Second Persian War, Themistocles scored stunning victories over Xerxes at the battles of Artemisium (480 B.C.) and Salamis (479 B.C.), which put an end to Persia's ambitions in mainland Greece. Despite these successes, Themistocles was forced to leave Athens in 471, as a result of the machinations of his political enemies, and after a brief sojourn in Sparta escaped to Persia, where he was welcomed by the king, Artaxerxes I, who made Themistocles the satrap of Magnesia-on-Meander.

Cavafy makes another reference to the poem in one of his private notes, dated November 29, 1903:

> Yesterday I vaguely considered, it crossed my thoughts, the possibility of literary failure, & I felt suddenly as if all charm would have left my life, I felt an acute pang at the very idea. I at once imagined my having the enjoyment of love—as I understand & want it—& even this seemed—& very clearly seemed—as if it would not have been sufficient to console me of the great deception [= "disappointment"].
> This proves the verity of "The Satrapy."

But Wise Men Apprehend What Is Imminent   *pg. 7*

This is the first poem that Cavafy wrote about Apollonius of Tyana, and its publication history sheds light on the growing importance that the sage and mystic had for him. An early version, entitled "Imminent Things," was written in February 1896 and published in December 1899. That poem also bore the epigraph from Philostratus's *Life,* but the poet's decision, later on, to use a citation from that work as the title of the revised poem marks a special desire to draw attention to the ancient text itself. The passage in question comes from Book 8 of the *Life,* a scene in which Apollonius defends himself to Domitian against charges of sorcery. Here the seer protests that his ability to perceive imminent disasters is due to the elevated state—what he calls a "subtlety of the senses"—that he is able to achieve through his ascetic regimen and diet, derived from the teachings of Pythagoras.

The poem occupies a strategic place in Cavafy's arrangement of

Poems 1905–1915 (and indeed in its precursors). It is the first of four that share a common theme: that is, the way in which men are called upon, and sometimes fail, to perceive crucial messages coming from outside their world. That this theme was of particular importance is evident in the placement of this set of four—the present poem, "Ides of March," "The Gods Abandon Antony," and "Theodotus"—immediately after the two opening poems, which, as George Savidis observed, constitute the portal through which the reader is meant to enter into these collections.

Ides of March *pg. 8*

Julius CAESAR was assassinated on the IDES (the 15th) of March in 44 B.C. As Caesar made his way that morning to the Senate, where he hoped to hear himself declared king of Rome, a Greek scholar called ARTEMIDORUS tried to place a letter into his hand warning him of the plot to kill him, but was rebuffed. This poem, like "Theodotus," uses Caesar's career as a vehicle for pondering the vagaries of fortune.

The God Abandons Antony *pg. 10*

The title of this poem, in Classical Greek, is a quotation from Plutarch's *Life of Antony,* chapter 75. Here Plutarch describes the last night of Marc Antony's life, when his troops had deserted him for Octavian and all Alexandria knew that Antony's cause was totally lost:

> It is said that, about halfway through this night, while inside the city all was quiet and dejected because of the fear and the anticipation of what was yet to come, suddenly there was heard the combined sounds of all sorts of instruments, and the shouting of a crowd, along with merrymaking and festive acrobatics, as if a procession were leaving the city with no little tumult . . . To those interpreting this sign it seemed as though the god to whom Antony once most likened himself [i.e., Dionysus] and to whom he was most dedicated, was now abandoning him.

Of special interest here is the emphasis on the faculty of hearing as the vehicle for apprehending the true significance of what is taking place, a connection that strongly links this poem to "But Wise Men Apprehend What Is Imminent," the first in this series of four poems about the wise man's preparedness—or lack thereof—for the uncertainties of life.

Theodotus pg. 11

This poem was written prior to 1911; Savidis identified that early version with a poem listed in one of Cavafy's chronological catalogues with the title "Victory." This final version was first published in 1915.

THEODOTUS of Chios, a rhetorician at the court of the Ptolemies in Alexandria, is said to have urged the murder of POMPEY (Gnaius Pompeius Magnus, 106–48 B.C.), the powerful rival of Julius Caesar. Pompey had once ruled Rome alongside Caesar, but his relationship with his onetime colleague disintegrated, and eventually the two met in a pitched battle at Pharsalus, where Pompey was defeated in 48. He then fled to Egypt, where he was stabbed to death on landing there, in September 48 B.C. Caesar was said to have been disgusted when his supporters, thinking to please him, brought him the severed head of the man whom, although a deadly rival, he admired greatly. It was at the foot of a statue of Pompey, erected in the Roman Senate, that Caesar himself was assassinated in 44 B.C. (the subject of "Ides of March").

Cavafy wrote a "self-commentary" in which he ponders the motif, which recurs strikingly throughout his work, of invisible and immaterial apparitions and their relation to the visible and material worlds. This motif was of interest not least because it was connected, in turn, to his larger interest, heavily influenced by his youthful reading of the Parnassian poets and the Symbolists, in the exalted status of poets, seers, and sages, and their special, privileged knowledge of the world's mysteries. Cavafy discussed these themes in connection with the present poem:

> What is ἄυλο [immaterial] is not always invisible. Things seen in hallucinations are "ἄυλα", but they are visible, at least to one person, although one who has the hallucination. Ghosts

are "ἄυλα" [immaterial], but not invisible (we are in the domain of poetry, of the imagination, it should be remembered).

As for the ἄυλος [immaterial] Theodotos bringing a head, it is, reasonably, taken as being understood that the head is "ἄυλο" [immaterial] too. Theodotus in the first part of the poem, & things pertaining to him, Alexandria, the tray, the head are in the concrete, in the material. In the next part of the poem, Theodotos passes in to the domain of the metaphysical, he is spiritual, he & the things he carries.

For more on the motif of invisible apparitions, see the note on "Since Nine—," pp. 399–400.

Monotony
pg. 12

The poem was first written in July 1898, with the title "Like a Past"; it was published with the present title in 1908. Like many of the poems written in the 1890s—particularly the Unpublished Poems "Builders" (1891) and "The Bank of the Future" (1897)—it offers a particularly bleak vision of future progress.

Ithaca
pg. 13

An early version was written in 1894; the present version was composed in October 1910 and published in November of the following year.

The addressee of the poem is Homer's Odysseus, the quintessential Greek wanderer with a quintessentially Greek mind: curious, avid, hungry for knowledge and experience. In the *Odyssey,* the monsters that Odysseus encounters on his ten-year voyage home from Troy include man-eating giants called LAESTRYGONIANS, as well as Polyphemus, one of the race of CYCLOPS (primitive, cannibalistic giants), whom Odysseus blinds in a famous episode recounted in Book 9 of the poem. Because Polyphemus is actually a son of the sea god POSEIDON, Poseidon vengefully pursues Odysseus thereafter, causing storms and shipwrecks, and punishing those who help the hero on his way home. The poverty of the rocky island kingdom of Ithaca was proverbial in the Homeric poems, and ruefully alluded to by its inhabitants; and yet (as Telemachus, Odysseus's son, remarks in Book 4 of the *Odyssey*) beloved of its people.

For more on Cavafy's early interest in the figure of Odysseus, see the note on "Second Odyssey," pp. 501–5.

Trojans *pg. 16*

The epic poems of Archaic Greece, among them Homer's *Iliad* and *Odyssey,* recall the ten-year-long siege of Troy by the invading Greeks, which ended in the utter destruction of the Trojans. The greatest of the Greek warriors was ACHILLES, and the greatest of the Trojans was Hector, the son of Troy's king and queen, PRIAM and HECUBA. The elderly royal couple lived long enough to see their son cut down by Achilles on the battlefield; the poignant scene in which the broken old king travels in secret to the Greek camp in order to beg Achilles to return his son's body to him for burial (*Iliad,* Book 24) is the subject of the Unpublished Poem "Priam's March by Night." Achilles himself did not survive to see the end of the war, but was killed by Hector's brother, Paris, who, aided by the Trojans' supernatural ally, Apollo, shot Achilles in the heel with an arrow. Troy nonetheless eventually fell, and during the brutal sack of the city by the Greeks, old King Priam was murdered, at an altar where he'd taken refuge, by Achilles' son, Neoptolemus. Hecuba was given as a slave to Odysseus, one of many Trojan women who were awarded as booty to the various Greek leaders.

To the early period of Cavafy's poetic production belong seven poems based on Greek myth. It is noteworthy that fully five of these are devoted to episodes or characters familiar from Homer's *Iliad:* the present poem, "Priam's March by Night," "The Horses of Achilles," "Suspicion," and "The Funeral of Sarpedon." This predilection is not without interest for our understanding of Cavafy's developing poetic consciousness, since the *Iliad* is traditionally identified as the more "historical" of the two Homeric epics; so we might say that in his early years of writing, Cavafy turned naturally to the canonical text that would best suit his already fixed interest in thinking poetically about history.

This poem, along with "Monotony," the early version of "The City" (entitled "Back in the Same City Again"), and the Unpublished Poem "Vulnerant Omnes, Ultima Necat" (1893), all reflect the disillusionment with progress that marked the later nineteenth-century Continental, and particularly French, poetry that influenced the young Cavafy.

King Demetrius *pg. 17*

DEMETRIUS POLIORCETES ("the Besieger of Cities") assumed the throne of Macedonia in the tumultuous years of dynastic struggle soon after the death of Alexander the Great. Born in 336 B.C., the son of Alexander's comrade Antigonus the One-Eyed, who later became king of Phrygia in Asia Minor, Demetrius distinguished himself in arms in the internecine wars between Alexander's Successors (the "Diadochi"), although the grueling yearlong siege of Cyprus in 305–304 B.C., to which he owes his epithet, was resolved finally in diplomatic negotiations. In 294 B.C. Demetrius, whose wife was the daughter of Macedonia's onetime regent, intervened in the dynastic intrigues in Macedon and declared himself king after murdering the young Alexander V.

Demetrius was given to displays of royal grandeur, and encouraged the kind of ruler-cults associated with the East. Determined to reconquer his father's former empire, he prepared a vast expedition against Asia Minor in 288, but failed to achieve his ambitions when two of the other Successors, Ptolemy I of Egypt and Seleucus of Babylonia, offered vigorous military resistance to his plans. Demetrius was eventually expelled from Macedonia, and his final struggle to maintain power ended in disgrace when his troops, tired of serving his overweening imperial ambitions and taste for luxury, deserted him to join the enemy leader, PYRRHUS. After a bit of further intriguing with Ptolemy, Demetrius eventually surrendered himself to Seleucus, and spent his final few years in captivity, where, embittered, he drank himself to death.

The epigraph, in Classical Greek, is taken from Plutarch's *Life of Demetrius,* 44.6, and describes Demetrius's departure from his camp after it became obvious that his men were deserting him en masse. It is worth noting that this Greek figure is paired, in Plutarch's *Parallel Lives,* with the Roman Marc Antony, a character dear to Cavafy: in Plutarch's words (1.3), both men "bore witness in particular to Plato's saying that the greatest natures exhibit great vices as well as great virtues. Both were great lovers, great drinkers, warlike, munificent, grandiose, overweening, and in their fortunes bore corresponding resemblances to each other."

In this poem, as in "The Seleucid's Displeasure," Cavafy uses shifts in register between katharevousa and demotic to underscore—with a particularly pointed irony in this case—the theme of a great ruler's sudden demotion in status (see the discussion in the Introduction, pp. xiii–xiv). The words used to describe the king when he "left" and cast aside his "clothes," in lines 5 and 6, are demotic; the two words used to describe the same action and the same object, in the case of the mere actor to whom the great king is being compared, are katharevousa. Hence my translation of the latter by means of the more elevated "departs" and "attire."

The Glory of the Ptolemies   *pg. 18*

For the dynastic names LAGID and SELEUCID, see the note on the Hellenistic dynasties above, pp. 368–70. Although the identities of the monarchs in question are not clarified, the entire Hellenistic period was characterized by vicious rivalries and wars among the ruling houses founded by Alexander's generals. As the present poem suggests, an ongoing theme in Cavafy's poetry about the Hellenistic world is another, nonmilitary competition among the various rulers: the sometimes pathetic, often poignant yearning, by these many, increasingly distant heirs to Alexander and his generals, to lay claim to Greek culture itself.

The Retinue of Dionysus   *pg. 19*

In the Greek, the poem is set in rhyming couplets. The last word of the poem is pronounced with the accent on the final syllable.

Cavafy's interest in craftsmen—sculptors, potters, jewelers, artists— an inheritance from his early involvement with the Parnassians, with their emphasis on formal beauty divorced from political and social content and Romantic self-dramatization, is evident in a number of poems, including "Maker of Wine Bowls" (*1903; 1912; 1921;* 1921), "Sculptor from Tyana" (*1893; 1903;* 1911), "In Stock" (*1912;* 1913), and "Painted" (*1914;* 1915).

The Battle of Magnesia   pg. 20

The poem concerns two rulers and the two great battles in which they fought, conflicts that effectively put an end to the political and military supremacy of the culturally Greek kingdoms of Alexander's Successors, and firmly established Roman domination over the Greek-speaking Hellenistic world. PHILIP V (238–179 B.C.), an expansionist king of Macedonia, was soundly defeated by the Romans under Flamininus at the Battle of Cynoscephalae in 197, a victory for the Romans that effectively made Greece a province of Rome. (For Philip as a leader of a short-lived Hellenic coalition against the Romans, see the Unfinished Poem "Agelaus.") Seven years later, the Romans under the Scipio brothers defeated the equally aggressive expansionist Seleucid king, ANTIOCHUS III ("the Great"), at the BATTLE OF MAGNESIA, after which his Seleucid empire (which included present-day Syria) ceased to be a major Mediterranean power. By this time, however, Philip, who had once allied himself with Antiochus—a secret treaty between the two kings was aimed at divvying up the overseas possessions of their mutual rivals, the Ptolemies in Egypt—had turned against his former ally, because the latter had failed to provide assistance to Philip at Cynoscephalae. Indeed, Philip, who had been confined to Macedon after his defeat by the Romans, and forced to pay an enormous indemnity to them and to give up his younger son as a hostage, had recently won favor for himself (and remission of both the indemnity and the son) by giving assistance to the Scipios as they crossed through northern Greece en route to Asia to make war on Antiochus. These historical details enhance our perception of the palpable aura of gloating that hovers over this poem, and which barely conceals the more pathetic emotions associated with Philip's shattered dreams.

Philip's request for roses to adorn his banquet was the subject of an amusing anecdote told by Cavafy's friend I. A. Sareyannis (who was a botanist) in his *Notes on Cavafy*. Here Sareyannis remarks that after around 1911 (when Cavafy was publishing regularly) the poet ceased any kind of systematic reading of contemporary literature, and instead devoted himself to reading the historical works from which he drew the matter for his poems—or which he might consult to confirm this or that detail of history (as does the narrator, Sareyannis notes, of "Caesarion"). Sareyannis recalls that in 1929, as he was composing a note on "The Battle of Magnesia," he wrote to Cavafy to say that he'd spotted what he thought was an error: given that the Battle of Magnesia took place in December—and given how speedily news could in fact travel at that point in Mediterranean history—Philip's banquet would likely have taken place late in December or early in January, months during which roses were, so Sareyannis thought, unlikely to be available. Cavafy replied with alacrity, crisply informing his abashed friend that there was in fact export of roses from Egypt to Italy during the winter, and indeed that in the first century A.D. Italy had begun to cultivate its own late-blooming winter roses, *Rosae hibernicae*.

The Seleucid's Displeasure   *pg. 21*

Like "The Battle of Magnesia," this poem has as its subject the decline of Greek cultural and political supremacy during the rise of Rome. The Greeks are here represented, as often in Cavafy's work, by members of the various dynasties founded by Alexander's Successors: in this case, DEMETRIUS I Soter ("the Savior") of the royal SELEUCID house of Babylonia, the grandson of that Antiochus III who figures in "The Battle of Magnesia"; and PTOLEMY VI Philometor of the LAGID dynasty in Egypt (the epithet, a conventional one, means "mother-loving," used here because Ptolemy ascended the throne at the age of six with his mother as co-ruler). The two men were virtually coevals: Demetrius was born in 187, and Ptolemy the year before, and both died in 150.

The dramatic date of the poem is 164 B.C., when Demetrius was living as a political hostage in Rome, where he had to sit passively as his father's empire passed first to his uncle, Antiochus IV, and then to his cousin. In that year, the twenty-two-year-old Ptolemy was expelled from Alexandria by his younger brother, also called Ptolemy (later Ptolemy VIII Euergetes, "the Benefactor"), with whom he had been jointly ruling along with their sister Cleopatra II. After coming to Rome to "beg" for help, the elder Ptolemy returned to Egypt the following year as sole ruler, his younger brother having been sent by the Roman Senate to rule the North African province of Cyrene. (The conflict between these two brothers, and Rome's settlement of their dispute, is the subject of "Envoys from Alexandria.") Eventually, the older Ptolemy was elected king of the Seleucid empire and ruled jointly with Demetrius II, son of the Demetrius mentioned here; the elder Demetrius eventually returned home from Rome, and both he and Ptolemy were ultimately killed in the same battle, against Alexander Balas, a pretender to the Seleucid throne.

The baroque family entanglements of the Ptolemies provided Cavafy with subject matter for several poems in addition to "Envoys from Alexandria": see also "Those Who Fought on Behalf of the Achaean League," "In Sparta," and the Unfinished Poems "Ptolemy the Benefactor (or Malefactor)" and "The Dynasty."

For dicussion of the technical features of this poem, see the Introduction, pp. xliv–xlv and liv.

Orophernes *pg. 23*

OROPHERNES played a small but intriguing role in the complex dynastic struggles that vexed the Seleucid dynasty in the second century B.C. He was (falsely) alleged by his mother, Antiochis, the daughter of Antiochus III "the Great," to be her son by her husband, Ariarathes IV of CAPPADOCIA (by whom Antiochis had another, legitimate son, Mithridates, who later ruled as Ariarathes V). It is worth noting, because Cavafy alludes to it (line 6), that the house of Ariarathes was a rather grand and ancient Persian one: the founding ancestor, Ariarathes I, was the Persian king Darius III's satrap, or provincial governor, when Alexander the Great overran Asia in the 330s B.C.; for resisting Alexander, this first Ariarathes was put to death at the age of eighty-two. Because Orophernes is illegitimate, such pedigrees—as, indeed, his alleged descent from STRATONIKE, the daughter of Demetrius Poliorcetes, who famously wedded her own stepson—are important to him.

Orophernes' supposed father, Ariarathes IV, had sided with Demetrius I Soter in his final stand against the Romans at Magnesia (in 190

B.C.; see "The Battle of Magnesia"), but after Demetrius's defeat Ariarathes wisely, to say nothing of opportunistically, switched his allegiance to the Romans. When conflict between his chosen son, Ariarathes V, and Orophernes arose, Rome intervened and divided Cappadocia between them, but eventually Ariarathes prevailed and Orophernes was expelled and took refuge with his protector Demetrius, whose throne he eventually tried to usurp.

Alexandrian Kings   *pg. 26*

The ceremony to which the poem refers was the propagandistic "Donations" of 34 B.C., organized by Marc Antony to promote the imperialistic claims of his alliance with CLEOPATRA. The elaborate titles given to her children were, of course, wholly symbolic, although they do suggest the scope of the couple's ambitions: all of the lands once ruled by Alexander the Great were, at least in name, distributed to the young royals. ALEXANDER Helios and PTOLEMY Philadelphus were Cleopatra's children by Antony; as his nickname suggests, CAESARION's father was said by Cleopatra to have been Julius Caesar, who had been her lover before his assassination ten years before the events narrated in this poem. (The child's official name was Ptolemy XV Caesar.) Antony and Cleopatra also had a daughter, Cleopatra Selene, Alexander's twin, who during the Donations was named queen of Cyrenaica in North Africa; interestingly, she does not figure in this poem.

At the time of the Donations, Caesarion would have been thirteen, Alexander six, and Ptolemy two years of age. A year after his parents' suicides in 31 B.C., Caesarion was murdered at the orders of Augustus. (See also "Caesarion.")

A remark Cavafy made to Timos Malanos confirms the poet's meticulous preoccupation with historical accuracy: "I dressed him in pink silk because at that time an ell of that sort of silk cost the equivalent of so-and-so many thousand drachmas."

Philhellene   *pg. 28*

Here as in other poems, such as "Potentate from Western Libya," Cavafy explores the fraught relationship of a non-Greek character to Greek culture—a relationship made more complex in this poem by the fact that the Greek civilization to which the speaker aspires had long since fallen under Roman domination. In this dramatic monologue, a princeling who rules some unnamed but clearly remote Eastern possession of the Roman Empire—ZÁGROS is the major mountain range of present-day Iran, and in ancient times constituted the border between Media and Mesopotamia; and PHRÁATA was the summer seat of the Parthian kings—issues orders for new coinage to be struck. Here as in many other poems, a certain tension between Greek cultural aspirations and Roman political realities is evident: the philhellenic ruler's swagger is undercut by the fact that he has to kowtow to the Roman proconsul (compare, for instance, "The Seleucid's Displeasure" and "Envoys from Alexandria"). But even his relationship to Greek culture, which he is so eager to advertise on his coinage, seems rather vexed. On the one hand, the speaker refers dismissively to the Hellenized intellectuals who occasionally visit his court as "devotees of puffery"; on the other hand, he uses the elevated Purist forms for the words "unhellenized" and "we are" in the last line—a hint, once more, at his desire to appear properly Greek.

The Steps

pg. 29

An early version was written in August 1893 and published in January 1897 under the heading "Ancient Days." The poem was reworked in December 1908 and published in September of the following year.

The Roman emperor NERO (Nero Claudius Caesar, 37–68 A.D.) was the son of Agrippina the Younger (15–59), the great-granddaughter of Augustus and sister of the emperor Gaius ("Caligula"), and of Gnaeus Domitius Ahenobarbus, a member of the distinguished old clan of the AHENOBARBI. Soon after the birth of her son, Agrippina was banished by her brother, but when Gaius was assassinated she was recalled by the new emperor, her uncle Claudius, who then married her. Agrippina is said to have poisoned her husband in order to hasten the accession of Nero (54 A.D.), but she soon fell out of favor with Nero, and in the spring of 59 was murdered at the seaside resort of Baiae on his instructions.

Nero himself proved a disastrous ruler: notorious for his passion for all things Greek (he "freed" the province of Achaea, i.e., Greece, after making a triumphant tour of it in 67), suspected of starting the fire that destroyed half of Rome in 64, moved by increasing paranoia to instigate numerous judicial murders of prominent Romans, he was finally chased from Rome during a widespread insurgency against him by generals in several provinces (including Galba in Spain: see "Nero's Deadline") and committed suicide on June 9, 68, at the age of thirty-seven.

In Roman religion, LARES were very ancient tutelary deities associated with crossroads, farms, and (as here) houses; typically a Roman house contained a private chapel or shrine called the *lararium* (Cavafy uses the Greek version, *lararion,* in line 7), inside of which were small images of these deities, who were also associated with the spirits of the family's ancestors.

Vengeance for the crime of matricide was, in Greek mythology, thought to be the province of creatures called ERINYES—"Furies"— winged apparitions who are described in Aeschylus's *Oresteia* as having doglike faces dripping with blood, and who pursued matricides and drove them mad.

Herodes Atticus pg. 30

HERODES ATTICUS (L. Vibullius Hipparchus Tiberius Claudius Atticus Herodes), ca. 101–177 A.D., was one of the premier figures of the so-called Second Sophistic of the second century A.D., a rhetorical movement that flourished between about 60 and 250, and which was marked by a renaissance of interest in the Greek literature of the High Classical period (i. e., the First Sophistic). The son of an extremely wealthy and distinguished Athenian who served in positions of considerable power in Rome under the emperor Hadrian, Herodes Atticus followed his father's example of exemplary public service, serving as a Roman senator, attaining the consulship in 143 A.D., and counting among his friends the emperors Hadrian, Antoninus, and Marcus Aurelius, whose mentor he was. But Herodes was even more distinguished for his intellectual and literary career: although his letters and treatises do not survive (we have only one Latin translation of a short parable about grief, preserved in the *Attic Nights* of Aulus Gellius, who heard Herodes lecture at Athens), his work was said to rival those of the ancient classics in its elegance and restraint. He was, indeed, a proponent of the archaizing Attic style in vogue among Greek writers during the Second Sophistic. A great philanthropist, Herodes was responsible for the magnificent concert hall, or odeum (Greek *odeon*), that stands at the base of the Acropolis in Athens, and which is still used for performances. The present poem is the only mature poem of Cavafy's in which Athens is mentioned.

Herodes, as his epithet indicates, was a bona fide Attic (rather than Asiatic) Greek, one who successfully reached, and remained at, the pinnacle of Roman society. As such, he is the natural object of Cavafy's interest—particularly since there was an ongoing intellectual and literary debate during the Second Sophistic about the merits of the purely "Attic" versus the "Asiatic" Greek style. The source of the subtle and humorous tension in the poem is, in fact, the implied competition between two claims to Greekness: that of Herodes "the Attic" and that of ALEXANDER OF SELEUCIA, the representative of the great Greek culture bequeathed to Asia by the Hellenistic monarchies. The prestige of the provincial sophists may be inferred from the career of this Alexander, who, despite the unkind nickname bestowed on him (the "Clay Plato"), taught in cities from Egypt to Antioch to Rome, and visited Athens itself, as this poem makes clear. In his *Lives of the Sophists,* Flavius Philostratus (on whom see the note on Apollonius of Tyana, pp. 357–60) tells us that Alexander appeared on an embassy on behalf of his native city before the emperor Antoninus Pius, and indeed went so far as to scold the emperor for not paying attention (Antoninus responded tartly with a dismissive comment about the eastern Greek's effeminate finery). He eventually led the important ministerial office known as *ab epistulis graecis,* which dealt with the emperor's Greek correspondence, under Marcus Aurelius.

The source for Cavafy's poem is a passage in the *Lives of the Sophists* that suggests the cachet that went with being able to draw an audience of bona fide Greeks—and with being one as well:

> Hearing that Herodes was sojourning in Marathon, and that all the young people had followed him there, he [Alexander of Seleucia] wrote him a letter, inviting the Greeks; "I shall come," Herodes said, "with the Greeks myself."

We have Cavafy's transcription of this passage into Modern Greek, and it is worth quoting because, in the subtle alterations it makes to the original, it sheds light on the process by which Cavafy transformed his source material into its final, poetic form:

> Alexander, having come to Athens from Seleucia in order to lecture, wrote to Herodes—who was staying in Marathon and had around him a numerous court of artists—announcing that he wished to speak and requiring of him his Greeks. Herodes, with great wit, replied that he too was coming with the Greeks.

The joke lies in Herodes' implication that these "real" Greeks will not come without him.

Sculptor from Tyana   pg. 32

TYANA was a city in Asia Minor, a place significant in Cavafy's work as the birthplace of the sage Apollonius. The sculptor-narrator is fictional; his subjects are both mythological and historical. The poem is organized around a series of subtle oppositions: the sculptor is of the Greek east, but seems to be living in Rome, where his clients are Romans; the mythic figures suggest his Greek roots, while the historical figures are, with one crucial exception, quintessentially Roman.

RHEA, the wife of Cronus, was the mother of Zeus, king of the gods; POSEIDON, Zeus's brother, was god of the sea, and also associated with horses; and HERMES, Zeus's son, often represented as a beautiful youth, particularly in Hellenistic art (as, for instance, in the famous statue by Praxiteles), was the messenger of the gods. PATROCLUS in Homer is represented as the dear friend of Achilles, although later Greek tradition made the two lovers.

It is worth noting that the Romans whom the sculptor has portrayed are key figures in the history of the Roman Republic. MARIUS (157–86 B.C.), of an equestrian rather than noble background and an uncle by marriage to the aristocratic Julius Caesar, rose to the consulship, and is widely seen as having contributed importantly to the decline of the

Republic by fostering the creation of client armies loyal to a single pow-
erful military figure rather than the State. LUCIUS AEMILIUS PAULLUS
MACEDONICUS (d. 160 B.C.), a highly distinguished figure noted for his
appreciation of Greek culture, was consul in 168, and in that year led
the Roman forces to a decisive victory in the Third Macedonian War—
the defeat that signaled the end to any mainland Greek resistance to
Roman authority—against Perseus of Macedon, the son of Philip V (see
"The Battle of Magnesia") and brother of Demetrius, who lived as a
hostage at Rome. SCIPIO AFRICANUS MAJOR (236–c. 183 B.C.), the
brother-in-law of Aemilius Paullus and the brother of the Scipio who
defeated Antiochus at the Battle of Magnesia, was, like Paullus, a great
enthusiast for Greek culture who yet presided over Roman fortunes at a
time when the autonomy of the Hellenistic kingdoms was coming to an
end under Roman expansionism; Africanus Major was best known,
however, for his crushing defeat of the Carthaginian leader Hannibal at
the Battle of Zama in 202 B.C.

The statue could, on the other hand, be of SCIPIO AFRICANUS
MINOR (185–129 B.C.), the son of Aemilius Paullus, who was later
adopted by the son of Scipio Africanus Major. A key figure in the Third
Punic War, against Carthage, he was also famous for his philhellenic out-
look: while in Greece for the Battle of Pydna, in which he served with
distinction, he befriended the historian Polybius. His deep admiration
of Greek culture and literature were typical of the so-called Scipionic
Circle, of which he was the preeminent member; that, along with his
strict Roman virtue, political prestige, and military distinction, made
Africanus Minor a figure much admired by Cicero, who made him a
character in several of his works. CAESARION (see "The Glory of the
Ptolemies" and "Caesarion") stands out as something of an anomaly
among this gallery of great Romans. He was the love-child of Cleopatra
and Julius Caesar; born in 47 B.C., he did not live long enough to
accomplish any deeds worthy of note before being murdered by Octa-
vian (later Augustus) in 30 B.C.

Cavafy's choice of his sculptor's subjects is hardly casual, and indeed
is highly suggestive in its implied comment on the relationship between
Roman and Greek culture, and on certain political ironies. Aemilius
Paullus and the two Scipios, all three famous for their philhellenism,

presided over Rome at the zenith of its consolidation of power through-
out the Mediterranean, at the expense of the Hellenistic kingdoms
whose culture the three so admired; Marius was responsible for a polit-
ical development that would lead Rome herself into her Imperial phase;
and Caesarion represents, in his parentage and his very person, the
failed dream of a truly Greco-Roman political and dynastic unity.

Among the visual arts, sculpture enjoys special place in Cavafy's
work, which both refers often to actual statues and bas-reliefs and
invokes statuary in its descriptions of ephebic beauty. For the former, see
"The Retinue of Dionysus," "In the Presence of the Statue of Endymion,"
and "Maker of Wine Bowls"; for the latter, see "I've Gazed So Much," "In
the Entrance to the Café," "That's How," and "Aristobulus."

The Tomb of Lysias the Grammarian   pg. 34

Diana Haas has made the interesting argument that the "maybe" in line
6, which hints at a gently ironic attitude toward the possibility of an
afterlife, connects this poem to "The Rest Shall I Tell in Hades to Those
Below," with its amused sophist half-smiling at the idea of an afterlife in
which life's secrets may finally be revealed.

Tomb of Eurion   pg. 35

The setting is, once again, the cultural melting pot of Hellenistic
Alexandria; ALABARCHS were magistrates of the Jewish community
there. While Eurion and his teachers are all invented, his interest in the
province of ARSINOÏTES is perhaps suggestive: this area (present-day
Fayûm, in Egypt) was named for the Ptolemaic queen Arsinoë II (ca.
316–270 B.C.), the daughter of Ptolemy I of Egypt and his queen,
Berenice I, and a woman of extraordinary allure and cunning. Married
at the age of about seventeen to the much older Lysimachus, a former
comrade-in-arms to her father and a companion and Successor of
Alexander the Great, she was widowed at thirty-six and eventually mar-
ried her brother, Ptolemy II Philadelphus; their court represented
Ptolemaic and Alexandrian culture at its zenith.

Just as the allure of Arsinoë hovers, perhaps ironically, over the
desert district named for her, which is the object of Eurion's disserta-

tion, so too Eurion's own allure—ironically unknowable from the data given here about the appearance of his tomb or from the facts of his life, education, and intellectual enthusiasms—hovers still in the mind of the speaker.

That Is He

pg. 36

The title, repeated in line 9, is an allusion to a passage from the work of the second-century A.D. belletrist LUCIAN OF SAMOSATA. Born in 120 A.D. in the capital city of the kingdom of Commagene (modern southeastern Turkey), Lucian traveled extensively, living for a while in Alexandria, where he held an official position, and in Athens; he died around 180.

An accomplished lecturer, satirist, and essayist, Lucian was famous above all for his mordant wit and biting condemnation of the pretensions of the contemporary intellectual and literary scene, with which his travels had made him all too familiar. Among his seventy or so published works are treatises exposing a popular magician as a fake; an attack on the pretensions of the Cynic philosopher Peregrinus (who later demonstrated his humorlessness by setting himself afire at the Olympic games of 165); a *How to Write History* in which he recommends impartiality and adherence to the known truth and wittily lampoons historians who employ superficially Thucydidean devices; and the *Teacher of Orators,* in which Lucian tartly observes that would-be orators can achieve success by including claptrap and impudent remarks in their speeches. He was particularly interested in exposing the contemporary mania, among Greek-speaking littérateurs of the Roman Empire, for aping the Attic style of the great Greek writers of the fifth and fourth centuries B.C. The Second Sophistic indeed saw a profusion of lexica of and guides to "acceptable" Greek words—acceptable, that is, because they could be found in the five-hundred-year-old works of Lysias, Demosthenes, Plato, and the like.

The allusion here is to chapter 11 of Lucian's *The Dream,* in which the author relates how he came to his literary career. In a dream, he writes, the figure of Culture, richly dressed, approached the then-impoverished and unknown Lucian and promised him such great fame as a writer that people would immediately recognize him wherever he went:

> And even if you go abroad, not even on foreign territory will
> you be unknown or without fame. For such are the marks of
> recognition that I will put on you, that each of those who
> look upon you will nudge the man next to him and say,
> pointing you out, "That is he."

The Unfinished Poem "And Above All Cynegirus" also owes its title, and
much of its point, to a citation from Lucian.

An EDESSENE was a citizen of Edessa, the capital city of the little Syr-
iac kingdom of Osrhoene, which was founded in 132 B.C. after the
breakup of the Seleucid empire, and which remained independent until
it was made a Roman province in the early third century A.D. Ruled
originally by a dynasty of Arab sheikhs, it was Christianized fairly early,
and (as Cavafy was surely aware) was the first state to have a Christian
king. It is tempting to imagine that the young Edessene of this poem is,
then, a Christian—one who has left his quaint hometown for the first
time to try his luck at a literary career, and who is dazzled to encounter,
in the much older and more splendid Antioch, one of the greatest
metropolises of its time.

Dangerous   pg. 37

For remarks on the significance of this poem in Cavafy's work, see the
Introduction, pp. xxxii–xxxiii. Appropriately for a poem that has as its
subject the tensions between pagan and Christian values, the dramatic
date of this verse is the joint reign of the two sons of Constantine the
Great (d. 337 A.D.), the emperor who officially made Christianity the
supreme religion of the Roman Empire. Constantine had three sons,
CONSTANS, Constantine II, and CONSTANTIUS II; unsurprisingly, the
period after their father's death was marked by strained alliances and
grim tensions among the three, who were meant to divide their father's
empire among them. Constans, who reigned in the West, killed Con-
stantine II in 340, and was himself killed in a coup ten years later; Con-
stantius died in January 361 while marching to do battle with his cousin,
Julian the Apostate, who after becoming emperor attempted to restore
pagan worship in Rome.

In the late third century A.D., the emperor Diocletian had introduced an administrative arrangement whereby the Roman Empire was divided into eastern and western regions, each ruled by an emperor bearing the title of AUGUSTUS; each *augustus* had serving under him a deputy bearing the title of *caesar,* who was expected in due time to succeed as *augustus.*

Manuel Comnenus *pg. 38*

The Byzantine emperor MANUEL I COMNENUS (born ca. 1120), son of John II, whom he succeeded in 1143, transformed the austere and pious court of his father into a center of glittering festivity, with tournaments borrowed from Western Europe. Always more oriented to the West than most Byzantine rulers, he never gave up his dream of restoring the former Roman Empire in its entirety, and to this end he neglected his Turkish neighbors while pursuing an aggressive policy of expansion into Italy, meddling in European politics to no little extent, and going so far as to ally himself with the pope against the Holy Roman Emperor. During his reign, he successfully incorporated Bosnia, Dalmatia, and Croatia into the empire; at home, substantial merchant colonies from various Italian cities established themselves at Constantinople.

Manuel's neglect of affairs closer to home cost him dearly: in 1176 his army was shattered by the Turks at the Battle of Myriocephalum, and he was said never to have laughed or smiled again. He died on September 24, 1180, and was succeeded by his son, Alexius II.

In the Church *pg. 39*

LABARA (singular *labarum*) refers to the standards carried in processions of the Greek Orthodox Church; the finials often take the form of seraphs' heads.

A fragmentary letter preserved in the Cavafy Archive and reconstructed by Diana Haas sheds light on the strong emotions that churches evoked in the poet:

> The ancient Byzantine churches are also most interesting. They are low & very small buildings whose outside has no imposing appearance but a charming old world look . . . the curious [?] painted pictured walls, the old carved wood seats

& pulpits . . . mellowed by the centuries, the quaintly gilt
Icones you feel transported into the dim & mystical enchant-
ing realm of [the] Middle Ages of Greece.

Another sentence refers to the "high silver candle sticks where the lights
of so many hopes & many fears have shone."

In his 1976 study, *Cavafy's Alexandria,* Edmund Keeley has drawn atten-
tion to the striking resemblance between this poem and a passage from
Oscar Wilde's *The Picture of Dorian Gray* that similarly shows great inter-
est in the aesthetic element of church ritual—a similarity that is to be
expected, given Cavafy's early attraction to the Decadents of the 1890s:

> [C]ertainly the Roman ritual had always a great attraction for
> him. . . . He loved to kneel down on the cold marble pave-
> ment, and watch the priest, in his stiff flowered dalmatic,
> slowly and with white hands moving aside the veil of the
> tabernacle, or raising aloft the jeweled lantern-shaped mon-
> strance with that pallid wafer that at times, one would fain
> think, is indeed the "*panis caelestis*", the bread of angels, or,
> robed in the garments of the Passion of Christ, breaking the
> Host into the chalice, and smiting his breast for his sins. The
> fuming censers, that the grave boys, in their lace and scarlet,
> tossed into the air like great gilt flowers, had their subtle fas-
> cination for him.

The phrase "OUR BYZANTINISM" merits some comment. Diana Haas
has made the important observation that Cavafy's strong feeling for
Byzantine culture as the conduit for true Greek identity from the
ancient to the modern era is often signaled by the use of the first-
person-plural pronoun. "Byzantinism" importantly suggests not so
much the empire itself as a historical entity, as rather the culture in the
abstract, one whose institutions, particularly the Greek language and
the Greek Orthodox Church, were the vehicle for the simultaneous
continuation and transformation of the pagan Greek identity. Cavafy
came across this concept of Byzantinism in the writings of the German
scholar Ferdinand Gregorovius (in an 1882 Greek translation), where
the author attaches special importance to the role of the church in the

transformation of the culture of the late Roman Empire into the Greek empire that would become Byzantium. "In Constantinople," he wrote, "as if in some great cauldron, the culture of the Greek and Roman pagan world, the Christian religion, the cosmopolitan mechanism of Roman imperial government, and the habits and mores of Asia, achieved a bond that became renowned throughout the world as Byzantinism." (In this context it is worth noting that a figure upon whom Gregorovius seizes as a symbol of this richly hybridized culture—the empress Eudocia, who began life as a pagan named Athenaïs and became the wife of Theodosius II—was the subject, almost certainly, of one of Cavafy's poems on "Byzantine Days.")

My translation of line 4 will seem strange to some. The Greek here is *mes s'ekklêsía tôn Graikôn,* literally "into a church of the Greeks." But Cavafy himself noted that such a translation would falsely connote a distance, perhaps even an estrangement, between the speaker and the church he enters. He was, after all, a Greek Orthodox himself; the meaning here is, rather, a Greek Orthodox church as opposed to a church of any number of other denominations, of which there was a surfeit in Alexandria. The English translation of George Valassopoulos ("When I enter the Church of the Greeks") was corrected by the poet himself thus: "When I enter the Greek Church."

Very Rarely   *pg. 40*

This poem and the three that follow constitute a mini cycle concerning the relationship between the artist and his work, and between Art and Nature.

In a self-commentary, Cavafy explained the title as "constituting a commentary on the poem." The phrase "very rarely," he went on to say, applied to those exceptional cases in which a work of art of special quality had the ability to touch future generations.

In Stock   *pg. 41*

The original is in rhymed couplets; with the exception of the final couplet, all of the rhymes are homophonous.

As a subset of Cavafy's general interest in artists and their relationship to their creations we can detect a narrower theme: that of a competition between Art and Nature, with a strong suggestion that the powers of the former are superior. This favorite theme of the Parnassian poets whom the young Cavafy read so avidly notably recurs here and in the poem "Artificial Flowers."

Morning Sea   *pg. 43*

The date of composition is unknown; the poem was first printed in 1915.

In one of his "Notes on Poetics and Ethics," written on July 5, 1902, Cavafy pondered the lack of feeling for Nature that marks his poetry:

> I have never lived in the country. I haven't even visited the country for short whiles, as others have done. Nevertheless, I wrote a poem in which I praise the countryside, where I write that my verses are a tribute to the countryside. The poem is insignificant. It is indeed the most insincere construction; a true fallacy.
>
> But, it crosses my mind—is that true insincerity? Does not art always lie? Or, rather, is it not that when art lies the most, it is then that it creates the most? When I wrote these verses, was it not an artistic achievement? (The fact that the verses were imperfect is not perhaps due to the lack of sincerity; for how very often one fails, even armed with the sincerest of impressions.) At the time when I wrote the verses, did I not possess an artificial sincerity? Did I not fantasize in such a way as if I had lived in the country indeed?

In an essay called "Cavafy: The Man of the Crowd," Cavafy's friend J. A. Sareyannis recalled that after his 1932 throat operation, in Athens, the poet went to a convalescent home in the village of Kifissia:

> He pulled me towards the window and showed me the marvelous view: in the foreground some huge cypresses, beyond the plain stretching out as far as Tatoï, and rising up in the

background the breathtakingly beautiful mountains of Parnes and Pendeli. With irritating gestures the poet indicated how oppressed he was by it all. "It bores me," he told me. (tr. Sasa Wheeler)

Song of Ionia   *pg. 44*

First written probably before 1891, an early version of this poem, called "Remembrance," was published in October 1896 and subsequently revised in July 1905 (with the title "Thessaly"); it was then revised once again and published, in its present form and with its present title, in July 1911.

One of the poet's reading notes on Gibbon, concerning the late Roman emperor Attalus (d. after 416 A.D.), is worth considering in connection with this poem in its final form. Of Attalus, Gibbon writes that he was a "degraded emperor [who] might aspire to the praise of a skillful musician," to which Cavafy responds:

> The subject for a beautiful sonnet, a sonnet full of sadness such as Verlaine would write—
>
> *"Je suis l'empire à la fin de la decadence."* Lost in the Gothic tumult and utterly bewildered, a melancholy emperor playing on the flute. An absurd emperor bustled in the crowd. Much applauded and much laughed at. And perhaps at times singing a touching song—some reminiscence of Ionia and of the days when the gods were not yet dead.

The reference to Ionia here is not gratuitous: Attalus, as Gibbon notes elsewhere, was born in Ionia and "had been educated in the pagan superstition" there. Hence although the original version of this poem predates Cavafy's reading note to Gibbon, it is tempting to think that the subsequent change in the setting of the poem from Thessaly to Ionia may have been influenced by the passage in Gibbon, to which Cavafy may well have returned at some point.

Diana Haas has noted that some time around 1900—which is to say, during the period when Cavafy was revising this poem—the poet read the Homeric *Hymn to Demeter,* which provided the subject matter for "Interruption," and suggests that at the same time he likely read the *Hymn to Hermes,* whose description of the buoyant young god, silently skimming the peaks of Cyllene at morning, is recalled in "Song of Ionia." Particularly worthy of note are the similarities between Cavafy's poem and the translation of the *Hymn to Hermes* by Shelley, a poet whom Cavafy knew and, indeed, translated:

> All night he worked in the serene moonshine—
> But when the light of day was spread abroad
> He sought his natal mountain peaks divine.
> On his long wandering, neither man nor god
> Had met him, since he killed Apollo's kine,
> Nor house-dog had barked at him upon his road;
> Now he obliquely through the key-hole past
> Like a thin mist, or an autumnal blast.

In the Entrance of the Café   pg. 45

An early version of this poem, now lost, entitled "By the Hands of Eros," was written in 1904; the final version was published in 1915. The title of the lost early version draws attention to a favorite motif here: the use of the language of sculpture to describe beautiful young men. See note on "Sculptor from Tyana," pp. 388–90.

Come Back   pg. 47

The original title of this poem was "Memory of Pleasure."

He Swears   pg. 49

According to Timos Malanos, this poem has its origins in the period of Cavafy's existence as a young man when he was living what we would call a "double life," perhaps soon after his 1885 return to Alexandria from Constantinople, where he had his first homosexual experiences with his cousin George. Malanos, in his 1957 book about Cavafy, recalls the poet telling him that as a young man he would pass his nights in "certain isolated quarters" of Alexandria as a "slave to his temptations." After such nights, apparently, the poet would repent and write, in large letters on a piece of paper, "I swear I won't do it again." An acquaintance of Cavafy's recalled years later that the young poet would bribe a servant to muss his bed back at home, in order to fool his family into thinking he had slept there. He kept, indeed, a room in a brothel on the corner of the Rue Mosquée Attarine, and he later recalled that one morning he took a piece of chalk and wrote on the window, "You're not to come here again, you're not to do it again."

Chandelier   *pg. 51*

The poet himself left a note in Greek explaining the "empty room" in this poem, the climactic placement of which, at the end of this collection, suggests the great significance it had for him:

> It's the life—or rather a few years, 8, 10, in the life of certain men—in which pleasure, eroticism hold sway so violently that it's like an "illness," and they dominate and remove or annihilate everything else so that the room of life ends up completely empty, and nothing remains apart from the chandelier itself (everything else in life takes place *en passant,* unconsciously, mechanically).
>
> The consequences aren't always terrible. Often they are, but in the end it is a fearless [the poet has written "fearful" here, but this is clearly a slip] body that is willing to achieve such a life. And that won't, out of fear—languishing in *désir*— remain outside the life that it wants, that it seeks.

Poems 1916–1918

Since Nine—   *pg. 55*

The poem was first written in 1917 with the title "Half Past Twelve."

The appearance of nocturnal apparitions is a motif that recurs significantly in Cavafy's work, from his early ghost story "In Broad Daylight" (ca. 1895), in which a black-clad male figure appears to a character in the dead of night, right through his mature period. The mid- to late 1910s in particular saw a striking preoccupation with this theme: "Theodotus" (<1911; 1915), in which the poet warns that the "invisible, immaterial" specter of the rhetorician Theodotus of Chios, threatening doom, might appear at any moment even in the tidiest, most well-organized lives; "Caesarion" (1914; 1918), in which the poet, after a restless night of intensive scholarly study, seems to see the murdered son of Antony and Cleopatra; and the Unfinished Poem "It Must Have Been the Spirits" (1919), in which the speaker imagines one night that his furniture vanishes, to be replaced by the figure of a youth he had met years before in Marseille.

The poet's interest in supernatural apparitions goes back to his earliest youth. In the travel journal he kept from his 1882 trip to Constantinople, he wrote that

> For my own part, I am apt to join in opinion with those who believe that *all* the *regions* of *Nature swarm* with *Spirits;* & that we have *multitudes* of *Spectators* on all our actions when we think ourselves most alone.

For Cavafy's "self-comment" on the theme of the invisible that is not, however, "immaterial," see the note on "Theodotus," pp. 376–7. Savidis, in his commentary on the Published Poems, notes that the poet's apartment did not have electricity, and was lighted by oil lamps or by candles.

In the Presence of the Statue of Endymion   pg. 57

For the poet's interest in statuary and sculpture, see the note on "Sculptor from Tyana," pp. 388–90.

Mount Latmus in Asia Minor, near the opulent ancient city of Miletus, was one of several cult sites dedicated to ENDYMION, a handsome mortal youth beloved in myth of the moon goddess, Selene. A marginal note on the text of Apollonius of Rhodes's *Argonautica* (a Hellenistic epic which elaborately retells the story of Selene and Endymion in the context of the poem's larger narrative about Jason, Medea, and the Argonauts) indicates that the myth of the love-struck goddess and her mortal beloved had been treated already by Sappho. A cave in Mount Latmus was said to be the spot where Endymion sleeps eternally and is visited periodically by the goddess.

The title is usually rendered as "Before the Statue of Endymion." But the Greek preposition that Cavafy uses, *enópion,* has a slightly stronger flavor than that suggested by "before"; its root is, in fact, the word for "face." The subtlety is one about which Cavafy clearly cared: an earlier title for this poem, subsequently discarded by the poet, was *Pro tou agalmatos tou Endimíonos,* the preposition *pro* there conveying precisely what the English "before" does.

Envoys from Alexandria   *pg. 58*

Like so many of Cavafy's historical poems, this one alludes to a bitter rivalry between Hellenistic kings, although in this case the two kings are brothers: Ptolemy VI Philometor ("the mother-loving") of Egypt's royal Lagid house, and his younger brother, Ptolemy VIII Euergetes ("the Benefactor"): the latter, and his epithet, are the objects of no little derision in the Unfinished Poem "Ptolemy the Benefactor (or Malefactor)." In 164 B.C., after he was expelled from Alexandria by his ambitious younger sibling, the elder Ptolemy appealed to Rome for assistance in winning back his throne—the incident to which "The Seleucid's Displeasure" also alludes. The Romans backed him, dispatching the younger sibling to rule Cyrene, in North Africa. The intervention of Rome, an empire on the rise, is thus starkly contrasted, as often in these historical poems, with the decline and disarray of the Hellenistic powers.

The allusion to the Delphic oracle (which also makes an appearance in "Nero's Timetable") adds a further layer to the restrained yet mordant ironies of this poem. From the earliest period in recorded Greek history down to the end of pagan worship, the oracle of Apollo at Delphi (in Central Greece) had enjoyed the greatest prestige—and political power. Envoys of states from all over the Greek world brought lavish gifts to the oracle (which were housed in elaborate "treasuries," each state constructing its own) in the hopes of receiving favorable responses to the questions they posed about the conduct of their domestic or international affairs. The interpretation of the usually vague oracular utterances could have important real-world ramifications. (Most famously when, during the Persian Wars, the Athenians asked the oracle how they should deal with the looming invasion by Persia; the oracle's response—that they take refuge "behind wooden walls"—was interpreted by most as an injunction to build a wall around the city, but others, led by the general Themistocles, persuaded the citizenry that the oracle was instructing them to build a powerful navy. The great Athenian naval victory over Persia that ended the war in 479 B.C. seems to bear out the latter interpretation—hindsight, of course, being the best-known aid to interpretation.)

Therefore, although there is no record of the two warring Ptolemies having appealed to Delphi for a settlement of their familial and political dispute, the dramatic situation represented in this poem is entirely plausible and dovetails nicely with the known facts. The dispute itself; the lavish gifts offered by each brother in the hope that he will receive a favorable response; the uneasiness of the priests (who clearly don't intend to leave things to the god) as to how they might word the response, given that one or the other of the two brothers (and benefactors of the shrine) must prevail; and then the unexpected and ironic revelation that Roman *Realpolitik,* rather than Apollo, has determined the outcome of the dispute—these threads come together beautifully in the last word in Cavafy's poem. *Moirasia* means, literally, "the allotment of portions," but the word *moira* that is at the heart of *moirasia* means, in Classical Greek, "fate" or "destiny." (It is helpful here to think of the similarly twofold connotations of the word "lot" in English.) Hence the destinies of the two Ptolemies are apportioned not by the Greek oracle, as in days of old, but rather "divvied up" crassly by the powers that be in Rome.

Aristobulus   pg. 59

The poem refers to a particularly grisly instance of dynastic maneuvering in ancient Judea, a territory whose history in the first century B.C. was, even by the standards of late Hellenistic times, embittered and complex; a tiny political entity in which nationalistic impulses raged against more than one occupying great power. During the mid-first century, both Rome and Parthia played for power in Judea, each empire designating its own choice of king: the Parthians selected Antigonus, a member of the old Judean royal family, the Hasmoneans; Rome, in the person of Marc Antony, had chosen Herod (73–74 B.C.; later Herod I the Great), the son of an ambitious vizier from the region of Idumaea. With Roman military assistance, Herod successfully established his rule in Judea. A great philhellene, he undertook ambitious building projects that included an artificial harbor at Caesarea, an amphitheater and theater for Jerusalem, and the rebuilding of the Temple, which he cannily entrusted to the priests. (Local opposition to foreign occupiers was traditionally ignited by pagan attempts to defile the Temple.)

Despite his shrewdness as a ruler, Herod was less skilled at managing domestic intrigues—which were numerous, to say the least, given that he had ten wives. One of these was MARIAMNE, the daughter of the Hasmonean throne princess, ALEXANDRA (who was the granddaughter of the Alexandra in the poem "Alexander Jannaeus, and Alexandra"). Mariamne's brother was ARISTOBULUS (53–35 B.C.), who was famed particularly for his beauty; according to the historian Josephus, the young prince's good looks caught the eye of his mother's great friend, Marc Antony. At the time of the incidents narrated in this poem, Aristobulus had recently been appointed by Herod as High Priest of the Temple at his mother's insistence; his popularity among the common people inevitably aroused the suspicions of the paranoid Herod, who, egged on by his mother, CYPROS, and his sister, SALOME (later the subject of Oscar Wilde's play; the name is pronounced with the accent on the second syllable), ordered the eighteen-year-old Aristobulus to be drowned while he was swimming in a pool at Alexandra's palace in Jericho. This savagery toward members of his own family was by no means unusual. Herod went on to order the execution of Mariamne herself six years later; her mother, Alexandra—the morally outraged figure in Cavafy's poem—is said to have testified against her daughter in order to save her own life, and was herself executed soon after. In the year 7 Herod ordered the executions of his two sons by Mariamne as well; a few days before his death, in 4 B.C., he ordered the murder of his eldest son.

The source for the events alluded to in this poem is Josephus's *Jewish*

Antiquities, 15.3.53–61, where we find a similar emphasis on Alexandra's rage and on her frustration at not being able to reveal the true cause of her son's death:

> Upon all this, Herod decided to carry out his plan against the young man. And so when the holiday was over, and he was feasting at Jericho with Alexandra, who had invited them there, he acted very kindly toward the youth, and took him aside to a deserted spot, showing himself perfectly willing to play with him and act the child with him, in a way that delighted the boy. It being rather hotter than usual in that place, they suddenly all went out en masse, as if gripped by a frenzy, and standing around the fishponds (those around the courtyard, which were large) they cooled themselves off from the midday heat. At first they merely watched Herod's servants and friends as they swam; but presently the youth, egged on by Herod, went into the water along with them, and as dusk fell those of Herod's friends to whom he had given the command dunked him as he was swimming, plunging him under the water as if it were being done in good fun; they didn't stop until the boy was completely drowned. This is how Aristobulus was murdered, having lived not quite eighteen years, and having occupied the high priesthood for only a year; an office that Ananelus now assumed again.
>
> When this calamity was related to the women they were immediately plunged into mourning, as they beheld the body that was laid out in front of them, and their grief knew no limits. As the news spread the entire city mourned excessively, each household making the calamity its own, as if it had not happened to someone else. But Alexandra was far more deeply affected, knowing as she did that it was murder; and yet while her grief was greater than that of the others, owing to her knowledge of how the murder had been committed, she had nonetheless to bear up, anticipating as she did even greater evils to come. Often she meant to cut her life short by her own hand, but she desisted in the hopes that she

would live long enough to avenge the unjust murder that had been plotted; indeed even more, she resolved to try to live even longer, never letting on that she might think that her son had been slain on purpose, so that she might take vengeance when she thought the moment propitious. Herod, meanwhile, made every effort to ensure that no one abroad imagined that the boy's death had been the result of any plot of his.

Caesarion

pg. 61

The first version of this poem, written in 1914, had the title "Of Ptolemy Caesar"—the latter being one of the names of Ptolemy XV Philopator Philometor (47–30 B.C.), the last monarch of the Lagid dynasty founded by Ptolemy I; better known as CAESARION ("Little Caesar"), he was the son of Julius Caesar and Cleopatra.

In the "Donations" of 34 B.C., when he was only thirteen years old (see "Alexandrian Kings"), Caesarion was grandly declared the "king of kings" by his stepfather, Marc Antony. A year after the suicides of Antony and Cleopatra in 30 B.C., Octavian (later Augustus) had Caesarion put to death; as he gave the order for the murder, one of his advisors is said to have complained sardonically of the dangers of *polykaisariê*, "too many Caesars." The Greek, *polykaisariê*, is a punning allusion to the Homeric coinage *polykoiraniê*, "too many rulers," which appears in Homer's *Iliad*, 2.203–6. In this famous passage, Odysseus berates the mutinous Greek troops who wish to abandon the siege of Troy and return home:

> *Not all of us Achaeans can be masters here;*
> *too many rulers [polykoiraniê] is no good thing; let one man rule,*
> *one king, to whom the crooked-minded son of Kronos gave*
> *the scepter and royal rights, that he may use them to be king.*

Etienne Combe, the last European director of the library in Alexandria from which Cavafy would borrow books, recalled that the poet would borrow collections of inscriptions such as those mentioned in this poem.

Nero's Deadline pg. 63

As the cruelties and egomaniacal excesses of the emperor NERO (on whom see the note on "The Eumenides' Footfalls." p. 482) worsened, a plot to overthrow him was instigated by C. Julius Vindex. (Among those excesses was Nero's ludicrous concert tour of Greece—known to the Romans as the province of ACHAEA—in the year 67, when he "liberated" the province.) Vindex invited the popular governor of Spain, Servius Sulpicius GALBA (3 B.C.–69 A.D.), a member of an extremely distinguished aristocratic family, to join the conspiracy. Galba eventually marched on Rome, and after Nero's suicide in 68 became emperor in his seventy-third year.

But this poem does much more than gently mock Nero's wholly unearned sense of security, which depends (as does the smugness of other Cavafian subjects) on a partial or imperfect knowledge or vision; a further irony is that Galba himself proved to be no great success. Indeed, his own avarice and tactlessness made him as unpopular among the legions as he would eventually be among certain of his political allies, and on January 15, 69, he was murdered by the praetorian guard at the instigation of M. Salvius Otho, a former co-conspirator against Nero who was disappointed when Galba failed to appoint him his heir. Further historical ironies ripple outward from this poem: Otho himself was emperor for only a few short months, fatally clashing with yet another of his former co-conspirators, Aulus Vitellius, who had also declared himself emperor. By the end of the year 69, four men had been emperor; the last was Titus Flavius Vespasianus (Vespasian: 9–79 A.D.), a practical man of relatively humble origins who successfully established himself as emperor and founded the Flavian dynasty.

The oracle given to Nero is recounted in Suetonius's *Life of Nero*, chapter 40:

> Astrologers had once predicted to Nero that he would one day be put away; whence that well-known saying of his: "Our humble art sustains us," by which he no doubt thought he might be indulged in his pursuit of the art of lyre-playing— an amusement for an emperor, but a necessity for a private

person. Some of the astrologers had promised him rule over the East, once he had been cast off, several referring by name to the rule of Jerusalem; rather more promised the restitution of all his former fortunes. Being inclined to this latter hope (having lost both Armenia and Britain and having recovered both), he reckoned that he had been acquitted of the bad luck for which he had been fated. And, after he had consulted the Delphic oracle and heard the response that he must beware the seventy-third year, taking this to mean that he would die only at that age, and taking no account of Galba's age, he felt such great confidence not only in his old age, but also in a constant and singular good fortune, that when he lost some extremely valuable articles in a shipwreck, he did not hesitate to say to his intimates that the fish would bring them back to him.

Safe Haven   *pg. 64*

This poem revisits, in a pagan context, a motif Cavafy had first treated twenty years earlier in a Christian one, in "Prayer" (*1896; 1898*): the drama of a young man's untimely death is poignantly contrasted with his family's earnest but futile hopes and prayers for his well-being. He would take up the theme again ten years later, in "Cleitus's Illness," in which both Christian and pagan prayers fail to save a gravely ill young man.

One of Their Gods   *pg. 65*

An early version of this poem, called "One of Them," was composed in 1899; this rewritten version was first printed in 1917.

Diana Haas has noted that this is the first extant poem by Cavafy in which the word "ephebe" appears, and in which, indeed, the drama of the poem, externally as well as emotionally, pivots on a studied confusion between a beautiful mortal and a beautiful god—one that recurs, for instance, in "Song of Ionia." In this context—and particularly given the date of composition of the earliest version of this poem, at the end of the decade in which Cavafy, heavily influenced by Baudelaire and the Parnassians, first started to write about elite beings gifted with a special sight—it is interesting to note that in the *Life of Apollonius of Tyana,* the great sage observes that the teachings of Pythagoras promised initiates that they would be able to know how to discern the presence of a god. For Cavafy's interest in supernatural apparitions and visitations more generally, see the note on "Since Nine—," pp. 399–400.

SELEUCIA was the name of a number of cities in the vast Seleucid empire; the name derives from that of the founder of the dynasty, Seleucus I. One of these was Seleucia-on-Tigris, founded on the river's left bank, below Baghdad, around 305 B.C., as the capital of the king-dom, but a likelier candidate for the setting of this poem is Seleucia Pieria, founded on the mouth of the Orontes River around 300 B.C. by Seleucus, who was buried there by his son, Antiochus. This Seleucia, which the historian Polybius describes as having boasted fine temples and civic architecture, suburbs, and a business quarter, was also an important naval base, and it could well have provided the decadent plea-sures to which Cavafy's subject is devoted.

Haas has also drawn attention to the way in which this poem reflects the extent of the poet's absorption of Gibbon, whose *Decline and Fall* contains the following passage (3.29) about the fourth-century general Stilicho:

> If Stilicho had not possessed the external advantages of strength and stature, the most flattering bard, in the pres-ence of so many thousand spectators, would have hesitated to affirm that he surpassed the measure of the demi-gods of antiquity; and that, whenever he moved with lofty steps, through the streets of the capital, the astonished crowd made room for the stranger, who displayed, in a private condition, the awful majesty of a hero.

Stilicho, one might add, was half Roman and half Vandal; the mixed her-itage of this impressive figure is an element recalled, perhaps, in the way that the citizens of Seleucia in the poem wonder whether the beautiful ephebe is a Syrian of Greek origin, or some kind of foreigner.

Tomb of Lanes *pg. 66*

The implied milieu of the poem is a pointedly cosmopolitan one, and therefore consonant with the poet's interest in the multicultural richness of life in the cities of Greater Greece: LANES is a name of uncertain provenance, MARCUS Roman, and RAMETICHOS Egyptian. HYACINTH, in Greek mythology, was a beautiful mortal youth, and the name became a byword for youthful male beauty. The myth is most famously retold by Ovid: beloved of Apollo, Hyacinth was killed by a jealous Zephyr; from his blood, as it spilled on the earth, sprang the flower that bears his name.

In a City of Osrhoene *pg. 68*

Another poem in which Cavafy introduces, with unusual explicitness and a characteristically delicate irony, the tension between the Classical Greek cultural inheritance and the vast sprawl of the later Greek-speaking world, through which that inheritance was disseminated.

For the setting of this poem, OSRHOENE, a Syriac kingdom, see the note on "That Is He," pp. 391–2. CHARMIDES, an Athenian youth famed for his beauty (and also Plato's uncle) was immortalized in the Platonic dialogue that bears his name: in it, Socrates, inspired by the perfection of his companion Charmides' beauty, seeks to define wisdom. The historical Charmides, as it happens, was killed in a political dispute, and there is, perhaps, a subtle invitation in this poem to compare the noble Athenian, martyred for his convictions and immortalized in high literature, with the young Rhemon, hurt in a barroom brawl and dragged to an inn by his ragtag band of ethnically mixed friends.

The body of a beautiful wounded youth, immobilized and lovingly tended, is a motif that can be traced to "The Funeral of Sarpedon," a poem that shares that motif with Oscar Wilde's "Charmides" (1881), which may well have influenced it: the original title of this poem was, in fact, "Charmides." For a possible connection between Wilde's and Cavafy's poems, see the note on "The Funeral of Sarpedon," pp. 469–70.

Tomb of Ignatius *pg. 69*

First written in April 1916 with the title "Tomb of Hieronymus."

In the early church, a lector (Greek *anagnostês*) was a lay person responsible for reading selections from the Old Testament and Epistles during the liturgy; later on, the position was held by clerics in minor orders. Since Cavafy, in a commentary on this poem, characterizes the position as being "semi-ecclesiastical," we can infer that the poem is set during the earlier rather than the later days of Christianity. The office might have held special interest for the poet, since a well-known item in the biography of Julian the Apostate was that he held the position of lector before abandoning his Christian faith.

In the Month of Hathor *pg. 70*

In this perhaps most remarkable of the "tomb" poems, Cavafy has re-created the appearance of a scholarly transcription of a funerary inscription. In such transcriptions, letters that are missing or illegible in the original (which can, however, be inferred from context) are rendered in brackets, so as to distinguish them from what is actually legible. This tension, between the traces that remain and what must be inferred, irradiates the entire poem.

HATHOR was the name of the cow-headed Egyptian goddess whose eponymous month came late in the autumn. In Greek, the letters KAPPA and ZETA (KZ), taken together, also represent the number 27, i.e., the age of the deceased.

For Ammon, Who Died at 29 Years of Age, in 610 *pg. 71*

The milieu of this poem is clearly Egyptian: AMMON is an Egyptian name, and the name RAPHAEL suggests that the boy is Coptic.

Aemilian Son of Monaës, an Alexandrian, 628–655 A.D. *pg. 72*

Savidis suggests that this poem was first written in 1898 with the title "On Guard," in a version comprising only the first two stanzas of this final version.

The dates that Cavafy invents for his fictional subject, together with the telling detail that he died in Sicily, point to a subtle historical irony. Mohammed's general, the Arab leader 'Amr, conquered Byzantine Alexandria in the year 642; although the Byzantines twice tried to recapture it soon afterward, it was to remain in Arab hands. Hence whatever his armor, whatever his boasts, we may take it that Aemilian was forced to flee his native city for his life.

I've Gazed So Much— pg. 75

The original title of this poem, in the first draft of 1911, was "For Beauty."

The Window of the Tobacco Shop pg. 77

The original title of this poem, in the first draft of 1907, was "In the Closed Carriage."

In Evening pg. 79

The poem's setting is Alexandria, as indicated by its original title, "Alexandrian."

Gray pg. 80

Cavafy takes conspicuous pains to conceal the sex of the beloved in this poem: in the Greek, no pronoun is given as the subject of either of the two active verbs—"departs" in line 5, and "lives" in line 7. I have rendered these lines so as to preserve this important ambiguity.

Below the House pg. 81

This taut and beautiful poem from the mid-1910s rather strikingly contains elements that would recur in poems of the late '20s and early '30s. The way in which the mundane neighborhood (*sinikía*) in the first line becomes the setting for a miraculous transformation of everything (*ipóstasis . . . óli*) into intense emotion (*idonikí sinkínisi*) in the last sentence is something we encounter again in "In the Same Place" (1929), where the everyday inventory of the poet's neighborhood (*sinikía*) again leads to a climactic and total transformation of everything into emotion (*esthimatopiíthikes olókliro*). Similarly, the collocation here of the imperfect verbs "standing" (*stekomoun*) and "gazing" (*ekíttaza*) that together lead to an erotic/pleasurable epiphany will reappear in "The Mirror in the Entrance" (1930), where the reflection of an athletic young tailor's assistant who was standing (*stékontan*) and gazing at himself (*kittázontan*) in a mirror causes the mirror to rejoice in the vision of "perfect beauty" that it has received on its surface.

Stratis Tsirkas (in *O Politikos Kavafis*, "The Political Cavafy") identified the germ of this poem in one of the irritated reading notes that Cavafy made between 1893 and 1896 on the text of Ruskin. The latter had argued that

> energetic admiration may be excited in certain minds by a display of fireworks, or a street of handsome shops; but the feeling is not poetical, because the grounds of it are false, and therefore ignoble. There is in reality nothing to deserve admiration either in the firing of packets of gunpowder, or in the display of the stocks of warehouses. But admiration excited by the budding of a flower is a poetical feeling, because it is impossible that this manifestation of spiritual power and vital beauty can ever be enough admired.

Cavafy retorted as follows:

> This confinement of Poetry in the prison of "noble grounds" is mistaken . . .
>
> Great and superior works can be created within the framework "of the street with handsome shops," by reason not of the nobility or the lack thereof—foolish words—of the "street etc.," but rather of the feeling, or the sensation, that will be connected with the "street" and that will surround it as if with a halo.

The Next Table *pg. 82*

As in "Gray," Cavafy's Greek makes it impossible to determine the gender of the object of the speaker's desire.

Days of 1903 *pg. 84*

Originally written in March 1909, with the title "March 1907," this is the first of the five "Days of . . ." poems that the poet published.

Poems 1919–1933

Of the Jews (50 A.D.) *pg. 89*

The dramatic date of the poem is crucial. The brief reign of the emperor Gaius ("Caligula": born 12 A.D., acceded in 37, assassinated in 41) was marked by explosions of violence against, and among, Jewish communities in the empire. In 39–40, riots broke out in Jerusalem and other cities with large Jewish populations after the emperor tried (in 38) to have a statue of himself placed in the Temple; in Alexandria, tensions between the Jewish community (which had benefited under a relatively disinterested Roman administration), and the majority of Alexandrian Greeks (who bitterly resented both the Romans and the increasingly assimilated Jews, who were showing ever-greater interest in acquiring Greek citizenship rights) exploded in a violent pogrom. Many Jews were massacred, synagogues were destroyed or defiled, and a ghetto was established. Only after the accession of the emperor Claudius, in 41, was calm restored for a time. The Jews were granted their civic rights once more, although they were denied Greek citizenship.

It is against this background of tensions among the various subcultures of the Roman East that Ianthes' oscillation between Hellenic culture and the Jewish identity, which sets him apart from Hellenism, must be read. (His name is Greek but his father's is Roman, which itself is suggestive of the cultural mixing that fired Cavafy's imagination.)

Imenus *pg. 90*

An early version of this poem, entitled "Love It More," was written in October 1915; however, it lacked the historical details provided in the second stanza of the poem in its current state, and hence the larger framework that suggests one possible reading of this strange short poem.

The Byzantine emperor MICHAEL III (839–867), nicknamed "the Drunkard," was the son of the emperor Theophilus and empress Theodosia; he inherited the throne as a child and, when he grew up, was known for his dissoluteness. (The intrigues of his mother and various protectors, and the ecclesiastical upheavals they caused, are likely the historical backdrop for the Unpublished Poem "Fugitives.") In his avidity for pleasure and his disdain for the right exercise of kingship, he resembled no one so much as Nero, to whom Gibbon compared him—unfavorably, indeed, since Michael, a devotee of drink and horse racing, did not even have Nero's artistic pretensions. Cavafy was familiar with Gibbon's devastating assessment of this deliciously immoral figure, from chapter 48, part 3, of *Decline and Fall*:

> Among the successors of Nero and Elagabalus, we have not hitherto found the imitation of their vices, the character of a Roman prince who considered pleasure as the object of life, and virtue as the enemy of pleasure. Whatever might have been the maternal care of Theodora in the education of Michael the Third, her unfortunate son was a king before he was a man. If the ambitious mother labored to check the progress of reason, she could not cool the ebullition of passion; and her selfish policy was justly repaid by the contempt and ingratitude of the headstrong youth. At the age of eighteen, he rejected her authority, without feeling his own incapacity to govern the empire and himself. With Theodora, all gravity and wisdom retired from the court; their place was supplied by the alternate dominion of vice and folly; and it was impossible, without forfeiting the public esteem, to acquire or preserve the favor of the emperor. The millions of

gold and silver which had been accumulated for the service of the state, were lavished on the vilest of men, who flattered his passions and shared his pleasures. . . . The unnatural lusts which had degraded even the manhood of Nero, were banished from the world; yet the strength of Michael was consumed by the indulgence of love and intemperance. In his midnight revels, when his passions were inflamed by wine, he was provoked to issue the most sanguinary commands; and if any feelings of humanity were left, he was reduced, with the return of sense, to approve the salutary disobedience of his servants. But the most extraordinary feature in the character of Michael, is the profane mockery of the religion of his country. . . . A buffoon of the court was invested in the robes of the patriarch: his twelve metropolitans, among whom the emperor was ranked, assumed their ecclesiastical garments: they used or abused the sacred vessels of the altar; and in their bacchanalian feasts, the holy communion was administered in a nauseous compound of vinegar and mustard. . . . By this extravagant conduct, the son of Theophilus became as contemptible as he was odious: every citizen was impatient for the deliverance of his country; and even the favorites of the moment were apprehensive that a caprice might snatch away what a caprice had bestowed. In the thirtieth year of his age, and in the hour of intoxication and sleep, Michael the Third was murdered in his chamber by the founder of a new dynasty, whom the emperor had raised to an equality of rank and power.

It is worth nothing here that Michael has the characteristics of various other Postclassical and Late Antique monarchs whom we meet in Cavafy's historical poems. Like Orophernes in the poem that bears his name, or the children of Cleopatra in "Alexandrian Kings," he was caught in political intrigues from earliest childhood; like Julian the Apostate, another rebel monarch, he was notable for his contempt for religion. But Michael lacks the poignancy or contrarian fascination of those figures; undistinguished, perhaps, for anything but the intensity of his decadent pursuits, he is of interest for Cavafy because his reign provides the decadent context in which other "unnatural" pleasures might emerge, as indeed they do here.

Aboard the Ship
pg. 91

The original title of this poem was "The Ionian Sea."

Of Demetrius Soter (162–150 B.C.)
pg. 92

For DEMETRIUS I SOTER ("the Savior"), see the note on "The Seleucid's Displeasure," pp. 382–3. Demetrius was the second son of SELEUCUS IV PHILOPATOR, a son of Antiochus III "the Great" of the Seleucid empire. It was under Antiochus III that the Seleucids were disastrously defeated by the Romans at the BATTLE OF MAGNESIA in 190 B.C. (on which see "The Battle of Magnesia"); afterwards his son, Seleucus IV, became the mere coregent of his ancestral domain. In 178 B.C., at the age of nine, Seleucus IV's son Demetrius went to live at Rome as a political hostage, a token of goodwill by the Seleucids to their new masters; he remained there for sixteen years, during which time first his uncle, Antiochus IV Epiphanes, and then his cousin, Antiochus V, supplanted him on the Seleucid throne. This Demetrius is the eponymous Seleucid of the poem "The Seleucid's Displeasure"; he is also mentioned briefly in "Orophernes."

In the year 162 B.C., at the age of twenty-five, Demetrius succeeded in escaping from Rome, with the help of no less a personage than the historian Polybius. Despite Rome's support of his rivals, Demetrius successfully (and somewhat ruthlessly) established himself as ruler in the empire of his forefathers after his return, and he took for himself the title *Sôter*, "Savior." He was killed in battle in 150, at the age of thirty-seven, defending his throne against the pretender Alexander BALAS (see "Orophernes" and "The Favor of Alexander Balas"), who claimed to be the son of Seleucus IV, and who, more importantly, had the support of the Romans as well as of the Egyptian and Pergamene rulers. Balas triumphed, but only briefly: after scarcely five years he was forced from the throne, with the Romans' blessing, by Attalus II of Pergamum, Ptolemy VI of Egypt, and an intriguer called HERACLEIDES, formerly satrap of Babylon, and subsequently murdered by the man with whom he had taken refuge.

If Indeed He Died pg. 94

An early version of this poem, entitled "Absence," was written in October 1897; Cavafy revised it in July 1910 and again in March 1920, when he printed it for private circulation. The text of this early draft is worth comparing to the final version:

ABSENCE

Where has he gone off to, where has the Sage been lost?
After his innumerable miracles
he suddenly disappeared, and nobody has heard
what's become of him, what he's done, where he's gone.
But they said that he will never die.
Perhaps the time has not yet come for his return
and for this reason he's been gone for sixteen
centuries.—But he will appear again.—
Or perhaps that story is true, the one in which
his assumption into heaven took place in Crete,
in the middle of the night, while virginal voices,
harmonious voices, and foreign to this earth,
hymned "Go from the earth, go up to heaven,
go," and to his native land he then returned.—
But after this, in Tyana, a young
man, a sophist, said that he had seen him.—

In both versions, the speaker is a pagan admirer of APOLLONIUS OF TYANA, Philostratus's biography of whom was alleged to have been based, in part, on a memoir of Apollonius by a disciple called DAMIS. The title of Cavafy's poem is the Classical Greek phrase *eige eteleuta,* a quotation from the closing of Philostratus's *Life:* "There are several versions of his death," Philostratus writes, "if indeed he died [*eige eteleuta*]."

In its final form, the poem pointedly juxtaposes the covert paganism of Cavafy's speaker with the famous Christian piety of the Eastern

Roman emperor JUSTIN I (ca. 435–527). Often overshadowed by his more illustrious nephew and heir Justinian (not least because the historian Procopius, to whom we owe much of our knowledge of Justin's court and that of his nephew, was implacably hostile to the lowborn Justin), Justin was in many ways a remarkable figure. The legend has it that, with little more than the clothes on his back, he traveled from his native Macedonia to the great capital of Constantinople as a young man, and rose through the ranks swiftly to become commander of the three hundred *excubitors,* or elite palace guard; this meant that he was the only commander of troops in the city. When, on the night of July 8, 518, the emperor Anastasius died without immediate heirs, Justin was acclaimed—unwillingly, or so he immediately wrote the pope in Rome, Hormisdas—the new emperor. He was distinguished in his personal life for a lack of self-indulgent excess (he remained married to the wife he had bought as a slave and subsequently freed) and, in his public life, for effecting a reconciliation of the Eastern and Western Churches, in 518.

Justin is known, indeed, for having supported other kinds of reconciliations as well. Two years before his death, he repealed a law that prohibited members of the senatorial classes from marrying women from the lower classes—presumably, it is thought, to allow his nephew and adopted heir, Justinian, to marry a former actress, Theodora, who later became empress. This repeal is credited with precipitating the disintegration of old class boundaries within the Byzantine court. It was as an alleged spy for Justin's court at Constantinople that Boethius, author of *The Consolation of Philosophy,* was put to death in Rome by the Ostrogothic king Theodoric, in 524.

Justin's reign was marked by ferocious theological disputes and schisms between various Christian sects, and it is against that perfervid and sometimes violent background that we must read the clandestine paganism of the speaker in the present poem, which like so many others (for instance, "On the Outskirts of Antioch") contrasts the fervor of the Christians with the decaying energies of Greco-Roman paganism. The addition of the Late Antique frame to the original poem of 1897 suggests, perhaps, a desire to represent subtly within the poem the poet's own complicated negotiations between pagan desires and Christian culture, between the permissible and the forbidden.

Young Men of Sidon (400 A.D.)

SIDON was an important commercial city of Phoenicia, located on the coast of present-day Lebanon; in antiquity it was a major producer of luxury goods, such as purple dye, and also of glass. The date of 400 A.D. is suggestive, marking as it does a historical moment not long after the triumph of Christianity in the Roman Empire, and not long before the advent of the barbarians; for this reason, the date Cavafy chooses for this poem evokes the short but clarion swan song of pagan Classical culture. ("Beyond the gardens of Sidon," Sareyannis wrote of this poem, "and the perfumed youths, we can make out in the background of the scene the shapes of the barbarians.") Cavafy uses the fraught date of 400 A.D. in the title of two other poems: "Theater of Sidon (400 A.D.)," and "Temethus, an Antiochene: 400 A.D."

The poem is organized, in part, around a perceived competition between purely literary pursuits and great historical events. The setting in luxurious Sidon, the perfumed room in which the recital is taking place, and in particular the choice of poets to be recited clearly suggest that, at least in the mind of the youth who speaks out, "poetry" is an exalted and rarefied realm which one ought proudly to inhabit; his and his friends' preference for epigrammatists known for their erotic verses suggests further that the proper subject of poetry is, to his mind, the passions. MELEAGER, a poet and philosopher from Gadara, in Syria, flourished around 100 B.C.; although he wrote in a variety of genres, he is most famous for his *Garland,* a collection of verse epigrams elaborately arranged by author and theme. His poems are nearly all erotic, addressed to both girls and boys. CRINAGORAS, from the city of Mytilene on Lesbos, was a poet of epigrams, many of them about members of the inner circle of the emperor Augustus; he himself was a member of official embassies to both Julius Caesar (in 48–47 and again in 45 B.C.) and Augustus (in 26–25 B.C.), and appears to have lived until about the time of the latter's death, in 14 A.D. RHIANUS of Crete was another epigrammatist. Born a slave about 275 B.C., he became a schoolteacher and scholar; best known as a composer of epics devoted to various regions of Greece, he also produced an edition of Homer and many erotic epigrams, of which very few survive.

At least part of the irony of Cavafy's poem is that "history" is here represented by the greatest of the poets recited in that Sidonian salon: the Athenian tragedian Aeschylus, who was born at Athens ca. 525, and died in the city of Gela, in Sicily, in 456 B.C. The actor in Cavafy's poem chooses to recite not a passage from one of Aeschylus's great dramas, such as those to which the agitated youth alludes, but rather Aeschylus's own verse epitaph, which, according to the later Greek authors Athenaeus and Pausanias, was composed by the playwright himself and (according to the largely apocryphal *Life* of Aeschylus) inscribed on the tomb erected for him by the people of Gela at their own expense. The epitaph, in four lines consisting of two elegiac couplets (alternating dactylic hexameter and dactylic pentameter), has been preserved, and runs as follows:

> Here lies Euphorion's son, Aeschylus, an Athenian, beneath this
>   tomb, dead in wheat-bearing Gela.
> His valour far-renowned the Marathonian lea may proclaim—
>   and the flowing-haired Mede, who knew it well.

The lines allude to the Athenian playwright's service during the Persian Wars of 490–479 B.C., and specifically at the Battle of Marathon in 490, the decisive encounter at which the Greeks defeated the Persian army; the Persians fought under the Median general DATIS and under ARTA-PHERNES, the brother of Darius I, the king who had instigated the war. It was in this battle that Aeschylus served and his brother was killed.

The implicit contrasts that run through this poem—between history and literature, between art and life—thus also include, subtly, the tension between the great Hellenic past and the later Mediterranean cultures, such as that of Late Antique Sidon, that were the heirs (the perhaps debased heirs) to high Hellenism.

That They Come— *pg. 98*

In her critical presentation of Cavafy's work, the French novelist Marguerite Yourcenar comments on the uncanny motif of the conjuration of ghosts, apparitions, and lost loved ones that persists throughout his poems (see the notes on "Theodotus," pp. 376–7, and "Since Nine—," pp. 399–400), and which in this poem includes a suggestion of occult magic:

> This is what gives him his strange quality of a genuine, which is to say well-concealed, esoterism. Hence, in "That They Come," and in "Caesarion," the darkness both allegorical and real, the image of the taper and of the extinguished lamp, seem to pass from the domain of literary ornament or even erotic fantasy into the domain of the occult; we cannot help but think of the sorcerer's formula *extinctis luminibus* ["with lights extinguished"].

Darius *pg. 99*

Cavafy sets his poem in the city of AMISUS in Pontus, a kingdom constituting the northern part of Asia Minor and extending as far south as the area known as Cappadocia, in central Asia Minor, during the reign of its last independent king, MITHRIDATES VI EUPATOR DIONYSUS ("the Great"), who was born about 132 B.C. and was another of Cavafy's doomed Hellenistic rulers living in the growing shadow of Roman supremacy. The scion of a dynasty that traced its roots to Persia, Mithridates was, indeed, the last Hellenistic monarch to be a serious threat to Roman power in the Mediterranean and Near East. By the time he was in his late forties, his own expansionist policies had made him the master of most of Asia Minor, much of Greece, and of the Aegean islands except for Rhodes—and thus a formidable foe of the Romans, with whom he fought three major wars, the so-called Mithridatic Wars, between 88 and 67 B.C. Like many of the Hellenistic figures who captured Cavafy's imagination, he straddled the non-Greek and Hellenic worlds: at once savage and incomprehensibly "barbarian" in many of his habits (he provoked the first Mithridatic War after massacring eighty thousand Roman citizens while overrunning Pontus in 88; after his final defeat he ordered his own harem to be killed), and Greek, an admirer and (in his coinage) imitator of Alexander the Great. He was said, too, to have a prodigious memory, and is famous for having attempted to make himself immune to poisons by taking sublethal doses of a variety of known toxins.

Mithridates' descent from associates of DARIUS THE GREAT of Persia (549–486 B.C.), the king who instigated the Persian Wars with the Greeks from 490 to 479 B.C., provides the occasion for the epic that the poet in Cavafy's poem is writing. The name Phernazes is Persian; as the fictional poet tries to imagine the lust for power that motivated the ancient Persian ruler to seize the throne, he learns that the contemporary, Persian-descended king has decided to make war on the Romans. The event described is most likely the onset of the Third Mithridatic War, in 74 B.C., in which Mithridates occupied Bithynia, a neighboring province, in response to a move by Rome to annex it. He was eventually driven out of Pontus by the Roman general Lucullus, and defeated at the Battle of Nicopolis by Pompey in 67 B.C. A few years later he was murdered, at the age of sixty-eight, by a guard while plotting to renew his anti-Roman activities.

The distinctive framing device found in this poem—that is, a Hellenistic poet's attempt to write a work about the Classical past—recurs most notably in the Unfinished Poem "Ptolemy the Benefactor (or Malefactor)"; but a number of other poems take the form of fictional verses embedded in later historical frames: see for example "Imenos," "For Those Who Fought on Behalf of the Achaean League," and the Unfinished Poem "Epitaph of a Samian."

Anna Comnena pg. 101

ANNA COMNENA (1083–1146) was the eldest daughter of the Byzantine emperor Alexius I Comnenus. After failing to usurp the succession on behalf of her husband, Nicephorus Bryennius, from her brother JOHN, who subsequently became emperor as John II, Anna retired to a convent and there wrote the ALEXIAD, an epic poem in fifteen books about the life of her father. The direct quotations from Anna's work that appear in Cavafy's poem come from chapter 4 of the Prologue; it is perhaps an intentional irony on the poet's part that the object of the lyric laments that he quotes is not, in fact, Anna's father, but rather her husband, Bryennius, whose premature death she mourns in terms that are hyperbolic, to say the least. ("The calamities of the past," she goes on to say, "in the face of this infinite disaster, I regard as a mere drop of rain compared with the whole Atlantic Ocean or the waves of the Adriatic Sea.") Our sympathy for Anna's copious tears may, however, be mitigated by the knowledge that she bitterly decried her husband's failure to help her seize the royal power on Alexius's death (see below).

Although Anna's encomiastic work and high-flown style have come in for favorable reappraisal in recent years, the general tenor of Cavafy's attitude toward his subject, at least, seems to reflect the censorious conclusions of Gibbon, who writes as follows about Anna Comnena and her paean to her father's virtues:

> The life of the emperor Alexius has been delineated by a favourite daughter, who was inspired by a tender regard for his person and a laudable zeal to perpetuate his virtues. Conscious of the just suspicion of her readers, the princess Anna Comnena repeatedly protests that, besides her personal knowledge, she had searched the discourse and writings of the most respectable veterans; that, after an interval of thirty years, forgotten by, and forgetful of, the world, her mournful solitude was inaccessible to hope and fear; and that truth, the naked perfect truth, was more dear and sacred than the memory of her parent. Yet, instead of the simplicity of style and narrative which wins our belief, an elaborate affectation of rhetoric and science betrays, in every page, the vanity of a female author.

Cavafy's decision to cite actual lines from Anna's *Alexiad* seems indeed to stem from an ironic impulse: her low and raw motives, after all, stand in stark contrast to the famed elevation and refinement of her Greek. Still, about this elevation and refinement there is little dispute, however varied the assessment of Anna herself. In a footnote to his rapturous description of the prosperous and cultivated reigns of the Byzantine emperor Basil and his son and successor Leo the Philosopher, Gibbon, referring to the "general knowledge" of the enlightened age that was Byzantium in the twelfth century, declares that

> Anna Comnena may boast of her Greek style (τὸ Ἑλληνίζειν ἐς ἄκρον ἐσπουδακυῖα) and Zonaras, her contemporary, but not her flatterer, may add with truth, γλῶτταν εἶχεν ἀκριβῶς Ἀττικιζοῦσαν ["she did indeed possess an Attic dic-

tion"]. The princess was conversant with the artful dialogues of Plato; and had studied the tetrakús, or quadrivium of astrology, geometry, arithmetic, and music.

And yet as Cavafy's poem makes clear, Anna's devotion to learning did not preclude a passion for power as well. This passion is exquisitely conveyed by Gibbon, whose description of the aftermath of Alexius's death (including his wife Irene's denunciation of the dying emperor as a "hypocrite") is vivid and witty:

> It was the wish of Irene to supplant the eldest of her surviving sons in favour of her daughter the princess Anna, whose philosophy would not have refused the weight of a diadem. But the order of male succession was asserted by the friends of their country; the lawful heir drew the royal signet from the finger of his insensible or conscious father; and the empire obeyed the master of the palace. Anna Comnena was stimulated by ambition and revenge to conspire against the life of her brother, and, when the design was prevented by the fears of scruples of her husband, she passionately exclaimed that nature had mistaken the two sexes and had endowed Bryennius with the soul of a woman.

The final sentence in particular is worth keeping in mind when we evaluate Cavafy's decision to quote Anna on her inconsolable grief at her husband's death. Although her plot against her brother merited death, John commuted the sentence; Gibbon pointedly notes that one achievement of John's beneficent reign was to abolish the death penalty throughout the empire.

Byzantine Noble, in Exile, Versifying

pg. 102

The imaginary speaker refers to events during the reigns of Michael VII, who was deposed in 1078, and NICEPHORUS III BOTANIATES, who deposed him. Three years later, in 1081, Botaniates was himself deposed by the founder of a new dynasty, Alexius I Comnenus. (Alexius was the husband of IRENE DUCAS and father of Anna Comnena: see "Anna Comnena" and "Anna Dalassene.")

The "HEROES OF THESSALY AND THE PELOPONNESE" are, very likely, the protagonists of the *Iliad*—Achilles, who was raised in Thessaly by the centaur Chiron, and the sons of Atreus, Agamemnon and Menelaus, kings of Mycenae and Sparta in the Peloponnese.

The references to matters both Byzantine and Classical in this poem clarify its underlying structure and a hidden irony. The poem falls into two sections, each of which is divided among religious and political themes. The first, Byzantine section begins by mentioning the speaker's expertise in religious and ecclesiastical matters (which apparently had made him invaluable to the now-deposed Botaniates) and then alludes to the turbulent politics of his time—his own exile at the order of Irene Ducas, the new empress, presumably because of his relationship with Botaniates. A similar progression structures the second, Classical part of the poem: first there is a reference to religion (to the trio of Greek gods about whom the speaker now composes his verses), and then to a mythic political struggle—the clash of wills between kings, Achilles and Agamemnon, which fuels the narrative of the *Iliad*.

The historical, mythological, and literary allusions crammed into this short poem reveal, in turn, its underlying irony—one that, as often in Cavafy, recalls to mind the power of poetry itself. Although the speaker presents his poetic efforts in exile as a mere "diversion" to alleviate his boredom, the subjects he has chosen (religion, internecine struggles between powerful rulers) in fact pointedly recall to mind the reasons he has been exiled in the first place. For this reason, his conclusion—that the littérateurs back in Byzantium censure his verses simply because they are jealous of his poetry's technical perfection—is revealed as being disingenuous.

The reference to CONSTANTINOPLE in line 18 is the only instance in which the name of the city occurs in Cavafy's published poetry.

Favour of Alexander Balas   *pg. 104*

The original title of this poem was "The Wheel of the Chariot."

ALEXANDER BALAS (d. 145 B.C.), a pretender to the Seleucid throne who claimed to be the son of Antiochus IV (see "For Antiochus Epiphanes"), wrested the kingship from Demetrius I Soter in 150 B.C. (see "Of Demetrius Soter," "The Seleucid's Displeasure," and "Orophernes") with the support of Rome and the rulers of the Hellenistic kingdoms of Egypt and Pergamum, suspicious as they always were of a resurgence of Seleucid power. Five years later Balas, who had proved an incompetent king notable for his deplorable excesses, was himself driven from the throne and killed.

The ephebic royal favorite who is Cavafy's narrator here is fictional.

Melancholy of Jason, Son of Cleander: Poet in Commagene: 595 A.D.

pg. 105

The original title of this poem was "Knife."

COMMAGENE, a territory in the northern part of ancient Syria (now in southeastern Turkey), was once a part of the Seleucid empire but became an independent principality in 162 B.C. after its governor revolted; its principal metropolis was Samosata, founded by King Samos in 150 B.C. During the first century B.C. and first century A.D. its fortunes as an independent state rose and fell: one ruler, Antiochus I (see "Epitaph for Antiochus, King of Commagene"), voluntarily submitted to the Romans, while at other times it was forcibly annexed. In later times, Commagene was part of the Byzantine empire, until it was conquered by the Arabs in 638 during their great expansion after the death of Mohammed.

The symbolic appeal that this little kingdom had for Cavafy is easy to see. It was, first of all, a hybrid of Greek and Asian elements: in Classical times, the kings of Commagene claimed descent from both Darius and Alexander, and the kingdom's religion was appropriately hybrid as well—a Hellenized form of Zoroastrianism. There was, too, the status of Commagene as a nominally Greek culture beleaguered by larger, non-Greek powers: the Romans at the beginning of its history, and the Arabs at the end. The date of 595 A.D. suggests that Jason's decline is meant to mirror that of his city, for that year fell about halfway between two landmarks in the decline of Commagene, the first being the brutal sack of the city by the Persian Sassanid monarch Chosroes I in 542, and the second the final conquest of the city by the Arabs in 638. It is worth noting further that this century-long death agony was alleviated—"for a while"—by a peace treaty between Chosroes' successor, Chosroes II, and the Byzantine emperor Maurice.

Demaratus   pg. 106

The dramatic date of the poem could well be the latter half of the fourth century A.D., the era of PORPHYRY, a scholar, philosopher, theologian, and student of Plotinus, the founder of Neoplatonism. Porphyry was born in the Phoenician city of Tyre in 234 A.D., and died around 305; in 263, he moved to Rome, where he became Plotinus's student and friend. (Plotinus, in turn, was a student of Ammonius Saccas, who is mentioned in "From the School of the Renowned Philosopher.") Best known for having organized and edited Plotinus's teachings into a collection of texts now known as the *Enneads,* Porphyry, who was as interested in Aristotle as his fellows were in Plato, also wrote a valuable commentary on Aristotle's *Categories,* a *Life of Plotinus,* and a number of original philosophical texts of his own.

Porphyry, on the other hand, was a common name in Late Antiquity, and it may be that the teacher in question is not, in fact, supposed to be the great Neoplatonist (who, as the scholar Christopher Jones reminds me, is unlikely to have been setting exercises for young students).

The theme to which this intriguing Porphyry's young student applies himself concerns a figure from the remote period, nearly eight hundred years earlier, of the Persian Wars (490–480 B.C.) during which a coalition of small Greek city-states repulsed invasions by the Persian kings DARIUS and XERXES. The Spartan king DEMARATUS (or Damaratus) ruled between 510 and 491 B.C. In his *Histories,* Herodotus recounts how Demaratus's co-ruler, Cleomenes I, conspired with a Spartan called LEOTYCHIDES to force Demaratus from the throne: Cleomenes bribed the Delphic Oracle to say that Demaratus was not the legitimate son of his father, King ARISTON, and therefore was ineligible to be king himself. Furious and seething with resentment, Demaratus fled Sparta and offered his services as an expert on Greek ways to Darius, who rewarded him with the satrapy of Mysia (for which see "The Satrapy").

Timos Malanos recollected Cavafy's own interpretation of this complicated character: "The poem shows that Demaratus is not a traitor.

Deep down in his conscience he rejoices when he hears that the Greeks are winning."

From the School of the Renowned Philosopher   *pg. 109*

AMMONIUS SACCAS (d. 242 A.D.), "the Socrates of Neoplatonism," was an Alexandrian Christian, famous as the teacher of two much better known and crucially important figures in Christian Neoplatonism, Plotinus and Origen. The teachings of these fellow students of Cavafy's fictional protagonist are worth bearing in mind when reading this poem. Plotinus (205 to 269–70 A.D.) maintained that the soul stood halfway between pure mind and the inferior flesh, and that moral choices were, therefore, choices between the aspirations of the former and the primitive urges of the latter. (His student Porphyry, another important figure in Late Classical Christian theology—see the note on "Demaratus"— began his biography of his teacher with the observation that Plotinus always seemed ashamed of being in his body.) Origen (185–86 to 254– 55 A.D.) also adapted Platonic models to Christian theology. A central concern of his theological writings (most of which consisted of commentary on biblical passages) was to refute the predestinarianism of the Gnostics of the century before; he maintained that the workings of human reason enabled individuals to choose between good and evil acts.

It is, perhaps, with these alternative models of what Ammonius Saccas's teaching might lead to that we ought to read Cavafy's poem about a shallow young man vacillating between religious, cultural, and moral poles. This vivid young character is one that the poet had experimented with earlier: an Unfinished Poem entitled "And Above All Cynegirus," dated July 1919, is narrated by a young Roman making a Grand Tour of the Greek east, whose ability to concentrate on the lofty literary lecture he is attending is compromised by thoughts of erotic ecstasies to come that evening.

Maker of Wine Bowls   *pg. 111*

First written in November 1903 with the title "The Amphora Maker," the poem was reworked in July 1912, when it was given its current title, and again in December 1921, when it was printed for the first time.

The dramatic date is fifteen years after the decisive Roman defeat of the Seleucid king Antiochus III at the BATTLE OF MAGNESIA, which took place in 190 B.C.—hence around 175 B.C. (See "The Battle of Magnesia"; for the significance of the battle, see the note on pp. 381–2.) HERACLEIDES was the all-powerful treasurer of Antiochus IV Epiphanes, a son of Antiochus III who illegally succeeded his brother Seleucus IV as ruler of the empire (see "Of Demetrius Soter," "The Seleucid's Displeasure," and "Temethus, Antiochene: 400 A.D.").

Those Who Fought on Behalf of the Achaean League   *pg. 112*

The title of the poem, in Classical Greek, purports to be from an epigram written (as the last lines indicate) during the reign of the Hellenistic Egyptian king Ptolemy IX Soter ("Savior"), nicknamed *Lathyros,* or "CHICKPEA." Ptolemy, born about 141 B.C., was elected co-ruler of Egypt with his (extremely unwilling) mother, Cleopatra III, in 116, on the death of his father, Ptolemy VIII (on whom see "Envoys from Alexandria"). This puts the dramatic date of the poem in 110–109 B.C.

The ACHAEAN LEAGUE, an association of Greek city-states formed in 280 B.C. as a successor to an earlier confederation, consisted eventually of nearly the entire Peloponnese and much of central Greece, and was the chief Greek political power during the period that saw the rise, and eventual triumph, of Rome—a period, as so many poems make clear, of great interest to Cavafy. In the early 140s B.C., long-simmering conflicts between the Spartans and other League members exploded, and Sparta appealed to Rome for intervention; the Romans sent envoys to demand that Sparta, Corinth, and Argos, the complainants, be released from the League. League officials, however, insulted the Roman officials, with the result that the Roman forces stationed in Macedon (which had already been conquered by the Romans) marched south and defeated the League's forces, who were serving under the incompetent commanders DIAEUS and CRITOLAUS, in 146 B.C. (The historian Polybius, in his account of the Achaean War in book 38 of his *Histories,* denounces the two as "ignorant and ill-disposed" in their blind and foolish belief that the Romans, preoccupied with the prosecution of the Third Punic War in Africa and campaigns in Spain, would be unwilling to engage the Greeks as well. "But empty heads have empty notions," the *Histories* go on to declare.) After the victories against the Achaeans by the Roman commanders Metellus and Mummius, Corinth was sacked, its men killed and its women and children sold into slavery; the League was dissolved; and Central Greece and the Peloponnese were added to the province of Macedon as Roman possessions. The defeat of which Cavafy's fictional poet writes, then, marks the final military and political subjugation of Greece to Rome.

The incompetent and doomed struggle to assert an independent Greek identity against the *Realpolitik,* to say nothing of military might, of Rome is a theme that runs through both parts of this poem—which is to say, not only the wistful epigram lauding the doomed Greek struggle of 146 B.C., but also the closing couplet, with its allusion to Ptolemaic Egypt. For the reign of "Chickpea" was characterized by a level of intrigue and instability—to say nothing of Roman intervention in Hellenistic Egyptian affairs—that was unusual even for the infamously intrigue-ridden Egyptian dynasty. After serving as governor of Cyprus during his father's last years, Ptolemy married first one of his sisters, then divorced her to marry another; was made to rule jointly with his hostile mother, and then forced by Rome into a co-kingship with his younger brother. An armed insurrection by this younger brother compelled Ptolemy to flee first to Cyprus, then to Seleucid territory, during which time the younger brother acceded as Ptolemy X Alexander I. Ptolemy IX, however, struck back and reconquered Cyprus, subsequently defeating a coalition between his mother's forces and those of the Jewish state; in 89–88, he reconquered Egypt and reestablished himself as king (at which time his brother Ptolemy X was killed in a naval battle).

Other poems about the disastrous Ptolemies include "Envoys from Alexandria," "The Seleucid's Displeasure," "The Glory of the Ptolemies," and the Unfinished Poems "Ptolemy the Benefactor (or Malefactor)" and "The Dynasty."

For Antiochus Epiphanes *pg. 113*

The poem, with its original title "Antiochus Epiphanes," was most likely written first in November 1911, and then reworked and printed for the first time in February 1922.

Like "Those Who Fought on Behalf of the Achaean League" and many others, this poem explores the melancholies and ironies associated with the decline of Hellenistic Greek culture and political power during the last two centuries B.C., when Rome rose to Mediterranean preeminence. ANTIOCHUS IV EPIPHANES (ca. 215–163 B.C.) was the third son of Antiochus III "the Great," the ruler of the Seleucid empire who was defeated by the Romans at the Battle of Magnesia in 190 B.C. (See "The Battle of Magnesia" and "Temethus, Antiochene: 400 B.C."). The Treaty of Apamea (188 B.C.), concluded after Magnesia, imposed harsh indemnities on the Seleucids, which prevented further military adventures in the West; it also established Antiochus III's second son, Seleucus IV, as co-ruler. Although Seleucus observed the treaty's terms following the death of his father, he did maintain good relations with the two Hellenistic dynasties that had not yet succumbed to Roman rule, the kingdoms of Macedon and Egypt; his daughter Laodice was given as a wife to Perseus, the son of the Macedonian king Philip V.

Following Seleucus IV's death in 175, his younger brother acceded to the throne as Antiochus IV Epiphanes. Antiochus IV followed a policy of urbanization and Hellenization, which made for more efficient rule throughout his territories; unfortunately for his subsequent reputation, these policies aroused great hostility in Judea, where the Jews rebelled against him. (His desecration of the Temple in Jerusalem led to events commemorated by the holiday known as Hanukkah.) Although he refrained from becoming involved in the West—particularly the consolidation of Greek power and expansionist policies of the Macedonian king Perseus, his nephew by marriage, which eventually precipitated war with Rome—Antiochus did have ambitions in both Egypt and the East, and died while on campaign in Parthia in 163. His son, Antiochus V, ruled briefly, until he was deposed by Demetrius I Soter upon his return from Rome (see "Of Demetrius Soter").

In 168 B.C., Perseus was defeated by the Roman general Aemilius Paullus at the Battle of PYDNA, after which Greece became a province of Rome known as Achaea.

The youthful favorite of Antiochus IV in Cavafy's poem is fictional; he may be the "Emonides" who, in "Temethus, Antiochene: 400 A.D.," is mentioned as being Antiochus's favorite, and whose name is used as the title to a poem about homosexual love. That this youth comes from Antioch is no minor detail: ANTIOCH, the capital of the Seleucid empire, was founded in 300 B.C. by Seleucus I, and became one of the great metropolises of the ancient Near East, remaining a wealthy and sophisticated urban center for nearly a millennium, until the Persian and Arab invasions. Built on the banks of the Orontes River, about fifteen miles from the sea (its port, Seleucia, appears in "One of Their Gods"), it owed its great wealth to its situation on the important trade route connecting Asia to the Mediterranean, at the edge of a fertile plain that produced abundant wine and olives; its wealth in turn generated a cosmopolitan culture that boasted great intellectual and artistic activity. As a culturally and ethnically rich urban center—its original settlers were Athenian and Macedonian veterans of Alexander's campaigns, but it also boasted a large and privileged Jewish community— the city bore a strong resemblance to that queen of Hellenistic capitals, Alexandria, and for this reason features prominently in Cavafy's work as an urban model of the cultural diversity of the Hellenic diaspora. "After the great, the wonderful Alexandria," Cavafy wrote, "this center of Hellenism attracts my imagination."

In an Old Book   *pg. 114*

The original title of this poem was "The Book."

Julian, Seeing Indifference   *pg. 116*

This poem strikingly contains direct quotations from a primary source, a device that Cavafy also uses in "Apollonius of Tyana in Rhodes" and a number of other poems. The text in question is a letter from the emperor Julian to the high priest Theodorus, in which Julian appointed Theodorus "governor of all the temples in Asia, with power to appoint all the priests." The letter's references to what Julian saw as the sad state of neglect into which worship of the pagan gods has fallen provides a vehicle for a rather self-important discourse about religion and piety— the kind of humorless severity in the emperor for which Cavafy has such disdain—that culminates in a lengthy encomium of the Jews, for whose piety and willingness to die rather than break their laws Julian professed great admiration. The passage quoted in this poem comes immediately prior to the reference to the Jews:

> Being that they [the pagan gods] have come to be neglected and corrupted, with wealth and luxury triumphing over them, I believe it's necessary to consider them from, as it were, the cradle. Seeing, therefore, that there is considerable indifference among us toward the gods, and that all due reverence for the greater powers has been driven out by impure and vulgar luxury, I was always privately grieved by that state of affairs; for while those who turned their minds to the practices of the Jews' religion were so ardent that they choose to die on its behalf . . . our attitude toward the gods is so casual that we have forgotten the customs of our fathers.

Epitaph of Antiochus, King of Commagene   *pg. 117*

For the significance of COMMAGENE, see the note on "Melancholy of Jason, Son of Cleander: Poet in Commagene: 595 A.D.," pp. 426–7. Formerly part of the Seleucid empire, Commagene became independent in 162 B.C., after the empire had been considerably weakened following defeats at the hands of the Romans. Several subsequent rulers of this principality were called Antiochus; the most likely candidate for the subject of this poem is ANTIOCHUS I, the ruler who brought Commagenian independence to an end when, in 64 B.C., he submitted to the Roman general Pompey in return for territory in Mesopotamia. A quarter century later, he was probably deposed by Marc Antony in favor of his brother, Mithridates.

Antiochus's role as the puppet of Roman triumvirs is just one factor that gives, perhaps, a certain poignancy to the claims of the fictional epitaph in Cavafy's poem. Another would be the fact that the real Antiochus is known not so much for his modesty but, rather, for the grandiose funerary monuments he erected: one for his father at the royal burial place at Arsameia (Eski Kahta in present-day Turkey), which features the lengthiest funerary inscription in western Turkey; and one for himself on Mt. Taurus (Nemrut Dagi, "Mt. Nemrud," in present-day Turkey). The latter featured statues of the dead monarch seated among colossal images of the gods, still visible today. This monument was, moreover, not at all purely Hellenic, but, with its blend of Persian and Greek elements, reflected the hybrid nature of Commagenian cult.

The word I have translated as "Hellenic," *ellinikos,* is a particularly resonant one for Cavafy, with subtle and complex overtones. It suggests, as I have tried to convey, a person of broad Greek culture—not, that is, merely someone who is Greek by nationality, which could easily have been suggested by the word *Ellin,* the usual Greek word for "Greek." Not "a Greek," then, but "Hellenic," in outlook, culture, and taste; a state of mind rather than a nationality. In a famous comment reported by Cavafy's early biographer Timos Malanos in his 1935 book *Peri Kavafis* (*On Cavafy*), the poet is said to have remarked, "I, too, am Hellenic [*ellinikos*]. Mind you, not Greek [*Ellin*], nor Grecified [*Ellinizon*], but Hellenic."

Theater of Sidon (400 A.D.) *pg. 118*

For SIDON, and for the significance of the date, see the note on "Young Men of Sidon (400 A.D.)," pp. 419–20.

"THOSE WHO WEAR GRAY CLOTHES" is a reference to Christians.

Julian in Nicomedia *pg. 119*

The poem is set in the second of the two periods that Julian spent in the port city of NICOMEDIA, the capital of the Roman province of Bithynia, in the northwest part of Asia Minor. Julian had lived there between the ages of five and ten, after he was orphaned by the assassinations of his family; he returned there as a young man of nineteen in 351 A.D., the year in which this poem is set. This was the period in which Julian began to show a marked interest in pagan worship, although he was obliged to hide this illicit enthusiasm both from his uncle, the emperor CONSTANTIUS II, and from his half brother, GALLUS, who were Christian. Julian's attraction to pagan practices was fostered by the Neoplatonic philosophers CHRYSANTHIUS and Chrysanthius's friend MAXIMUS of Ephesus, who initiated Julian into theurgic rites. MARDONIUS, a eunuch, served as Julian's tutor.

The theme of the young Julian's hypocrisy—here, his willingness to play-act at being a Christian in order to avoid suspicion—recurs in Cavafy's negative portrayal of the emperor; the theme of a devious young man and the morally vacant fluidity with which he moves between pagan and Christian activity recalls "Dangerous," another poem that Cavafy set during the reign of Constantius.

The Year 31 B.C. in Alexandria   pg. 122

After Octavian (later Augustus Caesar) resoundingly defeated the combined forces of Antony and Cleopatra at the battle of Actium in 31 B.C., the couple fled to Alexandria, where Cleopatra, in an attempt to keep the news of the disaster from her people, appeared in a triumphant victory parade. The reaction to the news of Antony and Cleopatra's defeat, as a vehicle for pondering the unexpected vagaries of Fate, reappears in the poem "In a Municipality of Asia Minor."

John Cantacuzenus Triumphs   pg. 123

The narrator of this poem on Byzantine historical themes is an aristocratic supporter of the ultimately failed coup d'état of Admiral Apocaucus, Patriarch John Calecas (the "BISHOP"), and the scheming dowager empress ANNA of Savoy, widow of ANDRONICUS III; their grab for power precipitated the Civil War of 1341–1347, in which the noble JOHN CANTACUZENUS, "the reluctant emperor," ultimately prevailed. The poem should be read in the light of two salient facts that, in hindsight, undercut, with different degrees of irony, the narrator's anxiety. The first is that the leniency for which the narrator hopes (either from John himself or from his wife, IRENE) was, in the event, forthcoming: John Cantacuzenus was indeed far more lenient than might have been expected by Anna and her party, and Gibbon reports of his accession that "a general amnesty quieted the apprehensions, and confirmed the property, of the most guilty subjects." Hence the narrator's foolishness

435

in supporting the vicious and venal Apocaucus and his party is, if anything, the more clear. The second is that, as we know, Cantacuzenus's triumph was to be fairly short-lived, since after only five years as co-emperor with John V, he would be forced to abdicate after yet another civil conflict—one in which, this time, he did not "triumph."

To the student intimate with Byzantine history, this poem's opening allusions to the narrator's great wealth will inevitably call to mind a crucial aspect of the Civil War of 1341. After John declared himself emperor in Thrace, in October 1341, his enemy Apocaucus, back home in Constantinople, incited an ugly mob to sack and destroy the properties of Cantacuzenus and his family; the staggered mob's glimpse of the fantastic luxuries to which aristocrats such as John and his mother were accustomed gave a nasty economic twist to the civil unrest that was to follow, and which would involve mob attacks and confiscations all over the empire against the upper class. The specific possessions to which this poem's narrator refers as he anxiously surveys his intact estate (land, chattels, plate) were—as Cantacuzenus himself records in his memoirs—the very items that aroused such rage on the part of the poor when they broke into both his mother's estate in Constantinople, where hoards of gold and silver plate and jewelry were discovered, and his own. (The former emperor records that the expropriation of his estates in Macedonia alone during the Civil War cost him five thousand head of cattle, one thousand draft animals, fifty thousand pigs, seventy thousand sheep, and two hundred camels.) But, as we know, John refrained from inflicting comparable expropriations on those who supported his enemies, such as the poem's narrator.

Temethus, an Antiochene: 400 A.D. *pg. 125*

With the exception of ANTIOCHUS EPIPHANES, the Seleucid ruler who lived from 215 to 163 B.C. (see "For Antiochus Epiphanes" and note on pp. 430–2), the characters here—both the poet Temethus in 400 A.D. and Emonides, Antiochus's favorite more than five centuries earlier— are fictional. ("Emonides" is pronounced with the accent on the third syllable.) The reference in this poem to a favorite of Antiochus suggests a self-conscious connection to "For Antiochus Epiphanes," in which

Cavafy describes a "young man of Antioch" who is the king's favorite; for all we know, that young man could be Emonides. SAMOSATA was the principal metropolis of Commagene, founded in 150 B.C. by King Samos.

"YEAR ONE-THIRTY-SEVEN OF THE GREEK'S DOMINION" refers (if we count from the establishment of the Seleucids at Babylon in 312 B.C.) to the year 175 B.C., during Antiochus's reign—the same year, it's worth noting, in which "Maker of Wine Bowls" is set; a moment, in other words, well after the end of Seleucid supremacy. Here as elsewhere in Cavafy's work, 400 A.D. is a date whose significance lies in the fact that it falls not long before the onslaught of the barbarians who would put an end to Greco-Roman culture: see also "Young Men of Sidon (400 A.D.)" and "Theater of Sidon (400 A.D.)."

Of Colored Glass   pg. 126

After the Civil War of 1341–47, JOHN VI CANTACUZENUS was crowned emperor of Byzantium in the BLACHERNAE Palace, the chief residence of the imperial family, on May 21, 1347, with the fifteen-year-old John V Palaeologus, son of Cantacuzenus's friend the late emperor Andronicus III, as co-emperor. The DETAIL to which Cavafy refers is related in Book 15 of the thirty-seven-book *Roman History* by the polymath and historian Nicephorus Gregoras (ca. 1293–1360), a contemporary and supporter of Cantacuzenus and his family, whose history serves as an important witness to the first half of the fourteenth century. In a long passage devoted to the emperor's coronation, Gregoras describes the sorry state of the imperial household after the deprivations of the Civil War, during which John's archenemy, the widowed empress ANNA OF SAVOY, emptied the treasuries and sold off the palace treasures in order to finance her schemes:

> Such was the poverty of the royal household at that time, that there were no silver or gold cups or goblets; but some were of tin, and all the others were earthenware or clay. From which anyone who is not simple in such matters can understand where things stood with respect to other neces-

sities, which it was not possible to see to in the wonted fashion; for such was the force of the penury among those who then ruled, in deeds and words and counsel. I shall forbear to mention, that the royal diadems and robes of that ceremony, for the most part, had the appearance of being of gold and indeed of precious stones: but the former were of leather, dyed gold in the way that leatherers sometimes do; and the latter were of glass, gleaming in a myriad of colors. There were, here and there, valuable stones that had a genuine gleam, and also the glitter of pearls, which cannot deceive the eye. So ruined, so utterly extinguished, so brought low were the ancient good fortune and magnificence of the Romaic [= Byzantine] world, that I cannot now expound the narrative of these affairs without shame.

Although we clearly find here the "detail" that inspired Cavafy's poem, the last line of the passage in question also betrays considerable tension between the source material and the poem itself: whereas Gregoras feels "shame" about the lowly state to which the once-illustrious court had been reduced, Cavafy emphasizes that he sees nothing cheap or unseemly about it, focusing instead on the genuine nobility of the man who was forced to wear those fake jewels; and indeed sees the fake jewels as a symbol for the poignant ironies of history. (Gibbon, for his part, introduces the story of the fake jewels with the pithy remark that "the festival of the coronation and nuptials [of Cantacuzenus's daughter Helena and the co-emperor, John V] was celebrated with the appearance of concord and magnificence, and both were equally fallacious.")

In the context of Cavafy's overt editorializing in this poem about the meaning of the vignette he is relating, it is worth noting that whereas Gregoras rejected a deterministic view of history, John VI Cantacuzenus, in his own historical memoirs, the *Historiai*, saw—unsurprisingly, given the disappointing outcome of his rule—"Fate" (*Tyche*) and "Necessity" (*Anankê*) as the great forces at work in human affairs. The Unfinished Poem "On Epiphany" (1925) similarly contrasts the respective histories of Gregoras and Contacuzenus to pointed effect.

The repetition of the phrase "ANDRONICUS ASEN'S DAUGHTER" as an epithet for Cantacuzenus's wife, Irene Asenina Cantacuzene, is pointed:

at the beginning of the Civil War, in 1341, Irene's father shockingly joined her husband's enemies, Anna of Savoy, Apocaucus, and the patriarch Calecas, in declaring John Cantacuzenus a public enemy—the act that marked the climax of a concerted campaign of harassment against John and his family, and which sparked the beginning of civil strife.

The 25th Year of His Life   pg. 127

Savidis notes that the poem was likely composed in June 1918 with the title "The 23rd Year of My Life, in Winter," and was first published in June 1925. Of particular note is the shift from the first person, in the first version, to the third person, in the title of the finished work.

On an Italian Seashore   pg. 128

The poem alludes to the aftermath of the Roman triumph over the Achaean League in 146 B.C., the final chapter in the story of Rome's ascent over Greece during the third and second centuries B.C. (See "Those Who Fought on Behalf of the Achaean League.") After crushing the Greeks, who had labored under the command of the incompetent Diaeus, the Roman consul and general Mummius sacked CORINTH, as an example to Greeks contemplating future resistance. The population of the famously luxurious and pleasure-loving city was put to the sword, and the city was stripped of its great treasures, which were then shipped to Italy. ITALIOTE refers to an ethnically Greek inhabitant of southern Italy—a person of typically Cavafian mixed identities and loyalties (see, for example, "Poseidonians," in which this specialized term can also be found).

Apollonius of Tyana in Rhodes   pg. 130

The incident narrated in the present poem is, like other anecdotes about Apollonius, taken from Philostratus's *Life of Apollonius of Tyana,* and indeed Apollonius's response to the Rhodian is cited, in this poem, in the original Classical Greek of that text. Part of the effect of the poem is the contrast between the "high" Classical Greek of Philostratus (whose hero, Apollonius, here admires the "high" art of pagan Greece) and the demotic diction of the rest of the poem—a contrast meant, perhaps, to reflect that between gold and clay.

In antiquity, the most famous cult images of pagan Greek temples (for example, the great statue of Athena in the Parthenon, and that of Zeus in the temple of Zeus at Olympia) were chryselephantine: that is, composed of gold and ivory plates hung on a wooden core.

Cleitus's Illness   pg. 131

The milieu is Alexandria at a time when pagan and Christian forms of worship flourished side by side—the same setting as those we find in poems such as "Dangerous," "Priest of the Serapeum," and "Myres: Alexandria in 340 A.D." For this reason, we are probably meant to imagine the action taking place around the fourth century A.D.

The motif of mortal prayers that go unanswered by inscrutable deities clearly had a gentle hold on Cavafy's imagination; the present poem seems to be a culmination of sorts. He had treated it thirty years earlier in "Prayer" (1896; 1898), in which a woman prays to the Virgin for her son's safe return from sea; and a decade before composing the present poem he had written "Safe Haven" (1917; 1918), in which the death of a young man far from home is contrasted, with similar poignancy, to the ignorant hopes of his parents. The setting of the present poem allows Cavafy to juxtapose the Christian and the pagan prayers—all of them, in this case, futile.

In a Municipality of Asia Minor   pg. 132

For the defeat of Antony and Cleopatra and the reaction to it, see the note on "The Year 31 B.C. in Alexandria," p. 435. Apropos of this poem, C. M. Bowra observed that "He shows the fundamental indifference of the ruled to their rulers. No doubt he had observed this in Egypt."

Priest of the Serapeum   pg. 133

Since its importation to Alexandria by Ptolemy I in around 300 B.C., the cult of the god SERAPIS was vigorously promoted by the Ptolemaic monarchs of Egypt, who saw its potential as a vehicle for cultural unity. Although the god himself was thought to have originated as an amalgam of two Egyptian deities, the death god Osiris and the bull god Apis, responsibility for the creation of the formal cult in Alexandria belonged, almost exclusively, to Greeks; it is no accident that the deity combined aspects of many Greek deities: Zeus, Hades, Asclepius (who was thought particularly to be a healer), Dionysus, Helius. As such, the god—a native deity overlaid with Hellenic characteristics—was an apt symbol of the hybrid cultures of the Hellenistic kingdoms after Alexander. Worship of Serapis was extremely widespread throughout the Mediterranean and the Greek East.

The temple of Serapis, or SERAPEUM, at Alexandria was considered one of the wonders of the world. Gibbon, in chapter 28 of the *Decline and Fall,* gives a vivid description of the destruction, in 390 A.D., of this fabulous edifice, on the orders of the archbishop of Alexandria, Theophilus, for whose religious fanaticism the Enlightenment historian does not hide his contempt.

In the Taverns pg. 134

The milieu of the poem is the cosmopolitan ancient Levant. An EPARCH was the governor of a large district, or *eparchy.*

A Great Procession of Priests and Laymen pg. 135

An early version of this poem, entitled "The Cross," which may have been written in September 1892, was included in the group of poems entitled "The Beginnings of Christianity."

JULIAN the Apostate died of wounds he received in battle on June 26, 363, at the age of thirty-one. He was succeeded by his contemporary JOVIAN (Flavius Jovianus), who had served on the Persian campaign, and who on his elevation to the throne immediately concluded an unpopular peace with Persia. In stark contrast to Julian, Jovian—who died within a year of becoming emperor, before he reached Constantinople—was a devout Christian. The procession referred to in the poem is invented, although the Christian Antiochenes' hostility to Julian is well documented, and is the subject of the poems "Julian and the Antiochenes" and "On the Outskirts of Antioch."

Sophist Departing from Syria   pg. 136

For ANTIOCH, see the note on "For Antiochus Epiphanes," pp. 430–2.

Julian and the Antiochenes   pg. 137

From July 362 A.D. to March 363, when he went off on the campaign against Persia in which he would perish, Julian resided at Antioch—a visit that was in every way disastrous for his relations with his Christian subjects. His restoration of numerous pagan shrines and temples and desecration of Christian shrines hardly endeared him to the Antiochenes, and his ostentatious asceticism and arcane and antipopulist philosophical program made him an object of ridicule in the eyes of the notoriously pleasure-loving local population (whose frivolity had, over the centuries, indeed aroused the contempt of observers as different as the emperor Hadrian and St. John Chrysostom). Local wags openly wrote satiric verses about him. His response was to compose a long and bitter diatribe entitled MISOPOGON ("Beard Hater"), which takes the form of a satire of himself—the title refers to the much-despised affectation of growing a philosopher's beard—but is really a vehicle for expressing his derision for the Antiochenes, whose decadence he contrasts with his unkempt simplicity: his beard crawling with lice, his breast as shaggy as a lion, his fingers stained with ink. This lengthy and extraordinary composition, which also bore the title *Antiokhikos,* "Antiochene Speech" (the form of the title normally denotes a speech given in praise of a city) and which Julian caused to be displayed outside the imperial palace in Antioch, has been called by one classicist "one of the most incredible things that a Roman emperor, supposed to be in his right senses, ever did."

The epigraph to this poem is a citation from that work. Julian has just roundly chastised the citizens of Antioch for their incessant frivolity and insulting behavior toward him; he then addresses their sardonic observation that, compared to Julian—with his renovations of the pagan temples of Antioch and his desecrations of Christian shrines (outrages to which "On the Outskirts of Antioch" refers)—neither his predecessor, the Christian emperor Constantius (represented by the letter *K*, "KAPPA," the first letter of his name as spelled in Greek), nor Christ himself (represented by the letter *X*, "CHI," the first letter of the Greek spelling of *Christ*) had harmed their city. Citing this witticism, Julian seeks to undermine the Antiochenes' admiration for both Constantius and Christ, alluding to the avarice of the former and suggesting that Christ was a weak god, since he was unable to save the Christian shrines of Emesa, which were destroyed by a pagan mob.

This poem stands as one of the most cogent expressions of Cavafy's vision, so important for our understanding of his intellectual and poetic attitude concerning Greek identity, of Christian Byzantium as a truer expression of the cosmopolitan Greek spirit and élan than Julian's drearily puritan paganism was. Cavafy's choice of the theater, with its combination of the erotic and the aesthetic, as the particular symbol of the Hellenic spirit in this poem is hardly accidental: in the *Misopogon,* Julian singles out theatergoing for particular scorn in a passage that well conveys the prissiness that his enemies derided, and which may well have been in the poet's mind when he composed this poem:

> As you judge it, true beauty of the soul consists of a lascivious life . . . for my part I never saw a theater until I had more hair on my chin than on my head, and even then it was not my own doing. . . . Believe you me, by Zeus and the Muses, my tutor told me many times when I was still yet a boy, "Don't ever let the throng of your agemates who flock to the theaters persuade you to crave that sort of spectacle."

Anna Dalassene *pg. 138*

ANNA DALASSENE (1025–1102) was the sister-in-law of Emperor Isaac I Comnenus, and the mother of ALEXIUS I COMNENUS (1048–1118), who acceded to his uncle's throne in 1081. In that year, Alexius departed for a military campaign and entrusted his mother with full imperial powers in his absence. In the Byzantine state bureaucracy, documents containing imperial decrees of special importance bore a solid gold seal, or CHRYSOBULL (Greek *khrysoboullon*); the word chryso-bull came, in time, to denote the document itself.

The final line of Cavafy's poem is a quotation from the *Alexiad,* the verse epic about Alexius I Comnenus written by his daughter, Anna Comnena (see "Anna Comnena"). About her father's relationship with his mother, Anna Comnena writes as follows:

> It may cause some surprise that my father the Emperor had raised his mother to such a position of honor, and that he had handed complete power over to her. Yielding up the reins of government, one might say, he ran alongside her as she drove the imperial chariot. . . .
>
> My father reserved for himself the waging of wars against the barbarians, while he entrusted to his mother the adminis-tration of state affairs, the choosing of civil servants, and the fiscal management of the empire's revenues and expenses. One might perhaps, in reading this, blame my father's deci-sion to entrust the imperial government to the gyneceum [women's quarters]. But once you understood the ability of this woman, her excellence, her good sense, and her remark-able capacity for hard work, you would turn from criticism to admiration.
>
> For my grandmother really had the gift of conducting the affairs of state. She knew so well how to organize and admin-ister that she was capable of governing not only the Roman Empire but also every other kingdom under the sun. . . . She was very shrewd in seizing on whatever was called for, and clever in carrying it out with certitude. Not only did she have an outstanding intelligence, but her powers of speech matched it. She was a truly persuasive orator, in no way wordy or long-winded. . . .
>
> She was ripe in years when she ascended the imperial throne, at the moment when her mental powers were at their most vigorous. . . .
>
> As for her compassion toward the poor and the lavishness of her hand toward the destitute, how can words describe

these things? Her house was a shelter for her needy relatives, and it was no less a haven for strangers. . . . Her expression, which revealed her true character, demanded the worship of the angels but struck terror among demons. (tr. Elizabeth A. S. Dawes)

Greek Since Ancient Times *pg. 142*

An ancient legend concerning the great Hellenistic capital of ANTIOCH (for which sees the notes on "For Antiochus Epiphanes," pp. 430–2, and "Julian and the Antiochenes," pp. 442–3) held that the city was founded on the site of an earlier town called IONÊ, which had been settled by Argives on the site where the mythic princess Io is said to have died. In the myth, Zeus loved Io, whose father, INACHUS, was king of ARGOS; to protect the girl from his jealous wife, Hera, Zeus transformed her into a cow. Hera soon found out, however, and sent a gadfly to pursue the hapless girl, who thereupon wandered all through the known world until, in Egypt, she was restored to human form by a touch of Zeus's hand. She thereupon bore the god a son, Epaphus ("Touch"), through whom she was the ancestress of the Egyptian maidens known as the Danaids, who in the myth fled to their Greek ancestral homeland to escape their brutish suitors. In more than one way, therefore, Io links Greek and non-Greek cultures together.

Days of 1901 *pg. 143*

The poem, first printed in October 1927, was originally given the title "Days of 1900," which was subsequently changed to "Days of 1898" before acquiring its final form.

You Didn't Understand *pg. 144*

Immediately prior to his departure for Antioch in the summer of 362 A.D., Julian the Apostate issued an edict known as the School Edict, in which he forbade the use of pagan texts by Christian teachers. ("If they want to learn literature, they have Luke and Mark. Let them go back to their Church and expound on *them*.") Widely condemned even by pagans, who understood that the great literature of the pagan past was the common cultural heritage of all Hellenes, the edict was manifestly aimed at eventually eliminating Christians from the empire's elite. The present poem is based on an incident, reported in Sozomenus's *Ecclesiastical History,* in which Julian attempted to mock the efforts of Christian prelates to adapt Classical texts to Christian purposes.

The poem's tart humor rests on an elaborate linguistic play. What Julian said to the Antiochenes was *anegnôn, egnôn, kategnôn:* "I read, I understood, I condemned"; in Greek, these three words constitute a subtle and multilayered pun, since all three words have the same root, the verb *gignôskô,* "to know" or "to understand." *Anegnôn,* "I read," is a past tense of the verb *anagignôskô* (from the prefix *ana-,* literally "up," + *gignôskô*); *egnôn,* "I understood," is a past tense of *gignôskô;* and *kategnôn,* "I condemned," is a past tense of the verb *katagignôskô* (from the prefix *kata-,* "down," + *gignôskô*). Hence although Julian's meaning is straightforward, to the Greek eye his words look something like this: "I up-knew it, I knew it, I down-knew it." Cavafy applauds the Christians' swift and equally witty appropriation of the emperor's remark.

In Sparta *pg. 146*

The context of the poem is a complex and subtle opposition between the Classical and the Hellenistic that also contraposes mainland Greece and the greater Greek-speaking world of the Hellenistic era.

The Spartan king CLEOMENES III (c. 260–219 B.C.; acceded 235 B.C.) was a social reformer who—inspired, it would seem, by dreams of restoring Sparta to the greatness she enjoyed during her Archaic and Classical past—drastically reorganized the Spartan state during the 220s B.C., and embarked on ambitious military campaigns. Early military successes against Sparta's Peloponnesian neighbors emboldened Cleomenes to seize total power, after which he canceled debts (mortgage indenture had been a crushing social problem), initiated redistributions of land, and increased the dangerously low number of full Spartiates by including resident aliens and inhabitants of neighboring areas in the citizen body.

Cleomenes' dazzling successes in campaigns that ranged increasingly far north brought him, inevitably, into conflict not only with the Achaean

League (see the note on "Those Who Fought on Behalf of the Achaean League" pp. 429–30) but also with the great northern power, Macedon, and its king, Antigonus III. As a result, Cleomenes sought an alliance with Antigonus's enemy, the Egyptian king PTOLEMY III EUERGETES ("Bene-factor," of the Lagid dynasty), who agreed to aid Cleomenes on the con-dition that the Spartan king's mother, Cratesicleia, and his children be sent to Alexandria as political hostages. Cavafy's poetic account of Cleomenes' and his mother's reactions to this demand very closely follows the version of these events that we find in Plutarch's *Life of Cleomenes,* which was clearly the poet's source:

> For a long while Cleomenes did not dare to declare to his mother the Egyptian king's demand; going frequently to her chamber to discuss it with her, he found that whenever he was on the verge of opening his mouth, he did not have the courage, and remained silent. Seeing his embarrassment, his mother became suspicious, and asked those who were in most regular contact with him, whether her son did not desire something of her that he dared not mention. When at last Cleomenes had pulled himself together and explained to her that matter as it stood, she began laughing with all her might. "What," she said to him, "is that what you've so often wanted to say to me, and dared not reveal? Would that you would put me on a ship straightaway, and send me without delay wherever you think my body will be useful to Sparta, before old age comes to destroy it and use it up in inactivity and sloth."
>
> When all was in readiness for the voyage, they traveled by land to Cape Taenarus, accompanied by the entire army. When Cratesicleia was about to embark, she drew her son aside and led him, alone, to the temple of Poseidon. There she held him in a long embrace, and sensing that he was much dejected and so affected that he too had dissolved into tears, said to him: "Come now, King of the Lacedaemonians, so that when we leave the temple, no one might see us weep-ing, or doing anything unworthy of Sparta. For this alone is in our power; as for our fortunes, they will continue so long

as the god provides." Having spoken thus, she dried her face, returned to the vessel holding her grandson in her arms, and ordered the pilot to leave without delay.

Ptolemy III, however, died soon afterward, and his son was unsympathetic to Cleomenes' cause. The hostages soon found themselves prisoners, and after the failure of a daring rescue mission led by Cleomenes himself, all of the Spartans were executed.

The sad outcomes of the event alluded to in this poem should color our appreciation of the antique Spartan values so boldly asserted here in the face of Ptolemaic crassness. And yet the fact that the speaker in this poem, a king of Sparta, seems to be both fearful of and apparently ruled by his mother is itself, perhaps, meant as a melancholy marker of that city-state's own decline from the standards of its Classical apogee. In this context, two historical items are of particular note. First, in pursuing his bold social schemes, Cleomenes was following in the footsteps of his predecessor, Agis IV, whose widow, Agiatis, he had married: clearly he was a man who listened to his women. Second, Ptolemy III himself had famously complicated maternal relations. His own mother, Arsinoë I of Egypt, was the first wife of Ptolemy II and a daughter of Alexander's friend and general Lysimachus; she was exiled from Egypt for plotting to have her husband murdered. Ptolemy II then married his sister, Arsinoë II, who until her death presided over the most dazzling court in Ptolemaic history (see the note on "Tomb of Eurion," pp. 390–1) and presumably, adopted Ptolemy III as her son.

The relationship between the Sparta that Cleomenes helped revivify and the rest of the Greek world, both mainland Greece and the Hellenistic Greater Greece, would come to preoccupy Cavafy in the final years of his life. In "In the Year 200 B.C.," first published in 1931, the speaker's mockery of Spartan isolationism during Alexander's campaigns is itself subtly mocked by the fact that his exultant endorsement of pan-Hellenic world culture comes just a few years before the Roman triumph over the Hellenistic world. In one of the Unfinished Poems, entitled "Nothing About the Lacedaemonians" (1930; the title is an allusion to Alexander's snub of the isolationist Spartans), the speaker smugly suggests that there ought to be limits to the high principles articulated by Cleomenes' mother in "In Sparta"—a character whose noble sacrifice for her country indeed reappears as the subject of another of Cavafy's published poems, "Come, O King of the Lacedaemonians," which was inspired by the second speech of Cratesicleia in Plutarch's account, cited above.

In a Large Greek Colony, 200 B.C. *pg. 148*

The date of 200 B.C. is a significant one for Cavafy, who uses it again in the title of another of the Published Poems, "In 200 B.C.," and alludes to it in a number of other poems as well, including the Unfinished Poems "Nothing About the Lacedaemonians," composed the same year as the present poem, and "Agelaus," composed two years later. Coming a mere three years before the disastrous Battle of Cynoscephalae, in which the forces of Philip V of Macedon were routed by the Roman general Flamininus, and ten years before the Battle of Magnesia, which was the first of several crushing blows dealt by Rome to the independent Hellenistic kingdoms of Asia, this date suggests less (as the speakers in those poems smugly believe) an invincible acme of Hellenistic Greek civilization as, much more ironically, its imminent fall.

Potentate from Western Libya *pg. 150*

LIBYA was the Greek name for the entire continent of Africa; it is difficult to know where, precisely, Cavafy's fictitious potentate, a short-term visitor to Hellenistic Alexandria, is supposed to come from. Although the intersection of Hellenic and non-Hellenic cultures is, of course, a major Cavafian preoccupation, this poem—with its subtle presentation, at once sympathetic and ironic, of a non-Greek who is enthusiastically philhellenic (and yet reveals himself as a philistine)—may be read with particular profit together with "Philhellene."

Cimon Son of Learchus, 22 Years Old, Teacher of Greek Letters (in Cyrene) *pg. 152*

CYRENE was the great commercial and cultural capital of what is now Libya, birthplace of such distinguished Hellenistic figures as the philosopher Aristippus and the scholar and poet Callimachus. It has a special appeal, perhaps, to Cavafy because of a richly documented history that began in the Archaic period of Greece—it was founded as a colony of Thera in the seventh century B.C.—and continued turbulently through the Ptolemaic and Roman occupations.

On the March to Sinope   pg. 154

MITHRIDATES was the name of six rulers of the kingdom of Pontus, which stretched along the northern coast of Asia Minor below the Black Sea. The kings of Pontus, who claimed descent from Darius the Great, were eventually related by marriage to the Seleucid royal family—another of the numerous integrations of the Asian and the Greek that characterized the Hellenistic world.

MITHRIDATES V EUERGETES ("Benefactor") welcomed Hellenizing influences even as he pursued pro-Roman policies; in return for his support of Rome in the last Punic War, he received the province of Phrygia. This was just one of a number of instances of territorial expansions that marked Mithridates' vigorous reign. In 120 B.C. he was murdered at SINOPE, his capital city, by his wife Laodice, who is said to have opposed his expansionist policies. (His son, Mithridates VI Eupator Dionysus, is the subject of "Darius.")

Although the incident of the seer is invented, Mithridates V's ancestor, MITHRIDATES I, was indeed saved by his friend Demetrius (later Demetrius Poliorcetes: see "King Demetrius"), the son of Antigonus I "the One-Eyed," who had been one of Alexander's generals. Antigonus had already had Mithridates' brother killed and was intending to kill Mithridates himself when Demetrius warned his friend to flee.

Days of 1909, '10, and '11   pg. 156

On the way in which Cavafy uses tensions between katharevousa and demotic in this poem to suggest the difference between the male courtesans of glorious Alexandria in days of old and the sordid life of the beautiful boy in the present, see the Introduction, p. xliv. In a self-comment dedicated to this poem, Cavafy elaborated on this difference in illuminating terms. Because (he writes) a beautiful youth of those earlier times did not have to contend with social prohibitions, and because such relations weren't considered aberrant or shameful, he was able to enjoy his fame "in broad daylight" and could afford to have his beauty immortalized in paint or stone—unlike the beautiful boy in the present day, burdened with rough work that soon ruins his looks.

Myres: Alexandria in 340 A.D.   *pg. 157*

This is the longest poem that Cavafy published.

The specificity of the date in the title places Myres' death during the tumultuous joint reign of Constans and Constantius, the sons of Constantine the Great (the setting of "Dangerous," the first explicitly erotic and homosexual poem that Cavafy published; see the note on pp. 392–3). It was a period marked by internecine divisions within the state and within the church, and hence the ideal setting for the poem's delineation of the speaker's growing awareness of a division between himself, a pagan, and his dead beloved, a Christian.

Alexander Jannaeus, and Alexandra   *pg. 160*

Like "Aristobulus," this poem has as its subtext the political and cultural tensions between the heritage of ancient Judea and the larger Hellenistic world that had absorbed it. The area known as Palestine had been under the control first of the Persians, then of Alexander's empire; in the year 200 B.C. it became part of the Seleucid empire. By 167, the program of Hellenization that was part of a larger unifying effort by the Seleucid monarch Antiochus IV "Epiphanes" (see "For Antiochus Epiphanes") had helped to anger both religious and nationalistic sentiments in Jerusalem; in that year, Antiochus outraged both Jewish and patriotic sentiment by dedicating the Temple to Olympian Zeus and installing a garrison in the city. A popular uprising, led by JUDAH MAC-CABEE, a member of the priestly house of Hashmon, and his brothers Jonathan and Simon, eventually led to the expulsion of the Syrian occupiers in the year 142, and for the next eight decades the Hasmonean dynasty ruled Judea independently and with great vigor.

ALEXANDER JANNAEUS, a grandson of Simon Maccabee, acceded to the throne in 103 B.C. on the death of his elder brother, Aristobulus I, whose widow, ALEXANDRA-SALOME, Alexander married soon after. (This Alexandra was the grandmother of the Alexandra who, in "Aristobulus," mourns the murder of her son.) It was Alexander Jannaeus's elder brother who established the Hasmoneans as a secular dynasty, abandoning the title of High Priest for that of king, and Alexander himself added greatly to Judea's territorial possessions. As Cavafy well knew, Alexander Jannaeus's reign and its emphasis on aggressive military expansion saw the beginning of certain tensions—between the popular Pharisees and the aristocratic Sadducees, between political and military leaders—that would eventually lead to the downfall of the Hasmonean dynasty. These tensions were temporarily quieted under Alexandra, who became queen upon Alexander's death in 76 B.C.—the only queen regnant in the history of Judea—and who ruled peacefully until her own death in 67. But they soon exploded once again when her two sons, Hyrcanus II and Aristobulus II, fought for supremacy, bringing in various outside powers as allies; and it was only the intervention of the Romans—first Pompey, in 63 B.C., and then Marc Antony in the late 40s B.C.—that restored peace to Judea, which subsequently became a Roman administrative province.

Hence it seems right to take as ironic the speaker's assertion that Alexander and Alexandra presided over the conclusion of the "great work" initiated under the Maccabees: for their reigns saw the unleashing of the forces that would bring Judean independence itself to an end.

Beautiful, White Flowers As They Went So Well pg. 161

White flowers conventionally adorned the coffins of the young; Liddell, in his biography of Cavafy, records a remark made to him by a Greek undertaker that purple flowers would have been considered appropriate for an older person.

Come Now, King of the Lacedaemonians pg. 163

For the particulars of the story of the Spartan king Cleomenes and his mother, and Cavafy's adaptation of Plutarch's account of this tale, see the note on "In Sparta," pp. 446–9; the passage from which the title of the present poem is taken can be found on pp. 447–8.

In the Same Space

pg. 164

This remarkably terse and moving poem perhaps brings to mind an apothegm from the *Fusées* of Baudelaire (17), a poet of considerable importance to Cavafy: "In certain almost supernatural states of mind, life's profoundness reveals itself completely in the spectacle, however ordinary it may be, that one has before one's eyes. It becomes its Symbol."

The Mirror in the Entrance

pg. 165

In a note dated June 29, 1906, Cavafy wrote about the particular aesthetic and erotic effect that working-class youths had on him:

> I do like and I am moved by the beauty of the folk, of the poor youth. Servants, workers, petty commercial clerks, shop attendants. This is the recompense, one guesses, for their deprivations. All this physical work and exercise make their bodies beautiful and symmetrical. They are almost always lean. Their faces, either pale when their work is indoors, or sunburned when they are outdoors, have an attractive, poetic hue. They are a contrast to the affluent youth who are either sickly and physiologically dirty, or filled with fat and stains from too much food and drink, and [indulgence in too many] quilts; you think that in their bloated or dimpled faces you can discern the ugliness of the theft and robbery of their inheritance and its interest.

Should Have Taken the Trouble

pg. 168

The poem is set during the 120s B.C., when the Seleucid empire was tottering and subject to interference by venal foreign powers. "MALE-FACTOR" was the bitter nickname given by his people to Ptolemy VIII of

Egypt (170–116 B.C.), whose official epithet was *Euergetes,* "Benefactor" (see "Envoys from Alexandria," and also the Unfinished Poem "Ptolemy the Benefactor [or Malefactor]"). ZABINAS ("Slave") was the nickname of Alexander, the son of the usurper of the Seleucid throne, Alexander Balas (see "Of Demetrius Soter" and "The Favour of Alexander Balas"); between 128 and 123 B.C., Zabinas himself usurped the Syrian throne. He reigned until he was deposed and killed by Antiochus VIII (whose nickname, GRYPUS, means "Hook-nosed"). JOHN HYRCANUS was a son of the High Priest and freedom fighter Simon Maccabee (brother of Judah), and the father of Alexander Jannaeus (see "Alexander Jannaeus"). John's interests were naturally served by the chaos in Syria, to which Judea had belonged before it gained independence in 142.

According to the Formulas of Ancient
Greco-Syrian Magicians   *pg. 170*

For the aura of occultism in this poem, which makes itself felt so often in the poet's work, see the note on "That They Come—," pp. 420–1. In connection with this stark yet delicate poem, it's worth recalling a deeply poignant episode from Cavafy's final illness that was recorded by Rika Sengopoulos:

> Once in all his dreadful illness Cavafy wept. It was the day on which he was to go into hospital. We brought a little suitcase to take some papers with him and a few bits of clothing he wanted. When he saw the suitcase he was overcome by tears. We tried to calm him in this heart-rending moment when he was leaving his house for ever. He took the block [on which the poet, after his tracheotomy, wrote in order to communicate with those around him] and wrote: "I bought this suitcase 30 years ago, in a hurry one evening, to go to Cairo for pleasure. Then I was young and strong, and not ugly."

In 200 B.C.   *pg. 171*

An early version of this poem, entitled "Except the Lacedaemonians," was probably written in June 1916.

The opening line is a quotation from the message from Alexander the Great to the Athenians accompanying the three hundred Persian panoplies that he sent to Athens to commemorate his victory over the forces of Darius III, the king of Persia, at GRANICUS—one of the three battles that marked his conquest of the Persian empire (the others being Issus and ARBELA). Of the Greek states, only Sparta refused to join in Alexander's panhellenic campaign against Persia, proudly unwilling, as the Spartans were, to serve under a non-Spartan general. And yet this ostensibly high-minded and nationalistic pride cost them dearly, since in refusing to join the Macedonian's expedition into Asia, the Spartans missed out on the greatest military conquests the world had ever seen: conquests that took Alexander and his armies as far east as BACTRIA, a province located in the north of the present-day Afghanistan, and India. The COMMON GREEK LANGUAGE refers to what scholars call Koinê ("Common"), the Greek language that became the lingua franca of the Hellenistic world after Alexander's conquest.

For the significance of the year 200 B.C.—a moment immediately preceding the culminating Roman defeats of Hellenistic Greek monarchs, and therefore a date that marks the imminent absorption of the Greek world by Rome—see the note on "In a Large Greek Colony, 200 B.C.," p. 449. The significance of this date thus undercuts the swagger of the poem's narrator, with his supreme confidence in the greatness of the Greek civilization of the Hellenistic world: everything of which he boasts will soon be the property of Rome. That Cavafy was preoccupied with issues of Hellenic cultural and political unity in the years following the disastrous conclusion of the Greco-Turkish War of 1919–22 is demonstrated by the recurrence of allusions to this crucial date of 200 B.C. in a number of poems he was working and reworking at the beginning of the 1930s: the present poem, "In a Large Greek Colony, 200 B.C." (1928), and the two Unfinished Poems "Nothing About the Spartans" (1930) and "Agelaus" (1932).

Days of 1908 *pg. 173*

A prior version, entitled "The Summer of 1895," was probably written in July 1921.

On the Outskirts of Antioch

pg. 175

The poem alludes to a famous incident from the last year of Julian the Apostate's life, described at length by Gibbon. In July 362 Julian had set forth from the capital at Constantinople to ANTIOCH, which was to serve as the base for his Persian campaign (see "Julian and the Antiochenes," and the note on pp. 442–3). While there, he ordered the sanctuary of the god Apollo at DAPHNE, near Antioch, to be cleared of the Christian tombs that had been built there over the years. One of these tombs, to which a church had been attached, was that of BABYLAS, bishop of Antioch from 237 to 250 and a martyr of the church. (Ironically, his remains had been transferred to the vicinity of Apollo's temple in the first place by Julian's brother, Gallus, a fervent Christian, when the latter was serving as *caesar* in the East.) Heeding the complaints of Apollo's priests, Julian ordered the church demolished and the saint's relic moved elsewhere. Soon afterward, in October 362, Apollo's temple and the cult statue of the god were destroyed by a fire that, Julian alleged, the Christians had started. The incident proved the nadir of Julian's abysmal relationship with Antioch's Christian community: the emperor had already been insulted by the Christian populace, and the hostile town council had blocked relief efforts he organized during a famine that occurred there, in order to blacken his reputation. It was in response to this hostility from his Christian subjects in and around Antioch that Julian wrote the *Misopogon,* which is cited in the epigraph to "Julian and the Antiochenes."

Gibbon describes the incident as follows:

> When Julian, on the day of the annual festival, hastened to adore the Apollo of Daphne, his devotion was raised to the highest pitch of eagerness and impatience. His lively imagination anticipated the grateful pomp of victims, of libations and of incense; a long procession of youths and virgins, clothed in white robes, the symbol of their innocence; and the tumultuous concourse of an innumerable people. But the zeal of Antioch was diverted, since the reign of Christianity, into a different channel. Instead of hecatombs of fat

oxen sacrificed by the tribes of a wealthy city to their tutelar deity the emperor complains that he found only a single goose, provided at the expense of a priest, the pale and solitary inhabitant of this decayed temple. The altar was deserted, the oracle had been reduced to silence, and the holy ground was profaned by the introduction of Christian and funereal rites. After Babylas (a bishop of Antioch, who died in prison in the persecution of Decius) had rested near a century in his grave, his body, by the order of Cæsar Gallus, was transported into the midst of the grove of Daphne. A magnificent church was erected over his remains; a portion of the sacred lands was usurped for the maintenance of the clergy, and for the burial of the Christians at Antioch, who were ambitious of lying at the feet of their bishop; and the priests of Apollo retired, with their affrighted and indignant votaries. As soon as another revolution seemed to restore the fortune of Paganism, the church of St. Babylas was demolished, and new buildings were added to the mouldering edifice which had been raised by the piety of Syrian kings. But the first and most serious care of Julian was to deliver his oppressed deity from the odious presence of the dead and living Christians, who had so effectually suppressed the voice of fraud or enthusiasm. The scene of infection was purified, according to the forms of ancient rituals; the bodies were decently removed; and the ministers of the church were permitted to convey the remains of St. Babylas to their former habitation within the walls of Antioch. The modest behavior which might have assuaged the jealousy of a hostile government was neglected, on this occasion, by the zeal of the Christians. The lofty car, that transported the relics of Babylas, was followed, and accompanied, and received, by an innumerable multitude; who chanted, with thundering acclamations, the Psalms of David [that were] the most expressive of their contempt for idols and idolaters. The return of the saint was a triumph; and the triumph was an insult on the religion of the emperor, who exerted his pride

to dissemble his resentment. During the night which termi-
nated this indiscreet procession, the temple of Daphne was
in flames; the statue of Apollo was consumed; and the walls
of the edifice were left a naked and awful monument of ruin.
The Christians of Antioch asserted, with religious confi-
dence, that the powerful intercession of St. Babylas had
pointed the lightnings of heaven against the devoted roof:
but as Julian was reduced to the alternative of believing
either a crime or a miracle, he chose, without hesitation,
without evidence, but with some color of probability, to
impute the fire of Daphne to the revenge of the Galilæans.
Their offence, had it been sufficiently proved, might have
justified the retaliation, which was immediately executed by
the order of Julian, of shutting the doors, and confiscating
the wealth, of the cathedral of Antioch. To discover the
criminals who were guilty of the tumult, of the fire, or of
secreting the riches of the church, several of the ecclesiastics
were tortured; and a Presbyter, of the name of Theodoret,
was beheaded by the sentence of the Count of the East. But
this hasty act was blamed by the emperor; who lamented,
with real or affected concern, that the imprudent zeal of his
ministers would tarnish his reign with the disgrace of perse-
cution.

Cavafy had finished correcting the proofs of this poem, but had not yet
returned them to the printer, when he died on April 29, 1933, his sev-
entieth birthday.

Poems Published 1897–1904

Voices   *pg. 180*

The first version of this poem was written in July 1894 and published in
December of that year as "Sweet Voices" (now one of the Repudiated
Poems); a subsequent revision was done in December 1903 and pub-
lished in this form in August 1904.

The translation of the first word of the poem, the plural adjective *idanikés,* is a notoriously vexed issue. Strictly speaking, the word means "ideal"; but elsewhere in Cavafy's poetry, for instance in the Unpublished Poem "King Claudius," the poet clearly intends it to mean "unreal" or "imaginary." Hence my rendering of the word as "imagined," which imparts to the rather abstract dictionary definition the flavor of cerebral activity implied by Cavafy's usage elsewhere.

Candles   *pg. 182*

Writing in the mid-1890s to his friend Pericles Anastassiades, Cavafy referred to this poem as "one of the best things I ever wrote." A decade later, in December 1906, he made the following note apropos of this poem and two others that follow closely, "An Old Man" and "Old Men's Souls":

> What a deceitful thing Art can be, when you want to apply sincerity. You sit down and write—often speculatively— about emotions, and then, over time, you doubt yourself. I wrote "Candles," "The Souls of Old Men" and "An Old Man" about old age. Advancing towards old (or middle) age, I discovered that this last poem of mine does not contain a correct evaluation. "The Souls of Old Men" I still think correct; but when I reach seventy years I might find it wanting too. "Candles" I hope is safe.
>
> Descriptive poetry—historical events, the photographing (what an ugly word!) of nature—is perhaps safe. But it is a small and rather short-lived thing.

An Old Man   *pg. 183*

First written in 1894 and listed under the heading of "Fleeting Years," this poem was first published in the anthology *Ethnikon Imerologion . . . tou etous 1898* (1897) along with two other poems, "The Horses of Achilles" and "Horace in Athens." Apropos of Horace, it is noteworthy that "An Old Man" originally bore, as a subtitle, the Latin words *Eheu fugaces,* which is a quotation from an ode by that poet (*Odes* 2.14): *eheu fugaces . . . labuntur anni,* "alas, the fleeting years slip away."

One of Cavafy's *Unpublished Notes on Poetics and Ethics,* written in English, refers to "An Old Man," as follows:

> I distinctly felt 1 evening in January 1904 that I should have felt more at ease, with a fuller life, had I to remember a satisfactory morning or day to my craving for a f[uck?]; which is proof to the verity of "ι *Γέρος*" [= the Greek title of "An Old Man"].

In another of these notes (see above on "Candles"), written in Greek and dated 1906, the poet found this poem wanting in comparison to "Candles" and "The Souls of Old Men."

Prayer pg. 184

For the motif of mortals praying to impassive or unresponsive deities, see also "Safe Haven" and "Cleitus's Illness."

In his youth, Cavafy wrote with great emotion about the icon of the Mother of God: in an 1893 review of the poetry of Georgios Stratigis, commenting on a poem called "Before the Iconostasis," he observed that

> [i]n it I find as it were an echo of the dream-like and mystical devotion that the Greek people nurture toward the Mother of Christ—a feeling that causes it to regard her blessed icon as a great symbol of consolation; a feeling that . . . exalts and vivifies and honors [the Greek people].

Old Men's Souls pg. 185

The poem was originally classified under the heading "Prisons." For Cavafy's note on this poem, see above notes on "Candles" and "An Old Man."

The First Step   pg. 186

One of the most famous poets of the Alexandrian school, THEOCRITUS
(c. 300–260 B.C.) was born in Syracuse, on Sicily, but spent most of his
life in Alexandria. What little we know about him is gleaned from details
in his poems—for instance, that he'd appealed to Hieron, the ruler of
Sicily, before finding a patron in Ptolemy II Philadelphus of Egypt, at
whose brilliant court Theocritus seems to have remained thereafter.
Although he composed poems of every kind, Theocritus remains a
favorite above all for his pastoral "Idylls," with their elegant feeling and
witty descriptions of loves among rural and mythic characters.

Interruption   pg. 187

The references here are to two mythic interruptions by humans that had
disastrous results for divine plans. In the Homeric *Hymn to Demeter*—
which we know Cavafy had read around 1900, and which was clearly
the inspiration for this poem—DEMETER, goddess of the harvest, runs
amok on earth in her grief for her ravished daughter Persephone; even-
tually she comes to the town of ELEUSIS, where, disguised as an old
woman, she ends up working in the house of the king as a nurse to his
infant son. There she begins the arcane process of transforming the baby
into an immortal (as compensation for her own lost daughter, an
immortal who has become "mortal" by reason of her close proximity to
Hades) by placing him each night among the glowing embers of the
hearth-fire. One night, his mother the queen, METANEIRA, enters the
room and interrupts Demeter, who in a rage hurls the boy to the ground
and stalks out of the royal palace.

   THETIS and PELEUS were the parents of the Greek hero Achilles.
An immortal sea nymph unwillingly wed to a mortal man, Thetis
attempted to render her child virtually immortal by dipping him in the
terrible waters of the river Styx, contact with which would leave him
invulnerable. Cavafy here imagines that Peleus, in his palace at PHTHIA
(in the central Greek region of Thessaly), interrupts this process much
as Metaneira does in the Homeric *Hymn,* with the result that Thetis
neglects to dip the place on her child's ankle where she's been holding

him. This, of course, turned out to be the one vulnerable part of Achilles' body, and the location of the fatal wound he received as the Trojan War was nearing its end.

Thermopylae pg. 188

The battle of THERMOPYLAE was one of the most important battles of the Persian Wars (490–479 B.C.), in which the Persian empire, first under Darius the Great and then under his son Xerxes, attempted to subjugate the cities of mainland Greece. Despite being overwhelmingly outnumbered, a coalition of Greek states, led by Athens and Sparta, resisted the Persians with great bravery, and won the war in 479 after the decisive victories at Salamis and Plataea.

No act of bravery, however, was greater than that shown by the Spartans at Thermopylae, a pass between the mountains and the sea in north-central Greece through which the Persian army hoped to pass en route to Athens. As Herodotus relates in his *History* (7.201–233), a Greek force of between six and seven thousand troops bravely held the narrow mountain pass for two days, until a local man called Ephialtes betrayed them, showing the Persians an alternative route round the pass. After this, nearly all the Greeks withdrew or panicked, leaving about three hundred men behind, mostly Spartans, who heroically fought a rear-guard action until the last man had been killed; this action gave the departing force time enough to leave the vicinity safely. (According to one source, four thousand Persians were killed, to the Spartans' three hundred.)

Thermopylae has thereafter stood as a symbol of extraordinary bravery against unbeatable odds—and, too, of a supreme, rather stylish disdain for danger, such as truly brave men show. According to Herodotus, Xerxes sent a spy to see how many Greeks were ready to resist him in the pass, and the man he sent was astonished to see that, in the face of daunting odds, the Spartan soldiers were exercising and combing their long hair, "for it is the custom of these men to dress their hair," as the Spartan turncoat Demaratus (see "Demaratus") told Xerxes, "whenever they are about to put their lives in jeopardy."

Che Fece . . . Il Gran Rifiuto pg. 189

The title—which means "who made . . . the great refusal"—is a partial quotation of a line from Canto III of Dante's *Inferno*, which describes Dante and Vergil as they pass through the Gates of Hell ("Abandon hope, all ye who enter here"). The sight that greets their eyes, once through the gates, is an astoundingly long line of those souls "displeasing both to God and to his enemy" because they committed themselves neither to good nor to evil and therefore "had never been alive"—a failure that clearly fascinated the poet for his own reasons. Among these damned, according to Dante, was Pope Celestine V, a saintly and ascetic hermit who, having been elected to the papacy at the age of eighty, in 1294, resigned the office only a few months later. This extraordinary rejection of the Holy See—the "great refusal"—earned Dante's contempt primarily because it paved the way for the election of Boniface VIII, a pope for whom Dante had a special loathing.

The title of this poem quotes Dante's line about Celestine with one significant deletion. The lines in question are:

> *Vidi e conobbi l'ombra di colei*
> *che fece per viltate il gran rifiuto.*

> I saw and recognized the shade of him
> Who out of cowardice made the great refusal.

Cavafy, who is likely to have known Celestine's story and understood that the saintly man resigned less out of cowardice than out of humility and recognition of his own unsuitability for worldly office, shows more humanity here than Dante does, in deleting the phrase *per viltate,* "out of cowardice," in the second line.

The entire passage, cited in the Longfellow translation, which Cavafy owned, reads as follows:

> And he to me: "This miserable mode
> Maintain the melancholy souls of those
> Who lived withouten infamy or praise.

Commingled are they with that caitiff choir
Of Angels, who have not rebellious been,
Nor faithful were to God, but were for self.

The heavens expelled them, not to be less fair;
Nor them the nethermore abyss received,
For glory none the damned would have from them."

And I: "O Master, what so grievous is
To these, that maketh them lament so sore?"
He answered: "I will tell thee very briefly.

These have no longer any hope of death;
And this blind life of theirs is so debased,
They envious are of every other fate.

No fame of them the world permits to be;
Misericord and Justice both disdain them.
Let us not speak of them, but look, and pass."

And I, who looked again, beheld a banner,
Which, whirling round, ran on so rapidly,
That of all pause it seemed to me indignant;

And after it there came so long a train
Of people, that I ne'er would have believed
That ever Death so many had undone.

When some among them I had recognised,
I looked, and I beheld the shade of him
Who made through cowardice the great refusal.

Forthwith I comprehended, and was certain,
That this the sect was of the caitiff wretches
Hateful to God and to his enemies.

These miscreants, who never were alive,
Were naked, and were stung exceedingly
By gadflies and by hornets that were there.

These did their faces irrigate with blood,
Which, with their tears commingled, at their feet
By the disgusting worms was gathered up.

Walls *pg. 191*

The first printed version of this poem bore an epigraph from Aeschylus's *Prometheus Bound:* "How do I suffer unjust things." Although published and republished over the years in various periodicals, the poem, which was translated into English by Cavafy's older brother John a few months after it was written, was included neither in the grouping of Repudiated Poems, nor however in the privately printed collections *Poems 1904* and *Poems 1910;* it makes its first appearance as part of a collection in the "Sengopoulos Notebook" version of *Poems 1910.*

For a detailed discussion of the formal complexities of this poem, see the Introduction, pp. xlvii–xlix.

Apropos of "Walls" Cavafy left a note in English:

> Besides, one lives, one hears and one understands and the poems one writes, though not true to one's actual life, are true to other lives . . . not generally, of course, but specially—and the reader to whose life the poem fits admits and feels the poem: which is proved by [playwright and author Gregory] Xenopoulos' liking *Walls, Candles. . . .*

And:

> If even for one day, or one hour I felt like the man within "Walls", or like the man of "Windows" the poem is based on a truth, a short-lived truth, but which, for the very reason of its having once existed, may repeat itself in another life, with perhaps as short duration, perhaps with longer.

Waiting for the Barbarians

pg. 192

The poem at first seems to be among the strongest expressions, on the part of the younger Cavafy, of the pessimistic lassitude and resistance to the idea of progress typical of the Decadents. And yet the poet left a strong note, dating to the period of his "Philosophical Scrutiny" of 1903–1904, suggesting that we must read this work in a more complex way:

> The poem assumes this kind of social situation.
>
> Possible situation; not likely; not my own prediction. My own notion concerning the future is more optimistic. Anyway, the poem is not at odds with my own optimistic notion; it can be taken as an episode in the progress towards Good.

The note suggests a certain impatience with the facile attitude of ennui that was characteristic of the Decadents whom he liked to mimic as a young poet, one which, as he evolved into his mature phase, seemed to him to be too unsubtle and lacking in intellectual nuance.

Betrayal

pg. 194

The epigraph of this poem comes from the conclusion of the second book of Plato's *Republic*. The context is a discussion about whether the gods can be evil, a proposition that Socrates vehemently rejects: it is only in the imperfect representations of the gods, he says (e.g., in theater and poetry), that the gods appear to be imperfect. In order to demonstrate his point, Socrates cites a passage from a play by Aeschylus (it is not known from which lost play the quotation comes) in which THETIS, the wife of PELEUS and mother of ACHILLES, claims to have been misled by APOLLO about the fate of her son.

Cavafy's citation of Plato (who is in turn reporting a citation by Socrates of Aeschylus) creates a particularly dense framework for interpreting his own poem. On the one hand, the Classical quotation he has marshaled as the epigraph for his poem is Plato's critique, in the *Republic,* of the veracity of poetry. This part of the *Republic* is, indeed, the first systematic attempt in the Western tradition at a reasoned critique of myth and its allied art (as the Greeks saw it), poetry, and in this context the tone of Cavafy's poem, which is rather detached, in the rather Thucydidean manner of a historian coolly reevaluating a myth, suggests an alliance with Plato.

On the other hand, whereas the title, "Betrayal," suggests that Apollo—and, therefore, "Poetry"—can and does indeed lie, the vehicle for our appreciation of this insight is, of course, the poem that Cavafy is writing, and which we are reading.

The myth to which the poem and its epigraph allude concerns Achilles, the greatest of the Greek heroes who went to Troy. Thetis—a sea-nymph and daughter of the Old Man of the Sea, Proteus—and Peleus, the son of Aeacus, were the parents of Achilles. Thetis had been pursued by Zeus, but when he learned of a prophecy predicting that any son she bore would be greater than his father, he quickly married her off to Peleus; their marriage was said to have been the last great occasion at which both mortals and immortals feasted together. The tradition is that soon after the birth of Achilles, Thetis dipped the child in the river Styx in order to grant him immortality, but the place where she had held him, at his heel, remained vulnerable—his one weak spot. (See "Interruption.") Achilles was taken away from his mother as a boy and given to the centaur Chiron to be brought up in the woodlands of THESSALY, in central Greece. A story goes that when the Achaean kings came to fetch him to the Trojan War, his mother spirited him away to the island of Skyros, dressed as a maiden; there he married Deidamia, who bore him a son, Neoptolemus. Eventually his ruse was discovered and he went to Troy. Although Achilles' death at the hands of Paris, the seducer of Helen, is not depicted in the *Iliad* itself, the poem does allude to it: for instance, when his divine horses admonish him (19.494) to remember that he will be cut down by both a god and a man—i.e., by Apollo and Paris, who, guided by the god, aims his arrow at Achilles' heel, thereby killing him.

The Funeral of Sarpedon   *pg. 196*

This poem exists in two versions, both of them published: one in December 1898, and the other (extensively revised and rewritten) in

August 1908. Like Cavafy's other poems dealing with High Classical subjects (as opposed to Hellenistic or Byzantine), it belongs to the earliest period of his work.

"The Funeral of Sarpedon" is closely linked, in terms of its Iliadic themes and content, to "The Horses of Achilles." Book 16 of the *Iliad* represents a kind of dramatic peak in the overall action of the poem: in it, Achilles' companion Patroclus, the son of MENOETIUS, goes into battle with the Trojans disguised in Achilles' armor, a ruse that has the effect of temporarily routing the Trojans. Until his death at the hands of the Trojan prince Hector, Patroclus slaughters many Trojans and Trojan allies in an escalating fury. As Homer narrates (*Iliad* 16.419 ff.), among those killed by Patroclus was SARPEDON, the king of LYCIA and the son of Zeus and Laodameia. Immediately prior to Sarpedon's death, Zeus, watching the proceedings from Olympus, ponders whether to go against the decrees of Fate and snatch Sarpedon off the battlefield (16.433–37), but his wife, Hera—an implacable foe of the Trojans—argues with him, claiming that such favoritism on Zeus's part would disgruntle the other gods. Hera's response is worth quoting in full, as it clearly provided Cavafy not only with the theme of his poem, one he returns to, in different incarnations, again and again—the way in which even the mighty must cope with defeat—but the details of the action, from the mission of Sleep and Death to the "tomb and the grave-stele" (*tymboi te stêlêi te,* 16.457; the modern Greek is *to mnima kai tin stili*):

In reply to him the wide-eyed lady Hera spoke:
"Dread son of Kronos, what kind of speech you have made!
Do you really wish to free a mortal man, whose fate
has long been sealed, from dreadful-sounding death?
Fine: but know you that we gods will never praise you.
And I'll tell you something more, and ponder it well:
if you send Sarpedon home still living,
consider whether some other god might then want
to send his own son out of the heavy fray;
for around Priam's high city are fighting many
sons of immortals, in whom you'll arouse great anger.
But even if he is so dear to you, and your own heart grieves,
still let him fall in the heavy fray

under the hands of Patroclus, Menoetius's son.
But then, when his soul and life have left him,
send Death and painless Sleep to carry him home
until they reach the people of broad Lycia,
and there his brothers and clansmen will give him burial
with grave-mound and pillar. For that is the honor due to the dead."

Later on in Book 16, after Patroclus has slain Sarpedon and the Greeks and Trojans are battling for possession of his body and armor, Homer relates how Zeus arranged for the burial rites of his son (16.666–75):

And then cloud-gathering Zeus spoke unto Apollo:
"On, now, dear Phoebus: clean from Sarpedon the dark gore,
taking him out of the battle, and then use the running waters
of the river to wash him and then anoint him with ambrosia
and clothe him with immortal garments;
then send him off to be born by swift escort,
by the twins Sleep and Death, who will swiftly
set him down among the rich folk of broad Lycia,
where his brothers and clansmen will bury him
with grave-mound and pillar. For that is the honor due to the dead."
So he spoke, nor did Apollo fail to heed his father.

The sensuous description of a beautiful corpse, carefully tended, shows a debt to the Decadents. Cavafy's verses recall, indeed, Oscar Wilde's long 1881 poem "Charmides," about a beautiful youth who makes love to a statue of Athena. After the youth dies, his body is the object of languid attentions very similar to those lavished on Cavafy's Sarpedon:

But some good Triton-god had ruth, and bare
The boy's drowned body back to Grecian land,
And mermaids combed his dank and dripping hair
And smoothed his brow, and loosed his clinching hand,
Some brought sweet spices from far Araby,
And others made the halcyon sing her softest lullaby.

. . . .

> Hither the billow brought him, and was glad
> Of such dear servitude, and where the land
> Was virgin of all waters laid the lad
> Upon the golden margent of the strand,
> And like a lingering lover oft returned
> To kiss those pallid limbs which once with intense
>   fire burned . . .

Whether Cavafy knew Wilde's poem (which Wilde considered his best), we cannot know; but it is interesting that he invokes the name Charmides in a later poem, "In a City of Osrhoene," in which a youth, after being beaten up in a street brawl, is brought to a room in a tavern, where the moonlight streams through a window, illuminating his immobile, beautiful form.

The Horses of Achilles *pg. 198*

By the sixteenth book of the *Iliad*'s narration of the final year of the Trojan War, the Greek forces are suffering badly because Achilles, the greatest of the Greek soldiers, has withdrawn both himself and his countrymen from the fighting after being insulted by the commander-in-chief, Agamemnon. Out of pity for the allies, Achilles' soft-hearted friend and companion, PATROCLUS, persuades Achilles to let him wear Achilles' famous armor into battle; by so doing, he hopes to fool the Trojans into thinking that Achilles himself has returned to the fighting, and thereby to frighten them away for a while. Driving a chariot pulled by Achilles' immortal horses, Balios and Xanthe ("Charger" and "Roan")—they are the offspring of the Zephyr, the West Wind, and the harpy Podarge ("Swift-foot")—Patroclus roars into the fray and, for a while, wreaks terrible damage on the Trojans. He becomes so caught up in bloodlust, however, that he forgets all caution and fails to turn back, as Achilles had instructed, and is eventually killed by Hector, the leader of the Trojans, after Apollo helps to reveal the ruse of the borrowed armor. (In Book 19, these same horses are given voice by the goddess Hera, and they remind Achilles that he, too, is fated to die young, at the hands both of Apollo, the god ultimately responsible for Patroclus's death, and of a man, Paris.)

Cavafy's poem is, at points, a fairly close adaptation of about twenty lines from Book 17, which tell of how the grief-stricken horses stood apart from the mêlée as Greeks and Trojans battled furiously over the body of Patroclus (*Iliad* 17.426–47):

> But the horses of Peleus's son stood apart from the fray and
> wept, ever since they first had learned that their driver
> had fallen in the dust at the hands of mankilling Hector.
> Now Automedon, the rugged son of Alkimos,
> kept lashing them, laying on with the darting whip,
> now coaxing them with gentle words, now swearing:
> But the two did not want to go either to the ships, on the broad
>   Hellespont,
> or back into the battle with the Achaeans,
> but as a pillar stands firm, that upon some tomb-mound
> of a man who had died, or a woman,
> so they remained, firmly, holding back the beauteous chariot,
> trailing their heads in the dust. Their warm tears
> flowed down from their eyes to the ground in mourning
> desire for their charioteer. Their luxuriant manes were dirtied
> streaming down from the yoke-pads, along either side of the yoke.
> And seeing the two of them mourning, the son of Kronos took pity
> and shaking his head spoke to his own deep heart:
> "O, you two wretches, why did I give you to lord Peleus,
> a mortal, when you two are ageless and immortal?
> So you could suffer pain alongside wretched men?
> For there is nothing more lamentable as man
> of all that breathe and crawl upon the earth."

REPUDIATED POEMS

(1886–1898)

Word and Silence pg. 205

The epigraph to this poem is a Greek transliteration—not a translation—
by Cavafy of an Egyptian Arabic maxim into Greek characters; the first
line of the poem is an approximate translation of the maxim. Given the
poem's preoccupation with language, silences, and meaning, it seems
wrong to translate the epigraph itself: Cavafy clearly meant the reader to
confront the (likely unintelligible) sound of the proverb in the original
Arabic before reaching the translation itself.

   I am indebted to Glen Bowersock for the correct English transliteration of the Arabic.

Sham-el-Nessim pg. 206

The title ("Breath of the Wind") is the name of an annual springtime
Egyptian festival that coincided, in Cavafy's time, with Easter Monday.
Misiri was the common Greek name for Egypt (from the Egyptians'
name for their own land, *Misr'*); Gabari, Mahmoudiya, Mex,
Moharram Bey, and Ramleh were all names of Alexandrian neigh-
borhoods. Ptah was an ancient Egyptian god associated with creativity
and artisanship. Moganni is a transliteration of an Egyptian Arabic
term for a folksinger.

Bard pg. 209

The latter part of 1892 saw the young Cavafy preoccupied more than
usually with the Parnassian themes of the poet's necessary rejection of
the material, the ordinary, and the positivistic. Diana Haas has observed
that, in addition to "The Hereafter" (written in August 1892), which

articulates these themes very concretely, that period saw the publication of Cavafy's article on Keats's *Lamia,* in which he quotes the following lines:

> Do not all charms fly
> At the mere touch of cold philosophy?
> There was an awful rainbow once in Heaven;
> We know her woof, her texture; she is given
> In the dull catalogue of common things.

About this passage Cavafy commented that "the poet describes the really destructive vandalism that science wreaks on the beauties of nature, explaining and analyzing everything in the most material fashion destroys the charm and nobility of the unknown."

Vulnerant Omnes, Ultima Necat *pg. 210*

The Latin title of the poem, which means "All of them wound, the last one kills," was a common inscription on clock faces and sundials from the Middle Ages at least into the nineteenth century.

The poem has several possible sources. Théophile Gautier's 1865 collection *España* contained a poem called "L'Horloge" ("The Clock") bearing the same Latin epigraph; Paul Verlaine's *Ardennes* also cites the well-known Latin text in its description of a village clock, which Verlaine chides for failing in the "warning" and "moralistic" role promised by the inscription. Baudelaire's *Les Fleurs du Mal* also includes a poem called "L'Horloge," which opens with an address to the "Impassive god! whose minatory hands / repeat their sinister and single charge: / *Remember!*" and ends with the line "from all / the message comes: 'Too late, old coward! Die!' " (tr. Richard Howard). Still, although the first part of the present poem is characterized by the typical fin-de-siècle ennui to be found in its possible models (Gautier's verse contains the famously exhausted line, "To be born is merely to begin to die"), Cavafy's poem turns in the end, like so much of his work of the early 1890s, to embrace the promise of redemption and rebirth offered by Christianity.

Good and Bad Weather

pg. 212

This is the first poem published by Cavafy that was written in demotic.

Timolaus the Syracusan

pg. 213

This poem was first published in an 1894 collection along with three other of the Repudiated Poems: "Athena's Vote," "The Inkwell," and "Sweet Voices."

This is the first poem that Cavafy published that is set in the ancient (as opposed to mythic) past. Timolaus himself, however, is clearly invented, as a note from Cavafy to his brother John (who planned to translate the poem into English) indicates: there Cavafy told his brother that if the name "Timolaus" proved to be metrically inconvenient, he could leave it blank for the time being and they would find another name.

Athena's Vote

pg. 215

The poem, which is the first that Cavafy published on a mythological theme, alludes to the founding of the Athenian law court known as the Areopagus, where, in Classical times, capital crimes were tried. The great literary account of how this court came to be founded occurs in the final play in Aeschylus's trilogy, *Oresteia:* having murdered his mother, Clytemnestra, the young prince Orestes stands trial and is defended by the god Apollo himself. The jury of twelve Athenians, however, is evenly split, and Orestes is acquitted only after ATHENA casts the tie-breaking vote in his favor.

Sweet Voices

pg. 219

This poem is one of a small number that allow us to witness, in some detail, Cavafy's evolution as a poet. Reprinted twice in 1896, "Sweet Voices" was eventually rewritten by Cavafy late in 1903 and published in its final form in 1904 as "Voices." Comparison between the two versions suggests the rigorous process of self-editing and paring down that transformed the poet's mature work.

Oedipus

pg. 223

The French painter Gustave Moreau (1826–1898) exhibited his painting of the confrontation between Oedipus and the Sphinx in 1864. Cavafy's poem is based on a description of the painting that appeared in a newspaper.

According to an ancient mythic tradition for which Sophocles' *Oedipus Tyrannus* and *Oedipus at Colonus* are the most famous dramatic vehicles, OEDIPUS was the child of the Theban king Laius and his wife, Jocasta. Fearful of a prophecy that a child of his would kill its father and marry its mother, Laius entrusted the newborn Oedipus to a servant to be exposed on Mt. Cithaeron. The servant, however, pitying the newborn child, secretly entrusted it to a shepherd who served the household of the Corinthian king, and this king subsequently raised the child as his own. Later on, the youthful Oedipus, having overheard rumors that he was not in fact the natural child of his royal father, set off to enquire about his true paternity at the oracle of Delphi; en route, he encountered the party of Laius, and during an altercation on the road Oedipus slew Laius and his attendants, thereby unwittingly fulfilling part of the prophecy.

Oedipus then made his way to Thebes, which at the time was being tormented by the Sphinx—a monster that was (in some versions) part human, part lion, with the wings of an eagle and the tail of a serpent. This creature, a sort of Turandot *avant la lettre,* asked all passersby a question, killing anyone who failed to answer it correctly. The question is traditionally given as follows: "What creature goes on four legs at morning, two at noon, and three in the evening?" Oedipus, perceiving that the riddle turned on a metaphorical equivalence between a day and the lifetime of a human being, correctly answered "Man," and thereupon slew the Sphinx and liberated the city. Soon after he married the queen, Jocasta, who was, of course, his own mother. Only many years later, after they had had four children together, was the terrible secret of Oedipus's true identity revealed. Sophocles' *Oedipus,* often dated to around 425 B.C., narrates the events of the day on which Oedipus learns who he really is. In a subsequent play, *Oedipus at Colonus* (406 B.C.), the aged playwright fleshed out the myth with an account of the aged Oedipus's final day on earth: blind, paupered, Oedipus wanders into the sacred grove of the Furies at COLONUS, a suburb of Athens, and it is there, after a series of final confrontations with his rebellious sons and loyal daughters, that Oedipus is purged, mysteriously, of all his guilt, and after dying is elevated to semidivine status.

Moreau's canvas is noteworthy for the dreamy, almost erotic gaze exchanged between the youthful Oedipus, perched in languid contrapposto, and the insinuating, bare-breasted Sphinx whose right hind leg presses against Oedipus's barely concealed genitals; and for the gruesome detail of the body parts of the Sphinx's victims that litter the landscape in which this encounter takes place.

Ode and Elegy of the Streets — pg. 224

First published in *Kosmos,* April 1896, and reprinted the following month in *To Asty.* In 1899 this poem was published in an anthology, *Aigyptiakon Imerologion tou etous 1900,* along with "But Wise Men Apprehend What Is Imminent" (under its original title, "Imminent") and "The First Step."

The Cavafy Archive contains a note, dated October 1909, left by the poet in connection with this poem: it seems from the context ("Perhaps the best thing is to let it alone," the note begins) that Cavafy had pondered revising the poem, but in the end he wonders whether it is better to make a selection of his "good work" written in katharevousa, including the present poem, "Walls," and "In the Cemetery."

Near an Open Window — pg. 225

The original title of this poem was "Night of a Symbolist Poet." Certainly the poet indulges here in the elaborate synesthetic "correspondences" already evoked in "Correspondences According to Baudelaire." Diana Haas has also noted a strong correlation between the poetic ecstasy described here and the ecstasy attributed to Pythagorean initiates in Edouard Schuré's *Les Grands initiés: Esquisse de l'histoire secrète des religions* ("The Great Initiates: A Sketch of the Secret History of Religions") (1889), an inspiration for a number of Cavafy's other early works:

> *Ecstasy* is defined as a vision of the spiritual world, in which good or evil spirits appear to the viewer in human form and communicate with him . . . Nothing can suggest, according to the accounts of the great ecstatics, either the beauty and the splendor of these visions, or the feeling of ineffable fusion with the divine essence which they bring, like a drunkenness of light and music.

A Love

pg. 226

This poem is based on the ballad "Auld Robin Gray," by Lady Anna Lindsay Barnard (1750–1825), a poem that Cavafy first translated into Greek as "Vain, Vain Love" in *Hesperus* in June 1886. The text of Barnard's ballad is worth looking at, since comparison with the original delineates the contours of Cavafy's special preoccupations:

> When the sheep are in the fauld, and the kye at hame,
> And a' the warld to rest are gane,
> The waes o' my heart fa' in showers frae my e'e,
> While my gudeman lies sound by me.
>
> Young Jamie lo'ed me weel, and sought me for his bride;
> But saving a croun he had naething else beside:
> To make the croun a pund, young Jamie gaed to sea;
> And the croun and the pund were baith for me.
>
> He hadna been awa' a week but only twa,
> When my father brak his arm, and the cow was stown awa;
> My mother she fell sick,—and my Jamie at the sea—
> And auld Robin Gray came a-courtin' me.
>
> My father couldna work, and my mother couldna spin;
> I toil'd day and night, but their bread I couldna win;

Auld Rob maintain'd them baith, and wi' tears in his e'e
Said, "Jennie, for their sakes, O, marry me!"

My heart it said nay; I look'd for Jamie back;
But the wind it blew high, and the ship it was a wrack;
His ship it was a wrack—Why didna Jamie dee?
Or why do I live to cry, Wae 's me?

My father urged me sair: my mother didna speak;
But she look'd in my face till my heart was like to break:
They gi'ed him my hand, tho' my heart was in the sea;
Sae auld Robin Gray he was gudeman to me.

I hadna been a wife a week but only four,
When mournfu' as I sat on the stane at the door,
I saw my Jamie's wraith,—for I couldna think it he,
Till he said, "I'm come hame to marry thee."

O sair, sair did we greet, and muckle did we say;
We took but ae kiss, and we tore ourselves away:
I wish that I were dead, but I'm no like to dee;
And why was I born to say, Wae 's me!

I gang like a ghaist, and I carena to spin;
I daurna think on Jamie, for that wad be a sin;
But I'll do my best a gude wife aye to be,
For auld Robin Gray he is kind unto me.

Tennyson's "Enoch Arden" (1864) was also inspired by Lady Barnard's ballad. For other poems in which Cavafy responds to Tennyson's work, see "Second Odyssey" and "Simeon," with their notes, pp. 501–5 and 531–3.

Remembrance   pg. 230

Another early version of one of the "canonical" poems that allows us to appraise Cavafy's artistic development. First written probably in 1886, according to Savidis, "Remembrance" was rewritten in July 1905 and given the title "Thessaly." The final version, entitled "Song of Ionia," was published in June 1911. For more on the evolution of this poem into its final, published form, see the note on "Song of Ionia," pp. 397–8.

The Death of the Emperor Tacitus pg. 231

This is the first of Cavafy's Published Poems that takes as its subject a specific event from ancient history and features a historical, as opposed to mythological or invented, figure from the past. First published in the journal *Kosmos,* in January 1897, this poem was reprinted in *Aigyptiakon Imerologion tou etous 1899* (Alexandria, 1898) along with "Voice from the Sea" and "The Steps of the Eumenides," and again reprinted, in 1898, in a broadsheet entitled *Ancient Days,* along with "The Tears of Phaethon's Sisters."

The Roman emperor TACITUS (Claudius Tacitus, 200–276 A.D.), allegedly related to the great historian, was a distinguished senator who rose to the consulship in 273. In 275, within a year of the assassination of the emperor Aurelian, the Senate elected the elderly and somewhat reluctant Tacitus emperor. His brief reign was marked by attempts to restore some autonomy to the Senate, and by fierce battles with the Goths. Unpopular with his troops, he died, probably as the result of foul play, while on campaign in Tyana, in the province of Cappadocia in Asia Minor, in April 276.

That Cavafy's inspiration for this poem came from his reading of Gibbon seems certain, given that the poet made a marginal note, in his copy of *Decline and Fall,* to the following passage (the phrase he marked appears here in italics):

> If we can prefer personal merit to accidental greatness, we shall esteem the birth of Tacitus more truly noble than that of kings. He claimed *his descent from the philosophic historian, whose writings will instruct the last generations of mankind.* The senator Tacitus was then seventy-five years of age.

This passage is followed by a detailed description of the emperor Tacitus's death, which is almost certainly the source of Cavafy's poem:

But the glory and life of Tacitus were of short duration. Transported, in the depth of winter, from the soft retirement of Campania to the foot of mount Caucasus, he sunk under the unaccustomed hardships of a military life. The fatigues of the body were aggravated by the cares of the mind. For awhile, the angry and selfish passions of the soldiers had been suspended by the enthusiasm of public virtue. They soon broke out with redoubled violence, and raged in the camp, and even in the tent, of the aged emperor. His mild and amiable character served only to inspire contempt; and he was incessantly tormented with factions which he could not assuage, and by demands which it was impossible to satisfy. Whatever flattering expectations he had conceived of reconciling the public disorders, Tacitus soon was convinced, that the licentiousness of the army disdained the feeble restraint of laws; and his last hour was hastened by anguish and disappointment. It may be doubtful whether the soldiers imbued their hands in the blood of this innocent prince. It is certain that their insolence was the cause of his death. He expired at Tyana in Cappadocia, after a reign of only six months and about twenty days.

In particular, Gibbon's references to "the soft retirement of Campania," "the fatigues of the body," "the unaccustomed hardships of a military life" appear to have made an impression on Cavafy and reappear, as it were almost verbatim, in his poem.

The following note by the poet, preserved in the Cavafy Archive, suggests the reasons why this poem was rewritten ten years after it was first composed late in 1896:

> The poem "The Death of the Emperor Tacitus" which was written in 1896—and thereafter published two more times— had to be rewritten—since it was rewritten in 1906—since— other reasons aside—the expression "spiteful" [*mochthirá*] was, historically, nonsense. The Senate did not display spite when it elected Tacitus.

The Eumenides' Footfalls

pg. 232

This poem was written in August 1893 and rewritten in December 1908 with the title "The Steps." The summer of 1893 marked the beginning of a period in which Cavafy composed six other poems on Greco-Roman themes: "Sculptor's Workshop" (later retitled "Sculptor of Tyana"); "Displeased Theatregoer," "Horace in Athens," " 'The Rest Shall I Tell to Those in Hades Below,' " and two works that have been lost, "A Hellenizing Patrician" and "Cato the Censor."

For NERO, see the note on "The Steps," pp. 385–6.

The Tears of Phaëthon's Sisters

pg. 233

Best known from Ovid's retelling of it in Book 2 of his *Metamorphoses,* the myth of Apollo's son Phaëthon goes back well into Greek antiquity, and indeed was the subject of a lost play of Aeschylus, *The Heliads.* Phaëthon, the son of Apollo, demanded as a proof of his divine paternity that Apollo allow him to drive the chariot of the sun. But the heavenly steeds proved impossible for the mortal youth to manage, with the result that the chariot veered wildly off course, burning some parts of the earth while freezing others; to prevent further damage, Apollo was forced to kill his child, who was flung from the chariot and plunged headlong to earth. On hearing of their brother's death, Phaëthon's sisters grieved so interminably that they were finally turned into weeping willow trees, crying tears of amber.

Ancient Tragedy

pg. 235

In addition to references to the three principal tragedians of the Classical Greek theater, the poem makes an allusion to the playwright AGATHON (448–400), a younger contemporary of Euripides who was known for his innovations; Aristotle, in the *Poetics,* remarks that he wrote plays that were not based on mythological subjects. Agathon appears as a character in Plato's *Symposium,* discoursing on love; his delicate effeminacy is mocked in Aristophanes' *Thesmophoriazusae.*

Horace in Athens pg. 237

This poem was first published in the anthology *Ethnikon Imerolo-gion . . . tou etous 1898* (1897) along with "The Horses of Achilles" and "An Old Man"; interestingly, "An Old Man" bore, as a subtitle, a quotation from Horace: the Latin words *Eheu fugaces,* "Alas the fleeting [years]," appear in the first line of *Odes* 2.14.

HORACE (Quintus Horatius Flaccus, 65–8 B.C.) was the greatest lyric poet of Roman literature. A former slave's son who ended his life as the intimate friend of the emperor Augustus, he brought Roman verse to new heights of sophistication and subtlety by adapting the Latin tongue to intricate and refined Greek meters. This technical feat, which marked the apogee of Latin lyric expression, was twined with a distinctive philosophical agenda: throughout Horace's work, the passions and agonies celebrated in Greek lyric were replaced by a benign, almost avuncular geniality barely concealing a practical Roman hard-headedness. Life is short, he says again and again, so we must seize the day and enjoy the modest pleasures that a well-balanced existence affords us. (The phrase *carpe diem* is, in fact, a quote from Horace.)

Horace's intimate familiarity with Greek literature, so evident throughout his distinctive work, was polished during the years in his early twenties when he studied, as well-off Roman youths often did, in Athens. It was in Greece that the youthful Horace had his one bruising experience with high political passions and grandiose world events: while there, the twenty-year-old student learned of Julius Caesar's assassination and subsequently joined the doomed republican forces of Cassius and Brutus against those of Octavian. Horace barely escaped from the Battle of Philippi with his life, slinking back to Rome "with clipped wings," as he wrote in one of his poems. Whatever his youthful republicanism, Horace would go on to flourish under the patronage and friendship of the man he had once fought against, Octavian, who went on to become the first Roman emperor, Augustus Caesar.

Voice from the Sea

pg. 238

The early 1890s found Cavafy preoccupied with mortality and the fear of death, an anxiety that seems to have caused him to embrace the consolation offered by Christian compassion. The decade began, indeed, with the publication of an essay about Shakespeare ("*O Sakespiros peri tis zoïs*," "Shakespeare on Life"), which focuses on the terror of death expressed by Claudio in *Measure for Measure* (3:116–32), lines which Cavafy took pains to translate into Greek, and which conclude with this cold statement:

> The weariest and most loathed worldly life
> That age, ache, penury and imprisonment
> Can lay on nature is a paradise
> To what we fear of death.

The embrace of the consolatory message of Christianity may be seen in the present poem and also, for instance, in "The Hereafter" (1892), "In the Cemetery" (1893), and "Vulnerant Omnes, Ultima Necat" (1893), with its culminating embrace of the "rekindling" and "birth" promised by the church.

The Tarentines Have Their Fun

pg. 241

This poem was first published in the anthology *Ethnikon Imerologion . . . tou etous 1899* (1898), in which the first published version of "The Funeral of Sarpedon" (see note on pp. 467–70) also appeared.

The poem alludes to a historical incident of the third century B.C. In the late 280s, Rome had been consolidating its power throughout southern Italy, attacking a number of Greek colonies there—a state of affairs that caused no little alarm in Tarentum, then the largest Greek colony in that area. Fear of a Roman attack was exacerbating political factionalism, too, since the democratic party was bitterly anti-Roman, while the outnumbered aristocrats hoped that a Roman intervention might restore them to power. In the summer of 282, the Tarentines, who happened to be gathered in their seaside theater, saw a number of Roman ships sailing into their harbor. As this was a violation of an agreement the two cities had signed, the Tarentines sent some ships to attack the Roman fleet, and the Greeks were successful in sinking several of the Roman ships and killing a number of sailors. The outraged Romans sent a delegation of officials demanding reparations, but they had the bad luck to arrive in the autumn, during the local Dionysiac festival, which was also held in the theater. The Romans were led to the stage of the theater and asked to state their purpose, and when the chief envoy, the senator L. Postumius, addressed the crowd, his awkward Greek was ridiculed by the Tarentines, one of whom later threw garbage at the Roman's toga. "Laugh now," he is said to have declared to them then, "but this toga will not be cleansed until it is washed in your blood." The Romans later attacked and plundered Tarentum.

It is certainly significant that this incident is cited in Julian the Apostate's *Misopogon* (see the note on "Julian and the Antiochenes," pp. 442–3), a text with which Cavafy was familiar:

> The Tarentines once paid the price to the Romans for such wisecracking when, having gotten drunk at the festival of Dionysus, they insulted the Romans' delegation. But you are far more fortunate in every wise, for you give yourselves over to pleasure for the whole year instead of only a few days, and you outrage not foreign ambassadors but your own sovereign—the hair on his chin and the devices on his coins.

In November 1903, just as Cavafy was engaged in the intense "Philosophical Scrutiny" of his work, Gregory Xenopoulos, an Athenian writer whom the poet had met during his 1901 trip to Athens, published an article in which he recalled how the poet, who had sent him a selection of poems the previous year, asked him to return one of those poems; the reason Cavafy gave was that the poem, which was "The Tarentines Have Their Fun," wasn't "worthy of the honor" of being in Xenopoulos's hands. "I was very sorry," Xenopoulos wrote, "but as I respect the idiosyncrasies of poets, I sent it back."

The Funeral of Sarpedon *pg. 242*

Savidis believes that the earliest version of this poem was written in November 1892, thus making it the first of a total of seven poems with Homeric themes, the other six being "Priam's March by Night," "Second Odyssey," "Achilles' Horses," "Trojans," "Betrayal," and "Ithaca."

For SARPEDON, the son of Zeus whose death in battle is recounted in Book 16 of Homer's *Iliad,* see the note on the Published Poem "The Funeral of Sarpedon" (pp. 467–70), which was the final version of this poem, rewritten in 1908.

III

UNPUBLISHED POEMS

(1877?–1923)

The Beyzade to His Lady-Love   *pg. 247*

"Beyzade" (Greek *beïzades,* Turkish *beyzade*) was a ceremonial title given to the young sons of great figures of the Ottoman court. Cavafy composed the poem during the period of his stay in Constantinople, from July 1882 to October 1885.

Dünya Güzeli   *pg. 248*

The title is a Turkish expression meaning "the most beautiful sight in the world." Savidis suggests that at an earlier phase this poem was called "Harem."

When, My Friends, I Was in Love . . .   *pg. 249*

Cavafy grouped this poem, together with "La Jeunesse Blanche," under the heading "Fleeting Years."

Nichori   *pg. 251*

"Nichori" (Turkish *Yeniköy;* the Greek name derives from *Neokhorion,* "New Village") was a Greek neighborhood on the western shore of the Bosporus, where Cavafy's maternal grandfather had a country house in which the poet and his family lived during their flight from Alexandria. Cavafy left a note describing this poem as "autobiographical."

Song of the Heart   *pg. 253*

A note to the poem indicates that it was written on the morning of February 12, 1886.

To Stephanos Skilitsis

STEPHANOS SKILITSIS (or "Stephen Schilizzi") was one of Cavafy's two closest friends from the days when he, his widowed mother, and his two immediately older brothers, John and Paul, returned to Alexandria from England in the autumn of 1877. The building in which they lived on Rue Mahmoud Pacha el Falaki boasted a garden, and it was here that Cavafy first met both Skilitsis and his other close friend from those days, Michael Ralli. That the youths were very close is evident from the number of letters (in English) that survive from them to him in the Cavafy Archive; although none of the poet's letters to his friends survive, those from his friends shed light on his adolescent days. Not least among these is a letter from Skilitsis to Cavafy during the latter's stay in Constantinople from 1882 to 1885, which suggests that the adolescent Cavafy was reticent about his private life even with his two closest friends:

> You write me nothing about your private life. How can you
> be so secret? Don't you put confidence in us, or what the
> devil? Not a word is to be taken from you in any way.

In response to a letter in which Cavafy had mentioned (perhaps as a sop to his friends, or perhaps as a conveniently misleading reference to his first homosexual experiences, with his cousin George Psilliary, in 1883) his "bonnes fortunes" in the "demi-monde," Skilitsis displayed an amused curiosity:

> . . . my dear, this phrase "vaut un aveu". I hazard myself on
> this subject at the risk of displeasing you. But I am not to
> blame, the temptation is so much greater as such mentions
> are rare on your part.

Skilitsis died on April 8, 1886, at the age of nineteen; Cavafy saved a copy of the death notice that appeared in the Alexandrian paper *Telegraphos.* Ralli died in October 1889 of typhoid; Cavafy kept a short journal of his friend's illness.

Correspondences According to Baudelaire *pg. 255*

As noted in the Introduction, the last decade of the 1890s marked a period of intense interest on Cavafy's part in the "Esoteric" movement in European letters. Much influenced by his reading of Schuré's *Les grands initiés,* and of writers such as Viatte, Mercier, and Michaud, as well as Mallarmé, Pater, Swinburne, Maeterlinck, Arthur Symons, and many others, Cavafy was particularly attracted to the notion of the poet as a kind of seer whose special insight gave him access to visions of the hidden beauties of the cosmos—beauties appreciated, moreover, by the kind of synesthesis to which this poem refers, and which is present as well in Baudelaire's poem, which Cavafy's both paraphrases and cites verbatim. Although Cavafy was eventually to shrug off the stylistic influence of the writers he so fervently read in his late twenties and early thirties, his interest in special sight and insight, and particularly in figures (whether poets or bona fide mystics, such as Apollonius of Tyana, on whom see pp. 357–60), persisted throughout his creative career.

Since the extent to which the present poem borrows from its French model may only be gauged by direct comparison, I quote the Baudelaire in its entirety:

CORRESPONDANCES

La nature est un temple où de vivants pilliers
Laissent parfois sortir de confuses paroles;
L'homme y passe à travers des forêts de symboles
Qui l'observent avec des regards familiers.

Comme de longs échos qui de loin se confondent
Dans une ténébreuse et profonde unité,
Vaste comme la nuit et comme la clarté,
Les parfums, les couleurs et les sons se répondent.

Il est des parfums frais comme des chairs d'enfants,
Doux comme les hautbois, verts comme les prairies,
—Et d'autres corrompus, riches et triomphants,

Ayant l'expansion des choses infinies,
Comme l'ambre, le musc, le benjoin et l'encens
Qui chantent les transports de l'esprit et des sens.

CORRESPONDENCES

The pillars of Nature's temple are alive
and sometimes yield perplexing messages;
forest of symbols between us and the shrine
remark our passage with accustomed eyes.

Like long-held echoes, blending somewhere else
into one deep and shadowy unison
as limitless as darkness and as day,
the sounds, the scents, the colors correspond.

There are odors succulent as young flesh,
sweet as flutes, and green as any grass,
while others—rich, corrupt and masterful—

possess the power of such infinite things
as incense, amber, benjamin and musk,
to praise the senses' raptures and the mind's.

On September 22, 1907, Cavafy wrote the following note:

> Tonight I was reading about Baudelaire. And the author of
> the book I was reading was as if *épaté* [astounded] by the
> "Fleurs du Mal." It's time I reread the "Fleurs du Mal." From
> what I recall, they're not that *épatants*. And it seems to me
> that Baudelaire was enclosed within a very tight circle of
> pleasure. Yesterday night suddenly; or this past Thursday; and
> on many other occasions I've lived, and done, and imagined,
> and silently arranged stranger enjoyments.

[Fragment of an untitled poem] *pg. 257*

This rather exotic fragment provides an early glimpse of Cavafy the "poet-historian" at work, as he attempts to integrate a fictional narrative into a complex historical setting—a setting that, moreover, is characterized by a clash of ancient cultures, another theme that would dominate his mature work. The poem imagines the fate of an Ancient Egyptian girl, RHAMANAKTI, who had been murdered. The second stanza makes it clear that the poem is set in a rather late phase in the history of Ancient Egypt: either the Achaemenid Period (525–402 B.C., and then again from 343 to 332), when Egypt was ruled by Persian monarchs, or the period of Greek domination, which lasted from Alexander's conquest of Egypt in 332 until the death of Cleopatra, the last of the Ptolemies, in 30 B.C.

"Nous N'osons Plus Chanter les Roses" *pg. 258*

The title of the poem is a quotation of lines from "Printemps Oublié" ("Forgotten Spring") by René-François-Armand Sully Prudhomme (1839–1907), the French poet and essayist who was the first winner of the Nobel Prize in literature, in 1901. The poem, which appears in Sully Prudhomme's first published volume, *Stances et Poèmes* (1865), is preoccupied with the dangers of writing poetry on hackneyed themes:

> *Ce beau printemps qui vient de naître*
> *A peine goûté va finir;*
> *Nul de nous n'en fera connaître*
> *La grace aux peoples à venir.*
>
> *Nous n'osons plus parler des roses;*
> *Quand nous les chantons, on en rit;*
> *Car des plus adorable choses*
> *Le culte est si vieux qu'il périt.*

This lovely springtime, newly born,
Barely tasted, soon will end;

None of us can make its charm
Known to future generations of men.

We dare no more to speak of roses;
When we sing them, people laugh;
Since the worship of all the loveliest
Things is so old that it's already passed . . .

Sully Prudhomme was associated with the Parnassian movement, which exerted such a strong influence on the young Cavafy. An 1868 entry from Sully Prudhomme's *Journal Intime* nicely sums up the Parnassian's aesthetic ideology: "Compression seems to me more elevated, more worthy than expansiveness. To repress the heart's élan is to better count its beats, and a considered suffering is more noble than a suffering about which one cries aloud." The Parnassians' emphasis on formal polish led them, ultimately, back to the Ancient Greeks, always admired as the masters of form; a backward-looking antiquarianism, moreover, simultaneously served the Parnassians' ideological belief in separating poetry from vulgar utilitarian, political, or social concerns.

The extent to which Cavafy was preoccupied with Parnassian concerns for poetry's formal elements is clear from an article he published in October 1891, six months before composing "Nous n'osons plus chanter les roses." In a review of a work by P. Gritsanis called *Stichourgiki* ("Versification"), he argued that

Versification is the grammar of poetry, which every poet must learn well. Fantasy, the sublime, great ideas, in a word divine inspiration are the gifts that flow directly from nature, who alone knows their magic and hides it, having no intention for them to compete with her.

Parnassianism ultimately served as an important stage in the evolution (some would say devolution) of nineteenth-century poetry toward Symbolism and Decadence, movements that also held great interest for Cavafy.

Indian Image pg. 259

This is the first of the group of three poems treating ancient myths of Creation that Cavafy listed under the heading "Three Images": see the notes on "Pelasgian Image," pp. 494–5, and "Chaldean Image," pp. 509–10.

A certain fascination with Indian culture and history reveals itself in this poem and in a few others written in the early 1890s: "Eternity," which lifts an episode from the Bhagavad Gita; "A Samian's Epitaph," in which the poet imagines the life of a Greek who ends his life as a slave on the banks of the Ganges; and "Coins," in which Indian history (rather than that of Asia Minor, as is more typical in the poet's work) becomes the vehicle for a poetic reverie about the clash of Western and Eastern culture.

Although Cavafy's interest in India at this time surely owes something to his reading of Schuré's *Les grands initiés,* with its lengthy chapter on Krishna (for which see the note to "Eternity," pp. 507–8), it is worth remembering that India—at least, mythic India—was of considerable interest for the Parnassian poets. Ever since the publication of Victor Hugo's *Orientales* (1829), India and the East more generally, thought to be appealingly "exotic," had exerted considerable allure for a generation of French poets eager to break with a stale Romanticism (Sainte-Beuve waxed lyrical about the "*éclat éblouissant*" of Hugo's Orientalist verses); among the foremost of these indophile writers was Leconte de Lisle, Hugo's successor at the Académie Française and a leader of the Parnassians. The French poet's desire to anchor a poetics in the past ("*temps où l'homme et la terre étaient jeunes et dans l'éclosion de leur force et de leur beauté,*" "a time when man and earth were young and in the full flower of their power and beauty"), and even more his specific interest in seeing connections between the Hindu epics and Homer and the Greek tragedians, must have had an especially strong appeal for the young Cavafy.

The poem's particular interest in precious stones (shared by the other "Image" poems in the same group) is also noteworthy, recalling as it does a similar preoccupation on the part of the Parnassian and Decadent poets of the mid- to late-nineteenth century; the embrace of "Art for Art's sake," with an emphasis on emotional restraint and technical perfection, often found expression in elaborate praise of precious *objets d'art* and jewelry. This particular Parnassian motif occurs, in addition to the other two "Image" poems, in "Artificial Flowers" (originally composed 1894–96) and "In the House of the Soul" (1894); moreover, a chronological list of the poet's output makes reference to an 1891 composition called "Precious Stones," which does not survive. The interest in precious stones was to continue throughout his career: we find it in the descriptions of Nero's bed in "The Steps," for instance (1908–09), and of the amethyst and pearls adorning the costume of the half-Egyptian, half-Roman prince Caesarion in "Alexandrian Kings" (1912), and in the poignant detail of the Byzantine monarch so impoverished that he was reduced to using coronation regalia made of the eponymous materials in the 1925 poem "Of Colored Glass."

Not all of the poet's interest in this subject can be ascribed to the influence of the Parnassians, however. In his *Genealogy,* Cavafy noted that he was descended on his mother's side from prominent jewel merchants; in January 1886, at the age of twenty-two, partly in response to what he felt were insufficiently erudite press reports about an exhibition about coral that had taken place in London three years earlier, he published an article on the mythological significance of coral, the precious substance that more than any other appears in his work.

Pelasgian Image   *pg. 260*

The poet grouped this poem, along with "Indian Image" and "Chaldean Image," under the heading "Three Images." Each part of this triptych of poetic evocations of arcane myths of creation is dedicated to a different realm of ancient culture: India, Greece, and Babylonia.

PELASGIAN was the term used by Ancient Greek authors from Homer to Herodotus and by the later historians to refer to the indigenous ancient people who inhabited Greece prior to the arrival of the tribes who would become the Hellenic peoples; in Classical Greek thought, the Pelasgians were associated with a primitive or "barbaric" phase of culture, and the Pelasgian language in particular was thought to be barbarous.

The title's reference to a primitive stage of culture is mirrored in its

concern with a primitive phase of mythological history. The GIANTS
were a race of enormous creatures sprung from Earth (Gaia), fertilized
by the fluids released by the castration of Uranus (Sky). The poem
seems to refer to the most famous of the Giants, Enceladus, who during
the great battle between the Gods and the Giants was struck down by
Athena and buried in Sicily under Mount Etna (whose eruptions were
thought to be caused by the giant's movements). EPHIALTES, according
to Homer and other authors, was another giant and a classical type of
outrageous hubris: together with his twin brother, Otus, he attempted
to reach heaven by piling Mounts Pelion and Ossa on top of Mount
Olympus. They were also said to have attempted to rape Hera and
Artemis, and imprisoned the war god, Ares, in a brazen vessel. Still (as
Cavafy was undoubtedly aware), for all their outrageousness, the twins
were also associated in myth with the Muses.

The Hereafter

pg. 262

This poem was written in August 1892, the month in which Cavafy pub-
lished "Bard": for the theme of the poet's rejection of the material
world, see the note on that poem, pp. 473–4. The notion of one corpo-
real eye closing in death, even as the eye of the soul is opened to behold
a greater vision, recurs frequently in Schuré's Les grands initiés; for the
influence of this work on Cavafy, see the notes on "Correspondences
According to Baudelaire," pp. 489–90, and "Eternity," pp. 507–8.

The Mimiambs of Herodas

pg. 263

HERODAS (the name also appears as "Herondas") was a Hellenistic poet
active around the middle of the third century B.C. He was known for
his MIMIAMBS ("mime-iambs"), a genre that cast the southern Italian
genre called mime (dramatic dialogues) in a meter known as "limping
iambs" (an iambic line with two long syllables in the last foot which give
the line a "limping" feel). These mimiambs, in which the poet richly
evokes, through coarse language, humor, and spicy proverbs, the every-
day life of ordinary city- and townspeople, were known only through
fragmentary quotations until 1891, when the text of a papyrus in the

British Museum, containing seven complete poems and part of an eighth, was published to great excitement throughout the scholarly world.

Cavafy's poem makes reference to four of the seven complete texts by Herodas (which Cavafy is likely to have been aware of from scholarly publications). In Mimiamb 1, a married woman called METRICHE is approached by a elderly bawd on behalf of a besotted young man; she refuses the old woman's offer but kindly offers her a glass of wine. Mimiamb 2 (whose humor derives from its sly parody of legal rhetoric) is a monologue delivered by a brothel-owner, who rather shamelessly takes a merchant to court for having stolen one of his girls; lacking any hard evidence, he relies on an inflated courtroom style. In Mimiamb 4, set on the eastern Aegean island of Kos (for which reason Herodas is thought by some scholars to be a native of that island), two women visiting the temple of the god of healing, ASCLEPIUS, admire the various works of art on view—a vignette that is, among other things, a sly allusion to a similar scene in Euripides' *Ion*. The humor of Cavafy's seventh stanza, based on Mimiamb 7, about METRÔ's visit to a shoe or leather merchant, derives from the fact that when we first meet Metrô, in the sixth mimiamb, she is asking a friend where she got her dildo; it's to acquire one of her own that she goes to the shop of the shoemaker, whose footwear business is merely a cover for a more risqué line of products.

In the same year that this poem was written Cavafy published a review of a volume of poetry in which he commented on the way in which philological and archaeological discoveries could become inspiration for poetry:

> The sage archaeologists of the Museum of Giza are, without knowing it, benefactors of poetry—above all in an era when "there's nothing new under the sun" presses and oppresses us. Exhuming the bodies and treasures of the Rameses and the Thutmoses, plumbing and taking possession of the language and the history of that dead proud people, they bring to light not a few poetic subjects.

Azure Eyes *pg. 265*

CIRCASSIA was a region in the northern Caucasus whose people were famed for their beauty. The loveliness of the women, in particular, which gave them prized status in Ottoman harems, became a conventional literary theme from the Levant to Western Europe. In his *On Inoculation,* Voltaire observed that

> [t]he Circassians are poor, and their daughters are beautiful, and indeed it is in them that they chiefly trade. They furnish with those beauties the seraglios of the Turkish Sultan, of the Persian Sophy, and of all of those who are wealthy enough to purchase and maintain such precious merchandise. These maidens are very honorably and virtuously instructed how to fondle and caress men; are taught dances of a very polite and effeminate kind; and how to heighten by the most voluptuous artifices the pleasures of their disdainful masters for whom they are designed.

Similarly, Lord Byron's *Don Juan* (4.114) contains a conventional tribute to Circassian beauty:

> . . . fifteen hundred dollars
> For one Circassian, a sweet girl, were given,
> Warranted virgin. Beauty's brightest colours
> Had decked her out in all the hues of heaven.
> Her sale sent home some disappointed bawlers,
> Who bade on till the hundreds reached the eleven,
> But when the offer went beyond, they knew
> 'Twas for the Sultan and at once withdrew.

Alexandrian Merchant *pg. 267*

In ancient times, the Aegean island of Samos, with its mountainous terrain and ideal climate for grape growing, was a leading producer of prized wines, which were usually known simply by the adjectival form "SAMIAN."

The Lagid's Hospitality pg. 268

PTOLEMY IV PHILOPATOR (244–205 B.C.; reigned 221–205) was the great-grandson of the first Ptolemy, and is generally held to have presided over the beginning of the decline of the Lagid dynasty. Devoted to the orgiastic worship of Dionysus (he had an ivy leaf tattooed on his body) and exclusively bent on his literary and rather complicated erotic and romantic pursuits—one of his mistresses was the sister of one of his male lovers—he reigned at first under the influence of an ambitious adviser called Sosibius (see "Great Feast at the House of Sosibius"), who was able to bend the young king, indifferent to affairs of state, to his own purposes. The reign began with the murder of Ptolemy's mother, an uncle, and his popular younger brother, who was scalded to death in his bath on Sosibius's orders. (Another figure who met his death as the result of Sosibius's machinations was the Spartan king Cleomenes III, who had come to Egypt to rescue his captive family during the reign of Ptolemy's father, a subject treated in "In Sparta" and "Come Now, King of the Lacedaemonians.")

Of particular interest for the present poem were Ptolemy's literary pretensions (he wrote a play called *Adonis,* for which his lover Agathocles obligingly wrote a commentary) and especially a notorious anecdote about his treatment of a visiting SOPHIST, the Stoic Sphaerus. Knowing that a precept of Stoicism was that the wise man would never yield to a false appearance, Ptolemy presented the visiting sage with a table filled with ingeniously contrived wax fruits; when the poor philosopher found himself with a mouthful of wax, the king asked him whether this was not a case in which a wise man had yielded to false appearances. Cavafy surely knew this story, which renders the hopefulness of his fictitious sophist, in this poem, rather poignant.

A *mna* was a unit of currency equal to 100 drachmas. Most classicists estimate that, in Classical times in Athens, one drachma was equal to the daily wage of a skilled worker; a *mna,* then, would have been worth about four months' wages. The tetradrachma (a single coin worth four drachmas) was, for the most part, the coin with the widest currency in Classical times, although Ptolemaic Egypt—the setting of this poem—produced gold and silver coins in denominations as high as fifteen drachmas. Cavafy's interest in ancient numismatics is evident in such poems as "Coins," "Orophernes," "Philhellene," and the fragmentary "Bondsman and Slave" (see *The Unfinished Poems,* p. 112).

In the Cemetery   pg. 269

The year 1893 produced two poems that show Cavafy's marked interest in Christian forgiveness: this poem and the Repudiated Poem "Voice from the Sea." In a note from 1909—which is to say, after the Philosophical Scrutiny—the poet referred to this poem as one of his "good poems in katharevousa," along with "Walls" and "Ode and Elegy of the Streets."

Priam's March by Night   pg. 270

In Book 24 of the *Iliad,* the Trojan king, PRIAM, makes a secret nocturnal journey to the Greek camp in order to beg Achilles for the body of his son, Hector, whom Achilles has killed in single combat. For Cavafy's interest in Homeric themes, and his other treatments of scenes from the story of the Trojan War, see the note on "Trojans," pp. 378–9.

Epitaph   pg. 272

This is the earliest instance of a poem in the form of a funerary inscription, a device that Cavafy would return to in a number of poems of the mid-1910s: see, for instance, "Tomb of Lanes" (*1916;* 1917), "Tomb of Iases" (*1917;* 1917), "Tomb of Ignatius" (*1916;* 1917), and "In the Month of Hathor" (*1917;* 1917). The dates of these poems, all of them about young men who died in their twenties, suggest that the carnage of the First World War was at least part of Cavafy's inspiration.

In 1925 Cavafy took up "Epitaph" once again and attempted to fashion a new work from it. In the rewritten version, which was never brought to a form that satisfied the poet, the original sonnet is "framed" by additional material which presents it as the work of a Hellenistic poet writing in the time of Antiochus IV Epiphanes. (See the note on "Epitaph of a Samian," in *The Unfinished Poems,* p. 24).

Displeased Theatregoer
pg. 273

The setting would appear to be the first part of the second century B.C., at a performance of one of the comedies of the Roman playwright TERENCE (Publius Terentius Afer, ?–ca. 158 B.C.). Born in Africa, most likely at the beginning of the century, and brought to Rome as a slave in the service of a senator, Terentius Lucanus, Terence was given a superior education and later freed by his master, who seems to have been impressed by his abilities. His first theatrical success took place in 166 B.C. From his work come two of the most famous lines in Western drama: "While there is life, there is hope," and "Nothing human is alien to me." He is said to have died either during, or returning from, a trip to Greece.

Of the two great Roman playwrights (the other being Plautus, his slightly older contemporary), Terence was considered to be the more refined. Even so, his work unabashedly owed much to the style, and indeed the content, of the Greek comic playwright MENANDER (ca. 342–291), whose work Terence had translated into Latin. Menander was the great master of the New Comedy, the situational comedy that flourished in the fourth century B.C.; some of Terence's comedies are essentially little more than pastiches of Menander's works—a fact to which the fictitious speaker in this poem clearly has strong objections. The cultural snobberies of the speaker, who appears to be a Greek visitor to Italy, are made clear by his condescending reference to ATELLAN FARCE, the native Italian comic theater that treated the lives of lower-class people and that, like New Comedy, featured certain stock figures (forerunners of those found in the Commedia dell'Arte).

Before Jerusalem
pg. 274

This poem appears in two versions: the first in katharevousa, and the second in a more demotic form.

Cavafy had a particular interest in the First Crusade (1096–1099), perhaps because, like so much of the history that fired his imagination, it was a perfect vehicle for subtle thinking about the clash between Western and Eastern cultures—and indeed, not only between Christian

Europe and Muslim Asia, but between the Catholics of Western Europe and the Orthodox Christians of Byzantium. According to one standard account of the origins of the first Crusade, the grand enterprise was set in motion when the Byzantine emperor Alexius I Comnenus sent desperate letters to the West appealing for aid against the Turks; considerable public interest in an eastward expedition was said to have been provoked by the circulation of what Gibbon refers to as the Byzantine emperor's "plaintive epistles." Gibbon's phrase, however, drew the ire of Cavafy, who like Paparrigopoulos doubted the authenticity of the letters, and who in a marginal note in his text of the *Decline and Fall* testily observed that the epistles had long been considered spurious. Cavafy's resistance to Gibbon's description here no doubt had something to do with his comprehension that the Byzantine Greeks generally had more to fear from the European Christians than from the Muslim Turks: in his text of Gibbon, he marked the phrase, "the Greek and Oriental Christians, whom experience had taught to prefer the Mahometan before the Latin yoke."

"Before Jerusalem" indeed demonstrates no little irony with respect to the motivations and the behavior of the European Crusaders. In June 1099—the moment in which the poem is set—the Frankish Crusaders, under Raymond IV of St. Gilles, reached Jerusalem and began their siege of the city; after just over a month, on July 15, they entered the city at last and undertook the wholesale slaughter of the entire Muslim and Jewish populations, a literal bloodbath ("the slaughter was so great that our men waded in blood up to their ankles," one contemporary historian recalled) that was the subject of a particularly indignant comment by Paparrigopoulos (4.12):

> In such fashion did they think they were serving the Divine, those champions of the Saviour and servants of his evangelical commands.

Second Odyssey   *pg. 275*

That Cavafy was preoccupied with the figure of Homer's Odysseus in the early part of 1894 is clear not only from this poem, which owes much to the rather revisionist vision of the restless hero found in Tennyson's *Ulysses* (1842), but also from an essay that he wrote in April of that year called "The End of Odysseus." That essay contains translations of passages from the Tennyson and also from the twenty-sixth canto of Dante's *Inferno*, the canto in which Dante and Vergil encounter Ulysses and Diomede. As these selections (which I reproduce below) suggest, what caught Cavafy's imagination was the theme of perpetual longing: the unceasing yearning for new adventure that, in these two poetic adaptations, cause Ulysses to disdain home, Penelope, and Telemachus—all that the Homeric Odysseus so ardently seeks—and instead to long eternally for new voyages.

DANTE, *Inferno,* CANTO 26:

"O ye, who are twofold within one fire,
If I deserved of you, while I was living,
If I deserved of you or much or little

When in the world I wrote the lofty verses,
Do not move on, but one of you declare
Whither, being lost, he went away to die."

[. . . . .]

Then of the antique flame the greater horn,
Murmuring, began to wave itself about
Even as a flame doth which the wind fatigues.

Thereafterward, the summit to and fro
Moving as if it were the tongue that spake,
It uttered forth a voice, and said: "When I

From Circe had departed, who concealed me
More than a year there near unto Gaeta,
Or ever yet Aeneas named it so,

Nor fondness for my son, nor reverence
For my old father, nor the due affection
Which joyous should have made Penelope,

Could overcome within me the desire
I had to be experienced of the world,
And of the vice and virtue of mankind;

But I put forth on the high open sea
With one sole ship, and that small company
By which I never had deserted been.

Both of the shores I saw as far as Spain,
Far as Morocco, and the isle of Sardes,
And the others which that sea bathes round about.

I and my company were old and slow
When at that narrow passage we arrived
Where Hercules his landmarks set as signals,

That man no farther onward should adventure.
On the right hand behind me left I Seville,
And on the other already had left Ceuta.

'O brothers, who amid a hundred thousand
Perils,' I said, 'have come unto the West,
To this so inconsiderable vigil

Which is remaining of your senses still
Be ye unwilling to deny the knowledge,
Following the sun, of the unpeopled world.

Consider ye the seed from which ye sprang;
Ye were not made to live like unto brutes,
But for pursuit of virtue and of knowledge.'

So eager did I render my companions,
With this brief exhortation, for the voyage,
That then I hardly could have held them back.

[. . . . .]

When there appeared to us a mountain, dim
From distance, and it seemed to me so high
As I had never any one beheld.

Joyful were we, and soon it turned to weeping;
For out of the new land a whirlwind rose,
And smote upon the fore part of the ship.

Three times it made her whirl with all the waters,
At the fourth time it made the stern uplift,
And the prow downward go, as pleased Another,

Until the sea above us closed again."

Alfred Lord Tennyson, *Ulysses:*

Myself not least, but honour'd of them all;
[. . . . .]
This is my son, mine own Telemachus,
To whom I leave the sceptre and the isle,—
Well-loved of me, discerning to fulfill
This labour, by slow prudence to make mild
A rugged people, and thro' soft degrees
Subdue them to the useful and the good.
Most blameless is he, centred in the sphere
Of common duties, decent not to fail
In offices of tenderness, and pay
Meet adoration to my household gods,
When I am gone. He works his work, I mine.
[. . . . .]

It may be we shall touch the Happy Isles,
And see the great Achilles, whom we knew.

The Pawn
pg. 278

An early version of this poem had the following variant for line 24, which suggests at one point that the poet had considered giving the poem an erotic flavor:

for the queen, whom he loved

the same version contained the following additional lines:

This is how the lofty effort ends
This is how the lofty effort is fulfilled
This is how much the lofty effort cost

Dread
pg. 280

Like "In the Cemetery" (1893) and "Voice from the Sea" (1893), this poem suggests the extent to which the idea of Christian forgiveness, and particularly of divine protection from unnamed but overwhelming temptations, appealed to the poet as he entered his thirties. Haas has drawn attention to the way in which the language of this poem, particularly in the opening lines, echoes that of the bedtime prayer said by Orthodox Christians, which entreats the Virgin for protection from "the darksome sleep of sin and from every lurid and nocturnal lasciviousness."

In the House of the Soul
pg. 281

This poem and "La Jeunesse Blanche" ("White Youth") were clearly inspired by Cavafy's reading of the Belgian Symbolist poet and novelist Georges Rodenbach (1855–1898), whose work influenced other poems as well. (See the note on "Rain," p. 506.) Trained as a lawyer and a journalist, Rodenbach eventually moved to Paris, where he was a friend of the Goncourt brothers. He started publishing his poetry in 1877, but it was his fourth collection of poems, "La Jeunesse Blanche" (1886), that won him broad renown outside of Belgium. His appeal for Cavafy undoubtedly lay in the rejection of positivism and "progress," shared by Baudelaire, that is evident in the nostalgic evocation of a mystical union between the soul of the writer and the "soul" of his native city, present in both his poems and his novel *Bruges-la-Morte*. (To a fellow Belgian author he wrote: "As for producing literature in Belgium, in my view it is impossible. Our nation is above all positivistic and material. It won't hear a word of poetry.") Rodenbach's poetry and prose are characterized by an obsession with solitude, loss, exhaustion, and hopeless yearning, which the writer saw as the core of all high art: "The essence of art that is at all noble is the DREAM, and this dream dwells only upon what is distant, absent, vanished, unattainable."

Rain   *pg. 282*

Cavafy's immersion in the works of Rodenbach during the mid-1890s may well have inspired the composition of this atmospheric exercise in moody scene setting: the Belgian author often evoked the mists, canals, and rains of Bruges, particularly in his novel *Bruges-la-Morte,* whose protagonist, a middle-aged widower, finds his feelings for his dead wife reflected in the constant rains (and in virtually everything else about the haunted, rather dead old city). But rain figures prominently in the poetry as well. (*"C'est l'automne, la pluie et la mort de l'année,"* "It's autumn, rain and the death of the year!")

La Jeunesse Blanche   *pg. 284*

See the note on "In the House of the Soul," pp. 505–6.

Distinguishing Marks   *pg. 285*

The epigraph comes from the *Logoi* ("Speeches") of the fourth-century A.D. sophist and rhetorician HIMERIUS (ca. 315–386), a pagan master of the Greek style whose students included two great figures of the early Christian church, Gregory of Nazianzus (a favorite source of Cavafy's historical poems) and Bishop Basil the Great; among his other attainments, he acted as private secretary to the apostate emperor Julian. His career reveals much about the cosmopolitan culture of the Greek-speaking world in the years immediately following the division of the Roman Empire. Born in Prusa, in Bithynia (in the northwest of Asia Minor), he eventually settled at Athens, where his school became world renowned; in recognition of his contributions to Greek literature he was granted Athenian citizenship. Unlike his one-time employer Julian, however, Himerius showed no hostility toward Christianity, and thereby embodied the cosmopolitan breadth of culture and tolerance of the greater Greek world in Late Antiquity—one possible reason that Cavafy, implacably disdainful of the apostate, approvingly and apparently ingenuously quotes Himerius's encomium to Athens.

Eternity   pg. 286

The poem is based, ultimately, on a passage from the Bhagavad Gita. In this text, revered as sacred in the Hindu tradition, the divine narrator Krishna (an avatar of Vishnu, the supreme deity) converses with the warrior-hero, the Pandava prince Arjuna, immediately prior to a great battle; during the conversation, the divinity tries to soothe the young warrior, who has grown anxious prior to his trial, with accounts of various philosophical and spiritual doctrines.

Cavafy was almost certainly not familiar with the Bhagavad Gita itself, but rather with an account of the poem given in Schuré's *Les grands initiés*. The passage that seems to have inspired Cavafy is the following, from chapter 7 of Schuré's book, which is devoted to Krishna:

> Learned men grieve neither for the living nor the dead. You and I and these captains of men have always existed and will never cease to exist in the future. . . . No man can destroy the Inexhaustible. All these bodies will not endure, as you know. But seers know, too, that the incarnate soul is eternal,

indestructible, and infinite. And so: go you into battle, scion of Bharat!

Confusion

pg. 287

Diana Haas observes that the motif of the soul (the "keyword" of the 1890s), wasting away in an isolated confinement, runs through the 1889 collection *Serres chaudes* ("Hothouses") of another of the Belgian Symbolists to whom Cavafy was drawn during the 1890s, Maurice Maeterlinck, whose *Trésor des Humbles* was in Cavafy's library.

Salome

pg. 288

The date of this poem is significant. A note accompanying the manuscript indicates that the poet took his inspiration, with a typically scrupulous attention to details of the original, directly from "an antique Nubian Bible"; he goes on to cite the passage in question:

> Now Salome offered the head of the Baptist on a golden platter to the young Greek scholar who disdained love. But he said: "It is your head, Salome, that I would like." He spoke thus in jest, and the next day a slave brought to him the blond head of the Lover. The Scholar no longer remembered his Vow of the day before: he ordered the bloody thing to be taken away, and continued his reading of Plato.

The note ends with a reference to a newspaper article, dated February 11, 1896, about a performance of Wilde's *Salome*, a work bound to be of interest to Cavafy not least because of his evident interest in the Decadents and Symbolists. What is of interest here is that the poet wasn't, in fact, influenced by Wilde's version, but rather seems to be responding to it. If anything, Cavafy disdained Wilde's play, whose historical inaccuracies he ridiculed as an example of the errors to which "poetic license" with history was likely to lead.

Chaldean Image *pg. 289*

This is the third of the three elaborate mythological poems that the poet grouped under the heading "Three Images": see the notes on "Indian Image" and "Pelasgian Image," pp. 493–4 and 494–5.

CHALDEAN is often a synonym for "Babylonian," but in this context is a more specialized reference to the mythologies and cosmologies of the ancient Assyrian, Akkadian, Babylonian, and Sumerian civilizations of Mesopotamia. Chaldean wizards, oracles, and astronomers figure prominently in the history and mythology of the Ancient Near East. According to the Enuma Elish (the name given to the text of the great Babylonian Creation story), APSU and TIAMAT were the two primeval gods, Apsu the divinity of fresh waters, and Tiamat, his sister and wife, the divinity of salt waters. In the Enuma Elish, all of the gods were born of the union between Apsu and Tiamat (among them EA, the god of wisdom):

> When in the height heaven was not named,
> And the earth beneath did not yet bear a name,
> And the primeval Apsu, who begat them,
> And chaos, Tiamut, the mother of them both
> Their waters were mingled together,
> And no field was formed, no marsh was to be seen;
> When of the gods none had been called into being,
> And none bore a name, and no destinies were ordained;
> Then were created the gods in the midst of heaven,
> Lahmu and Lahamu were called into being . . .

Apsu, along with the vizier MUMMU, plans to destroy these other gods, but Tiamat foils his plan by enlisting the aid of Ea; they kill Apsu and banish Mummu. Ea becomes the greatest of the gods, and eventually fathers Marduk, who ultimately becomes the supreme god. Tiamat finally rebels against Marduk, and creates a race of monsters to do battle with him:

> They banded themselves together and at the side of Tiamat they
>   advanced;
> They were furious; they devised mischief without resting night
>   and day.

They prepared for battle, fuming and raging;
They joined their forces and made war,
Ummu-Hubur [Tiamat] who formed all things,
Made in addition weapons invincible; she spawned monster-serpents,
Sharp of tooth, and merciless of fang;
With poison, instead of blood, she filled their bodies.
Fierce monster-vipers she clothed with terror,
With splendor she decked them, she made them of lofty stature.
Whoever beheld them, terror overcame him,
Their bodies reared up and none could withstand their attack.
She set up vipers and dragons, and the monster Lahamu,
And hurricanes, and raging hounds, and scorpion-men,
And mighty tempests, and fish-men, and rams;
They bore cruel weapons, without fear of the fight.
Her commands were mighty, none could resist them;
After this fashion, huge of stature, she made eleven [kinds of]
    monsters . . .
  (tr. Leonard William King, 1902)

These excerpts suggest the degree to which Cavafy sought to re-create the rhythms and the rather stilted feel of the original. The text of the Enuma Elish was discovered in 1849 and published in 1876.

Julian at the Mysteries pg. 290

The inspiration for this poem is an episode from the youth of Julian the Apostate. At the age of twenty, Julian was initiated into the Eleusinian Mysteries, the secret ancient rites associated with the goddesses Demeter and Persephone which were supposed to have held out to true believers a promise of eternal life. Because of the strict secrecy enjoined on initiates, little is known about what actually happened during the ceremonies themselves, although (as will be seen from the following passage from Gibbon, who is the source of Cavafy's information for the episode on which this poem is based) flashing lights of some kind seem to have been involved. According to Gibbon, who derives the story from Gregory of Nazianzus, these lights (and whatever special effects might have accompanied them) so terrified the young Julian during the ceremonies that he reflexively made the sign of the cross when he saw them:

> He obtained the privilege of a solemn initiation into the mysteries of Eleusis, which, amidst the general decay of the Grecian worship, still retained some vestiges of their primaeval sanctity; and such was the zeal of Julian, that he afterwards invited the Eleusinian pontiff to the court of Gaul, for the sole purpose of consummating, by mystic rites and sacrifices, the great work of his sanctification. As these ceremonies were performed in the depth of caverns, and in the silence of the night, and as the inviolable secret of the mysteries was preserved by the discretion of the initiated, I shall not presume to describe the horrid sounds, and fiery apparitions, which were presented to the senses, or the imagination, of the credulous aspirant, till the visions of comfort and knowledge broke upon him in a blaze of celestial light.

It is at this point that Gibbon inserts the note that is the kernel of Cavafy's poem:

> When Julian, in a momentary panic, made the sign of the cross the daemons instantly disappeared (Greg. Naz. Orat. iii. p. 71), Gregory supposes that they were frightened, but the priests declared that they were indignant. The reader, according to the measure of his faith, will determine this profound question.

What interests Cavafy, here as elsewhere in his Julian cycle (particularly in the Unfinished Poem "The Rescue of Julian"), is less the correct interpretation of the demons' flight than the suggestion of a deep hypocrisy on the part of Julian, who would go on to treat so contemptuously the Christians and their faith—one that, as this episode makes clear, was more deeply ingrained in him than he cared to acknowledge. One strongly feels, indeed, that the hint of a resistance to self-knowledge on Julian's part is what irritates Cavafy so greatly.

To appreciate the extent of the emperor's hypocrisy, as Cavafy saw it, it is worth reading Gibbon's further comments on the Christian upbringing Julian received "from his Christian preceptors," as the historian noted: "the education, not of a hero, but of a saint." Gibbon's account is colored, as so often, by an ingrained hostility to religious fervor; but its attempt to fashion a psychological explanation for Julian's apostasy is nonetheless fascinating:

> . . . Julian publicly read the Holy Scriptures in the church of Nicomedia. The study of religion, which they assiduously cultivated, appeared to produce the fairest fruits of faith and devotion. They [Julian and his elder brother, Gallus] prayed, they fasted, they distributed alms to the poor, gifts to the clergy, and oblations to the tombs of the martyrs; and the splendid monument of St. Mamas, at Caesarea, was erected, or at least was undertaken, by the joint labor of Gallus and Julian. They respectfully conversed with the bishops, who were eminent for superior sanctity, and solicited the benediction of the monks and hermits, who had introduced into Cappadocia the voluntary hardships of the ascetic life. As the two princes advanced towards the years of manhood, they discovered, in their religious sentiments, the difference of their characters. The dull and obstinate understanding of Gallus embraced, with implicit zeal, the doctrines of Christianity; which never influenced his conduct, or moderated his passions. The mild disposition of the younger brother was less repugnant to the precepts of the gospel; and his active curiosity might have been gratified by a theological system, which explains the mysterious essence of the Deity, and opens the boundless prospect of invisible and future worlds. But the independent spirit of Julian refused to yield the passive and unresisting obedience which was required, in the name of religion, by the haughty ministers of the church.

Gibbon goes on to describe the intensity of the adult Julian's devotion to the pagan gods, which as usual excites the Enlightenment historian's disdain; what is noteworthy in this description, and what may well be yet another reason for Cavafy's complicated lifelong fascination with this emperor, is the reference to the nocturnal apparitions of the pagan gods, with whom, according to Julian, he would regularly discourse:

> Notwithstanding the modest silence of Julian himself, we may learn from his faithful friend, the orator Libanius, that he lived in a perpetual intercourse with the gods and goddesses; that they descended upon earth to enjoy the conversation of their favorite hero; that they gently interrupted his slumbers by touching his hand or his hair; that they warned him of every impending danger, and conducted him, by their infallible wisdom, in every action of his life; and that he had acquired such an intimate knowledge of his heavenly guests, as readily to distinguish the voice of Jupiter from that of Minerva, and the form of Apollo from the figure of Hercules. These sleeping or waking visions, the ordinary effects of abstinence and fanaticism, would almost degrade the emperor to the level of an Egyptian monk. But the useless lives of Antony or Pachomius were consumed in these vain occupations. Julian could break from the dream of superstition to arm himself for battle; and after vanquishing in the field the enemies of Rome, he calmly retired into his tent, to dictate the wise and salutary laws of an empire, or to indulge his genius in the elegant pursuits of literature and philosophy.

The motif of nighttime visions was one that exerted a powerful allure for Cavafy throughout his life: see the note on "Since Nine—," pp. 399–400.

The Cat   *pg. 292*

Cavafy himself gave a date of "1897 or before" to this poem. On stylistic grounds (the use of strict katharevousa), Savidis placed the date of composition before 1894, and possibly even before 1891. He notes that the likely inspiration for this odd poem was the publication, in 1893, of Roidis's "History of a Cat," although there is a strong influence exerted by the symbolic cats of Baudelaire, who was so important to Cavafy during the years when his tastes were being formed. In his comment on this poem (in "Offering of Three New Poems to K. Th. Dimaras,"

1985), Savidis particularly noted the following passage from Baudelaire's *Fusées* (19), first published in 1887:

> *Pourquoi les démocrates n'aiment pas les chats, il est facile de le deviner. Le chat est beau; il révèle des idées de luxe, de propreté, de volupté, etc. . . . .*

> Why democrats don't like cats is easy to guess. The cat is beautiful; it displays ideas of luxury, of cleanliness, of pleasure, etc. . . . .

We might also note another text of Baudelaire's, "Chat" ("Cat"), from *Spleen et Idéal,* with its evocation of the "sleek and proud" cat, "so discreet / in making known his will," and its "uncanny voice / —seraphic, alien— . . .":

> Familiar spirit, genius, judge,
> the cat presides—inspires
> events that he seems to spurn
> half goblin and half god!

Cavafy (who owned a dearly loved cat from 1898 to 1908) attempted to rewrite this poem in 1901; and as late as 1917, in a fanciful description of what an earthly paradise might look like, wrote the following lines:

> Seven cats at the least—or two jet-black,
> and two as white as snow, for contrast's sake.

BUBASTIS was a city in the Nile delta named for the ancient Egyptian cat deity, Bastet.

Impossible Things   pg. 294

The poet to whom Cavafy here refers is Keats, on whose *Lamia* he had written an article in 1892 (see the note on "But Wise Men Apprehend

What Is Imminent," pp. 374–5). In the "Ode on a Grecian Urn," Keats writes that "Heard melodies are sweet, but those unheard / Are sweeter . . ."

Addition *pg. 295*

Cavafy classified this poem, along with "Walls," "The Windows," "Lohengrin," and "Suspicion," as being about "difficulty."

This is one of the poems that Cavafy's brother John translated, and the poet's reaction to his brother's rendering sheds light on his understanding of its meaning. The extant translation by John of the first two and a half lines of this poem reads as follows:

> Whether I am happy or unhappy, it is not my care
> to examine. But of this have I the joy to be aware
> that in their immense addition . . .

Evidently, John's original translation of the first line went something like

> Whether I am happy or unhappy I have not the smallest care

because Cavafy takes his brother to task for using the dismissive phrase "smallest care":

> On all accounts the "*smallest* care" must come out. It's a thing I didn't say in my poem, a thing I had no intention of saying and that I don't believe I shall ever write. It's a dangerous "statement" . . . and is opposed to the spirit of previous poems already translated ("The Walls," "The Windows," "Lohengrin," "The Suspicion," which are a complaint against unhappiness), and it will perhaps be opposed to the spirit of other poems that will be translated. Finally, it's a *profession* which I in no way want to make.
>
> What I wrote is that "I don't calculate" whether I'm happy or unhappy. That is, for the moment, the moment of writing, I describe the idea that gives me pleasure, that I'm not a

number in the Addition, and doing this I don't examine if I am happy or unhappy. *I don't examine,* not *I don't care.*

The substitution of other words for *smallest care* will, I know, be very difficult, but it must be done. I wonder if the rhyme "share" could be used? "Whether I have or I have not a share of happiness." Or "Even if I have not a share of happiness." But these phrases are bosh.

Garlands

pg. 296

With its connection of beauty to evil (already the subject of the lost 1893 poem "The Beauty of Evil"), this poem's debt to Baudelaire's *Fleurs du Mal* is evident. This later poem can be seen as a kind of bridge between Cavafy's interest in Baudelaire and (with what Diana Haas has called its "spirit of sensual perversity") his later flirtation with the Decadents.

Lohengrin

pg. 297

Cavafy's library contained an Italian translation of the libretto of Wagner's 1850 opera *Lohengrin,* a work that may well have been of interest to the poet because its Medieval setting, like so many of the milieus that interested him, juxtaposes pre-Christian worship with Christianity. Given his familiarity with Edouard Schuré's *Les grands initiés* (see the note on "Eternity," pp. 507–8), moreover, it is tempting to think that the same author's *Le Drame musical en France,* I: *Richard Wagner, son oeuvre et son idée* (Paris, 1875) played some part in the poet's use of this opera. Haas has noted that all of the elements to which Cavafy's poem refers are in fact to be found in Schuré's summary.

In the opera, King Henry of Germany has come to Antwerp in an attempt to raise an army to defend Germany from the invading Hungarians, only to find that the region is in the grip of a power struggle with a bizarre history. In the absence of the legitimate heir, Godfrey, who disappeared years earlier, the dukedom has been claimed by Frederick of Telramund, whose wife, the darkly beautiful Ortrud, secretly worships the old gods; both Frederick and Ortrud accuse Godfrey's sister, Elsa, of having killed her brother in order to seize power for herself. Henry declares that the issue is to be decided by a single combat between Frederick and whoever volunteers to be Elsa's champion. The Herald is instructed to issue a fanfare calling for a champion to fight for Elsa. Despite Elsa's confidence that such a champion will materialize—for she has seen him in a vision—at first no one appears. Only after the third sounding of the Herald's trumpet does a mysterious swan-drawn boat appear, bearing a great knight (who, as we later find out, is Lohengrin). He declares his love for Elsa and agrees to fight for her—but only on the condition that she never ask to know his name or origins. She agrees, and he defeats Telramund, who is sentenced to be exiled. Cavafy's poem is based on this first act of the opera.

In the latter part of the opera (which provides the inspiration for the poem "Suspicion") we find Telramund and Ortrud plotting Elsa's downfall as she prepares to wed her champion. The former attempts to kill the mysterious knight, but instead is slain by him; the latter uses her wiles to plant in Elsa's mind jealous suspicions about her husband-to-be. Eventually she succeeds, and at the climax of the opera the knight—who, because Elsa has violated her promise, must now leave her and return to the place he came from—reveals that he is Lohengrin, son of Parsifal, the knight of the Holy Grail. Having uncovered his secret, he steps into the swan-drawn boat again and prepares to depart. At this point Ortrud makes a revelation of her own—a malicious one: the swan who draws Lohengrin's boat is none other than the long-lost Godfrey, Elsa's brother and the rightful heir to the dukedom, whom long ago she had transformed into a swan using her unholy magic. Had Elsa not violated her promise, Ortrud declares, the swan would have been able to resume human form. Lohengrin, however, is able to use his holy powers to save Godfrey, and at the moment when the young man reassumes human form, Lohengrin departs and Elsa collapses, dead, in her brother's arms.

Suspicion   *pg. 299*

For the plot of Wagner's 1850 opera *Lohengrin,* on which this poem is based, see the previous note, on "Lohengrin."

The Intervention of the Gods

Commenting on this poem, Cavafy wrote the following note in English: "This is a good poem, but the second quotation is objectionable." Like a number of other poems of the 1890s—for instance, "Builders" (*1891;* 1891), "The Bank of the Future" (*1897*), "Trojans" (*1900;* 1905)—this poem develops the theme of the futility of progress and of human action. Here, the theme is given a notionally classical Greek cast: the reference to the theatrical convention of the "god from the machine" (*deus ex machina*) in line 11 evokes the world of Greek tragedy, in which insoluble complications of destiny, fate, and plot were resolved by the eleventh-hour appearance of a god (*deus*) who often makes a closing pronouncement meant to put things right. (The phrase *deus ex machina* refers to the mechanical crane, *mêchanê* in Greek and *machina* in Latin, used to raise and lower the actor playing the god.) Here, the allusion to the *deus ex machina* is of course ironic; nothing is put right by the intervention of the gods, all is futility.

The first epigraph comes from Emerson's 1846 poem "Give All to Love," an exhortation to devote ourselves passionately to love that ends, somewhat startlingly, with an allusion to the fickleness of the beloved and the inevitable disappointment of the lover. A few stanzas will suffice to provide useful context:

> Give all to love;
> Obey thy heart;
> Friends, kindred, days,
> Estate, good-fame,
> Plans, credit and the Muse,
> Nothing refuse.
>
> . . . .
> Cling with life to the maid;
> But when the surprise,
> First vague shadow of surmise
> Flits across her bosom young,
> Of a joy apart from thee,
> Free be she, fancy-free;

Nor thou detain her vesture's hem,
Nor the palest rose she flung
From her summer diadem.

. . . .

Though thou loved her as thyself,
As a self of purer clay,
Though her parting dims the day,
Stealing grace from all alive;
Heartily know,
When the half-gods go,
The gods arrive.

It is easy to see why the resonant final lines (quoted by Kipling, too), with their suggestion that life's cruel disappointments and separations lead nonetheless to an apprehension of a deeper truth, appealed to the Cavafy of the 1890s, which as we know was a decade of devastating personal loss for the poet.

This solemn vision may explain Cavafy's later objection to the second quotation, which he could well have seen, on reflection, as unduly frivolous: the lines come from Dumas's rather sensational 1876 play *L'Etrangère* (The Foreign Woman), which treated infidelity, daringly modern marital arrangements, and race (the title character, played by Sarah Bernhardt in the original Paris production, is the illegitimate daughter of a Carolina planter and a mulatto slave), all set among the higher echelons of the French aristocracy. Savagely dismissed by Henry James in a review, the play nonetheless inspired his novel *The Americans*.

King Claudius   *pg. 302*

This is the longest extant poem in Cavafy's corpus. His interest in Shakespeare was already apparent in his articles "Shakespeare on Life" and "Greek Traces in Shakespeare" (see the note on "Voice from the Sea," p. 484). *Hamlet* in particular seems to have fired his imagination, since in addition to the present poem he wrote two other poems based on that play, of which we have only the titles: "Lights, Lights, Lights" (1893) and "The Downfall of Denmark" (1899).

Several of Cavafy's poems of the 1890s take the form of a (usually ironic) rewriting of well-known literary or historical episodes: see also "When the Watchman Saw the Light" (Aeschylus's *Agamemnon*), "The Naval Battle" (Aeschylus's *Persians*), and "Lohengrin" and "Suspicion" (Wagner's *Lohengrin*).

The Naval Battle   *pg. 306*

Like "When the Watchman Saw the Light," this poem takes an Aeschylean subject as the starting point for a rewriting; in this case, the play in question is *Persians*, Aeschylus's 472 B.C. dramatization of the unlikely Greek defeat of the vast Persian expeditionary forces in the Second Persian War of 480–479. The climactic battle of this conflict was the Greek victory over the Persian fleet in the narrow straits of Salamis, where the superior Persian numbers were of no avail. The inarticulate exclamations of the Persian chorus in this poem are direct borrowings from Aeschylus's text.

ECBATANA, SUSA, and PERSEPOLIS were all great cities under the Achaemenid dynasty of Persia, to which both Darius I and his son Xerxes, leaders of the two invasions of Greece from 490 to 479 B.C., belonged.

When the Watchman Saw the Light   *pg. 307*

The poem takes its inspiration from Aeschylus's *Agamemnon,* which opens with a watchman on the roof of Agamemnon's palace in Mycenae describing the lonely years he has spent, on Clytemnestra's orders, looking for the beacon that will signal the fall of Troy and the return of her husband, Agamemnon (leader of the Greek forces that had set sail for Troy ten years earlier). As we know, the queen, now the lover of her husband's cousin, Aegisthus, and bitter still over Agamemnon's sacrifice of their daughter, Iphigenia, eagerly awaits her long-absent king so that she might kill him. The present poem assumes the voice of the play's chorus, composed of elders of the strife-riven city.

ARACHNAEUM (or Arachnaion) was a mountain in the Argolid plain where Mycenae is situated; its twin peak would have been an ideal location for the last of the signal fires that the Watchman looks for. ATREIDS refers to the royal family of Mycenae: Agamemnon and his brother, Menelaus, were the sons of Atreus, from whom the dynastic name derives. By referring to the family in this way, Cavafy invokes a broader history of internecine violence that runs in this particular family: Atreus had murdered the children of his brother Thyestes, of whom the sole survivor was Aegisthus, who later usurped Agamemnon's throne and bed.

Artificial Flowers   pg. 309

The poet's interest in flowers, particularly as a vehicle for expressing alienation from Nature, is evident here as well as in "Garlands": among his unpublished texts he left what he called a "paraphrase" in Greek of the following two lines of the British poet Arthur Symons:

> Where under hot-house glass the flowers forget
> How the sun shines and how the cool wind blows.

The rejection of Nature in favor of exquisite artistic fabrications is a trope familiar from the Decadents of the 1890s; the most famous example is in Huysmans's 1884 novel *À rebours,* in which the hero inlays his pet tortoise's shell with flowers made of jewels.

September of 1903   pg. 311

In the margin of the manuscript of this poem and of "December 1903" and "January 1904," the poet penciled the initials "A. M.," almost certainly a reference to Alexander Mavroudis, a young man with literary ambitions whom Cavafy met during his 1903 visit to Athens, and who seems to have been the object of an intense but unconsummated crush. In November 1903 the poet wrote the following note in English, which refers to "2 Ms"—that is, two poems whose titles are the names of months:

> No poems were sincerer than the "2 Ms" written during and immediately after the great crisis of libidinousness succeeding on my departure from Athens. Now say that in time Ale.

> Mav. comes to be indifferent to me, like Sul. (I was very
> much in love with him before my departure for Athens), or
> Bra.; will the poems—so true when they were made—
> become false? Certainly, certainly not. They will remain true
> in the past, and though not applicable any more in my life,
> seeing that they remind me of a day and perhaps different
> impressions, they will be applicable to other lives.

In the context of Cavafy's relationship with Mavroudis, whatever form
it may have taken, it is interesting to note that the Greek word in line 7
that I have translated as "wear black mourning," *mavroforoun* (literally,
"wear black") bears more than a passing resemblance to the surname
Mavroudis.

December 1903 *pg. 312*

See the note above on "September of 1903."

January of 1904 *pg. 313*

See the note above on "September of 1903."

Poseidonians *pg. 316*

The favorite themes of once-great civilizations that are ultimately
superseded and, in particular, of peripheral cultures eagerly trying to
stake a claim to Hellenism, haunts this poem in a number of ways. The
POSEIDONIANS were the inhabitants of Poseidonia, a significant Greek
colony in Italy, which was founded in the seventh century B.C. by set-
tlers from Sybaris and became a Roman colony in 273 B.C., at the time
when Rome was consolidating its hold on the coastal cities of southern
Italy—the same historical event that inspired "The Tarentines Have Their
Fun." Under the Romans, Poseidonia was known as Paestum. The refer-
ence to TYRRHENIANS similarly evokes superseded cultures: this was
the name by which the Greeks referred to the Etruscans, the indigenous
people who inhabited the Italian peninsula until they too were effaced

by the Romans (also called LATINS). ITALIOTES refers to the Greek population of southern Italy, which during the seventh and sixth centuries B.C. was heavily colonized by Greek settlers.

The epigraph is of some interest. Much has been made of the differences between the original text of Athenaeus (who is here quoting Aristoxenus, a musician from Tarentum in Italy who in this passage invokes the decay of the Poseidonians as a parallel to what he saw as the decay of music) and Cavafy's citation of it here, which elides certain elements. Interestingly, save for the elision of one final sentence, the text as Cavafy cites it reproduces exactly the text of Athenaeus as it is quoted in John Addington Symonds's *Sketches and Studies in Italy and Greece* (1883), in a passage about a visit to Paestum:

> "We do the same," said Aristoxenus in his Convivial Miscellanies, "as the men of Poseidonia, who dwell on the Tyrrhenian Gulf. It befell them, having been at first true Hellenes, to be utterly barbarized, changing to Tyrrhenes or Romans, and altering their language, together with their other customs. Yet they still observe one Hellenic festival, when they meet together and call to remembrance their old names and bygone institutions; and having lamented one to the other, and shed bitter tears, they afterwards depart to their own homes. Even thus a few of us also, now that our theatres have been barbarized, and this art of music has gone to ruin and vulgarity, meet together and remember what once music was."

The similarity of the two citations suggests that the passage in Symonds—the homosexual English writer whose work Cavafy knew—rather than a reading of Athenaeus himself, was what inspired the present poem. This is, I think, borne out by the way in which Symonds presents the Athenaeus citation, emphasizing a cultural pathos that would have had great resonance for the poet:

> This passage has a strange pathos, considering how it was penned, and how it has come down to us, tossed by the dark

indifferent stream of time. The Aristoxenus who wrote it was a pupil of the Peripatetic School, born at Tarentum, and therefore familiar with the vicissitudes of Magna Graecia. The study of music was his chief preoccupation; and he used this episode in the agony of an enslaved Greek city, to point his own conservative disgust for innovations in an art of which we have no knowledge left. The works of Aristoxenus have perished, and the fragment I have quoted is embedded in the gossip of Egyptian Athenaeus. In this careless fashion has been opened for us, as it were, a little window on a grief now buried in the oblivion of a hundred generations. After reading his words one May morning, beneath the pediment of Paestum's noblest ruin, I could not refrain from thinking that if the sprits of those captive Hellenes were to revisit their old habitation, they would change their note of wailing into a thin ghostly paean, when they found that Romans and Lucanians had passed away, that Christians and Saracens had left alike no trace behind, while the houses of their own ἀντήλιοι θεοί—down-facing deities—were still abiding in the pride of immemorial strength.

If Cavafy's source was, in fact, Symonds, the Englishman's triumphant conclusion must surely color our interpretation of the poem as a whole.

The End of Antony

pg. 317

Given the representation of Cleopatra here as an exotic figure given to making "oriental" gestures, it is worth noting that, in one of his marginal notes to Gibbon's Decline and Fall, the poet heatedly defends the last of the Ptolemaic monarchs from Gibbon's dismissive characterization of her as a "barbarian queen." In chapter 3 of Decline and Fall, Gibbon paraphrases a speech of Augustus in which (Gibbon writes) the first Roman emperor declares that he could not in good conscience "abandon her [the Republic] to a degenerate Roman, and a barbarian queen"; footnoting this paraphrase, Gibbon cites the Greek historian Dio Cassius and the Roman historians Suetonius and Tacitus, preferring the latter two as sources "for the general language of Augustus." For Cavafy, who was acutely sensitive to gradations of Greekness, Cleopatra may have indulged in "Oriental" behavior, but she was no barbarian, as his note to Gibbon's text amply demonstrates: "I should much like to know," Cavafy wrote on a piece of paper which he inserted into his copy of Gibbon at this passage, "in which Greek or Latin author this extraordinary expression occurs." As Diana Haas has noted in her article about Cavafy's reading notes to Gibbon, Cavafy himself nowhere suggests that the last of the Ptolemies is anything but Greek; if anything, he is careful in this poem to distinguish the "Oriental" queen from the real "barbarians," her slave-women. Haas points to the 1914 Unpublished Poem "Homecoming from Greece," in which the hybrid nature of Greekness throughout Greater Greece is illuminated with some care:

> we too are Greek—what else could we be?—
> but with loves and with emotions that are Asia's,
> but with loves and with emotions
> that now and then are alien to Greek culture.

27 June 1906, 2 P.M. pg. 318

This poem was inspired by the Denshawi affair, a 1906 clash between British military personnel and Egyptian locals. The Englishmen, traveling between Alexandria and Cairo, stopped in the village of Denshawi and shot some pigeons belonging to the villagers; after violence erupted, one of the Englishmen was hit in the head with a stone and later died, of sunstroke, after making his way back to the British camp. The English responded by trying and hanging five of the villagers for murder, a punishment that Sir Reginal Storrs, an acquaintance of Cavafy's, referred to in his 1945 memoirs, *Orientations*, as "excessive and medieval." Cavafy, who was violently opposed to capital punishment ("whenever I have the opportunity I declare this," he wrote in a note of October 1902), was similarly revolted, although of course his sympathy in this poem has an erotic component.

Hidden

One of the poet's "Notes on Poetics and Ethics," dated December 1905, articulates, in prose, many of the sentiments expressed in this poem:

> The wretched laws of society—the result of neither sanitary nor critical judgment—have belittled my work. They have stifled my expression; they have prevented me from shedding light and emotion to those who are fashioned like me. Life's harsh circumstances have forced me to toil in order to master the English language. What a pity. If I toiled equally in French—if circumstances permitted it, if French was equally useful to me—then perhaps in this language—because of the facility provided by pronouns, which both declare and obscure—I could express myself more freely. Finally, what am I to do? I go to waste, aesthetically speaking. And I will remain an object of speculation; and I will be understood more fully by what I spurned.

A prose articulation of another important theme in this poem—the idea that although Cavafy himself lived in constrained times, he was aware that others who came later would be able to speak more freely than he could—may be found in the note of October 1902 in which he talks about his opposition to capital punishment (see above on "27 June 1906, 2 P.M."):

> I criticize, for example, the death penalty. I declare this at every available opportunity, not because I think that the states will abolish it tomorrow because of my saying so, but because I am convinced that stating it will contribute to the eventual triumph of my view. No matter if no one agrees with me. My word will not be in vain. Someone might repeat it, and it may fall on ears which will harken and be encouraged. Perhaps someone of those presently disagreeing might remember it—in a favorable circumstance in the future, and, through the coincidence of other cases, might be persuaded,

or might harbor doubts about his initial conviction. So in various other social matters, and in some that primarily necessitate Action. I know that I am a coward and I cannot act. That is why I only speak. But I do not think my words are needless. Someone else will act. But my many words—those of my cowardly self—will facilitate his deed. They clear the ground.

"The Rest Shall I Tell in Hades to Those Below" *pg. 321*

The title, which is in Classical Greek, is a quotation from the *Ajax* of Sophocles, first performed perhaps in the 440s B.C. In the play, the great hero of the *Iliad* commits suicide after he is tricked into disgracing himself by Athena, the divine protector of his archrival, Odysseus; the line that Cavafy quotes constitutes Ajax's last words before his suicide. It should be noted that the dynamics of silence and speech, of revealing and concealing—something that would have been of great interest to Cavafy for his own reasons—are famously prominent both in Sophocles' play and in other literary treatments of Ajax. Of the latter, the best-known and most often cited passage is to be found in Homer's *Odyssey*. There, in Book 11, Odysseus visits the Underworld and glimpses the ghost of Ajax, but when he tries to talk to his former enemy—who is still enraged at Odysseus for having unfairly won the arms of the dead Achilles—Ajax merely glares silently at him and stalks off. (This powerful scene was later adapted by Vergil in the *Aeneid,* where the ghost of the spurned Carthaginian queen, Dido, maintains a contemptuous silence when Aeneas tries to talk to her.) It is inconceivable that Cavafy was not aware of the Homeric passage, which gives a further irony to the poem as a whole: for Ajax did not, in fact, speak "in Hades to those below."

That's How *pg. 322*

This poem is the first of several that indicate an increasing interest on the poet's part in photography as he reached his sixties: the others are "The Bandaged Shoulder" (*1919*) and "From the Drawer" (*1923*). There is also an unfinished draft, now one of the Unfinished Poems, called "The Photograph," composed in 1924. The appeal that photography had for the aging Cavafy, its unmatched ability to preserve the beauty of bygone days that has been lost or eroded by time, is not hard to fathom.

Homecoming from Greece   pg. 323

Like "Philhellene" and "Potentate from Western Libya," this poem explores, not without some irony, the subtle problematics of Greek identity in the post-Classical Mediterranean. It is clear from the context that the speaker and his (significantly) silent companion, Hermippus, are men with some intellectual attainments—or, at least, pretensions: HERMIPPUS was the name both of a well-known literary biographer in the later 200s B.C. (famed both for an important biography of the head of the Stoic School, and for his sensational death scenes, he was an important source for Plutarch, a favorite of Cavafy's), and of a distinguished public speaker and author of the second century A.D., the author of a book about dreams, among other texts. The Hermippus of Cavafy's poem could be either of those men—or, indeed, neither, since the name is not an unusual one, and Cavafy's poems are peopled by sophists, grammarians, rhetoricians and other intellectuals who are likely as not to be fictional.

The salient factor, in this poem, is that the unresponsive Hermippus in the poem and his companion, both of them apparently attached to some kind of philosophical school, are clearly meant to be from the Greek East (as were the two historical Hermippus's); there is a strong suggestion that they have just been to Athens, the birthplace of the civilization of which these two intellectuals are the distant heirs. (The reference to rulers whose HELLENIZED or MACEDONIAN trappings ill-conceal their Arabian or Median [Iranian] backgrounds—like the tongue-tied eastern ruler in "Potentate from Western Libya"—indicates that their home is one of the farther reaches of the Greek world.) What is intriguing here is that the two characters would appear to have radically different feelings about their part-Hellenic, part-local cultural identities. For while the nameless narrator natters on about how relieved he is to be going home and how happily he accepts the "foreign," non-Greek aspect of his identity—more passionate, less coldly rational, we are meant to feel, than the Greek side (think of the "Oriental flailings" of Cleopatra in "The End of Antony," sharply contrasted with Antony's Stoic calm)—the silent Hermippus seems to have more complicated feelings about the issue. There is, indeed, a strong suggestion that, like a provincial academic returning from his first conference in a great metropolis, the "angry" Hermippus may be brooding precisely because he's just been exposed to the first time to a level of culture that is (as he thinks) far superior to that of his native city.

Fugitives   *pg. 325*

The title characters are clearly Byzantine Greeks who have been exiled from Constantinople. Although there has been some controversy about the precise historical setting of the poem, the reference to the Roman Church ("rather Latin," line 13) suggests to Savidis and others that the poem is set sometime after the banishment, in 867, of the Constantinopolitan patriarch Photius, well known as the author of the Schism between the Eastern and Roman Churches. Photius had become Patriarch in rather shady circumstances in 857, when his predecessor, Ignatius, was deposed and banished after refusing to give communion to Bardas, the regent for the child-emperor Michael III (see above, "Imenus") because Bardas had been carrying on an incestuous relationship with his daughter-in-law. After being rushed through Holy Orders in six days, Photius was ordained Patriarch by a bishop who had himself been excommunicated by Ignatius. These nefarious doings were viewed with great disapproval by the pope and the Latin bishops in the West, but their extreme measures against Photius and his supporters, which came to a head in the pope's threat to excommunicate the Patriarch, did nothing to shake him from his throne.

Photius reigned for ten years. In part because the pope and the Latin bishops had supported Ignatius against him, he was implacably opposed to Rome, and one of his last acts as patriarch was to excommunicate the pope and all the Latins. Then, in 867, Michael III was murdered by Basil I, who subsequently exiled Photius and his associates and restored Ignatius to the patriarchate. Photius spent the next seven years imprisoned in the monastery of Stenos on the Bosporus, staying in touch with his exiled friends and doing his utmost to win over the new emperor, which, astoundingly, he eventually did: he was recalled to Constantinople in 876 and appointed tutor to the emperor's son. On Ignatius's death the following year, Basil successfully intervened with the pope in Rome to have Photius reappointed Patriarch. He died in 897, having been once again deposed from the patriarchal throne by Basil's son and successor.

If the years of Photius's exile are indeed the setting for this poem, the reference to NONNUS has a particularly strong resonance. Nonnus, a native of Panopolis in Egypt (hence the epithet PANOPOLITE), was an epic poet who flourished in probably the late 400s A.D.; he was known above all for the *Dionysiaca,* a hexameter epic in forty-eight books about the god Dionysus's journey to India and back. (A good deal of other material of various sorts, including what one of his modern editors refers to as "his very inaccurate astronomical learning," is, inevitably, treated: Nonnus was known for his florid style and abstruse interests.) But he was also the author of a verse paraphrase of the Gospel of St. John, a fact of interest because it indicates that at some point he converted to Christianity.

Theophilos Palaeologus

pg. 326

An early version of this poem was written at an unknown date and rewritten in March 1903 with the title "I'd Rather Die Than Live"; the current version was written in 1914 or afterward.

On May 29, 1453, the Byzantine empire came to an end with the fall of Constantinople to the Ottoman sultan, Mehmet II. By that time, the capital city was virtually all that remained of the once-sprawling empire, and in the months leading up to the city's fall it was clear that resistance by the isolated forces of the last emperor, Constantine XI, could only achieve a symbolic significance at best. During the climactic battle for the city, Constantine's cousin, THEOPHILUS PALAEOLOGUS, a scholar and mathematician, is said to have fought alongside him and uttered the words *thélo thaneín mállon ê zên,* "I'd rather die than live," as he threw himself into the mêlée.

A Great Feast at the House of Sosibius *pg. 330*

For Sosibius, the murderous chief minister of Ptolemy IV, see the note on "The Lagid's Hospitality," pp. 498–9.

Simeon *pg. 331*

The Christian martyr SIMEON STYLITES (395–451) was the subject of an abiding fascination for Cavafy, and the object of great admiration. To Gibbon's extended description of the life and sufferings of this remarkable figure, Cavafy appended a long note in English; both are worth quoting here, not least because Gibbon's Enlightenment dismay at Simeon's religious zeal stands in stark counterpoint to Cavafy's admiration, which combines religiosity with something else—a taste for the rigor of solitude, and admiration for those who subject themselves to it.

Here is Gibbon:

> The most perfect hermits are supposed to have passed many days without food, many nights without sleep, and many years without speaking; and glorious was the *man* (I abuse that name) who contrived any cell, or seat, of a peculiar construction, which might expose him, in the most inconvenient posture, to the inclemency of the seasons.
>
> Among these heroes of the monastic life, the name and genius of Simeon Stylites have been immortalized by the singular invention of an aërial penance. At the age of thirteen, the young Syrian deserted the profession of a shepherd, and threw himself into an austere monastery. After a long and painful noviciate, in which Simeon was repeatedly saved from suicide, he established his residence on a mountain, about thirty or forty miles to the east of Antioch. Within the space of a *mandra,* or circle of stones, to which he had attached himself by a ponderous chain, he ascended a column, which was successively raised from the height of nine, to that of sixty, feet from the ground. In this last, and lofty, station, the Syrian Anachoret resisted the heat of thirty sum-

mers, and the cold of as many winters. Habit and exercise instructed him to maintain his dangerous situation without fear or giddiness, and successively to assume the different postures of devotion. He sometimes prayed in an erect attitude, with his out-stretched arms, in the figure of a cross; but his most familiar practice was that of bending his meager skeleton from the forehead to the feet; and a curious spectator, after numbering twelve hundred and forty-four repetitions, at length desisted from the endless account. The progress of an ulcer in his thigh might shorten, but it could not disturb, this *celestial* life; and the patient Hermit expired, without descending from his column. A prince, who should capriciously inflict such tortures, would be deemed a tyrant; but it would surpass the power of a tyrant, to impose a long and miserable existence on the reluctant victims of his cruelty. This voluntary martyrdom must have gradually destroyed the sensibility both of the mind and body; nor can it be presumed that the fanatics, who torment themselves, are susceptible of any lively affection for the rest of mankind. A cruel unfeeling temper has distinguished the monks of every age and country: their stern indifference, which is seldom mollified by personal friendship, is inflamed by religious hatred; and their merciless zeal has strenuously administered the holy office of the Inquisition.

It is interesting to compare Gibbon's contempt for monastic fanaticism to the almost ecstatic note of Cavafy, whose concluding special emphasis on the word "man" ("so wonderful a man") is surely a riposte to Gibbon's snide dismissal of monks as undeserving of the name of "man" ("I abuse the name"):

This great, this wonderful saint is surely an object to be singled out in ecclesiastical history for admiration and study. He has been, perhaps, the only man who has dared to be really *alone*. . . .
    The glory of Simeon filled and astounded the earth. Innu-

merable pilgrims crowded round his column. Poeple [sic] came from the farthest West and from the farthest East, from Britain and from India, to gaze on the unique sight—on this candle of faith (such is the magnificent language of the historian Theodoret) set up and lit on a lofty chandelier.

I have met with only one poem on Simeon Stylites, but it is in no way worthy of the subject.

The poem of Tennyson ["Saint Simeon Stylites," 1842], though it contains some well-made verses, fails in tone. Its great defect lies in its form of a monologue. The complaints of Simeon, his eagerness for the "meed of saints, the white robe and the palm," his dubious humility, his latent vanity, are not objectionable in themselves and may be [sic] were necessary to the poem, but they have been handled in a common, almost a vulgar manner. It was a very difficult task—a task reserved, perhaps, for some mighty king of art—to find fitting language for so great a saint, so wonderful a man.

Two things are worthy of our attention here. First, in his own poem Cavafy solves the problem he observed in Tennyson by making the narrator of the poem not Simeon, but an observer: in this way the poet emphasizes the remarkable *effect* of Simeon's solitude and suffering. Second, the reading note makes plain both his profound admiration for Simeon, particularly his fearlessness in the face of solitude—something that Cavafy sought himself, and which he explored in his poetry—and his awareness of the difficulty of creating a work worthy of such a figure ("a very difficult task . . . for some mighty king of art"). Both, it seems safe to say, help explain why Cavafy felt he could not publish his own poem about Simeon.

A fascinating element of Simeon's biography connects this figure to another for whom Cavafy had profound feelings: Apollonius of Tyana, the mage whose telepathy and ability to see into the future so intrigued Cavafy. Simeon's fifth-century biographer Theodoret reports that the Stylite was able to sense "what, in the future, was close at hand, what was imminent," and cites as an example a drought that Simeon had predicted two years in advance.

Coins pg. 334

As in "Epitaph," this poem reveals a fascination with the reaches—or perhaps the limits—of Hellenism, following the conquests of Alexander the Great. The names on the coins belong to various members of the dynasty of Indo-Hellenic kings who ruled in the northwestern part of the Indian subcontinent during the second and first centuries B.C. The civilization of the Indo-Hellenic kingdoms were showcases for the hybridization set in motion by Alexander's Asian campaigns: Hellenic elements permeated the local arts, the various Indian languages were combined with Greek, and Greek, Hindu, and Buddhist elements combined in religion as well. One of the kings referred to here, MENANDER I, converted to Buddhism.

It Was Taken pg. 335

Cavafy's interest in popular folk songs is well attested. In 1914 he published a long review-article on the subject, and between 1919 and 1920, immediately before he wrote this poem, he collaborated on an anthology. In the 1914 article, he writes at length about the "marvelous expressive power" to be found in folk songs about the Fall of Constantinople ("the CITY"). As so often with Cavafy, the philological and the emotional are here inextricably entwined under the rubric of Hellenism: the beginning of this poem, with its glimpse of the poet indulging his arcane interests only to come across an item that has a powerful emotional effect on him, is strongly reminiscent of "Caesarion," which charts a similar shift from an ostensibly scholarly and wholly cerebral interest in some episode of Hellenic history (one in which, indeed, something Greek was ultimately destroyed) to intense emotion.

TREBIZOND was a medieval Hellenic empire, located on the southern shore of the Black Sea, which had once been part of Byzantium; because it was the last of the former Byzantine realms to fall to the Ottoman Turks (in 1461), it is referred to as "the last Greek Empire." As he often does with Classical Greek, Cavafy here cites passages of a text—in this case, songs in the Trapezuntine dialect, which retains many aspects of the grammar and pronunciation of Classical Greek, and hence has an "archaic" flavor—in the original. ROMANY (*Romanía,* in Greek) was the name by which the Byzantine empire was popularly known during the Middle Ages.

Poems Written in English

[More Happy Thou, Performing Member] *pg. 347*

Because the original manuscript gives no title, the first line of the poem, bracketed, traditionally provides the name of the poem. However derivative its content and primitive its prosody, this poem is interesting inasmuch as it suggests that already in his late teens and early twenties, certain themes—the special knowledge of the elect; the uncanny power of strong gazes—had appeared in the poet's work.

Leaving Therápia *pg. 349*

The poem was written in July 1882. Therápia was a town near Yenikoÿ, where Haricleia Cavafy's father had a house. She and five of her sons fled to safety with her family in Constantinople after the anti-European riots of 1882 in Alexandria; they stayed briefly in Therápia before moving to a small house in Cadíkoy that her father rented for them.

Darkness and Shadows *pg. 350*

The manuscript is written in the hand of Cavafy's brother John, who translated a number of the poet's Greek poems; the subtitle indicates that this text is an English "transcription" of a poem that Cavafy had written in French. Cavafy occasionally used his mother's maiden name, Photiades, as his middle name, instead of Petrou, a form of his father's first name; hence the use of the initials "C. F. C." here, where the letter "F," in John's transcription, stands for "Photiades." Savidis suggests that the basis of this poem was the introductory poem "Fonction du Poète" ("The Poet's Function") in Victor Hugo's collection *Les rayons et les*

Ombres ("Sunlight and Shadows," 1840), which Cavafy owned; that poem exalts poetry as the "star that leads kings and shepherds to God!" The epigraph of this poem indicates that Cavafy wrote verse in French as well as English, although the original of this poem, "L'Ombre et les ombres," written sometime before January 1883, has been lost.

FURTHER READING

The following books will be of value to the general reader interested in further exploring Cavafy's life, work, and intellectual world:

The Mind and Art of C. P. Cavafy (Denise Harvey & Co., 1983). An appealingly diverse collection of the classic essays on Cavafy and his work by E. M. Forster, George Seferis, Patrick Leigh Fermor, W. H. Auden, and others.

G. W. Bowersock. *Julian the Apostate* (Harvard University Press, 1978). A refreshingly brisk and vigorous short study of the historical figure who fascinated Cavafy more than any other.

Peter Brown. *The World of Late Antiquity AD 150–750* (W. W. Norton, 1989). An expansive survey of the history and culture of a period that represents one of Cavafy's historial "margins"—long neglected by traditional classicists but of paramount interest to the poet.

E. M. Forster. *Alexandria: A History and a Guide* (1922; repr. Oxford, 1986). A survey *cum* guidebook that savors seductively of Cavafy's own era, by the English novelist who befriended Cavafy there during World War I, and who was responsible for first bringing the poet to the attention of English readers and critics. (With an Introduction by Lawrence Durrell, whose *Alexandria Quartet* is required reading for anyone interested in the city that shaped Cavafy's poetry.)

Peter Green. *The Hellenistic Age* (Modern Library Chronicles, 2007). An excellent brief introduction to the era that provided a setting for so many of Cavafy's poems; for those not daunted by its thousand pages, the same author's magisterial *Alexander to Actium: The Historical Evolution of the Hellenistic Age* (California, 1993) provides a magnificently detailed yet admirably lively account of the period.

Edmund Keeley. *Cavafy's Alexandria* (1976; repr. Princeton University Press, 1995). A meticulous analysis of the Cavafian corpus by the eminent translator and scholar, with a special emphasis on the crucial symbolic role of the city in the poet's work.

R. Liddell. *Cavafy: A Biography* (Duckworth, 1974; repr. 2000). Workmanlike but packed with useful information, this is still the only book-length biography of the poet in English.

John Julius Norwich. *A Short History of Byzantium* (Knopf, 1998). The abridged version of Norwich's magisterial three-volume study is the best popular introduction to the history of the Empire.

Philostratus, edited and translated by C. P. Jones. *Apollonius of Tyana* (Loeb Classical Library, 2006). This new translation brings to vivid life the sprawling quasi-novel that Cavafy considered a "storehouse of poetic material."

Christopher Robinson, *C. P. Cavafy*. Bristol Classical Press, 1988. An excellent short study of certain thematic motifs and linguistic subtleties in Cavafy's work; for readers with some Greek, the discussions of the poet's use of *katharevousa,* to which the present translation is indebted, will prove particularly illuminating.

ACKNOWLEDGMENTS

The preparation of this volume has taken more than a decade; during that time, I have been given invaluable and deeply appreciated assistance and advice by a number of friends, scholars, and institutions. It is a pleasure to be able to thank them here.

My work was originally supported by the Onassis Center for Modern Greek Studies at New York University, where I was a writer-in-residence in 1996, and by a Stanley Seeger Fellowship at Princeton University in 1999. I should say, apropos of my alma mater, that my interest in Modern Greek—not necessarily a given among classicists—has always been encouraged and supported with great warmth by Princeton's Program in Modern Greek Studies, from the early summer-travel grants I received when I was a graduate student, which gave me my first taste of the living Greece, to the very generous Seeger Fellowship just mentioned. Two individuals in particular there merit special thanks: first, Richard Burgi, who was my first Modern Greek teacher and who made me memorize Cavafy; and then Dimitri Gondicas, who has shown unflaggingly generous friendship and support to this somewhat unlikely Neohellenist, and eventually to this project, over the years. I'm deeply grateful to them both.

I am also indebted to the John Simon Guggenheim Foundation for a generous grant that allowed me to work on the translation and commentary of the Unfinished Poems.

The friends and colleagues who have shown interest in my Cavafy translations from the start are too numerous to name here; they know who they are, and they know how grateful I am to them. Among those whose comments and suggestions have meant particularly much to me are those great American *Cavafisti* Ben Sonnenberg and Walter Kaiser, as well as Alexander Nehamas; also Bob Gottlieb, and particularly Richard Howard, *witting and unwitting accomplice,* who provided invaluable support and insight; and Robert Silvers, to whom I owe so much, and who found a number of these translations a home where they could be appreciated before this volume was finished.

I must, however, single out for especially fervent thanks Pavlos Sfyroeras and Maria Hatjigeorgiou, whose enthusiasm, support, advice, and subtle insights into Cavafy are everywhere reflected here; Christopher Jones, who lavished on the manuscript more loving and meticulous attention than I could ever have hoped for; and finally Glen Bowersock, whose wisdom, scholarship, and attention to the smallest details, in commenting on my work in progress, more than once set me on the straight path when I was about to go astray. His friendship and interest in me and my work mean more to me than I can say, and I hope that the result, in the case of these translations and commentary, do some justice to his extraordinary kindnesses and to his example for more than twenty years now.

Anyone reading this text who is already familiar with the world of Cavafy and Cavafian scholarship will know how much I owe to those who have gone before me: my reliance on the vitally important work of George Savidis, Renata Lavagnini, Diana Haas, Edmund Keeley (another kindly presence at Princeton), Alexander Nehamas, Peter Bien, and many others will be obvious, as, I hope, will be gratitude to them. In this context, it is a pleasure to acknowledge the invaluable support, and the long-distance friendship, of Manuel Savidis, whose generosity in allowing me to quote from material in the Cavafy Archive, like his stewardship of that resource in general, shows how worthy a successor to his splendid father he is. That he has entrusted me with the first translation of the Unfinished Poems is an honor of which I hope I have shown myself worthy.

As always, Lydia Wills has been instrumental in bringing a project of mine to fruition; to expect anyone, even an agent, to master the intricacies of Cavafian rights and publication dates is probably to ask too much, but here as usual she showed her brilliant colors. Finally, I must say a word about my editor, Robin Desser. She assumed the care of this project ten years ago, and since then has shown a superhuman patience and understanding, as I gradually became aware of the magnitude of the task confronting me. Her enthusiasm, trust, and support for me over these years, in this and other things, are very precious to me.

INDEX OF TITLES

TEXTUAL PERMISSION

Grateful acknowledgment is made to David R. Godine, Publisher, Inc., for permission to reprint excerpts from *Les Fleurs du mal* by Charles Baudelaire, translated by Richard Howard, translation copyright © 1982 by Richard Howard. Reprinted by permission of David R. Godine, Publisher, Inc.

The following poems appeared, some of them in a slightly different form, in the following publications: "Alexandrian Kings," "Dangerous," "Envoys from Alexandria," "Herodes Atticus," "King Demetrius," and "The Seleucid's Displeasure" in *Arion;* "Sweet Voices" and "Voices" in *Gulf Coast;* "As Much As You Can," "Candles," "Very Rarely," "Windows," and "But Wise Men Perceive What Is Imminent," in *Meridian;* "Myres: Alexandria of 340 B.C.," "Nero's Timetable," "One of Their Gods," and "Philhellene" in *The New York Review of Books;* "Aboard the Ship," "In the Same Space," "Morning's Sea," and "The Retinue of Dionysus," in *The Paris Review.*

Grateful acknowledgment is made to Manuel Savidis and the Cavafy Archive at the Center for Neo-Hellenic Studies (Spoudasterio tou Neou Hellenismou) in Athens for permission to quote Mr. Savidis's translations of Cavafy's "Notes on Poetics and Ethics," and to quote the Greek-language poems that are copyright © Manuel Savidis, as well as other material in the Archive.

Daniel Mendelsohn was born on Long Island in 1960 and studied Classics at the University of Virginia and at Princeton, where he received his doctorate in 1994. His reviews and essays on literary and cultural subjects appear regularly in numerous publications, including *The New Yorker,* the *New York Times,* and *The New York Review of Books.* His previous books include *The Elusive Embrace,* a *New York Times* Notable Book and a *Los Angeles Times* Best Book of the Year, and the international best seller *The Lost: A Search for Six of Six Million,* which won the National Book Critics Circle Award, the Prix Médicis, and many other honors. Mr. Mendelsohn is also the recipient of a Guggenheim Fellowship, the National Book Critics Circle Citation for Excellence in Book Reviewing, and the George Jean Nathan Award for Dramatic Criticism. He teaches at Bard College.

A NOTE ON THE TYPE

The text of this book was set in a typeface named Perpetua, designed by the British artist Eric Gill (1882–1940) and cut by the Monotype Corporation of London in 1928–30. The shapes of the roman letters basically derive from stonecutting, a form of lettering in which Gill was eminent. The italic is essentially an inclined roman. The general effect of the typeface in reading sizes is one of lightness and grace. The larger display sizes of the type are extremely elegant and form what is one of the most distinguished series of inscriptional letters cut in the twentieth century.

Composed by North Market Street Graphics,
Lancaster, Pennsylvania
Printed and bound by Berryville Graphics,
Berryville, Virginia
Designed by Wesley Gott